Sacred Terror

Sacred Terror

How Faith Becomes Lethal

DANIEL E. PRICE

 PRAEGER

AN IMPRINT OF ABC-CLIO, LLC
Santa Barbara, California • Denver, Colorado • Oxford, England

Copyright 2012 by Daniel E. Price

Library of Congress Cataloging-in-Publication Data

Price, Daniel E., 1962–
   Sacred terror : how faith becomes lethal / Daniel E. Price.
     p. cm.
   Includes bibliographical references (p.) and index.
   ISBN 978-0-313-38638-1 (hardcopy : alk. paper) — ISBN 978-0-313-38639-8 (ebook)
1. Terrorism—Religious aspects. I. Title.
   BL65.T47P75 2012
   201'.763325—dc23   2012011931

ISBN: 978-0-313-38638-1
EISBN: 978-0-313-38639-8

16 15 14 13 12   1 2 3 4 5

This book is also available on the World Wide Web as an eBook.
Visit www.abc-clio.com for details.

Praeger
An Imprint of ABC-CLIO, LLC

ABC-CLIO, LLC
130 Cremona Drive, P.O. Box 1911
Santa Barbara, California 93116-1911

This book is printed on acid-free paper ∞

Manufactured in the United States of America

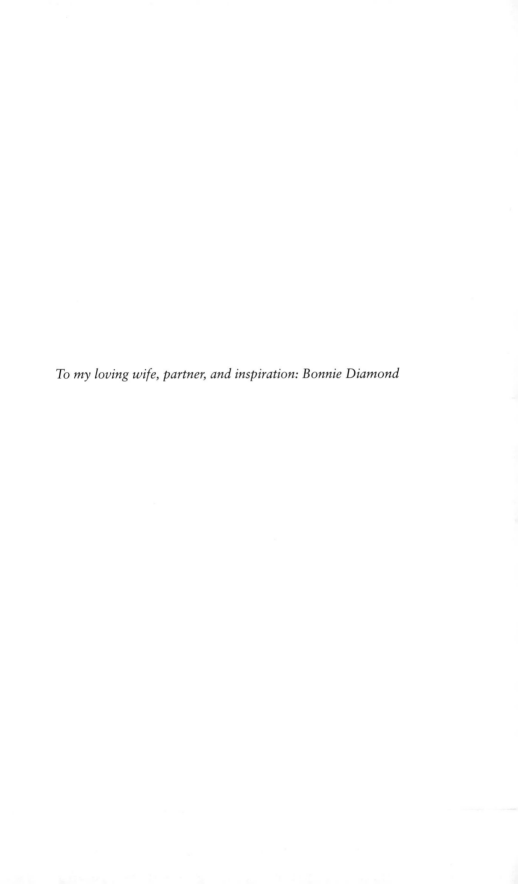

To my loving wife, partner, and inspiration: Bonnie Diamond

Contents

Preface

I have maintained a scholarly interest in religion for more than 25 years. I was first intrigued and frightened by religious Jewish settlers in the West Bank when I spent a year in Israel in 1984–1985 after I graduated college. Being Jewish, I wondered how individuals who shared my religious heritage could view the world in a way that was diametrically opposed to how I did. Consequently, I decided that I wanted to study the politics of Jewish extremism when I entered graduate school at the University of Texas in 1988. My MA thesis supervisor, Dr. Clement Henry, wisely suggested that I compare Israel's Jewish extremists with Egypt's Islamic extremists, which stimulated my interest in Islam. While writing my thesis, I discovered that there were profound theological similarities between Islam and Judaism and that Jewish and Islamic extremists had similar worldviews. However, I concluded that it was Israel and Egypt's very divergent political systems that had the greatest influence on shaping religious extremism in their respective countries.

My doctoral dissertation at Binghamton University examined the empirical relationship between Islam and democracy using comparative case studies and quantitative analysis. There, I concluded that, contrary to common perception, the lack of democracy in the Islamic world was not due to the Islamic religion but rather socioeconomic factors and the historical experiences of Islamic countries. Further research examining the relationship between Islam and human rights and civil liberties produced the same findings. Consequently, I concluded that Islam was not a regressive political force, as was commonly believed to be the case. The campaigns for democracy in the

Arab world in 2011 and demonstrations against rigged Iranian elections in 2009, along with the willingness of Islamic parties to take part in elections have supported my argument. Muslims are not only calling for democracy; they might be forming democracies that have their ideological roots in religion. Religion, therefore, is important in shaping the boundaries of public policy and legal systems, as Islamic democracies might include the intertwining of religion and state and a legal framework that emphasizes duties to society more than freedom from government intervention into citizens' lives. My conversations with numerous Moroccans during my residence in that country as a Fulbright scholar revealed that most supported democracy and a political system that was rooted in Islam.

The finding that Islam does not cause authoritarianism or the violation of human rights is not surprising as religious texts, traditions, and historical events can be found to support both democracy and authoritarianism, as well as both capitalism and socialism. In fact, the same verse from a religious text can often be used to support conflicting opinions on political and economic issues. The same textual and historical contradictions exist regarding war, violence, and terrorism—the focus of this book. Religion is important in that it provides moral justifications and rationalizations for those who advocate for political and economic policies or violence and terrorism. The significance of the vague, amorphous, and contradictory nature of religious texts, traditions, and histories was made clear to me when I studied Jewish law, the Talmud, and rabbinical commentaries on the Five Books of Moses during my year of rabbinical studies. At the same time, I discovered the verses from the Torah and the historical precedents that justified the actions of the Jewish extremists that had fascinated me 15 years previously. Given that these verses did not inspire me to become an Orthodox Jew, move to a West Bank settlement, and violently confront Palestinians and Israeli soldiers, I concluded that it had to be factors other than Judaism that shaped the worldview of my extremist coreligionists.

The notion that Islam was a dangerous and reactionary force surfaced with a vengeance following the attacks on September 11, 2001. In the past 10 years, Islam has been portrayed as being opposed to freedom, democracy, and liberty and as being a threat to America and Western society. Needless to say, I reject this notion, and this book will explain how the 9/11 attackers and other religion-based terrorists are primarily motivated by political, socioeconomic, psychological, and other secular grievances. It will also explain that Islam and Judaism are theologically similar and share many commonalities. On the other hand, Christianity has less in common with Judaism, which discounts the notion that Islam is a threat to the

Judeo-Christian ethic and tradition. I will also explain that, again, political and socioeconomic conditions, rather than religion, better explain why there is little Christian-based terror at this point in history. At the same time, I will show that this has not always been the case as Christianity has motivated wars and violence in the past.

It is important to note that explaining religion-based terror, particularly when using political, socioeconomic, and psychological factors, should not be seen as an attempt to justify the actions of the terrorists or to discount the severity of the harm and damage that they cause. Although I present the worldviews of the terrorists and the forces that combine to produce them, I am in no way condoning their actions. As a social scientist, I have tried to provide an objective and dispassionate analysis. However, my own background is bound to produce personal biases. Being a nontraditional and politically liberal Jew who supports the creation of a Palestinian state alongside a safe and secure Israel, I am probably the hardest on my own, Israeli Jewish extremists, who I believe are an impediment (one of many) to the realization of this goal. As a progressive American who strongly supports the separation of church and state, I feel a personal threat from right-wing Christian and antiabortion terrorists in the United States. My connection to Islam is more ambivalent, as I recognize the danger posed by global Islamic terrorism and the hatred espoused by many *jihadists* toward the United States, the West, and Jews. However, I don't think that Islamic faith is the cause of that threat or the hatred. At the same time, I am concerned by the Islamophobia that has followed 9/11 and the rallying of anti-Muslim sentiments for political purposes in the United States and other places.

The idea for this book was generated by teaching a class on religious extremism and terrorism at UMass Lowell in 2006. When preparing for the course, I could not find a text that was based on the notion that religion is not the primary cause of religion-based terrorism, so I decided to write one.

Acknowledgments

I am deeply indebted to Eve Buzawa, the chairperson of the Criminal Justice Department at UML, for calling me and asking me to teach the course and, later, hiring me as a full-time visiting professor. Because of her actions, I was able to resume my academic career after a year's hiatus and develop this new research interest. I am grateful to Michael Reison for his consistent but friendly encouragement to take on this project. This book would not have been possible without a STARS grant for pre-tenured faculty at Westfield State University, which provided me with a semester off from my teaching responsibilities to begin this project. I want to thank the Office of Academic Affairs for providing the grant, the Faculty Grant Advisory Committee for selecting my proposal, and my department chairperson, Judy McDonald, for juggling the schedule so that I could have the time off from teaching.

I am also indebted to my other colleagues in the Criminal Justice Department, including Chris Kudlac, Tom Roscoe, Audrelee Dallam-Murphy, Vic Ascollilo, Bill Cook, Scott White, Steve Smith, John Jones, Byung Jun Cho, and Brian Rizzo, for their support and encouragement and providing a wonderful work environment. My meetings with professors White, Roscoe, and Cho were particularly informative and helpful. I am blessed by the presence of my wife, Bonnie Diamond, who offered encouragement, consolation, and nourishment, when appropriate. My cat, Santino, was also helpful by being by my side during the process but refraining from jumping on the keyboard. Thanks are always due to my mother, Charlotte Price, who has made everything possible through a lifetime of support. I am also fortunate to have a wonderful family including my sisters, Rochelle and Miriam, their husbands, Steve and Paul, and nieces and nephews, Leah, Joseph, Alana, Josh, and Sarah. I also want to remember my friend and mentor Richard Hofferbert who passed away while I was finishing this book. He was an inspiration and a role model. Finally, thanks to all of my friends and family members for asking me how the book was going on a regular basis. I can now tell you that it's done.

Introduction

September 11, 2001, was a rude awakening for Americans to the problem of religion-based terrorism. Although religion-based terrorism is as old as organized religion and the current wave of *religion*-based terrorism began in the 1970s, the attacks on the World Trade Center, the Pentagon, and the attempted attack on either the U.S. Capitol or the White House was the first significant, successful incident of religious terrorism on American soil.[1]

Since then, religion-based terrorism, particularly Islamic extremism, has been labeled as the most significant threat to both U.S. and global security. In the United States, the 9/11 attacks were used as justification for launching wars in Afghanistan and Iraq, and the USA Patriot Act was quickly passed, which significantly enhanced the government's power to collect information on both citizens and noncitizens and weakened the protection of civil liberties. New government bureaucracies including the Department of Homeland Security and the Transportation Security Administration were created in order to protect Americans from this new threat. Also, a now discontinued color-coded terror alert system to warn Americans of the likelihood of a terrorist attack was instituted. Students across the country flocked to enroll in courses in Arabic language, Middle East Studies, and Islamic studies. The new threat to American and world safety, religious extremism, had been identified, and a campaign was launched to defeat the enemy.

The threat became clearer when we became more familiar with al Qaeda, the Islamic extremist organization headed by Osama bin Laden. Al Qaeda appeared to be particularly menacing because of its stated goal of replacing the current world order with a global Islamic nation ruled by Islamic law;

its hatred of the United States, the West, non-Islamic religions, and Muslims who were deemed to be apostates; it's not easily identifiable and cell-based organization; and it's successful use of suicide attacks. It was also realized that the Islamic Group, which had carried out the 1993 World Trade Center bombing, was loosely tied to al Qaeda and that its members have carried out or been associated with a number of attacks against U.S. interests overseas, including the bombing of the dormitories used by U.S. airmen in Saudi Arabia in 1996, the bombings of the U.S. embassies in Kenya and Tanzania in 1998, and the bombing of the USS *Cole* in Yemen in 2000. The threat from Islamic terror was magnified by incidents in the more distant past such as the takeover of the U.S. embassy in Iran in 1978 and the hostage crisis that followed, the suicide bombing that killed 243 U.S. Marines acting as peacekeepers in Beirut, Lebanon, in 1983, and the ambush of U.S. Army Rangers in Mogadishu Somalia, in 1993, which resulted in 18 deaths.

The conflict with radical Islam and Islamic terrorism becomes more apparent when viewed in global perspective, as other parts of the globe, particularly the Islamic world, have suffered from far more religious-based violence than the United States. At the time of 9/11, Israel was experiencing a wave of suicide bombings and attacks by Hamas, Islamic Jihad, and other Palestinian Islamic groups. Hezbollah, a Lebanese Shiite group associated with the attack on U.S. and French forces, was also launching attacks on Israel. Islamic extremist groups have carried out terrorist attacks in numerous countries across the Islamic world from Turkey to Indonesia. The current era of religious terrorism has not been limited to Islam and the Islamic world. Israel has a Jewish Underground that has engaged in terrorism against the Palestinian population and that country's prime minister, Yitzhak Rabin, was assassinated in 1995 by a Jewish extremist. Protestant Catholics and Protestants engaged in a 25-year campaign of terror and violence in Northern Ireland. Radical antiabortion Christians have murdered abortion providers in the United States, the most recent being Dr. George Tiller in May 2009. Sikhs, Hindus, and others have also engaged in religion-based terror and killed in the name of religion.

RESPONSES TO THE RISE OF RELIGION-BASED TERRORISM

It is clear that during the past 30 years the world has experienced an era of religion-based terrorism that is very likely to continue into the near future. However, is religion-based really the existential threat that some portray it to be? Will we be fighting the so-called war on terrorism against al Qaeda and other religion-based terrorists in 1,000 years or even 50 years?

Here, historical perspective is necessary. As was the case with the threat of communism and the Red Menace in the past, religion-based terrorism has been portrayed as a dark and irrational force that is a threat to very existence of the United States and Western society and values. As we know, communism is almost dead as an ideological force, and the great power, the Soviet Union, which fought to advance it, no longer exists. The other communist power, China, has fully embraced capitalism and holds a significant portion of America's national debt. It is also important to note that the radical communist and socialist terrorist groups in Europe, Japan, North America, and South America of the 1960s and 1970s have also disappeared. At the same time, religion-based terrorism was almost nonexistent during that period and did not emerge as a threat until the late 1970s.

Religion-based terrorists and terrorist groups are viewed as being irrational actors whose motivations are rooted in hatred and pure religious zeal, which makes them more dangerous than past enemies. Following 9/11, we were told that the terrorists hated us for our democracy, freedom, and way of life and would only be satisfied with our complete destruction.[2] When Iran was accused of developing nuclear weapons, we were warned that this had to be stopped because Iranian leader Mahmoud Ahmadinejad was a religious fanatic with a death wish.[3] In contrast, our Soviet counterparts could be trusted with nuclear weapons because they, like America and its allies, only had nuclear weapons so that they would not use them.[4] Noted scholar of Islam, Bernard Lewis, referred to the growing strength of political Islam in the 1970s as being a dark storm cloud that was overwhelming societies, as it had periodically done in the past. Lewis, however, wrote that the dark cloud is not necessarily a product of the Islamic religion, but, rather, significant political and economic transformation, and the relative decline of the Islamic world at the expense of the West.[5] However, scholars, pundits, and politicians still cling to the belief that religion, itself, causes some people to lose hold of their sanity and act in a destructive manner.

We are also warned that today's religious terrorists are more dangerous because they see themselves as part of historical struggle between good and evil. Thus, they are patient and are willing to keep on fighting and killing even if short-term victory seems impossible. Osama bin Laden compared the United States to the Crusaders of the 11th century and viewed his fight as part of the 1,400-year conflict between Islam and the West. Many of his communiqués and proclamations include a statement about the eventual fall of the United States. Israel's violent religious radicals view the Palestinians as being part of a long list of groups going back to the Bible that have tried to destroy the Jews. Because the Jews are different, they will always be hated, so they must be vigilant in defending themselves against their enemies. It is important to note that most Muslims and Jews have opted out of these eternal struggles. The late Osama bin Laden's global jihadists, who fight for the return of a unified Islamic *umma* ruled by Islamic law, like the one that existed during the time of the Prophet Muhammad, account for less than 30,000 of the world's 1.5 billion Muslims. Most of the world's Jews do not live in Israel and, therefore, are relatively certain that their gentile neighbors are not out to destroy them.

The dismay felt by Lewis and many others at the revitalization of religion as a political force is a result of religion being seen as a regressive influence, whose public role would decline as countries modernized. The primordial bonds and beliefs of religion were seen as disappearing remnants of traditional and illiterate societies. Modernity, development, and even democracy were thought to be incompatible with religion, which can be seen in the fear that the democracy movement in the Middle East might lead to the victory of Islamic political parties.[6] Given the alleged regressive nature of politicized religion, it is understandable as to why violence and terrorism in the name of religion are seen as more of a threat than violence and terrorism that are justified by secular ideologies. At the same time, politically motivated violence had seemed to be modernizing as almost all terrorism and political violence from the late 18th century to the late 1970s was motivated by secular ideologies such as anarchism, socialism, communism, and nationalism. Terrorism, perhaps because of this secular orientation or because of the competing threat of nuclear annihilation from the Cold War, was not seen as the severe threat that it is today. It is no surprise that dire warnings regarding the threat of religion-based terrorism and political violence began to surface in the 1990s following the fall of the Soviet Union and the concurrent discrediting of communism.

An early warning came from noted scholar Samuel Huntington in 1993 with the publication of his seminal article in *Foreign Affairs,* "The Clash of Civilizations." Huntington argued that the great conflicts of the 21st century would be fought between civilizations over cultural differences, such as religion. Huntington divided the world into seven civilizations (Western, Confucian, Japanese, Islamic, Slavic-Orthodox, Latin American, and African) and predicted that future wars would be fought along the fault lines between these civilizations. Huntington also claimed that Islam had bloody borders and that the Islamic civilization would be involved in much of this fighting and violence.[7] Huntington's article gained widespread attention and represented a paradigm shift in the study of international relations where the dominant realist school discounted the importance of culture and religion as causes of conflict in favor of conflicting national interests, struggles to maximize power, and competitions over vital natural resources. Given the apparent clash between Islam and the West and the increased significance of religion as a source of war, terror, and violence, Huntington, despite his many critics, appeared to have been prescient.[8]

Huntington suggests that these conflicts between civilizations over real cultural differences might actually be caused by factors other than religion. Some of the causes of the clash of civilizations, in addition to how cultures think and view the world, are the isolation caused by modernization, greater interaction between civilizations, and American world dominance.[9] These factors, of course, operate independently of religion and might be the real causes of violence in the 21st century. It is likely that many Muslims are angry at the United States not because the U.S. population is predominately Christian or because they hate freedom and democracy. Rather, the United States is the dominant power in the world, which causes it to exert its influence across the globe, which causes resentment among the lesser powers, just as it did when Great Britain was the dominant power. The other European powers still resisted Britain's world dominance, despite the fact that they were all Christians and some had value systems similar to their British adversary. It might also be the case that those displaced by modernization and globalization express their grievances in the language of religion, but the real cause of their grievances is the displacement, not the fact that their nations are not governed by religious law.

Noted scholar Mark Juergensmeyer also wrote about the increasing importance of religion as a cause of conflict in 1993. Juergensmeyer in *The New Cold War?: Religious Nationalism Confronts the Secular State* focused on religions as a source of domestic conflict and insurrection. Like Huntington, Juergensmeyer saw cultural forces as the emerging cause of conflict at the dawn of the 21st century. However, Juergensmeyer observed that the primary conflict would not be between different ethnic or religious cultures but, rather, between the emerging religious nationalists and the established secular political establishments across the globe.[10] Contrary to the claims of some scholars, the end of the Cold War between the United States and the Soviet Union did not result in an end of ideology with the triumph of Western democracy, liberalism, and capitalism.[11] The religious nationalists saw the Western secular orders, both liberal and socialist, as having failed and needed to be replaced by societies rooted in religious law and values. "Like those before them who challenge the existing order, the religious-nationalists often use violence to further their agendas. In many cases they are waging populist attacks against Western culture and political ideologies, and they aim to infuse public life with indigenous cultural symbols and moral values. Recent events also show that they can be hostile, dogmatic, and violent and that their confrontation with secular government that is virtually global in its reach."[12]

Juergensmeyer's argument about the rise of religious nationalism leads one to wonder as to what the causes were of this stringent and sometimes violent campaign to return to a society and a political system based on religious principles. Beginning with the Protestant Reformation and through the 1960s, religion's role in society was in constant decline. As mentioned, many scholars of political, social, and economic development contended that religion's influence on these institutions would be marginalized as countries modernized. It could be that just as Huntington's clash of civilization might be a product of nonreligious causes, Juergensmeyer's "new cold war" might also be the result of factors related to social and economic change. Perhaps disgruntled people are now using religion as a language to express their anger over political, social, and economic matters. In *The New Republic,* Lloyd and Susan Rudolph cautioned that the growth in politicized religion could not simply be attributed to religious belief, "When TV talking heads and op-ed contributors portray 'mobs' as 'frenzied' and believers as 'fanatic,' they have given up the task of discerning the human inducements and political calculations that make politics happen. They have given up making motives visible and showing how they are transformed."[13] One could suggest that this "new cold war" might not have taken place if democracy, socialism, and capitalism had succeeded in bringing about political systems that provided for people's basic material needs and protected human dignity. What will happen if the religious nationalists also fail to provide for their citizens? I imagine that a new language of discontent will develop or there will be a return to an old one.

Noted terrorism scholar Bruce Hoffman also wrote about the rise of religion-based violence in the 1990s. Hoffman was particularly concerned about the severity of religious terrorism. According to Hoffman, secular terrorists seek allies and attempt to build a new political order. In contrast, religious terrorists kill indiscriminately and are only concerned with the complete destruction of their enemies. For example, Islamic terrorists seek either to kill their enemies or convert their enemies.[14] Thus, religion-based terrorism is more dangerous than secular terrorism, and religious terrorists are more likely to use weapons of mass destruction. Again, one is reminded of contemporary Islamic terrorists like the late Osama bin Laden and the leaders of Islamic nations like Mahmoud Ahmadinejad of Iran, who are often accused of having a death wish. The latter's alleged religious fanaticism is often used as a justification for bombing Iran to prevent it from developing nuclear weapons.[15]

Hoffman also notes that religious terrorists use extremist interpretations of their religions to justify their terrorist activities and acts of violence. These interpretations vary significantly from mainstream interpretations of Islam, Judaism, and Christianity, which generally support peace and loving your neighbors.[16] The terrorists' deviant, violent interpretations of their religious traditions lead to an important question: What separates those who interpret religion in a way that leads them to kill in the name of God from those who do not? Given that religion is something that these two groups have in common, it must be nonreligious factors that are the causes of their very different expressions of their religious faith. It is also worthwhile to ask whether the religious worldview that supposedly facilitates indiscriminate killing is really all that different from the worldview of secular extremists. After all, Stalin, Hitler, Pol-Pot, and many other perpetrators of genocide have been motivated by secular ideologies such as Nazism, communism, and ethnocentrism. As suggested, religion might provide a language for those who feel marginalized and dehumanized to express their political, social, and economic grievances or their psychological dysfunctions.

The importance of anomie and fragmentation as causes of today's religion-based violence and terrorism are discussed in Gilles Kepel's discussion of the resurgence of religion as a general political force in the late 1970. Kepel wrote that the 1970s "brought hidden human miseries to light."[17] Many saw these miseries as being a result of the failure of communism and liberalism to produce wealth and prosperity for all. Rather, liberalism, in the West, led to selfish consumerism, and socialism led to poverty and repression in the Soviet bloc and the developing world. These failures, along with the dislocation caused by the rapid change that transformed societies and economies at the end of the 20th century led many to question the basic way in which their societies were organized. Across the globe, those who challenged the secular foundations of society, or not sufficiently religious foundations, all believed that God was necessary to create more human values.[18]

Kepel warns against simply viewing the new religious movements "as a dethronement of reason or manipulation by hidden forces."[19] Kepel then goes on to list some possible "parents"—literacy, computerization, and unemployment—of these "unwanted children" (the religious movements) of the end of the 20th century. These movements, according to Kepel "have a singular capacity to reveal the ills of society for which they have their own diagnosis."[20] In short, Kepel is making the point that one must look outside of religion to understand the growth of religious political movements.

Carrying Kepel's argument to the topic at hand, we will also have to look outside of religion to understand why some use religion as a justification for violence and terrorism. Kepel notes that not all religious political movements use violence or even desire to transform society. Rather some religious movements try to facilitate a peaceful transformation from within, while others seek to withdraw from society and its ills rather than to reform it.[21] Therefore, one of the tasks at hand is to understand the conditions and forces that increase the likelihood of a religious individual expressing his or her faith through violence and terror.

Two important books dealing with religion and terrorism, Jessica Stern's *Terror in the Name of God* and Juergensmeyer's *Terror in the Mind of God*, both point to the importance of the social, political, and economic roots of religion-based violence and terrorism. Part I of Stern's book lists alienation, humiliation, demographics, history, and territory as the grievances that give rise to holy war. Religion is noticeably absent from the list. One of the aims of Juergensmeyer's book is providing insight into "cultures of violence." Juergensmeyer's research shows that religion is only one of many components of these cultures of violence. The other components are the alienation, humiliation, marginalization, and unresolved political grievances that are discussed in Stern's book.[22] Stern and Juergensmeyer's books leave the impression that there are groups of angry people whose rage is deep enough to be lethal, which leads one to wonder about the conditions that produced their alienation and despair. Being religious, however, is certainly not the cause of their rage.

The current era of religion-based terrorism has been one of the catalysts for a number of books and a movie that condemn religion and advocate for atheism.[23] *The End of Faith* by Sam Harris begins by describing a suicide bombing by a Hamas terrorist and contains a list of all the conflicts that pit religion against religion. Perhaps, this terrible tragedy and all of the conflicts would not have taken place if religion had been driven from the face of the earth. My guess is that they would, as the world and the Palestinians have produced many secular terrorists and suicide bombers.[24] Religion has been around for thousands of years and, despite the wishes of critics, will continue to exist into the near future. During its long history, religion has been the motivating force behind both acts of charity and acts of violence. Religion, as is the case with all ideologies, leaves much room for interpretation. Although moderate interpretations of religion, as some claim, may be philosophically unsound and scientifically unverifiable, they are not responsible for violence and terror. To me, it makes more sense to try to understand what leads some to cling to extremist interpretations of religion than to argue the merits of a phenomenon that will continue to exist and that is a justification for action rather than a cause of action.

ARGUMENT AND OVERVIEW

In this book, I will investigate the causes of the contemporary wave of violence that has been waged in the name of God and religion. In doing so, I will seek to answer three important questions:

1. How do Islam, Christianity, and Judaism, supposedly facilitate violence and terrorism?
2. Are religious ideologies really that different than other ideologies that have motivated violence by radical groups in the past?
3. What separates the overwhelming majority of those who practice religion peacefully from those who kill in the name of religion? In other words, what are the nonreligious factors that lead people to interpret religion in a way that sanctions violence and terror?

The thesis of this book is counterintuitive because I will argue that religion is not the primary cause of religion-based terrorism. The potential for violence is inherent in Judaism, Christianity, and Islam, yet the overwhelming majority of Muslims, Christians, and Jews do not kill in the name of their religions. As will be discussed, religious texts and traditions can be used to support violence as well as peace and reconciliation. At the same time, war, terror, and violence are multicausal events. To reduce them to solely being a product of religion, even when the instigators' motives appear to be religious, is erroneous. Therefore, the important task is to identify the conditions that are favorable to interpretations of these texts and traditions that call for violence and terror.

While acknowledging that the contemporary era of religion-based violence and terror has included a diverse group of religions including Hinduism and Sikhism, as well as cults such as Aum Shinrikyo, I will limit my discussion to Islam, Christianity, and Judaism. Since one of my goals is to find commonalities in religious histories, texts, legal systems, and worldviews that facilitate terror, it makes sense to focus on religions that share a common heritage and have enough similarities to make comparison worthwhile. At the same time, the histories of these three faiths are intertwined, and each has had a profound effect on the others. The focus of the book will be on insurgent religion-based violence, including terrorism, assassination and guerilla warfare, against the state. Although the Islamic governments of Saudi Arabia, Iran, and the Sudan have terrible human rights records and have often used violence against their citizens, they are too small of a sample to facilitate a meaningful discussion of religion-based violence and terrorism by nation-states.

It appears that the current wave of religion-based terror and violence is primarily an Islamic phenomenon and that there is no need to include Judaism and Christianity in this analysis. As will be seen in case studies in chapters 6 and 7, there are significant occurrences of Christian and Jewish terror. The small number of Jewish terrorists can be explained by the simple fact that there are so few Jews in the world, approximately 14 million as opposed to 1.5 billion Muslims and 2.1 billion Christians. Given this small population, Jews are more than adequately represented in the world of religion-based terrorism. The small number of Christian terrorists is important evidence supporting the argument that religion-based terrorism is primarily caused by factors that have nothing to do with religion. One could argue that paucity of Christian terrorism is due to Christianity being a peaceful religion, while Judaism and Islam are not. Chapter 6, which provides a discussion of religion-based violence in Christianity, will demonstrate that this is not the case. Again, one must look outside the realm of religion to understand why Christianity is in a relatively peaceful period in comparison to Islam and Judaism.

An important caveat is in order before I outline the argument that will be presented in the chapters that follow. Although numerous potential determinants of religion-based violence will be identified and evidence of their significance will be offered, none of these factors can be considered a necessary or sufficient cause. In other words, none of these influences must be present for religion-based violence to take place, nor do they, by themselves, guarantee that groups and individuals will kill in the name of religion. Religion-based violence, like all human behavior and social phenomenon, is multicausal. As Assaf Moghadam succinctly states in his book on suicide bombings, "The causes of suicide attacks are complex and must be found in the interplay of personal motivations, strategic and tactical objectives of the sponsoring groups, and the larger societal and structural factors affecting the bomber and the group. In addition ideology is acquired by individuals having to do with emotions and beliefs—a complex process."[25] Thus, I am not providing an explanation that will explain every case but, rather, factors that increase the probability that religion-based violence will occur. It is also important to note that I am not claiming that religion has no role in violence and terrorism but that it serves as a justification for violence rather than a cause.

Chapter 1 will discuss the reasons why religion, in general, is frequently used to justify violence, particularly terrorism and suicide bombing. Here, I will look at key components of monotheistic religion, such as God, sacred texts, clerics, heaven, and communities of support, and religious worldviews such as good and evil, believers and nonbelievers, eschatology, sacrifice, and martyrdom. Chapter 2 will then explain why religion can't be the primary cause of religion-based violence. First, I will look at some of the characteristics and worldviews of religion that facilitate violence and show how they are present in secular ideologies and communities. At the same time, religious texts, traditions, and philosophies are vague, amorphous, and often contradictory. I will show that religion can be used to justify almost anything, and the same verse from a religious text such as the Torah or the *Quran* can be used to support conflicting positions as to whether and when violence and terror are acceptable.

Chapters 3 through 5 will outline the conditions that facilitate religion being interpreted in a way that facilitates terror and the taking of lives. Since religion-based terror is always political in nature, chapter 3 will consider political conditions and influences. Both domestic political structures, such as authoritarianism, and international influences, such as occupation, invasion, and American world hegemony, will be discussed. Special attention will be given to considering whether democracy suppresses or encourages religion-based terrorism. Chapter 4 continues the discussion of the conditions that facilitate religious violence by examining socioeconomic factors. This domain is important because, as mentioned earlier, most religious terrorists are marginal people who feel a strong sense of alienation from their nations of origin and the world as a whole. Some of the forces, which must be considered at both the national and international levels, that foster these feelings of alienation and despair are inequality, frustrated aspirations, rapid social change, enforced secularization, dislocation, and globalization. These socioeconomic grievances are often enhanced by ethnic cleavages, which also must be brought into an analysis of religion-based terrorism. The psychological and personal roots of religion-based terrorism are taken up in chapter 5. There is no definitive psychological profile of a religious terrorist, and research has suggested that most terrorists are, for the most part, mentally sound. However, group psychology has a profound influence on the behavior of suicide bombers and other terrorists. Here, groupthink and other important group dynamics will be considered.

Chapters 6 through 8 offer case studies to illustrate the argument outlined in the first five chapters that religion-based terrorism is caused by a number of factors including politics, society, economics, psychology, ethnic divisions, as well as religion. Chapter 6 focuses on Jewish terrorism in Israel including the assassination of Israeli prime minister Yitzhak Rabin by Yigal Amir and the activities of the Jewish Underground in the West Bank, who want that area to be annexed to Israel. Here, I will discuss how four important themes in Jewish history help shape the world view of contemporary Jewish extremists. Special consideration will also be given to the influence of democracy on religion-based terrorism. Christianity is considered in chapter 7, where I will discuss its significant theological differences with Judaism and Islam. The case of U.S. antiabortion terrorists is important because it represents religious terrorism that is native to America and that is occurring in a democracy. The conflict between Catholics and Protestants in Northern Ireland will show how religion is only one of many factors that cause groups to wage violence in the name of religion.

Islam, the subject of chapter 8, will provide the most difficult test of my argument because Muslim extremists are responsible for an overwhelming majority of the religion-based terrorism that has taken place in the past 30 years. The Palestinian group, Hamas, will be used to illustrate how opposition to Israel and its control of the West Bank went from being a largely nationalist struggle to one that has increasingly taken on religious overtones. Hezbollah, in Lebanon, will show that group's use of terror and violence is as much a result of political aspirations as it is an expression of religious fervor. Finally, al Qaeda, a group that appears to be motivated by blind hatred and religious zeal, will be considered. Here, it will become clear that al Qaeda's extremism is largely a product of authoritarianism, globalization, Osama bin Laden, and U.S. world dominance. In the conclusion, I will summarize my key findings, discuss the future of religion-based terrorism, and provide suggestions as to who to combat religious extremism and the violence that it produces.

Chapter 1

How Religion
Facilitates Terrorism

What is it about religion that leads people to kill in its name? People do not usually kill without reason, unless they are compelled to do so or are criminally insane. The histories of Judaism, Christianity, and Islam all contain many events of religion-based violence such as the Jewish Maccabean revolt, the Crusades, and the wars of Islamic expansion. Given this long association between faith and violence, religion must provide powerful justifications for shedding blood. The most powerful rationale is, of course, God. Religious warriors from King David to Muhammad always believed that they were fulfilling God's will, or defending God, and that their violence had been sanctified by divine authority. Religions also provide texts, either divine or divinely inspired, that are written records of God's will. These divine texts are often used to justify killing, as is the case with those who use the wars against the Amalekites in the Hebrew Bible as a precedent supporting violence against today's Palestinians. The violent interpretations of these texts often come from clergy such as Rabbi Meir Kahane and the leaders of the radical antiabortion movement in the United States, whose authority and revered status provide further justification for killing. Religion offers rewards in the afterlife for those who kill in its name. Many Islamic suicide bombers believe that they will receive 79 virgins when they get to heaven. Religion also provides a history of martyrs, such as Jesus and the Jewish Zealots at Masada who committed suicide rather than accept Roman rule, who sacrificed their lives or endured great suffering because of their faith.

Many who fight in the name of God believe that they are helping to bring about the end of history and are bringing about the World to Come by catalyzing events such as the second coming of Christ or the rebuilding of the Second Jewish Temple on Mt. Zion. These eschatological visions and the desire to bring about a World to Come often include a final struggle between good and evil. Followers of a religion believe that they are a force for good and justice, which makes it easy for them to label those who oppose them as being evil or the forces of the devil that must be destroyed.[1] Religion can easily be a very divisive force as it divides the world into believers and nonbelievers. Jews, historically, have viewed themselves as the chosen people and refer (often derisively) to non-Jews as *Goyyim* (nations of the earth). Islam categorizes individuals as Muslims, People of the Book, and People of Ignorance. In short, religion facilitates killing by dividing people into in-groups and out-groups, where the life of a member of the out-group is of less value and where members of the out-group are often seen as a threat. Finally, religion teaches the importance of personal sacrifice and provides communities emotional, spiritual, and logistical support for those who kill in the name of God.

GOD

God's role as the primary inspirational and legitimizing force behind religion-based violence was best illustrated by the battle cry "God wills it" that launched the First Crusade.[2] Wars and violence in the name of God began in the Hebrew Bible and continue today with al Qaeda and the murder of abortion providers. It is important to note that the first act of religion-based violence was committed by God, himself. Humanity, with the exception of Noah and his family, was destroyed in the great flood because God was angry. Lot's wife was turned into a pillar of salt for turning back to look at the burning cities of Sodom and Gomorrah, and countless numbers of Egyptians perished with the freeing of the Hebrew slaves in the Exodus story. God also intervened in battles as he aided the Children of Israel in their struggles with Amalek. J. Harold Ellens presents the metaphor of an angry God, whose wrath can be resolved only by someone, including his son (Jesus), being killed, which has resulted in the creation of a monster God in the psyches of monotheistic religions.[3] Given the existence of a God who has been willing to kill and has instructed his supporters to kill, it is not surprising that today's religious warriors believe that they are pleasing God by engaging in war, terror, and violence.

J. P. Larsson writes that it is often the fear of the wrath of an angry God for sins committed that leads some believers to engage in violence. These individuals feel that violence in God's name is a demonstration of their desire to win back the respect of the deity and to avoid being punished in the afterlife.[4] Thus, it is not surprising that the Christmas Day 2009 "Underwear Bomber," Umar Farouk Abdulmutallab, and the May 2010 Times Square bomber, Faisal Shahzad, had both engaged in sinful lifestyles prior to becoming Islamic terrorists. In essence, their failed attacks might have been acts of atonement aimed at regaining God's favor. As will be discussed, dying in holy war is viewed by some Islamists as a way of ensuring one's place in eternal paradise. As will be discussed, many other Jewish, Christian, and Islamic terrorists have also led secular and blasphemous lifestyles before renouncing their sins, becoming true believers, and engaging in religion-based violence.

Other religion-based terrorists do not see themselves as defending themselves from God's wrath but, rather, as defending God from those who attack him. Rabbi Kahane saw the Palestinians and the Israelis who wished to trade land for peace as attacking God because they sought to take or give away land that God had promised to the Jews. Kahane believed that God had always fought against his enemies beginning with the book of Exodus. In the 1980s, Kahane saw himself and his activists, who planned to blow up the Islamic holy sites on the Temple Mount, as instruments in the fight to defend God and his prescribed destiny for the Jews, occupation of all of the land promised in the Hebrew Bible, from the internal and external enemies who sought to thwart his plan.[5] Jessica Stern writes that Paul Hill, who shot a Pensacola, Florida, abortion provider in 1994, also believed that he was defending God. It was the abortion provider who was perpetrating the violence by violating God and Christ's principle of sanctifying life. Killing Dr. John Britton and his security escort was a defense of God and his law. Ultimately, Hill hoped to cause a civil war that would produce a Christian nation ruled in the name of God and Christ.[6]

Most religion-based terrorists believe that they are not only defending God but also fulfilling God's will. A true believer, of course, cannot act against God's will and must play a role in implementing that will, whatever it may be. It is quite common to hear people say that God has a plan for them or for society. Some of those individuals are content to let that plan play itself out through God's direction. Others try to further God's will through faith, prayer, and acts of charity. A small minority uses violence to implement the will of God. Ellens writes that the Western monotheistic religions maintain a theology that calls for humans to be responsible for the shape of society, while Eastern religions look inward for transcendence.[7] Thus, it is only natural that a fervent believer, who believes that he or she has insight into the will of God, might use violence to bring about his or her vision of a divine plan. Numerous examples of this tendency can be found in today's Islamic, Jewish, and Christian terrorism.

Sayyid Qutb, whose ideas are the inspiration for many of today's radical Islamic groups, wrote that it was an obligation to spread Islam until all are under the rule of God, free from the rule of man, and living under God's law, *Sharia* (Islamic law). According to Qutb, violence would be acceptable when resistance is encountered.[8] Osama bin Laden said the following when asked about the attack on September 11, 2001, "These actions were carried out by the zealous sons of Islam in defense of their religion and in response to the order of their God and prophet, may God's peace and blessings be upon him."[9] Paul Hill justified his killing of an abortion provider by stating that "If the state requires us to do what is contrary to God's law, we must obey God's law." He then goes on to say that the present abortion laws violate God's law and that it is his responsibility to see that God's will is not violated.[10] These ideas exemplify the notion that true faith shows itself through good works and righteous deeds. God's will must be carried out by his believers on earth, even if that means taking a life. War and terrorism, thus, become methods for the victory of God, which will lead to peace and harmony.[11] A true believer will receive a personal reward in the afterlife for acting in the name of God but will suffer grave consequences for failing to do so.

The notion of a rewarding and punishing God, whose will must be served, can merge with the belief that God's power is absolute. Jonathan Fox points out that because God is a divine or supernatural authority, extremists hold the view that mortal men can't question his will.[12] This notion is particularly ironic for Jewish extremists as Israel literally means to struggle with God in Hebrew.[13] However, Yigal Amir, who assassinated Israeli prime minister Yitzhak Rabin, believed that Rabin had to be killed because his intention of returning land promised to the Jews in the Bible was a violation of God's authority.[14] One meaning of the Arabic root from which the word Islam is derived is to submit.[15] As a result, Islamic extremism and terrorism include violently resisting those who oppose Islam as being part of completely submitting one's self to the will of God. Thus, Osama bin Laden has often made the claim that his attacks on the United States are defensive in nature because God requires resistance to those who attack Islam.

God also serves to sanctify killing by transcending ordinary meaning. Peter Berger talks about the process of cosmization by which activities in the world of human existence are simultaneously being enacted in the divine, supernatural realm, whose significance is beyond common human understanding.[16] In this regard, taking a life is not a simple act of murder but also a divine act, whose real significance, like other religious rituals, is divinely ordained. Regina Schwartz notes that once activity is legitimated by transcendence, it is elusive and inviolate.[17] This means that the religious justifications for violence and terrorism are beyond question and may not be understood by most individuals. Although murder is against the law, religion-based violence cannot be judged by human-made law because it is part of something far greater but incomprehensible to those who do not share the killer's state of enlightenment.

Religion-based terrorism, for those who seek to become closer to God through violence, can become a divinely ordained ritual. David Rapoport, in his discussion of early examples of Jewish, Islamic, and Hindu terrorism, writes that the religion embodies ritual and that strict ritualistic regulations governed the violent acts of the Assassins, a violent Islamic group in the Middle Ages. Adherence to these rules made their violence transcendent, and the rules could not be altered because they were divinely inspired.[18] Lloyd Steffen explains that when God is viewed as being the ultimate truth and the end limit of power, the morality of actions becomes certain. These actions, or rituals, must be performed without thought or error.[19] Mark Juergensmeyer, in his discussion of cosmic war, describes how the performance of religion-based terrorism resembles the performance of religious ritual. Dates of attacks are selected to correspond with religious holidays. The locations of attacks are selected based on their symbolic meaning for the victim or the attacker. Finally, the attacks must be carried out with ritualistic precision and must be performed with the same sense of holiness and awe that is required in performing other religious rituals.[20]

Baruch Goldstein's attack on Muslim worshippers at the Cave of the Patriarchs in Hebron, which resulted in 30 deaths, was carried out on Purim, a Jewish holiday commemorating the triumph of the Jews over their adversaries in ancient Persia. Goldstein viewed the Muslims' presence in a place that was sacred to Jews as offensive, and he was angry because he had been taunted by Muslims during a previous visit to the cave.[21] His choice of the Cave of the Patriarchs, where it is believed that Abraham, Isaac, and Jacob are buried, can be viewed as a defense of sacred space. Juergensmeyer discusses how Paul Hill looked on two incidents involving the murder and attempted murder of abortion providers with disfavor because they represented the improper performance of ritual. In the first case, Michael Griffin successfully killed Dr. David Gunn in Pensacola, Florida, but later tried to blame the pro-life movement for his actions in an attempt to reduce his sentence. According to Hill, Griffin had not performed the ritual with the proper intent. Shelly Shannon attempted to kill Dr. George Tiller in Wichita,

Kansas, but only wounded him. In this instance, Hill was disturbed because the ritual had been improperly performed.[22] The merging of religious ritual and violence is also evident at al Qaeda training camps, where religious and military instruction is combined. Accounts of the training of Palestinian suicide bombers describe a process that is very similar to the preparation for performance of major religious rituals.[23]

SACRED TEXTS AND THEOLOGY

The propensity to engage in violence in the name of God is strengthened by sacred texts where religious warriors can find justifications for the actions. Since true believers take it for granted that the Torah (Five Books of Moses), the New Testament, and the *Quran* are the word of God, these sacred texts are seen as instructions that must be followed in living one's daily life.[24] Charles Kimball writes that biblical verses serve as absolute truth claims that prove the righteousness of those who use violence in the name of religion.[25] These verses are proof that the religious warrior is acting out God's will when he or she blows up a bus or bombs a place of worship. It is no surprise that many Jewish and Christian extremists have cited Exodus 15:3, which states that "the Lord is a God of war," to justify their activities. According to Schwartz, the Bible and other sacred texts, when applied to contemporary issues and struggles, become manuals for politics.[26] Thus, the Jewish settler can use Genesis 12:7, where God promised the land of Israel to Abraham and his offspring, as justification for trying to force Palestinians off their land. Michael Bray, who was convicted in connection with the bombing of 10 women's health clinics where abortions were performed, also used the story of Abraham as a justification for his actions. He claimed that by being sent to prison for his crimes and leaving his children, he was like Abraham, who was willing to sacrifice his son to God in Genesis 22:1–12.

There are countless other examples of contemporary religious actors using sacred texts to justify violence and terrorism. It is important to note that, although these texts are manuals for contemporary politics, they are often vague, amorphous, and require interpretation, as is evident in Bray's claim. As a result, we can see instances of the same text or verse being used to support contradictory positions. For example, the rector of Egypt's Al Azhar University (authoritative voice of the country's Islamic establishment) used examples from the life of the Prophet Muhammad (*Sunna*) to justify launching the October 1973 war against Israel and the peace treaty signed between the two countries in 1979. It is also common to see the use of conflicting proof texts to justify opposing positions. In Matthew 5:38–40, Jesus tells his followers to turn the other cheek when they are struck by their enemies. Yet, in Matthew 10: 34–37, Jesus says that he comes not to bring peace but a sword. As a result, both those who want to use Jesus as a dove and as a hawk can find justification in scripture.

Theology, law, and other sacred works, although not as authoritative as divine texts, also provide justification for those who engage in religion-based violence. Scholars and theologians in Islam, Judaism, and Christianity have considered when war and violence are justified and produced the concept of the just war. The Christian notion of just war is rooted in the writings of St. Augustine and St. Thomas Aquinas. In general, a just war must be waged by a property authority, such as the state, must be for a just cause and not self gain, and must have the goal of peace and a return to order.[27] In the 20th century, the Protestant theologian Reinhold Niebuhr wrote that violence is sometimes necessary to combat injustice, particularly when that injustice is being supported by the overwhelming power of the modern state.[28] One of Niebuhr's peers, Dietrich Bonhoeffer, a Lutheran minister, participated in a failed plot to kill Adolf Hitler because he believed that violence could be used in the pursuit of a just cause and that human law can be broken if it contradicts divine law. Ironically, Michael Bray justified his participation in attacks on abortion clinics by citing Christian just-war theory, the writings of Niebuhr, and the example of Bonhoeffer.[29]

There are three types of war in Judaism, *Milhemet-hova* (obligatory war), *Milhemet-mitzvah* (commanded war), and *Milhemet-reshut* (discretionary war). The first two are nearly identical and involve obliterating the enemy, including every man, woman, and child. These wars, however, are considered terminated by most rabbinical authorities as they are limited to the biblical wars against the Amalekites and the Canaanites, peoples who no longer exist. The radical fringe of the religious-Zionist movement, however, views contemporary Palestinians as being the descendents of the Amalekites or analogous to them and calls for an obligatory war to eliminate them. The requirements for discretionary war, a Jewish king, the ancient Sanhedrin court, and the breastplate of the high priest, also do not exist in contemporary Israel, but debate exists as to whether the religious and state institutions of Israel can declare a discretionary war.[30] The notion of the *rodef* (one in pursuit of murder) was used as a justification for the assassination of Yitzhak Rabin. Under the *rodef* principle, a person who witnesses an attempted murder is obliged to intervene. Yigal Amir, who killed Rabin, justified his actions by claiming that trading land for peace would cause the death of Jews. Hence, it was his responsibility to kill Rabin before the prime minister could commit his act of murder.[31]

The concept of *jihad* in Islam is well known and is often used by Islamic terrorists and holy warriors. *Jihad* is a misunderstood and amorphous term that is commonly believed to mean holy war. *Jihad* is also often misconceived as an offensive war to conquer other nations and force them to convert to Islam. Rather, the word *jihad* is derived from the Arabic verb root, to exert. *Jihad* is an emphatic verb form of the root, meaning extreme exertion. Today the notion of *jihad* is often interpreted as being extreme exertion in fulfilling one's obligations as Muslim. To most Muslims, this means fulfilling the five pillars of Islam (prayer, charity, fasting during Ramadan, making the pilgrimage to Mecca, and the profession of one's faith) and observing Islamic law. For some, these obligations mean defending Islam when it is being attacked. *Jihad* was originally used in the context of holy war, Muhammad's campaigns against the pagan tribes against Mecca, and has been used to describe most wars involving Islamic forces. For the most part, *jihad*'s spiritual and internal meaning is more recent. Today's debate as to the real nature of *jihad* is a political one that is of little significance. What is important is that violent *jihad* is a part of Islamic history and that contemporary Islamic terrorists and heads of state call for violent *jihad*. Most who do, including Osama bin Laden, use *jihad* in a defensive context, as he believes that the United States declared a war on Islam by placing troops in Saudi Arabia during the 1990–1991 Gulf War and by supporting Israel. In short, *jihad,* for some, is a religious justification for war.[32]

CLERICS AND AUTHORITY FIGURES

Religious clerics, who provide authoritative interpretations of religious texts and traditions, are another justification for religion-based violence and terrorism. Clerics and religious scholars are considered men or women of God and, because of their training and status, are respected and revered. Thus, religious individuals often go to their clergy for advice on matters of daily affairs and guidance on religious issues. Kimball notes that religion requires obedience to the absolute and that, for some, this obedience is given to the absolute's mortal representatives, the clergy.[33] A violent antiabortion activist related that "I have talked to my pastor and this is what God wants us to do. We are protecting the unborn."[34] Yigal Amir sought the approval of a rabbi before assassinating Rabin for being a *rodef* but could not find one who would sanction the killing. Some rabbis may, however, have given the impression that Rabin was a *rodef* and a traitor. A judgment based on *Halachah* (Jewish law) was made that the Oslo Peace Accords were null and void, because it was illegal to relinquish ownership of any part of the land of

Israel to another people. Yaakov Ariel, the chief rabbi of Ramat Gan (a suburb of Tel Aviv), publicly reflected on whether Rabin was a *rodef*. Students at Israel's Orthodox university, Bar Ilan, discussed whether Rabin should die for his deeds. Rabbi Avigdor Eskin said an ancient Aramaic prayer, *Pulsa da Nura,* outside Rabin's residence in 1995, cursing the prime minister and calling for his death.[35]

The clergy's authority as interpreters of text and religious law enhances their ability to motivate their followers to engage in violence and terrorism. Avalos writes that the passing down of religious tradition orally through families, clans, and other social groups has become less common as society has modernized. As a result, religious traditions are increasingly being transmitted through written texts, and the interpretation of these texts is the domain of the clergy, which gives them more power and authority.[36] As mentioned, the president of Egypt, Anwar Sadat, sought a *fatwa* (interpretation of religious law) both when launching a war with Israel in 1973 and when making peace five years later. The Ayatollah Khomeini's status as an upper-echelon member of Iran's Shiite clergy and his promise of paradise for those who would meet their death certainly helped motivate thousands of Iranian teenagers to run through minefields during that country's war with Iraq in the 1980s. The motivation and authority of the mysterious and rarely seen Mullah Omar are credited with being a cause of the Taliban's easy takeover of Afghanistan in the mid-1990s. Rabbi Avraham Shapira, the head of an Israeli religious party, using rabbinic literature, issued a Jewish legal decision (*psak*) claiming that the obligation to settle the land of Israel is so important that one can put his or her life at risk when doing so.[37]

Religion often provides charismatic leaders who motivate their followers to violence through their representation of the divine and the force of their personality. Max Weber discusses the charismatic leader whose authority rests on his or her exceptional sanctity, heroism, or exemplary character. The charismatic leader's followers become devoted to the normative order that he or she has revealed or ordained. Weber's notion of the charismatic leader is based on the ancient prophets of Israel.[38] Thus, there is a strong connection between religion and charismatic leadership, as religious leaders are easily believed to be touched by the divine. Throughout history, religion has provided the archetypes of charismatic leadership such as Moses, Jesus, and Muhammad. Contemporary examples of religious charismatic leaders who have led their followers into battle include David Koresh of the Branch Davidian Christian cult in Waco, Texas. Koresh used biblical verses to justify his sleeping with any woman in the cult and, ultimately, inspired his followers to violently resist federal law enforcement agents when they attempted to take the Davidian's compound.

HEAVEN AND SALVATION

Clergy and sacred texts relate to another important determinant of religion-based violence, the promise of heaven and salvation for those who die fighting for God. Muslim holy warriors, apparently, are promised a place in heaven. "Think not of those who are slain in Allah's way as dead. Nay, they live, finding their sustenance from their Lord. They rejoice in the Bounty provided by Allah."[39] The following words from a member of the Pakistani militant group Harkat ul Mujahideen reflect one interpretation of this verse: "I pray for death every day. I decided to sacrifice my life for *jihad*. If I die in *jihad*, then I go to paradise. Allah will reward me. This is my dream."[40] He then goes on to comment that Muslims are not afraid of death because of the promise of life after death and paradise. The belief that 79 virgins and rivers of beer and wine await Islamic holy warriors when they get to heaven is well known. Israeli security forces reported that one Palestinian suicide bomber had wrapped his testicles in tin foil so that they would be intact when he arrived in paradise.[41] The notion of dying in battle for one's faith as guaranteeing entry to heaven is not limited to Islam. Soldiers participating in the Crusades were often promised entrance to heaven or a release from purgatory. Paul Hill, who murdered an abortion provider, looked forward to meeting God and was certain that he would go to heaven.[42]

Dying for God in holy war not only ensures the holy warrior's place in heaven but also means that he or she will be remembered as a martyr on earth. The parents of Palestinian suicide bombers often express pride in the exploits of their deceased children. The martyrs' funerals are often carried out in celebratory fashion with sweets provided and traditional wedding songs being sung. Pictures of the martyrs are posted in their communities, and their parents are paid compensation ranging up to 15,000 dollars.[43] Baruch Goldstein, the American-born Israel pediatrician who massacred 29 Palestinians at the Cave of the Patriarchs in Hebron, is viewed as a hero in the extremist, religious-Zionist community. A plaque with candles of mourning was erected in his memory in his hometown of Kiryat Arba on the West Bank. A web search of his name leads to a website that lauds him as a martyr and a hero.[44] Whether it is a place in heaven and an eternity in paradise with virgins and alcohol or being celebrated as a martyr after your death, religion gives some people the impression that dying is not only something not to be feared, but, rather, it is desirable and preferable to living. One must wonder as to the conditions that cause individuals to adopt this nihilistic view of life and death.

ESCHATOLOGY AND THE END OF DAYS

The significance of pleasing God, defending God, carrying out his will properly, authoritative religious texts, and martyrdom are directly related to eschatology (the study of the end of time). Monotheistic religions have visions as to what will happen at the end of time or the end of the world as we know it. The apocalyptic worldview can actually be traced back to the ancient pagan cultures of Mesopotamia and Egypt. Ellens writes that this fascination with the End of Days has always been ingrained in our psyche and can be seen today in numerous contemporary movies, books, and television shows.[45] Eschatological notions usually involve a period of trial and tribulation and pain and suffering prior to the arrival of a messiah figure, which brings about a world without suffering, eternal life, and people of faith are vindicated for their belief. The corrupt old era is ended and replaced with a new state of being where there is peace and happiness. Eschatological worldviews do not always lead to violence, as most believers are content to wait for God to decide when the time is right for redemption. Others hope to bring about the new era through faith, observing religious law, and acts of charity. A small minority, however, believes that they can help bring about the process of redemption through human artifice. Given that a period of war, violence, and conflict proceeds the dawn of redemption, it is inevitable that some will try to instigate violence in order to help the process play itself out.

There is a crucial messianic element to Jewish, Christian, and Shiite Islamic conceptions of the End of Days. Jews believe that the World to Come will be brought about by the coming of the *Mashiach* (Messiah).[46] The book of Isaiah contains numerous verses about the messianic era, and there are several rabbinic and Talmudic interpretations of the World to Come. It is generally agreed that there will be an ingathering of the Jews to the land of Israel. Solomon's Temple will be rebuilt on Mt. Zion, the persecution of Jews will end, and the Jews will live in peace. Some claim that the premessianic period (footsteps of the Messiah) will be filled with violence and tribulation. Following the exile from the land of Israel by the Romans in the 70 CE, the Jews of the Diaspora waited for the Messiah, and those who thought that they could bring about his return through human action, such as migrating to Israel, were strongly condemned. Israel's victory in the 1967 Six-Day War resulted in the capture of the old city of Jerusalem, which contains Mt. Zion where the first and second temples stood in ancient Israel, and the western support wall of the Second Temple, the holiest site in Judaism, still stands. As a result, a growing number of religious Jews began to come to the conclusion that the dawn of redemption had commenced and that it was their responsibility to speed up the process.[47]

Major obstacles, including the presence of Islamic holy sites, the Dome of the Rock and the al Aqsa Mosque, on the Temple Mount, the presence of 1.5 million Palestinians in the West Bank who wished to create a state on Jewish land, and governments that have negotiated to return that land to the Palestinians in a peace treaty, stood in their way. Some Orthodox Jews have prepared for the Messiah's return through nonviolent methods such as attempting to develop a red cow, which was offered as a sacrifice in the days of the Second Temple. Others have been engaging in a 15-year course of study to serve as priests when the temple is rebuilt. Paving the way for the coming of the Messiah has also been an important cause of Jewish violence and terrorism. Two attempts to blow up the Islamic holy sites were made in the 1980s. One group of plotters maintained that the Second Temple had to be rebuilt before the Messiah would come. The other group hoped that destroying the Islamic holy sites would cause a holy war between Muslims and Jews, in which the Messiah would intervene to bring victory to the Jews.[48]

The religious-Zionist movement in Israel has dedicated itself to maintaining Israeli control over East Jerusalem and the West Bank.[49] Rabbi Abraham Kook, the first chief rabbi of Israel, believed that the secular-socialist Jews who built and founded the state of Israel were doing God's work (although they did not realize or acknowledge it) by beginning the process of redemption. With capture of East Jerusalem and the West Bank, many Orthodox Jews, including Kook's son, Tzvi Yehuda, began to adopt the elder Kook's vision of modern Israel as a sign of messianic redemption.[50] The religious-Zionists then dedicated themselves to settling the newly captured lands so that they could not be returned in a peace settlement with the Palestinians. As will be discussed in chapter 6, extremist members of this group have launched numerous terrorist attacks against Palestinians and Amir assassinated Prime Minister Yitzhak Rabin for attempting to trade land for peace. This exchange could not be tolerated because yielding Jewish land could prevent or delay messianic redemption.

Christian End of Days theology builds on the Jewish scenarios described in the preceding text and is focused on the second coming of Jesus Christ and the rapture. Many evangelical Christians believe that the Jews must control the land of Israel, the Second Temple must be rebuilt, and the holy sites of the Muslims destroyed before Christ can return. Unfortunately, for the Jews, this process will instigate a cataclysmic period of wars known as Armageddon, which will result in the destruction of the Temple and the temporary ascendance of the anti-Christ. Jesus, ultimately, will lead the forces of God to victory. The 1,000-year kingdom of Christ will be followed by the Day of Judgment and the Rapture, when those who have accepted Christ as their savior will go to heaven and those who do not will be left behind to spend eternity in hell.[51] Given the prerequisite of Jewish control of the land of Israel and rebuilding of the Jewish Temple on Mt. Zion, many evangelical, millennial Christians are ardent supporters of the state of Israel.

The potential for violence in Christian eschatology lies with those who maintain a postmillennial theology. Premillennial theology holds that the 1,000-year reign of Christ will happen only after Christ's return, which will be facilitated by a cataclysmic historical event. This group tends to avoid politics and violence and focuses on trying to discern what that event will be and when it will take place. Postmillennial theology, on the other hand, holds that the 1,000-year kingdom of Christendom must occur before Christ will return. Consequently, this group, led by evangelicals such as Pat Robertson and the late Jerry Falwell, is very active in politics and is trying to turn the American nation into a Christian nation in order to bring about the second coming.[52] This group wishes to reconstruct society according to Christ's principles and capture important political, social, and educational institutions in the name of Christ.[53] As will be discussed in chapter 7, the violent extremist fringe of the antiabortion movement subscribes to postmillennial, Reconstruction theology and believes that abortion violates God's law and must be prevented, even violently, so that the 1,000-year reign of Christ can begin.

Islamic eschatological notions are based less on a messiah and going forward into a new World to Come than wanting to go back and re-create the conditions that existed at the time of the Prophet Muhammad. *Sharia*, Islamic law, is also a key element of Islamic conceptions of an ideal world. Islamic tradition contains the notion of the Mahdi, the guided one, who will come to rescue the Islamic community from corrupt and oppressive rulers and restore the true and just Islam that existed at the time of the Prophet. The notion of the Mahdi in the Sunni branch of Islam is limited to popular folklore and is not a part of formal doctrine. The Mahdi is firmly established in the Shiite branch of Islam and is believed to be the Hidden Imam, the divinely sanctioned successor to the Prophet Muhammad and the Caliph Ali (whose assassination led to the Sunni and Shiite split). Like Jesus, his rule will be divine and he will bring about an era of peace, justice, and righteousness.[54] There have been, however, few violent incidents aimed at facilitating the coming of the Mahdi, one exception being the seizure of the Grand Mosque in Mecca on the Islamic New Year in 1979 by a group whose leader claimed to be the Mahdi.

The dominant eschatological strain in Islam, as mentioned, is a desire to re-create the society that existed during the time of the Prophet Muhammad and his four rightly guided successors (caliphs). Islamic revivalists throughout the world call for the implementation of Islamic law, *Sharia*, which will create a humane and just society. Consequently, most Islamic terrorist organizations and revolutionary groups, such as the Taliban in Afghanistan, Islamic Jihad in Egypt (which assassinated President Anwar Sadat in 1981), and the Shabab in Somalia, seek to take over national governments and replace them with Islamic governments that will implement *Sharia*. As will be discussed in chapter 3, many of these groups have resorted to violence because of the lack of a peaceful alternative or because they have been excluded from legitimate politics. Al Qaeda is an exception in that it does not recognize nation-states and seeks to reestablish a universal Caliphate (Islamic theocracy) and believes that the whole world, rather than individual countries, would be ruled by *Sharia*. Al Qaeda has shown itself to be more than willing to use violence and terrorism to achieve this objective.

Eschatology further contributes to religion-based violence and terrorism by linking today's conflicts to timeless struggles that have been going on for centuries and that may extend indefinitely into the future. Mark Juergensmeyer writes that religion gives cosmic warriors the power to endure and to be certain that they will ultimately prevail, because scripture and history have already revealed the outcome of the battle, which they will ultimately win, because God is fighting alongside them. Dr. Abdul Aziz al Rantisi, a leader of Hamas (a Palestinian Islamic organization fighting to replace Israel with an Islamic state), remarked that the war for Palestine has been going on for hundreds of years and could continue for hundreds more. Al Rantisi views all defeats as temporary and is certain that Islam will triumph in the end.[55] One of al Rantisi's adversaries, Daniella Weiss, a leader of the religious-Zionist movement in the West Bank remarked that history put her where she is and will keep her there until redemption.[56] Both believe that the outcome of their conflict is in God's hands and that they are part of a timeless struggle that will lead to not only victory but also a World to Come that is beyond human comprehension or a return to a glorious past when perfection existed in the human realm.

GOOD AND EVIL

Eschatology relates to another cause of religion-based violence, the division of the world into good and evil. As discussed, the End of Days is preceded by a great struggle between the forces of good and evil and replaces a period of rule by a corrupt, tyrannical government that acts against religion. Ellens writes that the division of the world into good and evil, represented by God and the devil, is also a strong part of the human psyche and that this cosmic dualism becomes a lens that shapes people's worldview.[57] Lloyd Steffen calls this a dialectic between life-affirming and life-destroying forces.[58] Religious warriors see life as an endless struggle between good and evil, justice and injustice, chaos and order, and believers and nonbelievers.[59] The division of the world into good and evil is not limited to religion as former president George W. Bush labeled America's enemies the "axis of evil," and Communism was demonized as a force of evil during the Cold War. Religious notions of good and evil, however, are enduring and permanent, whereas secular notions of evil are more malleable to change. Russia, following the fall of Communism, ceased to be an enemy, and China is a major trading partner that holds much of our national debt.

Kimball points to Christianity's portrayal of Judaism as an example of how leaders of a religion create a binary world where they are good and their adversaries are evil. Although early Christians considered themselves a sect within Judaism, Christians began to see Jews, who denied that Jesus was the Messiah, as evil and an existential threat. The Gospel of John contains several passages that are critical of Jews.[60] Over the years, a myth developed where Jews captured and killed Christian children so that their blood could be used to make matzo (unleavened bread) for Passover. John Chrysostom, bishop of Antioch, said, "A synagogue is not only a whorehouse; it is a den of thieves and wild animals. It is a place where Christ is denied, a haunt of infidels, a hiding place of madmen under the damnation of God himself."[61] The portrayal of Jews as the earthly representation of the devil, the enemy of Christianity, and the killers of Christ facilitated nearly 2,000 years of Christian discrimination and violence against Jews including restrictions as to where Jews could live and what professions they could enter, the Crusades, the Spanish Inquisition, pogroms in Eastern Europe, and countless other massacres.

The division of the world into good and evil and the timeless struggle against the forces of the devil are in no way limited to Christianity. Sheik Yassin, the late spiritual leader of the Lebanese Shiite militia Hezbollah, said the following about the U.S. invasion of 1990–1991 to drive the Iraqis

out of Kuwait: "This is another episode in the fight between good and evil
(Islam and Christianity) and a hateful Christian plot against our religion,
our civilization and our land."[62] Osama bin Laden used the same image of
a dualistic conflict between two regions, "one of faith (Islam) where there is
no hypocrisy and another of infidelity (the West), from which we hope God
will protect us."[63] Once the world has been divided between good and evil,
it becomes a religious imperative to oppose the forces of darkness, as religion calls for its adherents to transform the world and improve humanity.
For the extremist, those who stand in the way of such transformation are
evil and can be killed. Ironically, religion's ultimate goal of peace and a just
world is often used to legitimate violence and bloodshed. The Islamic wars
of conquest, ostensibly, were to destroy idolatry, paganism, ignorance, and
barbarianism, while bringing Islam, a just and peaceful force, to the world.
The Crusades were waged to liberate the Holy Land from the heretical, bar-
barous, and evil forces of Islam.

Juergensmeyer points out that the struggle on a cosmic plane between
the good of religion and the evil of nonbelievers is often connected to real-
world political struggles.[64] When the late Ayatollah Khomeini (the motivating force behind Iran's Islamic revolution and its first leader) commented
that "life is faith and struggle" and that fighting is basic to human existence and on par with faith, he had specific enemies in mind—the United
States, Israel, and Westernized Muslims—not just vague evil. Consequently,
he prayed to God for the destruction of traitors and his enemies.[65] Here, we
see religion in its traditional role of fighting greater evil but with specific
and real-world enemies, such as foreign adversaries, corrupt secular governments, or governments that claim to rule in the name of religion but do not.
We can also understand why the most common form of religion-based violence is religious warriors attacking people of their own faith, as the devil
within is the greatest threat. As discussed, Yitzhak Rabin was assassinated
for his attempts to trade Jewish land for peace. In the months leading up to
his death, he was subjected to scurrilous personal attacks by members of the
religious-Zionist settler movement. Anwar Sadat was killed for being a traitor to Islam because he made peace with Israel. Osama bin Laden not only
viewed the United States as being his enemy and a force of evil but also saw
any Muslim who opposed him as being like Satan, particularly the leaders
of Islamic nations who supported the United States.

The dualist notion of a timeless struggle between good and evil culmi-
nates in the creation of an enemy that is less than human and that must be
destroyed. Bruce Hoffman writes that religious warriors come up with labels, such as infidels, sons of Satan, mud people, Christ killers, Zionist pigs,

and human excrement, which depict their enemies as being less than human. This collectivization and dehumanization of the enemy make it easier to kill them because they are stripped of their humanity.[66] The destruction of the inhuman enemy also becomes necessary so that the adversary's sinful ways do not corrupt the forces of good. Thus, the Canaanite nations that inhabited the land of Israel had to be destroyed when the Israelites sought to enter lest "they teach them to act according to their abominations that they performed for their Gods."[67] The enemy is seen as a form of pollution that must be obliterated. As Hoffman writes, the objective of religious warriors is not just to defeat their enemies but, rather, to wipe them from the face of the earth.[68] Amir Taheri quotes Hussein Musawi, a founder of Hezbollah: "We are not fighting so that the enemy recognizes us and offers us something. We are fighting to wipe out the enemy."[69]

BELIEVERS AND NONBELIEVERS

The division of the world into good and evil and the need to combat the wicked relate to religion's tendency to create insiders and outsiders. It is only natural that what brings a group of people together will separate them from everybody else. Members of the faith are accepted, and outsiders are viewed as a threat, which necessitates a constant watch of one's borders for those seeking to cause harm. Regina Schwartz writes that "Imagining identity is an act of distinguishing and separating from others, of boundary making and line-drawing, is the most frequent and fundamental act of violence we commit."[70] The boundaries that are drawn by monotheistic religions are particularly vulnerable to becoming places of conflict because of monotheistic religions' exclusive truth claims. J. P Larsson writes that because religions claim to have access to exclusive truth, their believers develop a sense of superiority and hostility. If one has select access to the truth, he or she should promote it, while viewing other truth claims as false. Judaism, Christianity, and Islam have unique ways of dividing the world between members of the faith and outsiders.

Jews, as mentioned, often refer to themselves as "the chosen people," and non-Jews are referred to as *Goyyim* (nations of the earth). Although non-Jews are permitted to dwell among Jews and are to be protected and treated with dignity in a state where citizenship would be defined by Jewish law, they do not have the same rights and responsibilities as Jews.[71] Although some Israeli religious extremists seek to expel all of the Palestinians living in Israel, East Jerusalem, and the West Bank, others would allow them to stay if they accept Jewish sovereignty and a diminished status. In either case, the fact that Palestinian Muslims and Christians are not Jews makes them of lesser value. As an Israeli once told me on a bus in Jerusalem, "the blood of Arabs is not equal to the blood of Jews." The major distinction made between Christians and other groups is whether one has been saved and accepted Jesus Christ as his or her savior. Those who have not are condemned to spend eternity in hell. The conversion of nonbelievers is one of the primary obligations of evangelical Christians and has, at times, been achieved through force. Many Jews and Muslims were forcibly converted to Christianity during the Spanish Inquisition. The Spanish brought Catholic missionaries, who enthusiastically supported the violent conquering of the native populations, with them to the New World. A recent article in *Harper's* describes a missionary zeal at the U.S. Air Force Academy and a growing number of members of the U.S. military who hope to fight a holy war against Islam.[72]

A question that will be dealt with later is why have Christian efforts at self-protection and proselytizing have become significantly less violent over the course of the past century. In contrast, Islam, as Huntington wrote in "The Clash of Civilizations," has bloody borders.[73] Islam divides humanity into three groups: Muslims, People of the Book, 'Ahal a Kittab (Jews, Christians, and Zoroastrians), and the People of Ignorance, 'Ahal al Jahilyah (pagans and pantheists). People of the Book were given protected status (*dhiminni*) in countries ruled by Islamic government. They were free to practice their religion and regulate the affairs of their community. However, they had to pay tribute, could not hold political office, and were considered second-class citizens. People of Ignorance were usually given the choice of submission to Islam or death. These categories exist primarily in theory today as most Islamic nations are ruled by secular governments and constitutions. The extreme severe vitriol and calls for violence by Muslim extremists, such as Ayatollah Khomeini, Osama bin Laden, al Rantisi, and Sheik Yassin, can be seen in the context of threats from Christianity and Judaism's competing exclusive truth claims, as represented by the United States and Israel.

The clash between opposing exclusive truth claims or between right and right often becomes violent or increases the severity of existing conflicts.[74] This process can be seen in the addition of a religious context in 1967 to the competing claims of the Palestinians and the Israelis over the same land. Prior to 1967, the Arab–Israel conflict was largely between competing nationalities and religion was of minor significance. Since 1967, the religious-Zionist settler movement has gained strength in Israel, while Hamas, an Islamic group, has challenged the nationalist Palestine Liberation Organization for leadership of the Palestinian Authority. Sworn enemies from the old nationalist leaderships, Yitzhak Rabin and Yasser Arafat, were able to reach a peace agreement in 1993–1994. The agreement has never been fully implemented because, in part, religious actors on both sides believe that their group has the exclusive right, granted by God, to control all of the land that is Israel or Palestine. Hence, Hamas has carried out suicide bombings and missile attacks, while Rabin was assassinated by a Jewish extremist, and religious-Zionists seek to grab as much land as possible in East Jerusalem and the West Bank in order to prevent the land being traded for peace.

The competition over land that results from drawing of boundaries between religious groups and the maintenance of exclusive truth claims will be considered further in the discussion of the conflict over Israel and Palestine in chapters 6 and 8. The importance of controlling land is related to a larger conflict between religions for what are believed to be scarce resources such as divine communications, scripture, and authoritative information from divine beings. Hector Avalos argues that religious violence is rooted in the competition over sacred texts and the authoritative interpretation of texts. The loss of control of these resources threatens a religion's claim to exclusive truth.[75] Consequently, religious leaders are very sensitive to responding to outside challenges because they threaten the legitimacy of their exclusive truth claims. Thus, threats are exaggerated or embellished to mobilize the faithful to arms. Sometimes, as reflected in the following comment by Pat Robertson, resistance is spiritual: "Satan has established certain strongholds. He goes after areas of our society which are crucial. He has gone after the education system and has been very successful in capturing it. Satan hates people. He desires to destroy people. We need to do spiritual warfare."[76] On other occasions, violent resistance is necessary, as is evident in al Rantisi's justification for suicide bombing, "War is our only option because we have been dispossessed for 50 years. We are under occupation. Jews have killed thousands of our people. All Israelis are combatants because they serve in the army. Jews killed 2000 in the first intifada, tens of hundreds in the mosques. They forced us to resist."[77]

The need for a vigilante defense of boundaries and the perception of threat are at the heart of Judaism, Christianity, and Islam, as all three faiths began as persecuted minorities, whose founders and saviors suffered for their beliefs. Abraham had to leave his homeland of idol worshippers in order to found Judaism and, by extension, Christianity and Islam. Moses was degraded as a slave and humiliated by the Pharaoh when he demanded that the Hebrew slaves be set free so that they could worship their God in their land. The Maccabees and the Zealots of Masada were Jewish minorities who

were persecuted and faced destruction but still held on to their faith. Jesus
was persecuted by Romans and mocked by his fellow Jews for his beliefs.
Eventually, he was tortured and crucified because he held on to his convic-
tions in the face of a hostile majority. The early Christians suffered the same
fate as they were also tortured and thrown to the lions.

Muhammad was mocked and forced to flee Mecca for his life when he
began to preach Islam, as he and his small group of followers also endured
persecution from the majority. Abraham, Moses, Jesus, and Muhammad all
spoke the truth to people in power and suffered. Yet, they persevered and
defended their truth claims and the boundaries of their weak communities.
Ultimately, they or their descendants prevailed. It is no surprise that today's religious warriors see themselves as following in the footsteps of their
founders and saviors, as they see themselves as persecuted minorities speak-
ing truth to those in power. This notion can be seen in Osama bin Laden's
diatribes against America, Israel, and the West; the defiance shown by the
killers of abortion providers, who cannot understand why a materialistic
and hedonistic America can permit legalized abortion; and the Jewish settlers who establish hilltop outposts in the West Bank surrounded by Arab
villages.

SACRIFICE

The suffering and humiliation endured by Moses, Jesus, Muhammad,
and other religious heroes, saints, and legends ties in with the importance
of sacrifice in religion. As Peter Berger notes, the history of religion is one
of sacrifice, death, suicide, mutilation, and minor acts of self-denial such
as fasting.[78] Judaism, Christianity, and Islam include many who have sacrificed their lives for their faiths including Jesus and the early Christians, the
Jewish zealots at Masada, and Hussein in Shiite Islam. Weber wrote that
religion has a power of psychic coercion on believers that leads them to
undertake acts of self-denial and mortification that they otherwise would
not. When communities are socialized to believe in salvation and union
with the divine, they develop norms that facilitate the acceptance of extreme pain and suffering.[79] Rene Girard views sacrifice as the cornerstone
of religion. Girard notes that people instinctively want things that other
people have, which results in competition. This competition, eventually,
leads to the death of one of the participants. The deceased becomes a martyr because he or she has brought an end to the conflict and peace. Religion
develops around these sacrificial events, and the objects that created the
crisis become taboo. Over time, humans produced scapegoats or symbolic

sacrifices to control violence. According to Girard, religion causes people to identify with the victim of the violence rather than to engage in more violence.[80]

Girard concludes that religion is a force that represses violence by creating scapegoats, empathy for the victims of violence, and symbolic violence to replace real violence, which is certainly true.[81] This taming of religious violence can often lead to honoring self-sacrifice, including suicide, as most of the first Christian saints were martyrs killed by the Romans. Judaism maintains the tradition of *kiddush Hashem* (sanctification of God) by dying rather than betraying one's allegiance to his or her faith. Thus, religion not only conveys the message to some believers that dying is not so bad but also, as mentioned earlier, has the potential to convey to some of its followers that it is honorable and that it is praiseworthy to take one's own life. Juergensmeyer writes that death in the name of God and faith can represent, to some, "the triumph of the sacred order over the chaos of the profane world."[82] The chaos of the profane world often includes significant pain and suffering, which religion often justifies as a necessary part of being a true believer. Again, the examples of Moses, Jesus, Muhammad, Job, and all of the other martyrs in Judaism, Christianity, and Islam bear witness to this necessity. This brings to mind the concept of theodicy, religion's promise of an ultimate reward for human suffering.[83]

The termination of the pain and suffering and the reward happen in an afterlife of eternal bliss for those who have followed religious law and who have been faithful and obedient. Consequently, the nobility of death is fortified by the rational calculus of an improvement in one's personal fortunes. The notion that dying for one's God and faith will end the misery of earthly life and bring about eternal happiness is made evident by a Palestinian suicide bomber from Gaza:

> With the first drop of his blood, the martyr is said to go straight to Paradise, his past sins wiped clean from the book of his life. He is buried in the clothes in which he dies, the bloodstains of his wounds serving as witness to his sacrificial death. . . . He will awaken not on earth but rather in the Garden of Delight, where he will be surrounded by all good things. Rather than the rivers of sewage, which run through the campus of Gaza, there will be rivers of holy wine, rivers of milk, rivers of honey, from which he will drink to his heart's content. He will recline on luxurious couches beneath trees without thorns. He will suffer neither heat nor cold. He will know no pain as we are told in *The Quran*, "God drives away his grief." He will enjoy forevermore the company of maidens who "neither man nor *jinn* (demons) has deflowered before."[84]

The mention of the terrible living conditions in Gaza suggests that there is connection between extreme disorder in one's earthly life, one's willingness to voluntarily leave that life, and the attractiveness of the afterlife.

The willingness to take one's own life as a sign of true belief combined with the belief that one is part of a persecuted minority facilitates the readiness of the suicide bomber to also take the life of another. Very often the religious warrior believes that he or she has no choice other than dying in battle for his or her cause because he or she is facing an overwhelmingly powerful enemy. The Palestinian suicide bomber faces the weapons, technology, and power of the Israeli Defense Forces, one of the most lethal fighting forces in the world. Al Qaeda, the Taliban, and the Iraqi militias that opposed the U.S. invasion and occupation of their countries are fighting against the most powerful nation in the world. Here, all of the factors that facilitate killing in the name of religion come together. The actor believes that he or she has carried out God's will. This belief is validated by sacred texts and traditions and approved or further motivated by a religious leader. Our religious warrior believes that he or she is part of a timeless struggle between good and evil, where the powerful opposition poses an existential threat to his or her faith and community. He or she is fighting, and likely dying, in a timeless struggle that will help bring about a utopia and his or her personal salvation.

COMMUNITIES OF SUPPORT

The final piece of the puzzle is the fellowship and community of support that religion often provides. A very small number of religion-based terrorists are lone wolves, who act without the assistance of a larger organization. Although this pattern might be changing as the three major attacks and attempted attacks on the United States in 2009–2010 were carried out by individuals acting on their own. (The three perpetrators of these incidents did have contact with terrorist groups prior to their attacks.)[85] The significance of a community of support for religion-based terrorists is directly related to the importance of fellowship and community in religion. Almost all important religious rituals are performed in the presence of a community of believers in places of worship. One of the key functions of religion and religious institutions is to provide community and to support those in need. Since religion, for the most part, is a group activity, it follows that religion-based terrorism should be as well.

The group provides three important types of support, logistical, spiritual, and emotional. Jessica Stern writes that one of the reasons why Palestinians groups, such as Hamas and the al Aqsa Martyrs Brigade, were able to carry out numerous successful suicide bomber attacks between 2000 and 2003 was the organization, training, and logistics provided by the groups. The attacks were planned, bombs were built and provided, and the martyr's family was provided for by the organizations. Very often the attacks are carried out in pairs, and there is a bonding between the partners that resembles a marriage.[86] Juergensmeyer describes a shadowy organization that provides logistical support for those who attack abortion providers.[87] Charles Selengut emphasizes the importance of the fellowship of religion-based terrorist groups and that because of bonding experiences, members have a strong need to fit in and are willing to engage in violence in order to remain part of the group.[88] Religious groups provide the cohesion, inspiration, mobilization, and support that enable individuals to engage in violence that they would not do so on their own. The significance of group psychological processes will be further explored in chapter 5.

This chapter has provided a list of reasons why monotheistic religions facilitate violence. In doing so, it has focused on factors that are common to Christianity, Islam, and Judaism. However, it might be that other ideologies such as nationalism, socialism, and anarchism have some of the same violence-producing characteristics of religions. At the same time, religious texts, traditions, and histories are often vague, amorphous, and contradictory. In the next chapter, I will argue that religion can be used to justify almost any behavior and that religion, like other ideologies, is used to make violence that is usually rooted in political, socioeconomic, and psychological causes seem not only acceptable but also morally just.

_____ *Chapter 2* _____

A More Complex Relationship between Religion and Terrorism

It would appear, following the discussion of the reasons why religion facilitates violence in the previous chapter, that it would be hard to argue that religion is not the primary cause of religion-based violence and terror. Despite the strong theoretical reasoning and the supporting evidence that was presented, an important question comes to mind. Why, if religion is a significant cause of violence and terrorism, are the overwhelming majorities of Muslims, Christians, and Jews nonviolent? Although there is no reliable way of counting the number of religion-based terrorists or the number of people who have engaged in violence in the name of religion, it is safe to assume that the number of religious warriors is far smaller than 1 percent of the world's 2.1 billion Christians, 1.5 billion Muslims, and 14 million Jews. In short, religion-based terrorists make up a miniscule portion of religious individuals and can be identified as extremists or people on the margins. If religion is a primary cause of violence and terrorism, there should be many more religion-based terrorists because this small number of cases does not confirm a strong relationship between religion and terrorism.

It is important to note that religion-based terrorists share a common faith tradition with the overwhelming majority of religious individuals who do not engage in terrorism and those who use religion as a justification for peacemaking and building bridges with other faiths. Therefore, there must be some intervening variables that are not related to religion, which cause these constituencies to interpret their faiths in such different ways. The variance in the interpretation of religion also tells us that just as there are important differences between religions that should not be overlooked there are also important differences within religions that must be considered. These differences are accounted for by religious texts, traditions, legal systems, and theologies that are vague, amorphous, and contradictory and that can be interpreted in an infinite number of ways. In this chapter, I will discuss the shared commonalities between religion and other ideologies that facilitate violence, the amorphous nature of religion, and the significance of how religion is interpreted. Religion, like other ideologies, has the potential to facilitate violence. However, it is political, social, economic, and psychological factors that cause some to interpret religion in a way that justifies violence and terrorism.

The strength of religion as a cause of terror and violence is also called into question by its variability over time. Religion, along with many nonreligious factors, was an important cause of war and terrorism, up until the 18th century. At that point, religion's role began to decline as the revolutions in America and France were rooted in secular concepts such as liberty, freedom, and equality. European colonization in the Islamic world was primarily, although not exclusively, based on the pursuit of political influence, raw materials, and markets rather than converting infidels to Christianity. The first instances of modern terrorism, in the second half of 19th century in Russia, were committed by anarchists. Waves of terror that followed offered other secular ideologies including nationalism and socialism. Religion did not become an important cause of terror until the 1980s with the beginning of the civil war in Lebanon, the Iranian Revolution, and the Camp David peace accords between Israel and Egypt. David Rapoport, who identifies four modern waves of terrorism, nihilist, anticolonial, New Left, and the current religious wave, notes that each of the first three waves eventually ran its course.[1] Consequently, it is likely that the current wave of religion-based terrorism will also end. If religion's strength as a cause of violence and terrorism varies, it must be nonreligious factors that are causing this variance as religion's basic tenets are stable.

The different waves of terror and the ideologies that were used to justify the violence that they produced demonstrate that religion is not the only dogma that can be taken to an extreme. An important historical perspective is provided by Mark Juergensmeyer who writes that secular nationalism became more religious as religion's influence declined. According to Juergensmeyer, the French Revolution had a religious zeal for democracy and the revolution took on the trappings of a church religion in the power given to its demagogue leaders and the slavish devotion to what it called the temple of reason.[2] This worship of reason and secular nationalism eventually resulted in the Reign of Terror where hundreds of enemies of the revolution were executed. Ideological justifications for terrorism, war, and violence that become too extreme ultimately fail to achieve their objectives, are repudiated by the moderate majority, and are replaced by a new revolutionary dogma.[3] It was the failure of socialism that helped spur the current wave of religion-based terror in the Islamic world. As will be seen, al Qaeda's seemingly indiscriminate use of violence has led to a growing sentiment against religion-based violence by most Muslims.

It is also important to ask whether religion shares commonalities with the other ideologies that have produced violence and terror. If so, these commonalities suggest that there is a uniform extremist mentality that causes ideologies to become violent. A look at the nine reasons why religion facilitates violence, which were presented in chapter 1, shows that only three— God, sacred texts, and heaven and salvation—are unique to religion. The other six—a focus on good and evil, division of the world into believers and nonbelievers, sacrifice and martyrdom, eschatology, reliance on authority figures and charismatic leaders, and communities of support—are also characteristics of nonreligious ideologies such as nationalism, ethnic chauvinism, and communism. Because religious ideologies and worldviews have much in common with secular ones, it could be that their violent strains are a reflection of human nature and a universal response to certain political, social, and economic conditions. The unique aspects of ideologies that are used to justify violence, such as God in religion and class struggle in communism, signify the need for a new revolutionary dogma to replace an old and discredited one.

COMMONALITIES BETWEEN RELIGION AND OTHER POTENTIALLY VIOLENT IDEOLOGIES

Good and Evil

The division of the world into good and evil is certainly not unique to religion. Nations involved in wars and conflicts with other nations have always portrayed their enemies as evil and satanic. A recent example of the division of the world into good and evil and the enemy as the devil worldview in a nationalist context is George W. Bush and his response to 9/11. Bush referred to America's enemies as "the axis of evil" and frequently claimed that the attacks of 9/11 were caused by al Qaeda's hatred of freedom and the American way of life.[4] America's enemies in war have always been portrayed as being less than human and given disparaging monikers such as "Gooks" (Vietnamese), "Ragheads" (Arabs), and "Heathens" (Filipinos in the Spanish American War). The division of the world into good and evil and the portrayal of one's enemy as being satanic can even be seen in the domestic politics of democracies such as the United States. "Birthers" went to great lengths to prove that Barack Obama is the enemy because he was really born in Kenya and is really a closet Muslim. Right-wing radio and TV hosts have gone as far as labeling him a Nazi, Fascist, and/or Communist whose true mission is the destruction of America from the inside. Like their religious extremist counterparts, they see the enemy within or the traitor to the cause as the greatest threat to the forces of righteousness.

Religion's dichotomizing tendency was certainly present in the Cold War between the United States and the Soviet Union. However, competing economic systems, capitalism, and communism, not faiths, were the ideological forces that stoked a 45-year global conflict that led to the brink of nuclear war with the 1962 Cuban Missile Crisis, the division of Europe into competing blocs, and wars by proxy throughout the developing world. Both sides frequently referred to the inherently evil nature of the opposition. The Communist world was known as "the Red Menace," and the saying "better dead than red" was common in the 1950s. Communism was seen as an ideology that stood for everything that we opposed: atheism, government control of the economy, and the restriction of individual rights and freedoms. The Soviets and their allies warned of the dire consequences of the free market such as the exploitation of the working class, the ruthless and violent pursuit of new markets, and the worship of materialism.

The belief in the inherent evil of communism caused domestic repression in the United States with the Red Scare following World War I, where suspected Communists were rounded up and deported, and the Communist Witch Hunt of the 1950s, when Senate hearings were held to root Communists out of important professions. Internal repression against the devil within in the Soviet Union was far more severe with Stalin's purges in the 1930s where millions were executed in an attempt to rid the Communist Party of counterrevolutionaries.[5] These responses to internal heretics are similar to the violence by religious extremists against traitors such as Yitzhak Rabin and Anwar Sadat. The view of communism as an inherently evil force can be seen in the American foreign policy of containing communism under Truman, rolling back the tide of communism under Eisenhower, and Reagan's labeling of the Soviet as "the evil empire." It can be argued that the fear of communism, as an ideological force, led to armed intervention in Vietnam, assisting in the overthrow of democratically elected regimes in Iran and Chile, and the Iran-Contra scandal.[6] The overestimation of the Communist threat (or, in the previously mentioned cases, socialist) can be compared to the worldview of religious warriors, who also view their enemies as evil and inflate the power of their enemies far beyond reality.

Division of the World into Believers and Nonbelievers

Religion divides the world into believers and nonbelievers, which creates a worldview where nonbelievers are viewed as being of lesser value, outsiders are viewed as a threat, and one must vigilantly guard his or her borders (both internal and external) from those seeking to cause harm. This division of the world into an in-group and an out-group, however, is not unique to religion, as it is also characteristic of groups involved in ethnic conflict and secular conflicts.[7] Although religion-based terrorism is the most common form of terrorism today, ethnic conflict remains an important cause of war, terror, violence, and genocide. Humans, throughout history, have demonstrated that they will defend their ethnic boundaries with the same ferocity with which they defend their religious boundaries. Recent atrocities motivated by ethnicity include the slaughter of Tutsi by Hutu in Rwanda, ethnic cleansing in the conflicts that resulted in the disintegration of Yugoslavia in the 1990s, and the use of chemical weapons against Iraqi Kurds by Saddam Hussein following the Gulf War 1991 to expel Iraq from Kuwait. At the same time, many conflicts that are often labeled as being religion-based, such as Israel-Palestine, Northern Ireland, and the former Yugoslavia, also have a strong ethnic cleavage that divides the warring parties.

Religions, as discussed in the previous chapter, divide groups into believers and nonbelievers, and an individual's status is dependent on whether or not he or she is a believer. Israeli religious extremists would expel Palestinians or treat them as resident aliens. Jews and Christians in countries governed by Islamic law would be protected but clearly would be second-class citizens. Secular-based nations have been known to make the same distinctions, but they usually have been based on race or ethnicity. A glaring example of a tiered society based on race was the treatment of African Americans in the American South, first as slaves and then under Jim Crow laws. The same division of society based on race was present in apartheid in South Africa, where residents were categorized into white, colored, mixed race, and African ethnicities. In both the American and South African cases, the nonwhite races were viewed as being inferior, given second-class legal status, and denied many of the rights and privileges, such as voting, that were given to whites. State-sponsored terror and vigilante terror in the American South and South Africa were also used to suppress those of lower status, as is the case in societies where people are divided by religion.

Adolf Hitler and the Nazi regime provide the most well-known and infamous example of violence being used to protect an ethnic group, the Aryans, from being polluted by another ethnic group, the Jews. At first glance, the Holocaust would appear to be a case of religion-based violence because it was primarily directed against the Jews, a religious group. This was not entirely the case as Hitler viewed the Jews as a nationality and distinct ethnic group. It was the fear that this inferior ethnic group would contaminate the superior Aryan race if the two groups continued to intermingle that caused the need for a final solution to the Jewish problem.[8] A major scientific research program was instituted by the Nazis that would produce a genetic and physiological method of identifying members of the Jewish race. At the same time, Jews who converted to Christianity were viewed as being Jewish and were killed, as were other inferior races such as Gypsies. Today's descendents of the Nazis—groups such as the Church of the Creator, the Aryan Brotherhood, and other racist extremist groups—also seek to defend the white race from inferior races such as African Americans, Hispanics, Arabs, and Jews. They, too, have shown a willingness to use violence in defense of ethnic purity.

Sacrifice and Martyrdom

Sacrifice and martyrdom, as shown in the previous chapter, are rooted in the histories and traditions of Islam, Christianity, and Judaism, as there are numerous heroes in each of the three monotheisms that are revered for their willingness to die for their faith. Throughout the ages, religion, however, has not been the only thing for which people have been willing to die. Leaving those aside who have given their lives for people with whom they have an intimate personal connection, such as family members, we find those who have died in service of their country. Dying for the nation is often viewed with the same honor and reverence by one's fellow countrymen as religious extremists feel for those who die fighting in the name of God. In fact, sacrifice and martyrdom for one's country is viewed as being heroic by the vast majority, while those, today, who die fighting for their faith are usually viewed as extremists. Thus, Nathan Hale, who is thought to have said, "I only regret that I have but one life to give for my country," before he was executed by the British for spying during the American Revolution is viewed as a hero.[9] In the same vein, Joseph Trumpeldor's words, "It doesn't matter. It is good to die for our country," are part of Israeli national folklore. Trumpeldor made this statement as he was dying of the wounds that he suffered while defending his Jewish settlement from an Arab attack in 1920

Palestine. Hale and Trumpeldor are evidence that nations, like religions, have martyr heroes.

It can be argued that dying for one's country is rational because an individual is dying for something tangible, one's land, home, and security. At the same time, many soldiers across the world are conscripted or join the military for economic reasons. Religious warriors, on the other hand, are thought to be irrational because they are willing to kill and die for abstract ideologies and concepts such as religion, heaven, and the World to Come. On the other hand, it is important to note that modern terrorists, whose violence is rooted in nationalism, economic justice, and political liberation, have often referred to themselves as "freedom fighters." To some extent, these terrorists are also martyring themselves for abstract ideologies and concepts such as justice and liberation. One of the rallying points for the American Revolution was Patrick Henry's statement, "Give me liberty or give me death," and the group that led illegal opposition to British rule in Boston was called the Sons of Liberty.[10] Just as nonreligious terrorists fight and die for abstract ideologies and concepts, I believe and will provide evidence that shows that those who martyr themselves in the name of religion are motivated, in part, by the same nationalist, economic, and political grievances of their nonreligious counterparts. Death, however, is more honorable when a warrior is fighting for a lofty ideology, be it religious or secular.

The recent wave of suicide bombings by Islamic terrorists has often been pointed to as being caused by a fanaticism and irrationality that is unique to religion, specifically Islam.[11] Suicide bombing in the past 40 years has primarily been the domain of Islamic terrorists. However, it is important to note that some terrorist suicide bombings have been carried out by nationalist groups such as the Tamil Tigers, who, until recently, were fighting to separate from Sri Lanka (which is ruled by the Sinhalese ethnic group) and create a Tamil homeland. Palestinian suicide bombings against Israel, in addition to being carried out by Islamic groups such as Hamas and Islamic Jihad, have also been used by the more nationalist-oriented al Aqsa Martyrs Brigade. Suicide bombings have also been used by nations in the conduct of conventional warfare, hence, the commonly used term "suicide mission." The most well-known example to Americans is the Japanese Kamikaze pilots who purposefully crashed their planes into American warships as World War II was drawing to a close. In addition to dying for their country, the Kamikaze pilots were also sacrificing their lives for their emperor. The Germans employed Neger submarines in World War II, which were, ostensibly, human torpedoes.

Eschatology

The promise of the End of Days and the creation of the World to Come often motivates religion-based terrorists. Furthermore, Judaism, Christianity, and Shiite Islam offer messiahs who will bring about the transformation to a blissful state of existence that is currently unknown to humankind. David Martin, in presenting his argument that Christianity does not cause war, reminds us that individuals, throughout history, have committed acts of violence in the name of other utopias and in the simple pursuit of power and wealth.[12] Communism is another ideology that offers a World to Come that is unlike the current state of human existence. Communism, like religion, is a historical-determinist theory of history, as Karl Marx argued that history is a progression from less developed to more developed relations of production. This evolution is historically predetermined and cannot be stopped by human activity or intervention. The economic systems produced by these relations of production are inherently unstable because of class conflicts. These economic systems also determine the shape of all other aspects of society, including politics and religion. Communism is the final stage in the progression from less developed to more advanced modes of production. Like the coming of the *Mashiach* (Messiah) and the second coming of Christ, it is the end of history. Just as Judaism and Christianity imagine a utopia in the World to Come, communism worker's paradise will be a world where all humans will be able to reach their full potentials.[13]

We see in communism an understanding of the world that is similar to that of religion. The world is controlled by a force greater than humans. History will play itself out, and a predetermined end point will eventually be reached. That end of history will be a utopia as Marxism predicts the withering away of the state and the creation of a worker's paradise, where all will live "from according to his ability, to each according to his means."[14] Just as there are religious warriors who hope to speed up the second coming of Christ, the coming of the *Mashiach,* or the re-creation of the Caliphate through violence, Communist revolutionaries have used violence to bring about working-class revolutions that would, ultimately, produce the worker's paradise. Vladimir Lenin provided a framework for the communist revolution in *What Is to Be Done,* which ultimately guided the Russian revolution that brought the world's first Communist government to power.[15] Future attempts to bring about Communist governments that would lead to workers' utopias took place in China, Cuba, Vietnam, and other nations. Acts of state terrorism such as Stalin's purges in the Soviet Union and Mao's

Cultural Revolution in China killed millions in order to ensure that internal enemies did prevent the perfection of the communist workers' paradise.

Charismatic Authority Figures

Religion, as noted in the previous chapter, offers leadership figures, which provide authoritative interpretations of texts, history, traditions, and theologies that justify terrorism and violence. Religious warriors are often motivated by the spiritual guidance of these clerics and, as was the case with Yigal Amir (Yitzhak Rabin's assassin), seek their approval for engaging in violent and terror. Leaders of secular oriented terrorist groups lack the spiritual and quasi-divine authority that comes with being a cleric. This does not, however, mean that nonreligious terrorist groups do not have ideologues that attain the same revered status as religious clerics. Che Guevara participated in several revolutionary campaigns, including the one in Cuba that brought Fidel Castro to power. He also served as an inspiration and role model, while his writings provided guidance for Marxist and socialist terrorists and revolutionary groups across the globe that fought for economic equality and the liberation of the masses.[16] The late William Pierce held a similar ideologue leader position in the American white supremacist movement as he headed the National Alliance (a white supremacist organization and publishing house) and wrote *The Turner Diaries* and *Hunter,* novels that have served as inspirations for right-wing racist extremist terrorists.[17]

Charismatic leadership, although the archetype for Weber's charismatic leadership was based on the prophets of the Hebrew Bible and the belief that someone has been touched by God is often a characteristic of a charismatic leader, is certainly not exclusive to religion or religious groups. The ability to engender loyalty and obedience based on the force of personality has been present in many secular leaders. Adolf Hitler and Benito Mussolini, ultranationalists, were two of the most well-known and notorious charismatic leaders of the 20th century. Nationalist and political terrorist groups, like their religious counterparts, are often led by charismatic leaders. For close to 40 years, Yasser Arafat was both the leader and the symbol of the Palestine Liberation Organization. Many Palestinians felt a strong personal connection to Arafat and that the force of his will would liberate their homeland.[18] It can be argued that a charismatic leader is almost necessary for the formation of any terrorist group because it takes such a personality to inspire others to sacrifice their own personal security and to lay down their lives for the cause.

Communities of Support

Communities of support, like charismatic leadership, are not unique to religion-based terrorist groups. Although religion-based groups have the added dimension of spiritual bonding, group cohesion, as will be discussed in chapter 5, is essential to all terrorist organizations. At the same time, lone-wolf nonreligious terrorists are as rare as lone-wolf religion-based terrorists. It is obvious that nationalist, economic, and politically based terrorist organizations would need to provide their members with the same logistical support as religion-based terrorist groups. Ideological bonding is also often present as Marxist terrorist organizations teach and indoctrinate their members in Marxist-Leninist theory, just as Islamic groups often provide Quranic and other religious instruction. Now that I have explained how six of the reasons why religion supports terrorism—viewing the world in terms of good and evil, division of humanity into believers and nonbelievers, eschatology, sacrifice and martyrdom, authoritative and charismatic leadership, and communities of support—are also characteristics of nonreligion-based terrorist groups, it is time to address the reasons that are unique to religion.

ARE RELIGION-BASED TERRORISTS MISINTERPRETING RELIGION?

God, sacred texts, and heaven now remain as the exclusive characteristics of religion that facilitate violence and terrorism. However, it is a tremendous leap to conclude that religion-based terrorism is primarily a function of God, heaven, and sacred texts. As mentioned at the beginning of the chapter, only a miniscule minority of religious individuals are religion-based terrorists. Religious believers, who wish to go to heaven or help bring about the End of Days, have many nonviolent alternatives such as prayer, charity and good works, doing well unto others, and following religious law. Why do the overwhelming majority of people of faith choose these options? Could it be that God communicates his desire for violence and mayhem directly to the select few who kill in God's name? This proposition is, of course, unverifiable. At the same time, it has not been confirmed in interviews with religion-based terrorists and their supporters as religion-based terrorists do not assert that they take orders directly from God. Even in religion-based terrorist circles, those who claim to speak with God are not taken seriously or are seen as being blasphemous. Since God does not directly command religion-based terrorists, how can they claim God wants them to kill?

It could be that religion-based terrorists are distorting or misinterpreting the texts and traditions of their faith.[19] In essence, religion-based terrorists are deviating from true religion. Following 9/11, it has often been claimed that al Qaeda and Osama bin laden's *jihadist* version of Islam is simply incorrect and a misrepresentation of true Islam.[20] Since bin Laden is not an *Alim* (religious scholar), his use of Islam to justify suicide bombing and killing innocent civilians is rooted in ignorance. Christians and Jews have also dismissed their violent extremists as being misguided. The Catholic Church and mainline Protestant denominations have denounced the take a life to save the lives of the unborn justification of pro-life extremists who murder abortion providers and set fire to abortion clinics. Yigal Amir, who assassinated Israeli prime minister Yitzhak Rabin, was condemned and denounced by Israel's chief rabbis, and his claim that Rabin was a *rodef* (someone who places Jewish lives in jeopardy) was also rejected. Like bin Laden, the abortion provider murderers and Amir misunderstood the teachings of their faiths, and their use of religion to justify violence was not representative of true Islam, Christianity, or Judaism.

There are two problems with the religion-based terrorism as a distortion of religion argument. First, many leaders and members of religion-based terrorist groups are clerics and religious scholars. As noted in the previous chapter, many Islamic terrorist groups are rooted in *madrasas* (institutions that provide instruction in the *Quran* and the Islamic religion). Antiabortion terrorists Paul Hill and Michael Bray were both ordained ministers. Rabbi Meir Kahane led the now-banned Kach political party, which called for the violent removal of all Arabs from Israel. Islamic terrorist organizations such as Hamas and Hezbollah count clerics among their founders and leaders. In short, individuals who are well versed in religious texts and traditions also interpret their religions as condoning terrorism. Ignorance is clearly not the problem. The claim that religion-based terrorists deviate from true religion is also problematic because religious fundamentalists also believe that they maintain ownership of true religion. Who is correct—as the violent extremists worship the same God, justify their actions with the same texts and traditions, and are products of the same historical legacy as the peaceful mainstream?

Both the extremists and the mainstream, actually, are correct—and incorrect—as the notion that there is one correct version or interpretation of any religion is contradicted by reality. Christianity is divided into Catholicism, Protestantism, Eastern Orthodox, and other variants. Protestantism is further divided into many denominations with sharply diverging theological orientations. Islam includes Sunni and Shiite, with many subgroups and splinter groups. Judaism is separated into the Orthodox, Conservative, Reform, and Reconstructionist movements. These divisions are caused by significant disagreement over the interpretation of sacred texts and traditions, the roles and authority of the clergy and individuals, and the extent to which religion can change to accommodate a constantly evolving world. It is the vague and amorphous nature of religion that facilitates these diverging interpretations. Just as Christianity was used to both justify and oppose slavery and the life of the Prophet Muhammad has been used to justify both capitalism and socialism, religion is used to justify nonviolence and terrorism. Disowning those who use scripture and tradition to justify things that we abhor means that we would also have to disown those who use them to justify peace and acts of charity.

Another possibility is that the interpretations of religion-based terrorists are wrong because of their miniscule minority status. In other words, Islam, Judaism, and Christianity are indeed diverse and facilitate a myriad of interpretations of their traditions. However, the tiny number of religion-based terrorists, itself, is enough to disqualify their claims to being legitimate Jews, Christians, and Muslims. Islam, Christianity, and Judaism, however, started out as being tiny groups consisting of their founders and a small group of followers. Their ideologies also contrasted sharply with that of mainstream society, and they, too, were considered radical minorities.[21] Disqualifying religion-based terrorists simply because they are small in number would mean that one would also have to disqualify the original Jewish, Christian, and Islamic communities because they too were small in number and were considered to be deviant. Finally, some of the smallest, yet nonviolent, religious movements and denominations, such as ultra-Orthodox Jews and Seventh Day Adventists, are the most strident in their claims of adherence to religious tradition.

RELIGION IS VAGUE AND AMORPHOUS

Religious warriors seeking to discern God's will, like their nonviolent coreligionists, must rely primarily on sacred texts and oral traditions to justify their actions. In order for those who claim to be killing in the name of God to be actually doing so, these texts, traditions, and legal systems must clearly and unequivocally state that God sanctions violence as an acceptable means to achieve their specific objectives. The reality, however, is that they do not. They do not provide clear instructions as to what to do regarding abortion being legal in the United States, the power imbalance between the Islamic world and the West, and the presence of 3 million Palestinians in the land of Israel that was promised by God to Abraham in the Bible. The religion-based terrorist is interpreting these texts and traditions and coming to conclusions that are at odds with those of the overwhelming majority, who believe that faith and good deeds will gain admission to heaven and bring about End of Days. Sacred texts and oral traditions facilitate divergent interpretations because:

- Core religious texts are most often composed of narratives of the lives of messiahs, prophets, and forefathers or foremothers.
- Religious texts are products of societies that existed 1,500 to 5,000 years ago.
- Religious texts are vague and amorphous.
- Religious texts are often self-contradicting.

Religion, particularly scripture and biblical quotes, has been used for every political purpose known to man, including a catalog of abuses.[22] Perhaps Shakespeare put it best when he wrote, "The devil can cite scripture for his purpose."[23] The flexible and malleable nature of religion is a common theme in scholarship on religion and sacred texts. As Regina Schwartz writes, "Since it (religion) seems to contain all things, it is useful for all ends."[24] Noted terrorism expert Walter Laqueur strikes a similar cord as he concludes that "Endorsements for nearly anything can be found in the holy writings of the major religions."[25] Lloyd Steffen addresses the specific question of terrorism, "Neither violence nor nonviolence is a necessary datum in defining religions. Violence, however, can reflect how people have chosen to enact their understanding of what it means to be a religious person."[26] This personal understanding is very much related to the historical, political, and cultural context in which one encounters religious texts and traditions.[27] A brief exploration of justifications for war in Judaism, Christianity, and Islam will illustrate how religion is used in accordance with temporal, cultural, and political contexts.

Judaism

Control of the land promised to the Children of Israel in the Bible is the primary justification for terror and violence in contemporary Judaism. Because this land is an inheritance promised by God to Abraham in several places in the Torah, as discussed in chapter 1, some believe that the Jews have the right to occupy this land and even use force to remove non-Jews who dwell in these lands. Others argue that Jewish control of that land, particularly Mt. Zion in Jerusalem where the first and second temples stood, will bring about the coming of the Messiah. This land is certainly promised to Abraham and his descendents in several places in the Hebrew Bible and Jews throughout history longed for the establishment of a Jewish state in that area.[28] Yet only a small number of contemporary Jews interpret this birthright as validating violence against Palestinians in the West Bank and against Israeli politicians willing to trade part of that land for peace. At the same time, Jewish efforts to settle the Land of Israel and create a new Jewish state (violently or peacefully) were almost nonexistent from the beginning of the Diaspora in 70 CE until the end of the 19th century. Those who tried to hasten the coming of the *Mashiach* were condemned to the point of excommunication. The current strain of violent land-based messianic Judaism only dates back to Israel's victory in the Six-Day War.[29]

Divinely sanctioned wars are seen throughout the Five Books of Moses and the books of the prophets. Victories, such as the campaign to destroy the Amalekites, were achieved through the will of God. The warrior God is seen in the description of the destruction of Pharaoh's army in the Red Sea as it pursued the fleeing Israelites, "The Lord is a warrior: the Lord is his name. The chariots of Pharaoh and his army he has cast in the sea. . . . Thy right hand, O Lord, is majestic in strength: thy right hand O Lord, shattered the enemy."[30] In the Book of Joshua, God provides an extended narrative of the peoples and nations, including the Amorites and the Moabites that he has defeated. In regard to the people of Jericho, God states that "The citizens of Jericho fought against you, but I delivered them into your hands. I spread panic before you, and it was this, not your sword or your bow, that drove out the two kings of the Amorites."[31] Postbiblical Jewish warriors such as the Maccabees of the Hanukkah story and the Zealots, who opposed the Romans, also believed that God would bring them victory. Thus, those who wage war to maintain the integrity of the Land of Israel certainly have reason to believe that God is fighting alongside them.

The *Tanakh* also contains images of a God who desires peace. King David makes preparations to build the Second Temple on Mt. Zion, but God rejects him because he has been a "fighting man who has shed blood."[32] The Prophet Jeremiah stated that the will of the Lord was that Israel should submit to the Babylonian king Nebuchadnezzar in order to prevent the loss of life and the destruction of Jerusalem. "Serve the king of Babylon and save your lives. Why should this city become a ruin?"[33] According to John Ferguson, surrender became not just a strategy but a religious obligation.[34] The *Tanakh* also contains the theme that humans should not instigate violence but, rather, should depend on God rather than military power, as is reflected in the words of Zachariah, "Not by might nor by power, but by my spirit, says the Lord of hosts."[35] God is also frequently portrayed as being a peacemaker, and his prophets often call on his children to seek peace. "They shall beat their swords into plow-shears and their spears into pruning knives; nation shall not lift sword against nation nor ever again be trained for war."[36] In short, those who seek peace or justification for returning holy land can also find support in scripture.

Those who fight for Zion today often view the Zealots of Masada as being heroic because they chose death rather than accept Roman rule of the holy land. On the other hand, Yochanan ben Zakhai smuggled himself out of Jerusalem in a coffin to the Roman camp. He was allowed to establish a yeshiva (religious school) and rabbinic court in Yavneh. Like Jeremiah, he was convinced that violent resistance was destructive, while recognition of alien rule would allow continued existence in the holy land and the perpetuation of the faith. Following the disastrous Jewish revolt against Roman rule and the resulting exile of a majority of the world's Jews from the land of Israel, a pacification of Judaism occurred in order to avoid a repeat of the tragedy. Judaism ceased to center around sacrifices in the Temple and became focused on the development of law and the exegesis of scripture.[37] Rabbi Mark Gopin provides an example of the desire of the sages of the rabbinical period to pacify the more violent aspects of the *Tanakh* in a *midrash* (rabbinical commentary) on Exodus 15:3 (the Lord is a man of war). Gopin describes how Rabbi Judah turns the references to God in military terms on their head and concludes that God hears the prayers of all humans and has compassion for all righteous people, not just Jews. God, regardless of a person's religion, only punishes the wicked. Finally, the description of God's use of multiple weapons actually implies that he does not need them but only his name.[38]

This hermeneutic of reworking of biblical texts to circumscribe their violent nature was commonly used in the rabbinic era.[39] One of the most important developments of the rabbinic era was the development of the definition of mandatory and optional war discussed in chapter 1. It appears that the rabbis intended on severely restricting the conditions for a just war. *Milhemet-hova* (obligatory war) and *Milhemet-mitzvah* (commanded war) involve obliterating the enemy, including every man, woman, and child. These wars, however, are limited to the biblical wars against the Amalekites and the Canaanites, groups that no longer exist. However, some have interpreted Exodus 17:16 ("The Lord will have war with Amalek from generation.") as meaning that all enemies of the Jews are the seed of Amalek. The requirements for *Milhemet-reshut* (discretionary war), a Jewish king, the ancient Sanhedrin court, and the breastplate of the high priest, also do not exist in contemporary Israel, but debate exists as to whether the religious and state institutions of Israel, substituting for the Sanhedrin court, can declare a discretionary war.[40] It is interesting to note that contemporary religious scholars are interpreting and applying the rules composed by medieval rabbis, who were interpreting and applying ancient texts to their time. So why did the scholars of the rabbinic period reach conclusions that discouraged war while some today use those conclusions to justify war?

The answer lies in the amorphous nature of the text and its relationship to a specific time and place. Are today's Palestinians the seed of Amalek? Is the prediction that God will have war with Amalek limited to biblical times and the direct descendents of Amalek or does it extend until the messianic period and all who seek to keep Israel from occupying the land promised in the Torah? At the same time, we have seen that there are verses from the *Tanakh* that call for peace and avoiding war. Hence, each individual and generation interprets according to its needs and the conditions of its existence. The authorities of the rabbinic era were scarred by devastating loss of the Land of Israel to the Romans and the resulting Diaspora. They saw war and violence in the context of the revolt against the Romans, which had proved to be a disaster. Hence, they hoped to discourage future holy wars. At the same time, Diaspora Jews were frequently persecuted and often violently attacked by the gentiles in whose lands they resided. Violence by Jews would only lead to further attacks and oppression by their neighbors. As mentioned, the failure of the Jewish revolt against the Romans also led to a strongly held belief that the re-creation of a Jewish nation in Israel would only come when God decided to send the *Mashiach*. Human attempts to create a Jewish state would violate God's will and be catastrophic.

Today's radical religious-Zionists, who justify violence against the Palestinians as being an obligatory or permissible optional war, operate in a very different context. Unlike their medieval Diaspora ancestors, they live in a period of strength, confidence, and progress. They reside in the modern state of Israel that was created through human artifice, seemingly, without messianic intervention. They see that the state of Israel was created in miraculous fashion from the ashes of the Holocaust and that the Six-Day War, another miraculous military victory, led to the capture of the Temple Mount in Jerusalem, Hebron, Bethlehem, Nablus, and other holy places promised to the Jews in the Bible. Some interpret these events as being signs that they are in the footsteps of the coming of the *Mashiach* and that their actions can speed up his appearance. Contemporary Israel is a technologically advanced nation with a very powerful army. Hence, the extreme religious-Zionists' active interpretation of scripture and tradition is not surprising. The righteousness of settling the land promised to Abraham is self-evident because much of territory, including Mt. Zion, has come under Jewish control in the past 100 years. Those who resist Jewish control, both Palestinians and Israeli politicians, are equivalent to the enemies who resisted Jewish occupation of the land in the *Tanakh*.

Christianity

A contemporary use of Christianity to justify terrorism and violence is the murder of abortion providers by pro-life extremists in the United States in order to save the lives of the unborn. They believe that the primacy of preserving life in Christianity justifies taking the lives of abortion providers because that will save the lives of countless unborn babies. As discussed in chapter 1, the pro-life terrorists often espouse Christian reconstruction and dominion ideologies, which hold that society needs to be rebuilt for Christ and that all important institutions need to be governed by Christians according to Christian principles. This reconstruction will eventually bring about the second coming of Jesus Christ and the rapture. Like their Jewish counterparts, the Christian terrorists have a unique interpretation of scripture and theology that is at odds with a majority of their coreligionists. In contrast to Jewish extremist religious-Zionists, they do not have direct links to scripture that justify their violence. Early Christians living at the time of the writing of the New Testament were largely a pacifist and persecuted minority rather than a people using violence to conquer their homeland (Jews) or expanding their empire through warfare (Muslims).

Jesus, as discussed, is noted for being a peaceful individual who lived a life that exemplified nonviolence and passive resistance. It is important to note that the passages in the *Tanakh* (most were written in the period directly prior to Jesus's appearance) dealing with the Messiah usually describe a character that is a military leader that conquers through violence. Psalm 2:9 states that "the Messiah will break the nations with a rod of Iron," and Ezra 4 describes a merciless conqueror of the Gentiles. Jesus in the New Testament, however, is presented as an antiviolent Messiah. He rejects Satan's temptation to possess the kingdoms of the world on terms (military) other than God's.[41] Jesus healed and commended the faith of a Roman soldier, a member of the enemy who sought to destroy him, and told his followers to "Love your enemies and pray for those who persecute you."[42] In probably his most famous proclamation of nonviolence, Jesus tells his followers, "You have heard that it was said, 'Eye for eye, and tooth for tooth.' But I tell you, do not resist an evil person. If someone strikes you on the right cheek, turn to him the other also."[43] Jesus, embodying a peaceful prophetic vision in Zachariah 9:9–10, made his messianic entrance into Jerusalem on a donkey, which symbolized his desire to make peace.[44]

There are, despite the generally pacifist orientation of the Gospels, violent and warlike themes in the New Testament that could serve as justification for antiabortion terrorists in the United States. Jesus used violence to drive the moneychangers out of the Temple because he viewed their activities as contaminating sacred space.[45] According to J. Harold Ellens, this incident set a precedent for Christians who wished to cleanse the world of pagans, Jews, and heretical Christians.[46] Ellens writes that the story also contains apocalyptical and martyrdom elements because this event helped set in motion the series of events that led to Jesus's Crucifixion.[47] Thus, those who use violence to bring about the World to Come and are willing to suffer while doing so have a biblical precedent. The New Testament also contains verses that seem to condone violence against nonbelievers and those who lack true faith.

> Do not think that I came to bring peace on the earth; I did not come to bring peace, but a sword. For I came to set a man against his father, and a daughter against her mother, and a daughter-in-law against her mother-in-law; and a man's enemies will be the members of his household. He who loves father or mother more than me is not worthy of me; and he who loves son or daughter more than me is not worthy of Me. And he who does not take his cross and follow after me is not worthy of me. He who has found his life will lose it, and he who has lost his life for my sake will find it.[48]

Christianity, like Judaism, has a concept of just war, which sets guidelines for the acceptable use of violence. It is important to remember that the consideration of any conditions under which war would be just did not come about until after Christianity had been established as the state religion of the Roman Empire and then the Holy Roman Empire. Here we see how Christian theologians, such as Ambrose, Augustine, and Thomas Aquinas, accommodated the pacifist messages of the New Testament and the example of nonviolent martyrdom from the early Christian community, which did not resist Roman persecution and eagerly celebrated their execution, to an environment where Christianity legitimated political authority. Ambrose, bishop of Milan, in praying for the victory of the Roman Empire over the Goths, reached back to the Old Testament to compare the Goths to the evil nation of Gog. He also claimed that the defense of the empire was holy because church and empire were interdependent. Augustine also used the Old

Testament in claiming that war was a tool of divine judgment against the wicked and was necessary to ensure the triumph of the righteous. He also limited the strictly pacifist message of the New Testament to personal relations. Augustine took the position that because sin was inherent in humankind, war was necessary as a cure for that sin.[49]

St. Thomas Aquinas, writing in the 13th century, developed the guiding normative for a just war and a rejection of absolute pacifism for the Catholic Church. It is important to note that by Aquinas's time Catholic priests were actively participating in war.[50] According to Aquinas, the three conditions necessary for a just war are:

1. The war must be waged by a sovereign authority, not an individual or a collection of individuals.
2. The war must be for a just cause, as the target must have committed wrongs against its citizens or seized property unjustly.
3. The war must be for the advancement of good and/or the avoidance of evil.[51]

The first requirement, the necessity of a sovereign authority, reflects the church's status as a political authority or a legitimator of political authority. Again, we see how religious texts and traditions facilitate changing interpretations according to the needs of the interpreter. Requirements two and three, just cause and advancement of good, are sufficiently vague and amorphous to justify almost anything. What qualifies as a wrong that is sufficiently evil to justify war? How are good and evil defined?

Those who kill abortion doctors can certainly claim that stopping the murder of unborn babies is a just cause and that they are both advancing good and preventing evil. However, they certainly cannot maintain that they are acting as sovereigns because they are actually violating the laws of the United States. One way that the radical antiabortionists get around the sovereign requirement is by claiming that the government of the United States is illegitimate because it violates God's law. As discussed in chapter 1, they also cite the theology of Reinhold Niebuhr, who wrote that violence is sometimes necessary to combat injustice, particularly when that injustice is being supported by the overwhelming power of the modern state.[52] The antiabortion terrorists also claim to be following the righteous example of one of Niebuhr's peers, Dietrich Bonhoeffer, a Lutheran minister, who participated in a failed plot to kill Adolf Hitler. Bonhoeffer believed that violence could be used in the pursuit of a just cause and that human law can be broken if it contradicts divine law.[53]

Islam

Jihad in defense of Islam against the West, Israel, or some other enemy is the most common justification used by Islamic religion–based terrorist groups. Al Qaeda holds that the West, led by the United States, attacked Islam by placing its troops in Saudi Arabia and other Muslim nations and tries to impose its secular and hedonistic culture on the Islamic world. Hence, its terrorist attacks are defensive operations to protect Islam from further onslaught. Hamas wages its *jihad* against Israel because that country is occupying Palestine and Jerusalem, Islamic land, and represses the Palestinian people. Following 9/11, the notion of *jihad* has become synonymous with Islamic terrorism and is often viewed as being a holy war to forcibly convert non-Muslims and non-Muslim nations to Islam. Some have wrongly identified *jihad* as being one of the five pillars of Islam. The definition of *jihad* as well as a Muslim's obligation to engage in *jihad,* however, is elusive, amorphous, and, like Christian and Jewish conceptions of holy war, has carried numerous interpretations during its history.

> Today the scholar must ask whether the word *jihad* has been degraded or has lost all coherence due to the multiple tasks for which the Muslim community has used it. . . . Is *jihad* still a grand religiously based form of warfare, designed to raise the world of Allah to its highest? Or is it the fact that any political and religious malcontent, such as Osama bin Laden, can label his struggle a *jihad,* caused it to lose all meaning . . . are these types of fighting related to the classical concept of *jihad* at all?[54]

There is debate, as discussed in chapter 1, over the true meaning of *jihad.* It is agreed that *jihad* is struggling or striving to follow in the path of Allah (God) and to be a good Muslim. Is the exertion and struggle violent or nonviolent? The answer, of course, is that it can and has been both throughout the 1,400-year history of Islam. Over the years, *jihad* has been segmented into the lesser *jihad* and the greater *jihad.* The greater *jihad* is the internal struggle against superstition, incorrect belief, carnal desires, and evil inclinations in the pursuit of spiritual enlightenment. The lesser *jihad* is an external campaign to expand the authority of the Islamic state and often involves warfare.[55] Later, Islamic jurists divided greater *jihad* into different types (depending on the target and the purpose) including polytheists, believers gone astray (committers of apostasy, fomenters of dissent, and bandits), People of the Book (Jews, Christians, and possibly Zoroastrians), and strengthening the borders (defensive).[56] The use of violence and the appropriate level of violence depend on the purpose and target.[57]

Scholars have concluded that *jihad* originally was conceived of as being the lesser *jihad* and has usually been viewed as warfare throughout most of Islamic history.[58] *Jihad* is mentioned frequently in the *Quran* with references that support both greater *jihad* and lesser *jihad*. Some, "Make war on them until idolatry shall cease and God's religion shall reign supreme. If they desist, God is cognizant of all their actions; but if they give no heed, know then that God will protect you," support the notion of an offensive war to convert non-Muslims or conquering lands held by non-Muslims.[59] Others refer to a defensive war to protect Islam from external attack.

> Fight in the way of God against those who fight you, but do not attack them first. God does not love the aggressors. Slay them wherever you find them. Drive them out of the places from which they drove you. Idolatry is worse than carnage. . . . Fight against them until idolatry is no more and God's religion reigns supreme. But if they desist, fight none except the evil-doers.[60]

Although this verse appears to argue that war should only be used as a defensive measure, it can also be used to justify terrorism. If one views the stationing of American troops in Saudi Arabia as an act of aggression, 9/11 can be justified as slaying the aggressors wherever you find them.

Given that the Prophet Muhammad and his followers were often under attack from local hostile tribes, attacking caravans to support their campaigns, and actively trying to spread the prophet's message, it is not surprising that a military oriented *jihad* is prevalent in the *Quran*, *Sunna*, and *Hadith*.[61] The frequent references to *jihad* in the context of war and conquest in the *Quran*, *Sunna*, and *Hadith* certainly support today's Islamic terrorists who claim to be waging a *jihad* to defend Islam from Israel, the United States, and the West. *Jihad* continued to be viewed in a largely military and violent context throughout the development and conquests of the Abbasid and Umayyad empires. David Cook writes that today's radical Islamic terrorists should be considered jihadists because of their regard for classical and contemporary Islamic law, their emphasis on the spiritual rewards of *jihad*, and their claim to be fighting for the sake of greater Islam.[62] Like their radical antiabortion Christian counterparts in the United States, who claim that their actions are a just war, they often ignore the requirement that *jihad* can only be declared by recognized authority, such as a caliph or an imam.[63] Also, their justifications for killing of civilians are based on textual sources or historical examples that are generally viewed as being exceptions, which they claim to be the rule.[64]

Those who advocate a peaceful interpretation of *jihad* that is rooted in the greater *jihad* also find support in Islamic texts, tradition, and history.

The notion that Islam seeks to forcibly convert non-Muslims is contradicted: "Let there be no compulsion in religion: Truth stands out clear from
error: whoever rejects evil and believes in Allah hath grasped the most trustworthy handhold, that never breaks. And Allah heareth and knoweth all
things."[65] It also appears that violence is only to be used as a last resort and
that the maintenance of peace is valued. "But if the enemy incline towards
peace, do thou (also) incline towards peace, and trust in God: for He is One
that heareth and knoweth (all things)."[66] As is the case with verses from
the *Quran* that support war and violence, peaceful passages are sufficiently
amorphous to invite interpretations that support violence. Individuals might
not be compelled to religion, but nations have been compelled to accept Islamic rule. The United States views itself as being a peace-loving nation, but
al Qaeda views its wars in Iraq and Afghanistan as being indications of its
hostility to Islam.

We have seen how Christian and Jewish theological and legal justifications of just war have changed according to the demands of different historical circumstances and the needs of various actors. The same is true of
Islamic interpretations of *jihad*. As the first era of Islamic expansion and
conquest drew to a close in the eighth and ninth century and opportunities to engage in the greater *jihad* became limited, an emphasis on spiritual (lesser) *jihad* became more common. This was particularly true in Sufi
(mystical) communities, which focus on turning inward and connecting
with the divine. Thus, the struggle and battle is an inward one and involves
combating negative emotions such as lust, fear, and acquisitiveness.[67] In the
19th and early 20th centuries, concepts of *jihad* were rooted in the experience of European colonialism and the Islamic world's decline relative to the
West. Late-19th-century reformers such as Jamal al-Afghani, Mohammed
Abduh, and Rashid Rida all called for the liberation of Islamic lands from
foreign rule followed by a reform and revival of Islam. Abdul Ala (Maulana)
Maududi, writing in India during the British colonial period, called for both
defensive *jihad* and armed resistance, as well as for an internal transformation of Islam and a focus on social reform and a return to the true Islam of
the *Quran* and *Sunna*.[68]

Today, the struggle over the meaning of *jihad* represents both conflicts
within the Muslim world and between the Muslim world and the West. The
power and influence that the United States wields in the Muslim world and
that Israel exerts over the Palestinians and Jerusalem is an affront to many
Muslims. Others see the secular and quasireligious governments in Islamic
countries as abominations. However, only a very small number of Muslims, despite textual and historical justification, have chosen to engage in a

violent "lesser *jihad*." Rather, there is a competing movement among Muslims that emphasizes the significance of the "greater *jihad*" and the reasoning behind the violent *jihad* against the West and the governments of Islamic nation is based on faulty interpretations of the *Quran, Sunna, Hadith,* and Islamic jurisprudence. As should now be clear, both the terrorists and the apologists can find ample justification for their position in sacred texts, traditions, and histories that are contradictory, vague, and amorphous.

The review of Judaic, Christian, and Islamic notions of the acceptability of war and the conditions that justify violence has only scratched the surface of the scripture, traditions, theologies, sacred histories, and jurisprudences of the three monotheistic religions. However, it did suggest that these religions can be interpreted in ways that support both war and peace. Despite the claims of apologists, the violent versions of Judaism, Christianity, and Islam are strongly rooted in sacred texts and traditions. The small numbers of individuals who cling to these violent interpretations of their faith and the variance in the use of religion as a justification for violence over time suggest that religion-based terrorism is strongly influenced by other factors. As was shown, religion, as an ideology, has many similarities with other ideologies, such as ethnocentrism, nationalism, anarchism, and communism, that have facilitated terrorism. Therefore, it is likely that the causes of these types of terrorism are also the causes of religion-based terrorism. The next three chapters will explore the political, socioeconomic, and psychological roots of religion-based terrorism.

_____ *Chapter 3* _____

Political Causes of Religion-Based Terrorism

Bernard Lewis writes that Islam is a great religion that has brought comfort and peace to many, "But Islam, like other religions, has also known periods when it inspired in some of its followers a mood of hatred and violence."[1] Although Lewis is asserting that Islam can cause hatred and violence, he then goes on to list a number of political grievances such as American support for Israel, despotic regimes in the Islamic world, and imperialism as possible explanations for the Islamic world's anger at the United States. Lewis, however, dismisses these political grievances and attributes the rage to a hatred of Western secularism and modernity and warns of a coming clash of civilizations. In the end, Lewis concludes that it is years of Western domination that has caused the rage that has led a minority of Muslims to cling to a violent interpretation of Islam.[2] Thus, it is not Islam, the religion, but the damage to the psyche of the Islamic world caused by alleged abuse by the West that facilitates the violence. Rage, perhaps, is the response of all nations, groups, and societies, even secular ones like the United States, when they feel threatened. How else would one explain the anger and hostility caused by plans to build an Islamic cultural center near the World Trade Center site in Manhattan? Some argue that, whatever the cause, fits of religious rage and the violence that often results from them are without purpose. Expressive violence is when the only objective of an act of violence is killing as many people as possible, and violence is both a means and an end. Thus, the goal of religion-based terrorism is destruction rather than achieving a political, economic, or social objective. This view harkens back to Lewis's claim that religion, itself, can be a dark and uncontrollable force that causes fits of rage. Several Harvard experts supported the notion that religion-based terror is purely expressive in an article in *Harvard Magazine*. Ashton Carter of Kennedy School of Government claimed that "The motivation for mass terror is a vengeful or messianic one rather than a politically purposeful one." Middle East expert, Eva Bellin, agreed and stated that "The aims of these terrorist networks are much more expressive than programmatic." Kennedy School resident terrorism expert, Jessica Stern, asserted that "Osama bin Laden's objectives are really expressive, not instrumental" because catastrophic attacks will not achieve the attackers' objectives.[3] To me, Stern's admission that al Qaeda's violence has objectives is evidence that it is instrumental violence to achieve some concrete end. It is also important to note that, as will be discussed in chapter 8, some of bin Laden's strategic objectives actually were achieved through 9/11. In this chapter, I will argue that religion-based terrorism, even al Qaeda's, like other forms of terrorism that preceded it, is rooted in political grievances and has political roots.

THE POLITICAL ROOTS OF RELIGION-BASED TERRORISM

Politics is the logical place to begin when explaining why some individuals interpret religion in a way that facilitates terrorism and violence. Until the 1990s, it was accepted that all terrorism was political in nature. Traditional terrorists sought to either replace a regime in power, change the existing political order, obtain rights and freedoms, or create a new political entity. Today's religion-based terrorists are viewed as being part of what is often referred to as "the new terrorism." These new terrorists, supposedly, have no political goals or objectives but only seek to kill as many people as possible, cause mass destruction, and create some sort of apocalypse.[4] The fact these new terrorists do not have political goals or aspirations is one of the things that make them more dangerous because they do not limit their violence in order to gain outside support. It is my contention that today's new religion-based terrorism is rooted in political environments that include authoritarianism, invasion and occupation, denial of self-determination, and anger at America's behavior as the remaining global power. Special consideration in this discussion of the political determinants of religion-based terrorism will be given to the relationship between democracy and religion-based terrorism.

All dissident terrorism is rooted in a grievance that a group has against a government or another group. Members of the dissident group must believe that their grievance is worth dying for and that resolution of the grievance through nonviolent means is not possible. Generally, the grievances of terrorists have been usually political and economic, as is evident in Dennis Rapoport's earlier discussed article, "The Four Waves of Rebel Terror and September 11." To review, the first wave, beginning in the 1880s, was anarchist and focused on weakening the control and power of autocratic government. The second wave, beginning in the 1920s, was anticolonial and involved groups such as the Irish seeking freedom and independence from colonial overlords. The third wave, New Leftist, began in the 1960s, and the objectives of terrorists were liberating masses in the developing world, weakening the power of the First World, and achieving self-determination or equality for dispossessed national and ethnic groups. The fourth wave, today's religion-based terrorism, aims at creating religion-based polities or a World to Come, also political objectives.[5]

It is important to note that Rapoport writes that the current wave of religion-based terror has its roots in the Iranian Revolution, which was a political revolt against the totalitarian, despotic, and repressive rule of the Shah Mohammed Pahlavi.[6] The revolution that toppled the Shah was orchestrated by a broad coalition of religious and secular groups, but the Ayatollah Khomeini later established the theocratic Islamic Republic through adroit political maneuvering aided by good fortune. If the CIA had not helped overthrow the democratically elected government of the socialist leaning Mohammed Mosaddegh in 1953 and if his government had been able to continue a program of reforms that were aimed at improving living conditions for all Iranians, the Iranian Revolution might not have occurred and as a result nor might the current wave of religion-based terrorism. Khomeini's anger at the United States was largely caused by America's support of the Shah. Here we see the significance of resentment toward outside powers that try to influence affairs in another country or region as a catalyst of religion-based violence.

The importance of invasion and occupation by an external power, a very severe form of outside interference, as a cause of today's religion-based terrorism can be seen in the successful guerilla war of the Mujahedeen in Afghanistan against the Soviets, who hoped to create a secular, socialist puppet state during the 1980s. The chaos and the corruption of ruling warlords following withdrawal of Soviet troops in 1989 led to the takeover of the Taliban, which was able to bring a semblance of order and a theocracy based on an extremely puritanical interpretation of Islam. It is also important to note that members of the Mujahedeen, who had been supported by the United States because of their opposition to the Soviets, went on to form al Qaeda. Thus, religion-based terrorists are capable of forming alliances with groups and nations with which they are ideologically opposed when it suits their strategic objectives. Such strategic behavior is certainly a sign of rational, goal-oriented behavior rather than pure religious zeal.

The desire to create a theocratic state is further evidence of the political roots of religion-based terrorism and violence, as the motivating grievance is a desire to change the basis of national political structures. As will be seen, the desire to replace a secular-based or insufficiently religious political order with a religious one is usually strongest in nations where governments are repressive and cannot meet the needs of their citizens or where an ethnic or national group is denied self-rule. Most Islamic terrorist groups operate or have operated in nations within authoritarian regimes such as Egypt, Syria, and Morocco, where elections have been tightly controlled and religious parties have usually been banned from participating. Even Osama bin Laden and al Qaeda have political goals as they seek a global Islamic state governed by *Sharia* law and ruled by a reestablished Caliphate. Also, bin Laden and fifteen of the nineteen 9/11 hijackers are from Saudi Arabia, a country that already has Islamic and *Sharia*-based government but is ruled by an autocratic and corrupt monarchy.[7] Religion, in short, is not a sufficient grievance for terrorism. Rather, the disgruntled group must feel that their religion is being attacked, repressed, and/or is not being given an opportunity to influence government.

AUTHORITARIANISM

Terrorism, religious or secular, is rare in democracies, and when it occurs in democratic settings, it usually fails. As mentioned, the current wave of religion-based terrorism is rooted in the Islamic world, where there are few real democracies. A look at the classifications provided by Freedom House shows that 22 of 34 nations with populations that are at least 75 percent Muslims are not free, while 10 are party free. Only two, Mali and Indonesia, are considered free, while only seven Islamic nations (Albania, Bangladesh, Bosnia, Indonesia, Mali, Senegal, and Turkey) are designated as being electoral democracies.[8] The grim state of freedom and democracy in the Islamic world suggests that terrorists are using religious terminology to express political grievances. Christian-based terrorism, in contrast, is almost nonexistent in Europe, the United States, and other Western nations, which are largely free and democratic. Israel and the United States are rare instances of democratic nations that have experienced native religion-based terrorism. The cases of Jewish terrorists in Israel and Christian terrorists in the United States provide opportunities to test the notion that democracy would moderate Islamic terrorism.

The ability of democracy to suppress terror becomes evident when looking back over the past 40 years. Many democratic nations including Italy (Red Brigade), Germany (Baader-Mieihof Gang), and Japan (Red Army) faced left-wing terrorist groups in the 1960s and the 1970s. Left-wing terrorist groups in the United States during this period included the Weather Underground, the Symbionese Liberation Army, and several Puerto Rican nationalist groups, while Canada faced sporadic terrorist attacks from separatist groups in Quebec. The most noteworthy aspect of all of these groups today is that they no longer exist. An important cause of their disappearance is the democratic governments that they sought to overthrow with violence and insurrection. However, all of the aforementioned terrorist groups were secular based. It might be that religion-based terrorist groups, because of their divine inspiration and eschatological goals, are not moderated by participatory government. Therefore, it is important to examine why the life expectancy of terrorist groups in democracies is so short and whether the same would be true if the Arab Spring of 2011 is successful and democracy takes root in the Islamic world.

Democracy is an important suppressor of terror because it provides legitimacy, the acceptance by the populous of a regime's right to rule over them. Noted political scientist Seymour Martin Lipset offered a succinct definition of legitimacy, "the capacity of a political system to engender and maintain the belief that existing political institutions are the most appropriate and proper ones for the society."[9] When regimes lose their legitimacy, they become unstable and lose their ability to govern. Regimes can draw on several sources to legitimize their rule such as charismatic authority, tradition (monarchies), religion, and rational-legal authority. The last form, as argued by John Locke and other Enlightenment figures, is government by the consent of the governed.[10] In short, citizens are most likely to accept the laws and policies made by elites when they have consented, through a social contract, to have those in power rule over them. It is interesting to note that several Islamic nations, where religion is used to legitimate authority such as Morocco and Saudi Arabia, have frequently been victimized by religion-based terrorists. These nations, however, are monarchies and are not democratic, which suggests that religion is not the primary grievance that is motivating the terrorists, rather it is authoritarianism.

It would seem that terrorism would be less likely in authoritarian and repressive political systems because these regimes can use all of the means at their disposal to repress discontent and disorder and are not constrained by the law. At the same time, they can prevent opposition opinions from being openly expressed through their control of the media and by outlawing dissent. Finally, they are not concerned with accommodating or winning over those who might support the goals of the terrorists but not their tactics.[11] It is important to remember that, in addition to having a grievance, the terrorist must believe that the status quo is so unbearable that it makes violence acceptable. The potential terrorist also has to have lost any hope that his or her grievance or injustice will be addressed through legitimate political channels.[12] Given these necessary conditions for terrorism, it is now clear as to how authoritarian political regimes facilitate terrorism. The lack of legitimate means for groups and individuals to pursue their political objectives provides the potential terrorist with a grievance and an injustice that is not being addressed. Living in a repressive society, where there is no hope for peaceful change makes the status quo unbearable and violence seem reasonable. Democracies and free societies, in contrast, offer the possibility of change through elections, interest groups, and petitioning elected officials. At the same time, the discontented and disgruntled at least have the opportunity to air their grievances and have their say.

Ted Gurr argues that backlash is crucial to the demise of terrorist groups in democracies. Gurr writes that terrorist groups hope that the government repression that usually follows terrorist attacks will help solidify support for their activities. Instead, the public's antipathy is directed at the terrorists because it believes that people have ample opportunity to seek redress for their grievances through legitimate and nonviolent political processes.[13] Thus, mainstream pro-life groups in America are forced to disassociate themselves from radical antiabortion activists who use violence against providers and clinics because they fear their cause will be stained by the violent extremists. In contrast, terrorists in authoritarian and repressive societies might expect more support from the general public, which views the ruling regime as being illegitimate. Also, citizens in democracies tend to be supportive when the government moves to control terrorists, while government repression in authoritarian societies, which is often collective, might lead to greater support for the terrorists. For example, the terrorist campaigns by leftist groups in Europe during the 1960s and 1970s led to strong support for governmental countermeasures. In contrast, Israeli reprisals against Hamas appear to strengthen Palestinian support for that group's suicide bombings and missile attacks.

Gurr also notes that democracies can redress the grievances of a majority of the members of a distressed group, leaving the radicals, who are willing to use violence, isolated. Thus, the achievements of the civil rights movement and the movement toward racial equality helped cause the marginalization of the Black Panthers.[14] It is also important to remember that terrorists must feel that there is no possibility of achieving change through legitimate politics and that their situation is desperate enough to warrant giving up everything and risking their lives for their cause. Because democracies offer social, economic, and political mobility, albeit limited in many cases, potential terrorists, radicals, and revolutionaries rarely reach the extreme level of despair that leads to terrorism. There is always another election on the horizon or interest group representing salient issues, such as the Occupy Movement or the Tea Party in America, which offers hope for change. Democracies have also shown an amazing ability to co-opt those who seek to destroy it. For evidence, one only needs to look at many of the radicals of the 1960s, both in North America and Europe, who went on to become part of the political establishment. The rewards—power, money, and status—offered to those who join the system and play by the rules are too much for most revolutionaries and radicals to pass up.

WOULD DEMOCRACY ALLEVIATE RELIGION-BASED TERRORISM?

The cases used to support Gurr's argument that democracy moderates terrorism all involve secular terrorist groups in the Western world. Would the same pacification take place with religion-based terrorist groups? Again, this is a question that primarily relates to Islamic countries, so it is important to look at the state of democracy in the Islamic world and the role that Islamic political groups have played in Muslim nations. As noted, free and open elections have been rare in the Islamic world, and when elections occur, Islamic political parties and groups have usually been banned from the political process. In Egypt, Tunisia, Algeria, and Syria, nationalist-oriented authoritarian presidents dominate (or dominated) the political system and closely monitor, control, and manage political competition. Parliaments and legislative bodies have largely served as rubber stamps for the head of state and his political party or movement. The opposition parties' activities and freedom to organize and criticize the political order have been severely restricted.

All of these nations with authoritarian regimes, to varying degrees, have experienced Islamic-based terrorism. Haffez al Assad, the late president of Syria, faced a significant challenge from the Muslim Brotherhood in the late 1970s, which included assassination of government leaders, attempts on al Assad's life, and the murder of 63 military cadets. Although the Syrian

Islamic Action Front was certainly rooted in religion, it called for free and fair elections, respect for human rights, and freedom of expression.[15] Al Assad's response was to launch a military attack that completely leveled the city of Hama, where the opposition was centered, and resulted in 15,000 deaths. The situation is repeating itself in 2011–2012 as Islamic groups are participating in the demonstrations and uprising against Assad's son, Bashar. Syria also raises the importance of ethnic cleavages that divide regimes from religion-based opposition as the Assads are from the minority Alawi sect, while the opposition is primarily Sunni.

The Muslim Brotherhood has been an opposition force to authoritarian government in Egypt, where it was born in the 1920s, since the reign of Gamal Abdel Nasser in the 1960s. Sayyid Qutb, who is often labeled as being the ideological inspiration for today's jihadists, wrote his manifesto, Signposts, while he was in prison for opposing the Nasser's Arab-Socialist regime. The Muslim Brotherhood, since the 1980s, has claimed to be a nonviolent group and unsuccessfully petitioned to run in parliamentary elections. Extremist groups such as the Islamic Jihad, on the other hand, have launched many terrorist attacks including the assassination of Nasser's successor, Anwar Sadat. Sadat had angered the Islamists by making peace with Israel and by leading a corrupt and authoritarian regime that made a small group of his cronies very wealthy, while the majority of Egyptians remained mired in poverty. Algeria, another Islamic nation with a strong nationalistic and socialist heritage and an authoritarian regime, began to open its political system in the 1990s. In 1989, the constitution was amended to separate the government from the ruling party, the National Liberation Front, create a multiparty system, and allow free elections. The main Islamic opposition group, Islamic Salvation Front, and other Islamic parties ran in municipal elections in 1990 and captured a majority of town councils. They also were on their way to winning national elections in 1991 when the army suspended the elections, declared a state of emergency, and set up a military government. A catastrophic civil war followed pitting Islamic militias against the regime, while splinter groups such as the Armed Islamic Group committed atrocities and acts of terrorism that caused the deaths of thousands.

Saudi Arabia, Morocco, Jordan Iran, and Sudan maintain authoritarian regimes, but their despots and monarchs claim to rule in the name of Islam, while repressing both religious and secular opposition. Many of these countries have parliaments, but their powers, to varying degrees, are limited, like those in secular-authoritarian Muslim countries. The regimes in these Islamic authoritarian countries view Islamic groups and parties as being particularly dangerous because their existence as a competing religious voice threatens regimes' ability to legitimate their rule with religion. The legitimacy of the Saudi monarchy is strongly rooted in Islam, as the ruling family claims to descend from the Prophet Muhammad; proclaims itself the guardian of Islam's two holiest cities, Mecca and Medina; and enforces a very strict interpretation of *Sharia* (Islamic law). The rule of the Saudi monarchy is absolute, and the regime, annually, is listed among the top abusers of civil and human rights. Given the autocratic rule in Saudi Arabia, it should come as no surprise that the country's brief history is filled with terrorism and insurrection. As discussed in chapter 1, a Shiite group launched an attack on the Grand Mosque in Mecca during celebration of the Islamic New Year in 1979. The Shiites are a persecuted minority in Saudi Arabia, where the ruling family is Sunni. Osama bin Laden and 15 of the 9/11 hijackers were of Saudi origin. Al Qaeda has launched or supported many attacks in Saudi Arabia, including the 1996 bombing of the Khobar Towers housing complex that killed 19 American servicemen.

Morocco also has a monarchy that claims direct descendancy to the Prophet Muhammad. The Moroccan king, as is the case in Saudi Arabia, is both the religious and political leader of the country. However, Morocco's legal system is primarily secular, its culture comfortably mixes Islamic and Western influences, and it has a parliament that is subservient to the king. Freedom of expression is tolerated, as long as the king and Islam are not criticized, and there are multiparty elections. Islamic parties are allowed to participate in elections, and the Justice and Development Party took a plurality of seats in the 2011 parliamentary elections.[16] Still, human rights abuses were common during the long reign of King Hassan II (1961–1999), and the political system is still firmly controlled by the monarchy. Given Morocco's controlled but expanding democracy that allows participation by Islamic parties, it would be expected that there would be less Islamic-based terrorism than in Saudi Arabia, and this, indeed, is the case. Major acts of terrorism are sporadic in Morocco with the latest being a suicide bombing at a Casablanca Internet café in 2007 and coordinated bombings in 2003 targeting a Spanish restaurant, a luxury hotel, a Jewish cemetery, a Jewish cultural center, a Jewish owned restaurant, and the Belgian consulate, which killed 33 civilians and 12 of the 14 terrorists. The attack was the most severe terrorist incident in Morocco's history and was linked to Salafia Jihadia, a group with ties to al Qaeda. However, thousands of Moroccans, led by the king, attended a solidarity rally against the attacks and in support of the country's small Jewish community.

The limited and brief discussion of terrorism in democracy in the Islamic world has suggested that Islamic terrorism is partly a product of repressive political systems and a lack of channels for legitimate political participation. If this is the case, terrorism should be limited in Indonesia and Mali, the two free nations (according to Freedom House) in the Islamic world. Given that Indonesia and Mali are relatively new democracies, more time is needed to determine whether representative government and a free society suppress religion-based terrorism in the Islamic world. For most of Indonesia's history, the country was ruled by the nationalist strongman Suharto and his Golkar political movement. Rioting in 1998 led to the Suharto's resignation and major constitutional reforms that created free and open elections and a multiparty system, which includes a number of Islamic parties. In recent elections, the established Islamic parties, particularly the United Development Party and the National Mandate Party, performed poorly, losing seats to secular parties and new more fundamentalist-oriented Islamic parties. All of the Islamic parties are loyal opposition and have support of the existing nationalist-dominated democratic political order.

It appears that democracy in Indonesia has not moderated the most radical and fringe religion-based terrorists as a militant training camp was recently uncovered in the remote Aceh province, and the radical Islamic terrorist group, Jemaah Islamiyah, remains a threat. Terrorism was frequent in the early years of Indonesian democracy with the bombing of the Jakarta Stock Exchange in 2000 and tourist hotels in Bali in 2002, which killed 202 people, and remains a threat. The government has tried to reform terrorists with rehabilitation programs, but these have been moderately successful. Also, the country's elite special forces, the Kopassus, has been frequently accused of war crimes and human rights violations.[17] Other factors that facilitate religion-based terrorism have also come into play in Indonesia. The government has a very difficult task in controlling the country's borders, as it is a 17,508 island archipelago. The country also has more than 300 distinct ethnicities with a small Chinese minority that controls a disproportionate amount of the country's wealth. Finally, al Qaeda has also established itself in Indonesia. Despite these obstacles, the population has become increasingly supportive of the government's campaign to combat terrorism. Originally, there was widespread belief that the Jakarta and Bali bombing were a Jewish, Western, and Chinese conspiracy. However, as attacks began to target Indonesians and the government tried the perpetrators in court, the media began to acknowledge that a radical group of Muslims that had gone astray was responsible.[18] This shift could represent democracy isolating radical extremists and leading the public to side with the government. Terrorism has been rare in Mali both before and after the transition to democracy.

RELIGION-BASED TERRORISM IN ISRAEL
AND THE UNITED STATES

The nature of the relationship between religion-based terrorism and democracy will be considered again in chapters 6 and 7 with the cases of Jewish extremists in Israel and radical antiabortion groups in the United States.
Israel is a democracy, but it is also a homeland for the Jewish people. However, its legal system is largely secular, and a majority of Israeli Jews are not
religious. As discussed, there is a religious-Zionist minority that has been
willing to use violence and terror when it has sensed that the Israeli government or the Palestinians are blocking their vision of an Israel that controls
all of the land promised to the Israelites in the Bible. Has the ability to pursue their goals through the political system limited or facilitated the violent
actions of the radical fringe? Antiabortion Christian terrorists in the United
States operate in a different context, a democracy where religion and state
are supposed to be separate. The antiabortion pro-life movement in America is sizable, is an active player in legitimate politics, and has been successful in limiting access to abortion and restricting the conditions under which
abortion is legal. Have their successes limited the amount of antiabortion
violence in the United States, or are the radicals unaffected by the events
taking place in the political system and the courts?

OCCUPATION

Occupation and the denial of self-determination have consistently been
significant causes of terrorism in the modern era. It is important to remember that the second and third waves of terror in Rapoport's "The Four
Waves of Rebel Terror and September 11" were both rooted in occupation and the denial of self-determination. In the second wave, colonial powers were often reluctant to let go of their colonies, so terrorism and armed
insurrection were often used to hasten their departure. One of the objectives of the third wave was self-determination for dispossessed national and
ethnic groups such as the Palestinians and the Catholics in Northern Ireland.[19] Thus, it is likely that much of today's religion-based terrorism, like
its secular-based predecessors, also has roots in occupation or other forms
of unwanted foreign influence.

Terrorism and asymmetrical warfare are the logical tools for groups and
peoples seeking to expel an occupying nation or to separate from an existing nation and gain independence. Because the occupying power or existing government has an army and a monopoly on the legitimate use of force,

the challengers are at a clear disadvantage. In most cases, attempts to defeat the occupier or the existing government through conventional warfare and direct confrontation are likely to fail. Thus, groups seeking independence or self-determination have always turned to terrorism and unconventional warfare to frustrate and enervate their powerful adversaries. Because terrorism and unconventional warfare involve attacks on civilians; nonmilitary targets such as civilian aircraft, schools, and entertainment venues; and tactics such as roadside bombs, hostage taking, and suicide missions, terrorists have always been viewed as being zealous fanatics, who place little value on human life.

The zealous fanatic label, as discussed, is standard for religion-based terrorists, whose violence, supposedly, has no real objective other than killing as many people as possible. On the other hand, the zealotry and fanaticism of some religion-based terrorists, like their predecessors in the previous waves of terror, could also be motivated by occupation, the desire for self-determination, or excessive cultural influence by an outside power. Robert Pape's study of suicide bombers found that their most common motivation is the defense of territory and the belief that they have been invaded by an alien culture that cannot easily be defeated. He also concluded that the suicide bombers are usually affiliated with organizations with well-defined strategies for eliminating the foreign presence.[20] James Rinehart found that millennial movements usually arise in a weak or colonized society in response to an invasion by a foreign power that attempts to impose its cultural values.[21] The use of terror to resist occupation goes all the way back to the Jewish Zealots who were struggling against Roman rule over ancient Israel. The American Revolution against the British can be seen as the first modern revolt against an occupying force that used terrorist tactics. The first violent acts against the British, who went from being viewed as fellow countrymen to an occupying force, were terrorist in nature, as government officials were harassed, kidnapped, tarred and feathered, and even killed. When the colonists openly rebelled, their guerilla, hit and run tactics were often labeled as unconventional and contrary to the accepted standards of warfare of the time.[22] Although most of the terrorist groups in Rapoport's second and third waves of terror were secular-based, some religion-based groups, such as the Muslim Brotherhood in Egypt and the Muslim League in India, were created, in part, to resist European colonial rule.[23] At the same time, the Palestinian struggle against Israeli occupation began as a largely nationalist campaign in the third wave but later took on religious overtones during the current wave of religion-based terrorism.

Palestine

The Palestinian case, which will be discussed at length in chapter 8, is the foremost example of occupation being a cause of religion-based terrorism. It is important to note that the conflict between Israel and the Palestinians is more than 100 years old but has taken on religious overtones only in the last 25 years. The campaign to create a Palestinian state is rooted in the competing claims of Jews and Arabs over the land that is the present-day State of Israel, the West Bank, and the Gaza Strip. The conflict began as a nationalist struggle between the growing number of Jewish settlers who arrived in Palestine during the first half of the 20th century and the Arab inhabitants of the area. At the same time, Zionists and Arabs both used violence and terror against the British colonial administration, which stood in the way of their aspirations for self-determination. After the state of Israel was created on the departure of the British, the conflict primarily became a series of conventional wars as the surrounding Arab nations took up the fight, promised a quick victory, and assured the Palestinians that they would soon be able to return to their homes.

Following the formation of the Palestine Liberation Organization (PLO) in 1964 and the cataclysmic defeat of the Arab armies in the 1967 Six-Day War, the Palestinians launched a terrorist campaign for the liberation of their homeland and a secular state, which was in line with other third wave struggles. As the PLO failed to bring about a Palestinian state either through terror and armed conflict or through the Oslo Peace Accords with Israel in 1994, the Palestinians in the West Bank and Gaza began to take the lead in the attempt to end Israeli rule by launching two uprisings (Intifada) in 1988–1990 and 2000–2006. The first Intifada marked the emergence of Hamas, an Islamic group that began to challenge to PLO for leadership of the Palestinian movement. Hamas's strength and popularity had grown significantly by the beginning of the second Intifada because it was seen as the leader of resistance against Israeli rule. Eventually, Hamas removed the PLO from power in the Gaza Strip. Hamas's ascendency and the second Intifada also marked the religionization of the Palestinian struggle and the use of suicide bombing. However, secular and nationalist Palestinian groups such as the al Aqsa Martyrs Brigade have also carried out suicide bombings.[24]

Afghanistan

Afghanistan presents two cases, the campaign against the Soviet Union invasion in 1979 and the opposition to the U.S. invasion following 9/11, of religion-based violence, terror, and insurrection being used to resist occupation by a foreign country. The Soviet invasion was sparked by a Marxist government instituting a series of reforms aimed at weakening Islam's role in society and creating a modern, socialist nation. The attempted reforms, in a very traditional Islamic society, along with the violent repression of opposition had led to the formation of the Mujahedeen opposition groups, which launched attacks on the Afghan army. In 1979, the government asked the Soviet Union to send troops in support of its ineffective army's attempts to quash the rebellions, which had spread through the country. The Soviets eventually sent 100,000 troops to the conflict and tried to pacify the country through massive bombings and depopulation. The Mujahedeen were assisted by volunteers from across the Muslim world as well as by arms from the United States channeled through Pakistan. The Soviets, failing in their attempts to pacify the country, withdrew in 1988–1989.[25] The resistance to the Soviets was rooted in Islam, and the Muslim volunteers from outside of Afghanistan came to participate in holy war.[26] However, it was the repressive nature of the Afghanistan government and its campaign against Islam that sparked the insurgency. The Soviet invasion and occupation caused the same response—violence and terror—that occurs wherever an outside power attempts to dominate another nation. If the Soviets had not invaded, they would not have been subject to attack by the Mujahedeen.

The American invasion of Afghanistan, following the attacks on 9/11 aimed at bringing down the Taliban government, which had given shelter to Osama bin Laden, has sparked the same resistance to foreign invasion and occupation that the Soviets encountered. Although the American-led Operation Enduring Freedom succeeded in toppling the Taliban regime and destroying most of al Qaeda's bases, armed resistance to the American forces, its allies, and the Afghan government under Hamid Karzai continues in 2012. However, it is difficult to label religion as being the primary cause of the opposition to American forces and the Karzai government. The Taliban are a rigorously puritanical Sunni Islamic group, which imposed a very strict interpretation of *Sharia* during its rule from 1996 to 2001. During that time, women were largely confined to their homes, and violators of laws against adultery were routinely stoned to death. However, many Afghans did not support the Taliban because of their theocratic rule and use of Islamic law. Rather, the Taliban brought order to a country that had been in chaos since the Soviet invasion, and they were seen as being less corrupt than the governments and warlords that had preceded them.

The importance of self-interest, rather than religion, was made evident when many of the warlords who had supported the Taliban were easily bought off, switched sides, and allied with the Americans and their Afghan allies during the 2001 invasion. Some former Taliban even joined the Karzai government. However, the 10-year occupation by American and NATO forces has led to a resurgence of the Taliban, which is now said to be a formidable fighting force that controls most of the southern part of the country.[27] Attempts to pacify resistance have led to many civilian casualties, which has helped gain supporters for the Taliban.[28] At the same time, the corruption and the ineffectiveness of the Karzai government has also led to more support for the Taliban and anger at its American benefactors. Thus, it appears that the longer the United States remains in Afghanistan, despite its efforts to rebuild the country and the introduction of 30,000 more troops in 2009–2010, the greater the resistance to its attempts to bring stability and democracy to that country. That resistance, however, is based more on a desire to see the foreign occupying force depart and an end to the ineffective and corrupt government that it supports than a desire for a return to the puritanical Islamic rule of the Taliban. It also appears that the Taliban are willing to use negotiation to gain power as they opened a political office in Qatar in December 2011 to facilitate peace talks.

Iraq

America's occupation of Iraq following the invasion of that country in 2003 also led to a campaign of terror and insurrection by Islamic groups. As was the case in Afghanistan, the original invasion and the toppling of the regime in power were completed with relative ease, and the Americans were viewed as liberators by some Iraqis. Saddam Hussein, a Sunni, had been a brutal dictator, who had repressed the country's Shiite and Kurdish populations and who had maintained power by using torture and murder to terrorize opposition. Resistance, however, developed as the United States attempted to occupy the country and create a government to replace the fallen regime of Saddam Hussein. The situation in Iraq was further complicated by the outbreak of a civil war between Sunnis and Shiites who were vying for power in the vacuum created by the American invasion. However, both groups, along with al Qaeda, used terror and guerrilla warfare against the United States and its British allies.[29] As was the case in Afghanistan, it was the struggle against occupation, not religion, which led to Islamic resistance against the United States. Iraqi Sunnis and Shiites would not have had reason to wage campaigns of terror and insurrection against the United States if its troops were not occupying their country.

The importance of self-interest and realpolitik can also be seen in the behavior of Islamic groups in Iraq. In December 2011, U.S. military involvement in Iraq ended, as the last combat troops left. It has often been claimed that the surge in 2007 that introduced an additional 20,000 American troops led to the decline in violence in Iraq, which facilitated America's withdrawal.[30] At the same time, the Shiite Mahdi Army, at the behest of their Iranian supporters, engaged in several ceasefires to encourage the Americans' departure.[31] Another turning point was the creation of the Sunni Awakening Councils, which took money from the Americans to stop fighting U.S. forces and focus their efforts on al Qaeda. In essence, this was a realization by the Sunnis that they were confronting too many enemies: the United States, al Qaeda (which had begun to challenge the local tribal chiefs), and the Shiite militias. Clearly, the losers in the civil war within Iraq and facing the al Qaeda challenge, the Sunni Awakening Councils came to the realization that the best method of securing their communities was allying with their former enemy and receiving weapons and payment. If they were truly motivated by religion, this move would not have been made.

Israel's Invasion of Lebanon (1982)

The Israeli invasion of Lebanon is another case where a foreign power invaded a country, was greeted as a liberator, overstayed its welcome, and, ultimately, facilitated the rise of religion-based terrorist groups. The Israelis entered Lebanon in 1982 to root out the PLO, which had developed a state within in a state in southern Lebanon from which it launched terrorist attacks into northern Israel. Israel was originally welcomed by the Shiites, who had suffered under de facto PLO rule. The Shiite militia, Amal, fought a prolonged battle with the Palestinians for control of the Sabra and Shatilla refugee camps in West Beirut and did not resist Israel's invasion. However, the Israelis set up a security zone in south Lebanon that they controlled in tandem with a Christian-dominated militia, the South Lebanese Army. Ultimately, a group of Amal members left the militia and with the backing of Iran started Hezbollah, which vowed to militarily resist Israel's presence in Lebanon. Since then, Hezbollah has launched numerous attacks against Israel and has joined the Palestinian group, Hamas, in vowing to fight for Israel's destruction.[32] Israel, eventually, launched a second invasion of Lebanon in the summer of 2006 in response to Hezbollah rocket attacks on northern Israel. The Shiites were also radicalized by the presence of U.S. and French forces in Lebanon in 1982, which were there as peacekeepers overseeing the departure of the PLO. Hezbollah and other militant Shiites, however, saw them as a tool of the Israelis in their attempt to dominate the country and install a Christian government.

STRATEGIC ALLIANCE OR CIVILIZATION RALLYING?

The consideration of occupation as a source of religion-based terrorism has also demonstrated that holy warriors and jihadists are more often motivated by utility maximization than religious fervor. It has been shown that, on many occasions, religion-based terrorist groups and militias will take assistance or align with a country or group that is of a different religion. As discussed, the Shiites in Lebanon originally saw the Israelis as allies in their struggles against Palestinians. The devoutly Islamic Mujahedeen in Afghanistan took aid and assistance from the United States, when they were fighting the Soviet Union. Some members and supporters of the Taliban were easily bribed to support the American invasion in 2001 and the Karzai government. The Sunni Awakening Councils in Iraq took American assistance and payments, when it became clear that an alliance with the United States was needed to protect them from al Qaeda and the Shiites. Their behavior contradicts Huntington's fear of "civilization rallying," where members of civilizations aid each other in wars against other civilizations.[33] Thus, it appears that many religion-based terrorists are, indeed, rational actors guided by political calculation more than religious loyalties.

DENIAL OF AUTONOMY AND SELF-DETERMINATION

The end of European colonialism and, later, the fall of the Soviet Union left many nation-states, such as the former Yugoslavia, with populations composed of a mixture of ethnic, tribal, linguistic, and/or religion groups. Many of these nation-states have endured wars, terrorism (both dissident and state), and insurrection as groups have fought to secede and achieve independence or autonomy, and governments have tried to suppress the secessionist movements. Many of these civil wars and insurrections have not involved religious divides as was the case in tribal conflicts in African countries, such as Rwanda and the Democratic Republic of the Congo, and purely ethnic conflicts such as the one between Kurds and Turks in Turkey and Kurds and Arabs in Iraq (All three groups are predominantly Muslim.). Many secessionist conflicts do involve religious divisions, such as Chechnya's fight for independence from Russia, the struggle by Black Africans (Christians and animists) in the Darfur region of Sudan against Arab-Muslims from the south, and Muslim separatists in predominantly Christian Philippines. Some of these insurrections involve two branches of the same religion such as Sunnis and Shiites in Iraq and Catholics and Protestants in Northern Ireland. The key issue for the conflicts that involve religious divides is the extent to which religion, as opposed to nonreligious factors such as ethnicity, class, denial of rights, and the desire for self-rule, is responsible for the terror and violence.

Only approximately 40 percent of the world's 267 cases of ethnic conflict involve religious divisions.[34] At the same time, nonreligious ethnic conflicts often produce savage violence and bloodshed as was seen in the civil war in Rwanda between Hutus and Tutsis, which resulted in 800,000 deaths.[35] Jonathan Fox has written a number of articles and books on ethno-religious violence. In a 1998 article, Fox wrote that religious motives for ethnic conflicts are usually complicated by political, social, economic, or autonomy issues. Fox concludes that "autonomy, or self-determination, is the issue that has most animated ethnic conflict in the twentieth century."[36] It is expected that demands for autonomy or self-determination would lead to violence because the dominant ethnic group usually fights to prevent the breakup of the state and the weakening of its power. According to Fox's analysis of the Minorities at Risk data set, religion is the primary cause of only a very small amount of ethno-religious conflicts.[37] Fox, in a quantitative study, looked at ethnic conflicts where religious divides support ethnic cleavages and found that religion was the primary issue of contention in only 12 percent of the cases of ethno-religious conflicts, was a secondary issue of contention in 61.9 percent of the cases, and not an issue at all in 26.7 percent of the cases.[38]

Religion, in most cases, only becomes a grievance that motivates ethnic conflict when there is a strong perception of religious discrimination by a minority group. Persecution and discrimination, of course, are also necessary conditions for nonreligion-based ethnic conflict, as minority and ethnic groups that are treated well have little reason to challenge the status quo.[39] Thus, religious groups behave the same way that other groups do when they feel that they are being systematically discriminated against and that the political system holds no means of recourse—they rebel. Perceptions of oppression and persecution are also relevant to the earlier discussion of invasion and occupation as causes of religion-based violence. There, the feelings of persecution and threat come from an external force rather than an internal one.

Religion does play an important role as an enhancer of ethnic conflicts, as Fox reports that when a group desires self-determination, the presence of religion doubles the intensity of the rebellion.[40] Religions, as Clifford Geertz suggests, are particularly salient in defining individual identity because they connect humans to a higher power. As a result, any challenge to an individual's religious framework is seen as an existential threat to both the believer and his or her greater community.[41] The salience of religion also explains why ethnic conflicts that involve religion are more likely to involve foreign intervention and civilization rallying, as some highly religious individuals, such as al Qaeda fighters, see attacks on coreligionists across the globe as threats to themselves. The intensity of religious loyalties, however, is often related to the overlapping of religion and nationalism.[42] This is certainly the case with Jewish and many Islamic terrorist groups because religion and state have, historically, been intertwined in Islam and Judaism. A quick review of a number of ethno-religious conflicts will illustrate the convergence of religion and national identity and show how other cleavages, including class and ethnicity, often enhance the divide between competing religious groups.

Northern Ireland

The conflict in Northern Ireland between Catholics and Protestants, which will be discussed at length in chapter 7, is a prime example of how ethno-religious conflicts often feature a number of cleavages that divide the disputing parties. The significance of religious differences in conflict in Northern Ireland is contradicted by the fact that Protestants and Catholics have coexisted peacefully elsewhere for the past 200 years. The Northern Ireland case is particularly complex because its roots go back to the 12th century and is directly caused by Queen Elizabeth I creating the Plantation of Ulster on the most prosperous agricultural land in Northern Ireland in the 16th century and giving it to English and Scottish Protestants to settle, while dispossessing the local Irish Catholics. Since then, the two groups have struggled with each other for control of the area. In addition to being divided by religion, the two communities have different national origins, cultural traditions, and languages. The Protestants dominated the political apparatus because of their ties to the English occupiers and thrived economically, while the Catholics were second-class citizens both politically and economically. In short, the Irish Catholics were a persecuted minority. The conflict in Northern Ireland was inflamed by British occupation, particularly with the arrival of troops in 1969 to quell civil disturbances.

Yugoslavia

The convergence of religious and ethnic identities is also a key characteristic of the civil wars and ethnic cleansing that took place in the former

Yugoslavia from 1991 to 1995. There, the conflict involved three competing ethno-religious groups: the Serbian Eastern Orthodox, the Croatian and
Slovenian Catholics, and the Bosnian Muslims. As is the case in Northern
Ireland, the roots of the contemporary violence go back hundreds of years.
Wars between Christians and Muslims in the Balkans began in the eighth
century, and Catholics and Orthodox Christians began fighting following
the rift that caused the Great Schism between Rome and Constantinople
in 1054. Since then, the groups have been contending for dominance in the
Balkan Peninsula with each holding resentments and grudges against the
others for past atrocities and persecutions. The creation of modern Yugoslavia following World War I did not end the animosity as the ethno-religious
groups fought during World War II with the Croats and the Bosnians generally supporting Nazi Germany and the Serbs primarily supporting the Soviet Union. Croats and Bosnians still resent the Serbian dominated state that
existed between the world wars, and Serb hostility is fueled by the ethnic
cleansing during World War II that resulted in the death of close to 400,000
Serbs.[43]

Joseph Tito (a Serb) was able to maintain relative peace and stability during his iron-fisted rule from the end of World War II until his death in 1980.
However, Croats and Bosnians frequently called for greater autonomy for
the country's ethnic groups with cycles of protest followed by repression.
Following Tito's death, Yugoslavia quickly disintegrated with Serbians resisting the demands of the Slovenians and the Croats for greater autonomy.
Wars followed when the Slovenians and the Croatians declared independence. Later, the Serbian army intervened in 1992 to help Serbs in Bosnia
and Herzegovina prevent a vote for a referendum on independence, which
was favored by Muslims. The war in Bosnia was particularly brutal with
the Serbs engaging in campaigns of shelling civilians, ethnic cleansing, and
genocide in attempts to create Serbian enclaves within Bosnia. The United
States and NATO eventually intervened and launched air strikes against the
Serbs. The Dayton Peace Accords in 1995 ended the conflict and created the
nations of Bosnia and Herzegovina and the Serb Republika Srpska. The war
resulted in approximately 100,000 casualties, of which roughly one-half
were civilians.[44]

The civil wars in the former Yugoslavia have been presented by Huntington and others as evidence of the clash of civilizations and the growing
importance of religion as a cause of conflict and violence. Religion's role as
a cause of the conflict, once again, is more complex than it appears at the
surface. As is the case in Northern Ireland, religious affiliation and ethnic
identification overlap and support each other. As Paul Mojzes writes,

The warfare in former Yugoslavia, indeed, did not begin as an explicitly re-ligious war, nor is the current character of the war primarily a religious one. These conflicts, however, do have distinct ethnoreligious characteristics be-cause ethnicity and religion have become so enmeshed that they cannot be separated. The fundamental causes of war are ethno-national yet many na-tionalists take on a religious label as way of expressing their identity and many religious institutions and leaders did not discourage this process.[45]

Mojzes goes onto argue that the Catholic Church, Eastern Orthodox Church, and Islamic authorities reinforced and often inflamed the nationalistic sen-timents in their respective communities. Despite the claims of leading cler-ics, religious institutions sanctioned and encouraged the use of their faiths in support of nationalist purposes.[46] For example, the Serbians claimed that the Bosnian Muslims were *mujahedeen* (holy warriors), who wanted to cre-ate an Islamic state based on *Sharia* law and to begin the Islamization of Europe, and tried to inspire their forces by stating that Kosovo was the holy land of the Serbian Orthodox Church because of a battle fought there against the Ottoman Turks in 1389.[47]

An important point to note in Mojzes's argument is that religion was not that cause of the conflict but, rather, was used as a tool to help stir national-ist feelings and to fan the flames of ethnic hatred. This, of course, is one of the central arguments of this book; religion is a justification or motivator for people who are engaging in violence and terror that is caused by other factors. The significance of religion as the primary cause of the civil war and state terror in Bosnia is further negated by the fact that the Bosnian Muslims are one of the most secularized Islamic communities in the world. Bosnian Muslims were known to drink alcohol and intermarry with Catholics and Eastern Orthodox prior to the civil war. Many saw Islam as being a cul-tural and social identity as much as a religious one.[48] Several scholars point to the importance of political factors, rather than primordial ethnic hatred as being the primary cause of the wars in the former Yugoslavia. Francine Friedman argues that politicians, who had lost the ideology (communism) that had supported their governance, turned to nationalism to legitimate their rule so that they could remain in power.[49] Susan Woodward writes that it was the failure to transform a communist polity into a democratic state that caused the conflict. Specifically, it was Yugoslavia's failed economic program, which led to a decline in the standard of living, which eroded the country's social fabric and led political leaders to appeal to ethnic and reli-gious prejudices to maintain their power.[50]

Another important factor mentioned by Fox that facilitates ethno-religious conflicts, the desire for autonomy and self-rule, is also crucial in the Yugoslavian case. For Serbian leaders who controlled the Yugoslavian government in the early 1990s, the dissolution of Yugoslavia and greater Serbia was unacceptable. At the same time, Slovenians and Croatians came to believe that independence was necessary when the Serbians resisted their demand for a loose federation of states. The Serb-dominated military, therefore, was used to force Slovenia and Croatia to remain part of greater Yugoslavia after those regions announced their intent to become independent. Naturally, the Slovenians and Croatians resisted when attacked by the Yugoslavian army. The Serbs found the possibility of an independent Bosnia even more troubling because of the large number of Serbs living in Bosnia and Herzegovina. Governments usually react with violence when an ethnic group, religious group, or geographic region attempts to break away from the nation, as was the case in the American Civil War. The secessionist group then responds with violence, often terrorism, because of its weakness relative to the country from which it is trying to secede.

Kashmir

The ongoing conflict over Kashmir is an ethno-religious conflict that also involves an interstate struggle between India and Pakistan. Following the end of British occupation in 1947, the rulers of states in British-controlled India with Muslim majorities were given a choice of joining India or Pakistan. The Hindu monarch of predominantly Muslim Jammu and Kashmir opted to align with India so that he could receive Indian military assistance in quelling a tribal rebellion. Pakistan sent troops of its own to the conflict, and the resulting war left predominantly Hindu India, with its secular government, controlling most of Kashmir with its Muslim majority. Since then, Pakistan has supported and armed Muslim guerillas and insurgents while claiming that these groups cannot be controlled, while India has held Pakistan responsible for Islamic terrorist activity in Kashmir. Consequently, the countries fought two more wars over Kashmir in 1965 and 1971. India maintains that Kashmir is an integral part of its territory and should remain a secularly governed area and that the 1947 Accession and the agreement ending the 1971 conflict affirmed its right to control the territory. Pakistan continues to label Kashmir a disputed territory and has called for a plebiscite where Kashmiris would determine their own future status.

An indigenous separatist movement began to develop in the late 1980s following disputed elections in Jammu and Kashmir that were claimed to be rigged.[51] Later, jihadists returning from the war against the Soviet Union in Afghanistan and supporters of the Taliban, allegedly with the assistance of

Pakistan, joined the fight on the side of the insurgents. The jihadist groups in Kashmir have been ruthless in their attacks on Hindu civilians, Muslims who cooperate with the Indian authorities, and the Indian army and local security forces. It is estimated that anywhere from 50,000 to 100,000 Hindus have been killed or forced to leave their homes.[52] At the same time, Indian forces and paramilitary groups have been equally ruthless and have committed extrajudicial killings, torture, and gang rape, while the disappearance of prisoners and Muslims suspected of supporting the insurrection is common. Security forces have also opened fire on peaceful demonstrations, claiming that their actions were in self-defense.[53] There has been a significant decline in militant violence in Indian-administered Kashmir over the past four years, which has been offset by a large number of demonstrations against Indian rule that have occurred during the same time frame.

The conflict and turmoil in Jammu and Kashmir certainly has religious roots, as Pakistan claims to be protecting the interests of the area's Muslims. Native Hindus wish to remain part of India, while native Muslims either seek independence or incorporation into Pakistan. At the same time, foreign fighters and Pakistanis have entered the conflict as part of a global campaign to liberate Muslim land and create Islamic states. The case of Kashmir, however, also supports Fox's argument that autonomy and self-determination are the most important determinants of the use of insurrection and terrorism in ethno-religious conflicts. Clearly, both violent and nonviolent methods of opposing Indian rule have brought strong repressive measures. An analogous situation exists in nearby Tibet, where the majority ethnic Tibetans, who are seeking independence or greater autonomy from China, have been severely repressed by the Chinese government, which has furthered its authority by bringing Han Chinese into the area and giving them favored status. Majority groups, be they religious, racial, or ethnic, react negatively when they are denied self-rule by an outside group or an internal minority, as was also the case with blacks in South Africa and Zimbabwe.

The policies and politics of India and Pakistan are also important causes of the insurrection in Kashmir. Jessica Stern writes that the Indian administration helped to create the intolerable and unstable situation in Kashmir, as the area was "essentially run as a kleptocracy."[54] Ironically, compliant Muslim politicians who controlled criminal and legal businesses were crucial supporters of Indian rule. Corruption, bribery, and extortion were common, while India ignored Kashmir's serious economic problems, illegally intervened in local politics, and rigged local elections.[55] Thus, the Muslim majority felt further victimized by a corrupt government that clearly had no respect for the rule of law. The insurgency in Kashmir was also inflamed by

political forces in India and Pakistan that used the conflict for domestic political gain. Indian Hindu nationalist politicians and parties have supported
the maintenance of control over Kashmir so that a precedent is not set for
Sikh separatists seeking self-rule in other parts of the country. At the same
time, Hindu nationalists gain support by using Kashmir to play on the fear
and dislike of Muslims within India. Pakistani politicians have supported
insurgents and terrorists in Kashmir to appease religious parties and extremists in their country. In short, some actors in both countries have felt that
maintaining the conflict is in their best domestic political interests.

SPILLOVER

The significance of occupation and persecution as causes of religion-based
terrorism and violence extends beyond the borders of the territory where the
occupation or the denial of autonomy occurs. The denial of freedom and
self-determination appear to inspire outrage among coreligionists across the
globe, which provides limited support for Huntington's notion of civilization rallying. The Soviet occupation of Afghanistan led to the creation of a
group known as the Afghan-Arabs, Muslims from the Arab world (including Osama bin Laden) who came to Afghanistan to aid the native Mujahedeen and later founded al Qaeda. Many of the Afghan-Arabs later went to
Bosnia to assist the Muslims in their civil war against the Eastern Orthodox
Christian Serbians and gravitated back to Afghanistan and Iraq following
the American invasions of those nations.[56] The Israeli occupation of the West
Bank, Gaza (until 2005), and, for some, all of Palestine is a significant motivating force for many non-Palestinian Muslim terrorists including al Qaeda.
In a 2008 video, Osama bin Laden stated that "We will continue our struggle against the Israelis and their allies. We are not going to give up an inch
of the land of Palestine." He also stated that Israel's occupation of Palestine was the most important cause of al Qaeda's struggle against the United
States and a motivation for the attacks of 9/11.[57] At the same time, several
governments of Muslim nations, including Iran and Saudi Arabia, have contributed arms and funds to Palestinian terrorist groups such as Hamas.

The American invasions and occupations of Afghanistan and Iraq also
inspired terrorism throughout the Muslim world. As noted previously, al
Qaeda did not have a presence in Iraq prior to the American invasion in
2001. However, Abu Musab al Zarqawi, a Jordanian, who had fled Afghanistan following the U.S. invasion of that country, joined and eventually
headed Ansar al-Islam in northern Iraq. In 2004, al Zarqawi swore allegiance to al Qaeda, and, since then, al Qaeda Iraq has carried out numerous

bombings; attacks on U.S. forces; and attacks on Iraqi civilians, security forces, and Shiites. Despite al Zarqawi's death in a U.S. air strike in 2006, the group remains active, and there are somewhere between several hundred and 3,000 foreign fighters in Iraq with 30–40 entering the country each month.[58] Although the U.S. invasion of Afghanistan greatly weakened al Qaeda in that country, it still remains active and has developed a greater presence across the border in neighboring Pakistan, with numerous foreign fighters taking part in terrorism and insurrection in both countries. Supporters of America's wars in Iraq and Afghanistan have also been the targets of Islamic terrorism. Al Qaeda set off bombs on four trains in Madrid, Spain, on March 11, 2004, killing 191, as punishment for that country's participation in the Iraq War. British Muslims sympathetic to al Qaeda attacked subways and busses on July 7, 2005, killing 56 people because of that country's supporting role in the U.S.-led wars in Iraq and Afghanistan.

The anger and hostility stirred by the U.S. invasions of Afghanistan and Iraq were strong enough to lead the National Intelligence Council to conclude that "The Iraq conflict has become the cause célèbre for jihadists, breeding a deep resentment of US involvement in the Muslim world and cultivating supporters for the global jihadist movement."[59] Also, a study by Peter Bergen and Paul Cruickshank at the Center for Law and Security at New York University found that there was a sharp increase in the number of terrorist attacks worldwide by Muslim groups in the three years following the U.S. invasion of Iraq. The authors share the NIC's conclusion that the invasion of Iraq helped motivate jihadist groups across the globe because of the anger and frustration that it has caused in the Muslim world.[60] The increase in global Islamic terrorism and the significant number of Muslims who are travelling to foreign countries to support Muslims who have been invaded and occupied or who are fighting for autonomy appear to support the notion of civilization rallying and that religion is a force that inspires people to violence. The Afghan-Arabs and others who travel the globe to join holy wars or launch terrorist attacks because of anger and frustration caused by U.S., Western, and Israeli aggression claim to be fighting in defense of their faith.

It is important, on the other hand, to remember that the cause of the outrage is the invasion and/or occupation of Islamic countries by stronger non-Muslim powers. At the same time, only a very small number of Muslims reach the level of indignation that is necessary to become a jihadist. This again leads one to wonder what separates this small minority from the majority that disapproves of U.S., Israeli, and Western behavior toward the Islamic world but does not engage in violence. Both groups are Muslims, read the same *Quran*, value the same oral traditions, and share the same history. This question will be taken up in chapter 5 when the socioeconomic causes of religion-based terrorism are considered. For the moment, it should be noted that religion-based terrorists are not the only ones who have travelled to other parts of the world to fight for an underdog that is under attack or who have launched terrorist attacks in solidarity with a dispossessed group. Approximately 32,000 foreigners volunteered to fight with the Republicans, who were the cause célèbre of left-leaning intelligentsia and working-class groups, during the Spanish Civil War.[61] The Japanese Red Army, a communist terrorist group, staged an attack at Israel's Lod Airport (now Ben Gurion) in support of the Palestinians, which killed 26 people.

The preceding discussion of authoritarianism, occupation, and self-determination suggests that people become violent when governmental authority is forced on them without their consent. Given that governmental authorities and occupying powers are reluctant to relinquish their power, it is likely that dissident groups will use violence to bring about a political system that represents their interest and desires. Because the opposition group is usually significantly weaker and has fewer resources than the government or the occupying power, it resorts to terrorism and other forms of asymmetrical warfare. This has been true for the American colonists rebelling against British rule, Communist rebels in Cuba, and the attempts of the Syrian Islamic Action Front to overthrow Haffez al Assad. Religion has played a role in some but not most of these insurrections. When religion has come into play, it has not been a direct cause of the terrorism and violence. Rather, it has been used as an ideology to further motivate people to violence and to justify the violence. In the next chapter, I will begin to look at another set of causes of religion-based violence, which relates to an individual's sense that he or she has been marginalized, lost status, and not achieved what he or she deserves in life.

_____ *Chapter 4* _____

Socioeconomic Causes of Religion-Based Terrorism

There is a common perception that religion-based terrorists come from the poorest, least educated, and most dispossessed social and economic segments of society. In fact, most contemporary holy warriors and jihadists, as was the case with the 9/11 hijackers, are usually well educated and have middle- or upper-class backgrounds. Assaf Moghadam found that there is no terrorism in the world's 49 least developed countries.[1] A 2004 analysis of Palestinian terrorists and Hezbollah in Lebanon concluded that increasing wealth raised the probability that an individual would be a terrorist.[2] A study of Pakistani Islamic terrorists found that a majority at least had a high school degree from public schools (as opposed to religious schools, *madrasas*) and were from middle- or upper-class backgrounds.[3] Jewish terrorists in Israel and antiabortion terrorists in the United States are also well-educated and well-off economically. The association between terrorism and wealth makes sense because poor people generally lack the education and skills that are necessary to plan and carry out sophisticated terrorist attacks like 9/11, where the plotters had to live in America without attracting unwanted attention and learn to fly airplanes. Thus, the notion of the illiterate peasant who is manipulated and brainwashed into religion-based violence because he or she does not know any better is often flawed. If religion-based terrorism is not a movement rooted in poverty, what are its socioeconomic roots?

Terrorists are often motivated by the perception that they are being threatened or persecuted by forces beyond their control and that extreme actions are necessary to counter those menacing influences. Chapter 3 described how groups and individuals respond with violence when authorities such as authoritarian governments, invading and occupying armies, police and security forces, and rival ethnic groups take away or repress freedom, democracy, self-determination, or national autonomy. A perceived loss of socioeconomic status or threat to one's place in society by internal or external forces can also cause disgruntled individuals to develop the level of anger, frustration, and despair necessary for violence. In short, religion- based terrorism is characteristic of individuals who believe that they have been pushed, or are threatened to be pushed, to the margins of society and that they deserve better than what they have. Thus, it makes sense that educated individuals with frustrated aspirations for a better life and vulnerable individuals with status to lose are more likely to become terrorists than those who are already at the bottom of society's socioeconomic ladder and are likely to have lost hope for a better future. When looking for the roots of religion-based terrorism, the place to begin is societies and segments of society that are experiencing rapid change that has promised much but delivered little and that has caused some to feel that what they value is threatened.

This chapter will examine some of the forces that have caused religion-based terrorists to believe that their status is being threatened and that they have been unjustly pushed to the margins of society. Forces of change such as rapid modernization, globalization, the advancement of technology, and the failure of governments to provide for their people often cause people to feel a profound sense of threat and precariousness. These larger factors have produced specific threats that cause marginalized individuals to turn to violence and to religion-based terrorist groups in order to regain the status and sense of empowerment that they feel that they have lost. Some of the threats, such as foreign cultures (Western) and nations (United States and Israel), are external. Others, such as inequality, frustrated aspirations, corruption and cronyism, women, and privileged minority groups, are internal. When individuals feel threatened and insecure, religion provides stability, comfort, and explanations as to why their world has gone awry. For a small minority, religion is used to justify lashing out with violence to regain a sense of empowerment.

MODERNIZATION

Modernization is a good place to begin when considering the sources of the change, disruption, and upheaval that have facilitated religion-based terrorism because it provided the context and the catalyst for other factors to be considered in the later text. Modernization also produced the breakthroughs in technology that led to revolutions in travel and communication and the rise of multinational corporations, which combined to create globalization and facilitate the perception of an onslaught from the West. Incorporation into the global economic system has primarily served to remind non-Western societies of their dependence on the West, the breakdown of their identities, and the loss of their status. Modernization has also been associated with Western ideologies, such as communism, liberalism, and secular nationalism, and values, such as consumerism, individualism, and hedonism, which are all viewed as threats to religious values. Concurrently, the West, with its powerful political, military, economic, and cultural forces, has often been seen as a hostile force that is assaulting and dominating local cultures and religions. Finally, modernization and the forces that it unleashed enticed many with the promise of freedom and prosperity but instead brought despair, frustration, and alienation.

Modernization, ironically, was supposed to lead to a decline in the role of religion in developing societies, as it had in the West. Early development theorists predicted that urbanization, literacy, and communication with the outside world would stimulate economic development and eventually democratization.[4] As individuals moved to the city, learned more about the outside world, and came in contact with a wider variety of people, they would develop the skills necessary to take part in modern economies and participatory societies. At the same time, traditional relationships, worldviews, and cultural forces, such as religion, would be broken down, destroyed, and eventually replaced by universal Western values such as secularism and liberalism. As individuals in traditional, religion-based societies became connected to the outside modern world and all that it had to offer, anything that prevented the enjoyment of its benefits, such as religion, would be cast aside.[5] These individuals would also come to believe that people, not uncontrollable forces like God and nature, controlled human destiny, which would result in increasing levels of education and technological development. As a result, religion's role as the set of principles and values that guided and provided order in society would, by necessity, decline, which is what had transpired in most of Europe and North America.[6]

What Went Wrong?

The gap between these high expectations and reality in the developing world and segments of the developed world in the early 21st century leads to a crucial question. Why and how did modernization go wrong to the point where it helped create the conditions that facilitate religion-based terrorism and violence? Although this book focuses on Christianity, Judaism,

and Islam, violence in the name of religion has occurred among Hindus and
Sikhs in India and among other religious traditions in the developing world.
It is important to note that a connection between socioeconomic transformation and religion-based violence has not been limited to the developing
world as globalization, the information revolution, and the move to a postmodern society have also brought rapid change to the developed world.
Jewish extremists in Israel have rejected the modern values of the State of
Israel, which are based on a secular oriented Labor-Zionist orientation that
is rooted in the West and which embrace modernity. Likewise, Christian antiabortion terrorists in the United States view the separation of church and
state in the United States as being illegitimate and call for a return to the
fundamentalist values of the Puritans. In all, it can be safely concluded that
change is disruptive and has the potential to produce violence that is often
justified with religion.

> The contemporary world has left the industrial era behind and entered a new
> era in which both social relationships and international affairs are being trans-
> formed in a way that we cannot easily categorize. . . . They (religious move-
> ments) are true children of our time; unwanted children, perhaps the bastards
> of computerization and unemployment or of the population explosion and
> increasing literacy and their cries and complaints in these closing years of the
> century.[7]

This quote from Gilles Kepel relates to the resurgence of the role of religion in global society that took place in the 1990s and its challenge to the
secular state. The disruption caused by modernization (and postmoderniza-
tion) is also commonly mentioned as being a cause of religion-based terrorism. Mark Juergensmeyer writes that the rapid change of modernization
often leads people to feel that they are frail and under siege, as global economic and communication systems have destroyed their status and sense of
power and control. "Religion provides men with a renewed sense of man-
hood and a justification for violence."[8] Others point to the importance
of the feelings of alienation and dislocation that are often brought on by
modernization. James Reinhart, in his discussion of apocalyptical religious
movements, writes that members of these groups feel that the end of life
as they knew it is upon them. The onslaught on their norms and customs
causes stress, tension, indignation, and, eventually, moral outrage as they
try to deal with rapid change. These feelings of righteous indignation often
lead to violence. Reinhart adds that industrialization and its resulting inequalities in the West in the 19th century also facilitated the development of
religious and secular millennial movements, including Marxism.[9] Therefore,

it is not surprising that Sayyid Qutb, who is viewed as providing an ideological inspiration for al Qaeda and other contemporary Islamic terrorist groups, wrote in the 1960s that Muslims have a responsibility to fight the elements of modernization that are hostile to Islam.[10]

Unmet Aspirations and Relative Deprivation

The rapid change and transformation, alone, brought on by modernization is not enough to cause individuals to turn to violence. Notice that Qutb mentioned that only the elements of modernity that are hostile to Islam need to be opposed, which means that modernity, as whole, is not unacceptable. Also, the overwhelming majority of people who turn to religion for comfort and shelter when faced with rapid change and dislocation do not become terrorists or lash out with violence. Modernization, at the same time, helped some individuals grow wealthy, gain status, and consolidate political power. Those individuals probably have few complaints about modernization, globalization, or Westernization and do not fill the ranks of religion-based terrorist groups. Rather, it was those with the cries and complaints, the individuals who grew to believe that modernization had failed to live up to its promises and who had been left behind, who became potential recruits for religion-based terrorist organizations. Modernization helped to enhance the divide between the haves and the have-nots both within nations and between nations. It also supplied many of the have-nots with the belief that they should have more, as they became educated and began to believe that achievement should have its reward. Llewellyn Howell concludes that the new terrorism is caused more by scarcity triggered by population growth and global and internal inequality that is magnified by increased awareness of the outside world than a clash of civilizations.[11]

Modernization, rapid change, and frustrated aspirations have often been used to explain revolution and other types of political violence. James C. Davies theorized that as citizens' expectations regarding their personnel well-being rise, governments must provide a reality that meets these aspirations. When a significant gap develops between expectations and reality, as is often the case in developing nations, the potential for revolution and political violence grows.[12] Although Davies was referring to individual economic expectations such as personal income, the theory should also hold true for aspirations in other areas such as liberty, equality, and fair and representative government. Ted Gurr expanded on Davies's theory with the notion of relative deprivation, which is the discrepancy between what people feel that they deserve from life and what they believe is actually obtainable.

Gurr writes that "The potential for collective violence varies strongly with the intensity and scope of relative deprivation among members of a collectivity."[13] Modernization, of course, is a primary cause of Davies's expectation gap and Gurr's relative deprivation because it causes people to believe that their future is not determined by uncontrollable forces, that they should be rewarded fairly for their labor, and that their own success is measured against that of others in society. The importance of frustrated aspirations in the realm of government and politics is made evident by Gurr's finding that a belief that the ruling regime was illegitimate significantly increases the probability of political violence.[14]

IRAN

The notion of modernization, rapid and disruptive economic growth, and change, leading to relative deprivation and frustrated aspirations can be applied to the Iranian Revolution, which led to the ascendency of the clerical-led theocratic government that endures more than 30 years later. Although the Iranian Revolution was largely peaceful and did not involve dissident terrorism, the regime that it brought to power has engaged in state-sponsored terrorism and has inspired, facilitated, and aided Islamic terrorist groups, including Hezbollah and Hamas, that hope to create Islamic governments in their countries. Ironically, the Shah Mohammed Pahlavi instituted the modernization campaign, the White Revolution, that was supposed to cause Iran to develop quickly enough to catch up with countries, such as Japan, by the close of the 20th century. As part of the White Revolution, women were given the right to vote, major land reforms were carried out, access to education and health care were greatly expanded, the country's agricultural industries were modernized, government industries were privatized, and government facilities and services were rapidly expanded. These changes, along with massive profits from the country's oil fields, led to astronomical economic growth and expansion. Between 1973 and 1975 alone, GNP rose 32 percent, government expenditures nearly tripled, and oil revenues quadrupled.

The period of economic growth, rapid modernization, and socioeconomic development played a significant role in the downfall of the Shah and the rise of the theocracy that eventually replaced him. The failed land reform program led to a massive migration to the cities and created a large disinherited and disheartened class that had trouble finding employment when Iran's economy crashed in the mid-1970s. Increased access to education and the media led to a demand for political participation, as university students within Iran and abroad were among the first to organize in opposition to the Shah. Many of these university graduates had been educated so that they could fill the ranks of Iran's government bureaucracies and modern industries. Instead, they turned on the Shah when their desire for political participation was thwarted. The hostility to the Shah intensified and spread when it became apparent that most of the oil wealth was ending up in the hands of the regime, corrupt government officials, and a small group of cronies. The rapid growth of the economy helped cause 41 percent inflation, which had the most adverse effect on the lower and middle classes. Finally, the waste of resources on grandiose projects, such as a subway system in Tehran, and the failure of to maintain basic services such as water and electricity caused further alienation.[15]

The failure to meet basic needs and the widening gap between rich and poor created an environment that was ripe for revolution. At the same time, many groups such as clerics, landholders, and traditional merchants saw their status decline under modernization, while the fortunes of women and minorities such as Jews appeared to be rising. It is no surprise that, in addition to removing the Shah, the Iranian Revolution, eventually attacked two forces, secularism and the United States, which were associated with the monarchy and which were viewed as being responsible for the Iran's downfall. Kepel points out that modernization, as was the case in Iran, has usually been accompanied by secularism. Consequently, secularism is often been blamed for the unemployment, inequality, repression, and anomie that have often resulted from modernization.[16] As will be seen in the discussion of Egypt later in this chapter, secularism is associated with the West and with imported Western ideologies such as liberalism and Marxism.

Secularism

Many religious political actors, such as the Ayatollah Khomeini, view secularism as a kind of religion that competes with Islam.[17] Because secularism is associated with the West and has pretentions of universality, it is seen as an ideological tool that makes cultural and economic imperialism possible because it provides a justification for the United States to spread its culture and way of life to the rest of the world.[18] Thus, secular oriented governments in the Muslim world are seen by religious extremists as being illegitimate and as being collaborators with the enemy. Bernard Lewis points out that in Islam secular ideas are seen as *asra al-muniya,* knowledge that is not from Islam and, as a result, is not knowledge at all.[19] Jewish extremists in Israel and radical antiabortion terrorists in the United States, as will be seen in chapters 6 and 7, maintain the same disdain for secularism and see it as a dangerous threat to their respective countries. A similar negative association between democracy and imperialism surfaced following the U.S. invasions of Afghanistan and Iraq in the early 2000s. Osama bin Laden has claimed that democracy is an American religion of ignorance that violates Islam by using man-made laws. He also stated that democracy "plays with the interest of the peoples and their blood by sacrificing soldiers and populations to achieve the interests of the major corporations."[20] The Taliban in Afghanistan have railed against elections and have used terror and intimidation to prevent people from voting because they are seen as an American tool to control the country through its proxy, the Karzai government.[21]

Secular nationalism's ultimate failure also helped to inspire religious radicalism and terrorism. Juergensmeyer suggests that if secular nationalism had succeeded in delivering material well-being, equality, representative government, and just societies instead of empowering a disconnected elite, we might not be experiencing today's religion-based violence.[22] Many members of the middle class in the Islamic world grew up with high expectations for secular nationalism because its virtues were extolled by leaders such as the Shah. The educated Iranians who had been taught that secularism would lead to a glorious future became disenchanted when this turned out to be a false promise. The crushing of these almost messianic-like hopes led to extreme disappointment when modernization's promises were unfulfilled.[23] In their despair, many turned to religion for solutions and comfort. The radical fringe that harbored the most extreme hostility toward secular nationalism used religion as a justification for lashing out with violence against the people and the ideology that had failed them. In this context, the victory of the religious faction in the uprising against the Shah and the struggle for power following his departure, as well as the disdain for the West and secularism by Khomeini and today's Iranian leaders, is understandable.

The United States and the West

Modernization, in addition to dashing the hopes of emerging elites, also threatened those who had already obtained power and status. The Shah's modernization programs and state-imposed secularization threatened the power of the clergy, merchant class, and land owners. All of these classes were traditionally minded and resented the regime's attempt to marginalize and to co-opt Islam. The anti-Western forces were further strengthened by the Shah's close ties to the United States, as he had risen to power in a coup facilitated by the CIA. America was a staunch ally that helped Iran produce its oil, train its army and feared security services (SAVAK), and modernize its economy. Thus, it was easy for many to blame Iran's enforced secularization and economic meltdown on the influence of the Americans. To make matters worse, the Shah maintained close military ties with Israel. All of these factors combined to produce the eventual victory of Khomeini and the ayatollahs in the struggle for power following the Shah's departure and a theocracy that remains virulently anti-Western and that has supported and trained Islamic terrorist groups such as Hezbollah and Hamas.

Khomeini clearly believed, as did bin Laden, in the existence of a bitter struggle, which is as much cultural and ideological as it is political and economic, between Islam and the West for dominance. In exile, he had warned against Westoxification, and as Iran's head of state, he sought to export the Islamic revolution to other countries, labeled America "the Great Satan," and called for the liberation of Jerusalem from Israel.[24] Thirty years later, Iran's president, Mahmoud Ahmadinejad, still focuses on the theme of the West's hatred for Islam and the struggle against its attempt to impose secularism on the Iran and the Muslim world when justifying Iran's development of nuclear reactors.[25] Ironically, the forces of globalization threaten Iran's theocracy today, as a reform movement that is angry over the country's high unemployment rate, corruption, and authoritarian rule used Facebook and Twitter to organize massive protests and demonstrations in June 2009 following rigged elections. As was the case in the late 1970s, they are rejecting an ideology that failed to deliver on its promises. This time, however, the ideology is not secularism but, rather, theocracy.

EGYPT

Nasser

The significance of the failure of modernization and secularization and its association with the West as a cause of religion-based terrorism can also be seen in Egypt with the murder of President Anwar Sadat in 1982 and frequent terrorist attacks by Islamic groups throughout the 1980s and 1990s. Gamal Abdel Nasser, following the Officer's Coup in 1952, engaged in a campaign of modernization and secularization that brought the country's religious authorities under the control of the state, relegated religious law to areas relating to personal status, and repressed the Muslim Brotherhood, which had helped him achieve power.[26] Like the Shah, Nasser instituted land reform, developed his country's infrastructure, and expanded literacy and higher education. Unlike the Shah, he enjoyed tremendous popularity, as he appeared to be fighting corruption and to be a man of the people. Nasser's popularity resulted from his successes in the international and regional political arenas, as he led the Arab Socialism, Pan-Arab and nonaligned movements; forced the British out of Egypt; and nationalized the Suez Canal.[27] He solidified his credentials as leader of the Arab world in 1956 Sinai Crisis when Israel, Great Britain, and France were forced to withdraw from the Sinai Peninsula by the United States and the Soviet Union. Although Egypt had lost the war, Nasser's status was enhanced because he had stood up to Israel and to Egypt's former colonial overlords and maintained its control over the Suez Canal. This victory, along with Nasser's charisma and popularity, allowed him to outlaw the Muslim Brotherhood and move Islam to the margins of Egyptian society.[28]

Nasser, eventually, led Egypt into the disastrous Six-Day War in 1967, which resulted in a catastrophic defeat to the Israelis and the loss of the Sinai Peninsula. Nasser had promised a decisive victory that would drive the Israelis into the sea. The disappointment and despair following the war led to a reevaluation of Nasser's regime and Arab Socialism, which were found wanting. As had been the case in Iran, many turned to religion for comfort and an explanation of the war's calamitous results.[29] A common rationalization for the defeat was that turning away from God and religion had led Egypt astray and to become morally bankrupt. The soldiers had not fought well because they lacked spiritual inspiration, and God had not come to the Arabs' rescue because they had ceased to follow his law. The regime was further criticized for selling out to the godless Soviets, Egypt's superpower patron and arms supplier, who had turned their back on Egypt and the Muslims in their time of need.[30] Sayyid Qutb railed against Nasser for abandoning Islam and portraying himself as a deity. Despite Nasser's populist appeal, Egypt remained a corrupt society with great inequality and a failed economy. Qutb called for the implementation of Islamic law and ridding the country of corrupting Western influence.[31]

Sadat

Nasser died in 1970 before an Islamist challenge could be mounted to his rule. His successor, Anwar Sadat, realized that Arab Socialism and secularism were failed ideologies, so he attempted to use Islam and Islamic groups to legitimate his rule. He emphasized his own personal piety, denounced socialism, threw the Soviets out of Egypt, and framed the 1973 war against Israel, a partial success, in a religious context by labeling it a *jihad* to reclaim lost Islamic lands and launching it during the holy month of Ramadan.

Of greatest importance, Sadat gave amnesty to the imprisoned members of the Muslim Brotherhood, legalized the group, and gave support to Islamic groups (ga'amat) on Egyptian university campuses. Sadat also constantly claimed that Egypt was an Islamic state and that *Sharia* would soon become the country's government and legal system.[32] Given Sadat's support for Islam and Islamic groups, he would seem to be an unlikely target of religion-based terrorists. However, his actions and policies betrayed his supposed commitment to creating an Islamic-based government and legal system. Committees were formed to codify *Sharia* into a modern legal system, but they never produced a finished product. Personal status laws were actually Westernized through Sadat's personal directive. Of greatest importance, Sadat went to Jerusalem in 1977; signed a peace treaty with Israel, the Camp David Accords, in 1978; and aligned Egypt with the United States.

Sadat, despite regaining the Sinai Peninsula in the peace treaty with Israel, became very unpopular as he was seen as being a tool of the Americans, who had sold out the Arab and Muslim worlds by making peace with Israel. At the same time, his *Infitah* policy, which focused on creating a capitalist-free market, allowed a small group of business owners, most of who were tied to the regime, to become wealthy at the expense of the rest of the country.[33] Sadat, like Nasser and the Shah, was now viewed as a corrupt ruler, who had sold out his country's best interests to a foreign power and a foreign ideology, capitalism. At the same time, Nasser and Sadat's modernization campaigns had led to an explosion in Egypt's urban population and a large class of college-educated but unemployed or underemployed young adults who were angered by the continued corruption and the lack of opportunity. Ironically, the Muslim Brotherhood and university ga'amat, which Sadat had aided, began to call for real Islamic government. Sadat's close ties to the United States caused many to believe that the Americans were the cause of the inequalities that resulted from Sadat's free market initiatives and of the country's moral bankruptcy. The World Bank and the International Monetary Fund, which were viewed as being extensions of the American government, pressured Egypt to cut its food subsidies, reduce its bureaucracy (an important source of employment), and further privatize.

The vast majority of the Islamic opposition under Sadat and his successor, Hosni Mubarak, were peaceful. The Muslim Brotherhood renounced violence and ran as independents in parliamentary elections in 1984 and 1987. To a great extent, the moderate Islamic opposition was a product of modernity, as they argued that Islamic law must be updated to function in modern society, developed Islamic banks that followed *Sharia* while participating in international financial markets, and claimed that Western technology and ideas are actually rooted in Islam.[34] However, several radical groups that used violence and terror also appeared in the 1980s and 1990s. These groups, such as the Islamic Jihad, Tanzim, Takfir wa al Hifjra, and al Gama'a al Islamiyya (Islamic Group), viewed Sadat as an apostate because he had not implemented *Sharia,* had abandoned the *jihad* against Israel, and had allowed the United States to spread its anti-Islamic culture in Egypt. These groups all traced their ideological roots to Qutb, who claimed that a true Muslim must wage violent *jihad* to create an Islamic state and that secular governments and outside influences, such as the United States, must be resisted with force. These groups are also the product of modernization, as many of their members were educated and radicalized during Nasser's period of secularization.

Saad Ibrahim interviewed several jailed members of Egyptian Islamic radical groups and found that most fit the profile of people whose lives had been disrupted and who had been disappointed by modernization. As is often the case, the radicals were first-generation immigrants to urban areas who were disgusted by the stark inequality between the haves and have-nots, rampant corruption, and the influence of Western culture.[35] Most had college degrees in science and technology and were unemployed and, consequently, unable to start families. Anomie, despair, and relative deprivation, as would be expected, produced recruits for religion-based terrorist groups. On October 6, 1981, Sadat was assassinated at a parade celebrating the crossing of the Suez Canal in the 1973 war by a group of military officers who had been recruited by the al Gama'a al Islamiyya and/or Islamic Jihad. Two days after the assassination, Islamic militants organized an insurrection in the city of Asyut in Upper Egypt. The rebels held several police stations and parts of the city for more than a week, and it took an attack by paratroopers to reassert government control. Islamic Jihad, the Islamic Group, and other Islamic terrorist groups have been responsible for several attacks since 1981, including an assassination attempt on the minister of the interior in 1990, an attack that killed 9 Israelis in 1992, an attack in Luxor in 1993 that killed 62 tourists, and bombings in Sharm el Sheik in the Sinai in 2005 that took 88 lives.

Two participants in Sadat's assassination later played key roles in terrorist attacks against the United States. Two weeks prior to Sadat's assassination, the Islamic Group's leader, Omar Abdel-Rahman, issued a *fatwa* calling for Sadat's death and the overthrow of the government. Abdel-Rahman later moved to the United States and was convicted of encouraging and planning the 1993 World Trade Center bombings and planned bombings of other sites in the New York area. Ayman al Zawahiri, an Islamic Jihad leader, who was also tried and convicted for planning Sadat's assassination, went on to merge the organization with al Qaeda in 1998 and became its leader after Osama bin Laden's death. Ironically, it was not Islamic terrorists, but peaceful demonstrations and protests by a broad spectrum of Egyptian society that eventually brought down the regime of Sadat's successor, Hosni Mubarak, in early 2011. Although the Muslim Brotherhood took part in the protests, it did not play a leadership role. Mubarak, like Nasser and Sadat, had imprisoned and tortured those who threatened the regime, including Islamists. The Muslim Brotherhood and other Islamic groups have expressed their support for democracy and took part in the 2011 parliamentary elections.

GLOBALIZATION

The individuals protesting for democracy in places like Egypt and Tunisia in 2011, ironically, share important traits—marginalization and frustrated aspirations—with religion-based terrorists.[36] The rapid change brought on by modernization that helped stimulate the Iranian Revolution and Islamic terrorism in Egypt pales in comparison with the massive transformation caused by the globalization of local economies, the global media, and the information age that characterize the opening decades of the 21st century. Robert Keohane and Joseph Nye write that today's globalization is particularly disruptive because its networks are thicker and more complex, it involves people from more regions and social classes, and it moves at such a rapid speed.[37] On a positive note, social media such as Facebook and Twitter helped facilitate the protests that brought down the autocratic regimes in Egypt and Tunisia. On the other hand, globalization has further strengthened the sense of peril, relative deprivation, anomie, and marginalization that can cause religion-based terrorism and violence. The threat of foreign cultures and values, particularly those associated with the United States and the West, has become more profound with the spread of the Internet and satellite TV. As a result, Western culture and all of its corrupting influences now easily penetrate nations and societies with the push of a remote control button and the click of a mouse. At the same time, multinational and foreign corporations appear to be overrunning local economies and leaving native businesses and elites in their wake.

A major disruptive element of globalization is the destruction of local cultures and values. Thomas Friedman, who generally sees globalization as a positive force that will improve the lot of all nations that embrace it because of its efficiency and competitive ethic, warns that the "anonymous transnational, homogenizing, standardizing market forces and technologies that make up today's global economic system can overrun every olive tree [the olive tree symbolizes local cultures and traditions] in sight, breakdown communities, steamroll environments, and crowd out traditions."[38] Friedman proposes the "Golden Arches Theory of Conflict Prevention," because countries with McDonald's restaurants had not gone to war with each other when he wrote *The Lexus and the Olive Tree*. To Friedman, this statistic symbolizes the development of a significant middle class, which would not want to go to war because it realizes that it would be bad for business.[39] Although the presence of McDonald's and a globalized middle class may prevent wars between countries, they may also fuel the anger of religious terrorists. To them, the McDonald's is an attack on local culture and a symbol of globalization and foreign penetration, which causes them to want to blow up the restaurant and lash out with terrorist acts to protect what is traditional and native. Friedman labels this as being the backlash against homogenization, as some are ready to go to war or use terrorism to protect their local culture from globalization.[40]

This violent backlash, as was the case in Iran and Egypt 30 years ago, is often justified with religion because it provides an ideological sword and shield to fight against globalization's onslaught. Almost 100 years ago, Hassan al Bannah, the founder of the Muslim Brotherhood and an inspiration for today's Islamic terrorists, railed against the atheism and lewd culture, which included half-naked women, liquor, theater, dance-halls, amusements, novels, whims, games, and vices, that came from the West and warned against "the devastation of religion and morality on the pretext of individualism and intellectual freedom."[41] Fast-forward to 2002 when Amrozi bin Nurhasyim was convicted for his role in a nightclub bombing in Bali, Indonesia, a spot frequented by Western tourists, and argued that foreigners introduced moral decay to his country through their TV and Western lifestyle. He viewed Bali's bars, nightclubs, and casinos as subtle and covert attacks on Islam.[42] To an extremist, the attack of the morally bankrupt and spiritually corrupting foreign culture and ideology must always be resisted with violence. In the age of globalization, this threat is amplified because the enemy is no longer off in the distance but is brought to one's doorstep by world tourism, the Internet, films, multinational corporations, and television.

Global Inequality

The cultural threat of globalism is heightened when it is delivered by the world's remaining superpower, the United States. Ismail Abu Shanab, a leader of the Palestinian group Hamas, who was assassinated in 2003, claimed that "Globalization is just a new colonial system. It is America's attempt to dominate the world economically and culturally rather than militarily. . . . America is trying to spread its consumer culture. These values are not good for human beings."[43] Mark Strauss argues that Shanab's ideas are common in the Arab-Muslim world where many see globalization as a Zionist-American plot to destroy Islam and erase its cultural borders.[44] An official with Iran's minister of culture and Islamic guidance called for a *jihad* against American television because "These programs prepared by international imperialism are part of an extensive plot to wipe out our religion and sacred values."[45] He went on to label satellite TV an enemy of the honorable Prophet Muhammad. Given that America, as the world's superpower, has used its military across the globe, particularly in the Middle East, it is no surprise that other angry men in the developing world such as the late Osama bin Laden and Ramzi Youssef (one of the participants in the 1993 attack on the World Trade Center) seek violent revenge on the United States for the turmoil that it has caused in their cultures and societies.[46] Globalization, in short, has helped spark terrorism by increasing contacts between societies with different values and allowing more powerful cultures to occupy weaker ones through media, values, and economics rather than through armies. As has always been the case, the weaker party is resisting with terrorism.

Inequality and the use of technology by the powerful to dominate the weak is another important way in which globalization has fueled the flames of religious extremism and violence. Benjamin Barber, like Friedman, writes about global capitalism's power to break down borders and homogenize the world by bringing societies into a world marketplace that makes everyplace the same.[47] Barber, unlike Friedman who sees globalization as a positive and inevitable force, focuses on the darker side of globalization, which is reflected in the title of his book, *Jihad vs. McWorld*. For Friedman, localism and native culture are represented by the quaint olive tree that will not disappear entirely but will serve to moderate the triumphant Lexus of globalization. Barber worries that the inequality and increasing divide between global haves and have-nots will result in violent resistance—*jihad*—to globalization. Strong evidence for the validity of Barber's concern are statistics that show how globalization has made the Islamic world poorer as a rapid population growth has been accompanied by a decreasing share of global trade and investment. In 1980, the Islamic world accounted for 13.5 percent of the world's exports, while in 2001, it accounted for only 4 percent. During that time period, the GNP of the Islamic world declined by 25 percent. In 2001, the entire Islamic world (approximately 1 billion people) received the same amount of investment as Sweden (a nation of 9 million people).[48] It is important to note that 1980–2001 is also the period when Islamic terrorism became a global problem. The situation will grow worse as the developed nations have free trade agreements, while China and India maintain protective tariffs leaving most of the Islamic world on the margins of global trade.[49]

The decline of the economic fortunes of the Islamic world and other parts of the developing world in the era of globalization also help further explain the hatred toward America that is part of *jihad*. Barber writes that American efforts to ensure prosperity at home seem like a rationalization for the oppression and the exploitation of others.[50] America's military incursions in the Islamic world—two invasions of Iraq, an invasion of Afghanistan, and bases and personnel throughout the region—along with its support of monarchs and dictators in Jordan, Saudi Arabia, Morocco, Yemen, Egypt, Tunisia, and the United Arab Emirates appear to be efforts to control the region's valuable natural resource, oil, for its own benefit. Barber argues that efforts by the United States to avoid international oversight and refusal to sign international treaties on global warming or the International Criminal Court are seen as signs of arrogance and imperialist intentions.[51] Friedman specifies that globalism leads to global arrogance based on soft power (culture, technology, and economy) rather than occupation and imperialism, "Global arrogance is when your culture and economic clout are so powerful and widely diffused that you know that you don't need to occupy other people to influence their lives."[52] Be it soft power or hard power, globalization, in much of the Islamic world, is viewed as a subterfuge for American domination, which must be resisted.

Globalization's Threat to the Islamic World

It is interesting to note that religion-based opposition to globalization is almost exclusively characteristic of the Islamic world. Other parts of the world such as India and China have welcomed globalization. Israelis, with the exception of the ultra-Orthodox, have embraced almost everything American. French resistance has been cultural as it has attempted to keep American words out of its language and banned the display of the golden arches by McDonald's. A common Muslim response is reflected in the words of a former Algerian prime minister, "This globalization you speak about is just another American conspiracy to keep the Arab world down, just like Zionism and imperialism."[53] The roots of the hostility felt by some in the

Islamic world toward contemporary globalization actually go back to the Crusades. John Esposito writes that memories of the Crusades, colonialism, and the establishment of the state of Israel are superimposed on contemporary events such as the war in Iraq, the Russian campaign against Islamic insurgents in Chechnya, and the Palestinian Intifada against Israel and create anti-American and anti-Christian sentiments.[54] Because Christianity was the religion of the Crusades 800 years ago and European imperialism 200 years ago, it is associated with Western attempts to control the Islamic world. Israel, a Jewish state in the predominately Muslim Middle East, is seen as a Western creation forced on the Muslim world.

Bernard Lewis sees today's hostility in the Muslim world toward the globalization that is associated with the United States as the latest chapter in a struggle between rival systems that goes back 1,400 years. For the first 1,000 years, Islam expanded from Arabia into the Levant, North Africa, Eastern Europe, Spain, and the gates of Vienna. At the same time, art, science, literature, philosophy, and mathematics flourished in the Islamic empires, while Europe was in the Dark Ages. Then, the tables were turned, and the European colonial empires extended into the Muslim world bringing with them foreign ideas, laws, ways of life, rulers, and settlers. The dominators became the dominated, and the culturally advanced became the culturally backward. The Muslims had been overwhelmed and overtaken by those who they viewed as being their inferiors.[55] The damage to the Muslim psyche caused by the military and cultural defeats was compounded by the religious dimension as Islam was supposed to supersede Christianity and become the dominant global religion. Thus, it is not surprising that for some in the Muslim world, including the former Algerian prime minister, the West is associated with hostility, aggression, and unwanted intrusions. As mentioned in the discussion of Iran and Egypt, the ideas and culture—modernity, secularism, and materialism—that the West brought with it are seen as being responsible for the continued relative decline of the Islamic world and for its tyranny and poverty.[56]

The hostility to Europe and its penetration of the Islamic world was transferred to the United States as it emerged as a superpower after World War II and more so when it became the world's sole superpower following the fall of the Soviet Union. America's time as the sole hegemon has coincided with the era of globalization, so its military, economic, and cultural power has made it the most visible agent of the rapid change that is undermining local cultures and values and that is producing corrupt and often secular leaders. Consequently, the United States is seen as heading a global conspiracy to control or destroy Islam, and all of its actions in the Islamic world are seen as having evil intent and requiring steadfast opposition. This could explain why several Egyptian Islamic groups reversed their condemnation of Saddam Hussein's invasion of Kuwait in 1990 and called for the defense of Iraq when the United States sent troops to defend the Kuwait.[57] It is easy to see why some in the Muslim world believe that the United States wants the rest of the world to adopt its culture and values, as America has played into these conspiracy theories by portraying itself as bringing universal values such as freedom, democracy, and the free market to the world.[58] As Huntington wrote in *The Clash of Civilizations,* "what is universalism to the West is imperialism to the rest."[59]

It should be no surprise that Islamic terrorists have been at the forefront of the resistance to the perceived onslaught of the United States. A Shiite suicide bomber in Lebanon was responsible for one of the first terrorist attacks by an Islamic group against the United States in October 1983 when he blew himself up at the headquarters for the Marines near the Beirut airport killing 241 American and 58 French soldiers. The Marines and French troops were brought to Beirut following the massacre of Palestinians by a Christian militia at two Beirut area refugee camps to restore and maintain order. However, they were soon seen as an occupying force that was in Lebanon to support the Christian government and the Israelis after they shelled Shiite and Druze neighborhoods in South Beirut. Even the Palestinian Islamic group, Hamas, which is not in direct conflict with the United States, referred to George Bush as the "leader of the forces of evil and the chief of the false Gods" following the first U.S. invasion of Iraq.[60] Osama bin Laden was the vanguard of opposition to U.S. global dominance until his death in 2011. His hostility toward America first surfaced in 1991, when he offered to lead a Muslim army to liberate Kuwait, but was refused in favor of American troops, whose presence on Islamic holy land, Saudi Arabia, was seen as an act of defilement. The choice of American troops over Muslims went right to the heart of the issue of the weakness of the Muslims, who were now dependent on the American descendents of the Crusaders for their protection. Since then, bin Laden and al Qaeda have been waging a global war against America, its allies, and other enemies of Islam. As will be discussed in chapter 9, al Qaeda is not only a response to globalism, it, ironically, is also its representative.

Inequality within Nations

Globalization, in addition to being seen as a source of international inequality that has been perceived as being a cause of the decline of the Islamic world and its domination by the West, has also caused inequity and marginalization within nations. Barber, like Friedman, believes that localism and tribalism are natural responses to the disruption and chaos that are caused by globalization, "*Jihad* in its most elemental negative form is a kind of animal fear propelled by anxiety in the face of uncertainty and relieved by self-sacrificing zealotry."[61] The anxiety and fear are often produced by the loss of status within one's society or a threat to one's economic well-being. When discussing the first wave of modernization that hit the developing world after World War II, I described how frustrated aspirations and relative deprivation helped facilitate religion-based terrorism. Globalization has increased the rate and intensity of the forces of change such as urbanization, industrialization, migration, mobility, literacy, and, of greatest importance, inequality. As a result, the number of marginal people in the world is also growing exponentially. Religion continues to provide comfort and solutions to those who seek a return to a perceived past where people led orderly and simple lives. For the angry and dispossessed, interpretations of religion that justify violence remain attractive.

Increasing literacy and access to higher education in much of the Muslim world continue to produce a large class of young educated males who cannot find adequate employment and are stymied by corrupt political and economic systems where bribes and connections are often necessary for advancement. Mike Mousseau argues that globalization is also a threat to people of power in clientist hierarchies that are common in the Islamic world. Mousseau writes that market-based economies brought on by globalization tend to overwhelm these networks because they introduce better quality goods and services that originate outside of the country. At the same time, a new group of elites that is tied to the globalization develops and is seen as a threat to the entrenched clientist hierarchies. Because loyalty to the group and supporting one's patron are important values in these networks, leaders can mobilize their clients on their behalf. Religion and anti-Americanism are used to rally anger against the forces of change that are unleashed by market economies because globalization is associated with the United States and the West. Mousseau, like Barber, warns that the disruption and social anarchy that are caused by globalization can lead those threatened with marginalization to violence. Consequently, Mousseau suggests that the terrorism that emerged in Indonesia following that country's move to democracy and a market economy in the early 2000s was a result of the threat that these transformations posed to those in power in that country's clientist hierarchies.[62]

Privileged Minorities

The economic strain and marginalization that are associated with rapid change and globalization have led to attacks against privileged minorities by religious extremists throughout the world. These minority religious groups are often viewed as being given special treatment or as an outside force that is causing chaos and turbulence. White supremacist groups such as the Church of the Creativity and Christian Identity in the United States that combine racism, anti-Semitism, and homophobia with Christianity are primarily populated by lower income whites who can no longer find well-paying factory jobs in the increasingly information- and education-based economy. Consequently, these individuals, who have seen their jobs exported to Mexico, Asia, and other developing nations, blame their bad fortune on gays, Jews, and minorities and justify their attacks on these groups with a very unique interpretation of the Bible.[63]

The Church of the Creator and the related Christian Identity movement espouse a version of Christianity that holds that Jesus was an Aryan, that a migrating tribe of blue-eyed Aryan Israelites who settled in Britain are the real Israelites, and that the group known as the Jews are imposters seeking to control the world.[64] Blacks and other nonwhites are commonly referred to as "mud people" and as being descendents of the devil. Timothy McVeigh, the perpetrator of the 1996 bombing of the Oklahoma City federal bombing; Eric Rudolph, an antiabortion activist who set off pipe bombs in Atlanta during the 1996 Olympics; and Buford Furrow, who attacked a preschool at a Jewish center in Granada Hills, California, were all inspired by or affiliated with the Christian Identity movement. All three were also white lower-middle class males, a group that sees its ascribed status as whites and males as being threatened by women, minorities, Jews, and gays; groups that have always been below them in the social pecking order.

Jews, the number one enemy of the American Christian Identity movement, have frequently been seen as an alien and foreign people who represent a threat to Christian and Muslim societies. The hatred for Jews that is a key part of the theology of Church of the Creativity and Christian Identity is partly based on the belief in a global Jewish conspiracy to dominate the world and American economies and eventually destroy them. Because of their stateless status until 1948, the Jews were frequently seen as a fifth column and international syndicate that was plotting world domination, usually through the world banking system and the media.[65] Thus, the Jews were the subversive dark forces of globalization of the early 20th century and the victims of organized violent attacks, pogroms, throughout Eastern Europe.

At the same time, anti-Semitism in the United States was socially accept-able until the 1960s and propagated by elites such as Henry Ford. Although Muslim terrorism against Jewish targets (outside of Israel), such as the 2003 suicide bomber attack in Casablanca on several Jewish institutions and busi-nesses; a 2002 bombing of a synagogue in Ghirba, Tunisia; and an attack on a Jewish center in Mumbai in 2008 (part of an assault on several targets), tends to be rooted in hatred of Israel, global Jewish conspiracy theories are widely accepted in the Muslim world. Japanese cult leader, Shuko Asahara, who planned the Aum Shinrikyo sarin gas attack on the Tokyo subway sys-tem in 1995, also referred to Jewish conspiracies in his writings.

Religion-based tension and violence that is related to economic marginal-ization and globalization can also be seen in conflicts between Hindus and Muslims in India. In one particularly violent episode, Hindus, encouraged by the Bharatiya Janata (a Hindu nationalist party), destroyed the Babri Mosque in Ayodhya in 1992, which caused weeks of intercommunal rioting and more than 2,000 deaths. Ten years later, Hindu plans to build a temple on the site led to a Muslim attack on a train carrying Hindu pilgrims and 58 deaths, which sparked another round of bloodletting. Susanne and Lloyd Rudolph, however, believe that Hindu aggressive behavior toward Muslims was motivated more by frustrated aspirations and the perception that they were being left behind at the expensive of India's Muslim minority, which they viewed as being privileged, pampered, and benefitting from India's glo-balized economy. According to the Rudolphs, Hindu expectations caused by India's rapidly growing economy, which was largely a product of global-ization and the entrance of foreign companies, were not being matched by opportunities. Encouraged by Hindu nationalists, the Hindus viewed their Muslim neighbors as being the source of their problems.[66]

Jessica Stern writes of violence between Christians and Muslims in Mu-luku, Indonesia, in 1999–2002 that left 6,000 dead and created 700,000 ref-ugees. Christians had long dominated in the region and had been favored by the Dutch during the colonial period. After independence, Muslims began to immigrate to the area and became a slim majority. The former dictator, Suharto, appointed Muslims to key political and economic posts in order to consolidate power, which angered the Christians. Although both sides feared that the other was trying to religionize the region, it was primarily a conflict between immigrants (Muslims) and natives (Christians), who felt that they were being marginalized and losing status to the newcomers. At the same time, interreligious social networks, Pela Gandong, based on eth-nicity had broken down because the new immigrants did not participate.[67] Violence by Muslims against Egypt's Christian Copts is another example of hostility toward a religious minority that is viewed as being tied to outsiders. Because the Copts are Christian, they are seen as being an arm of the West. Anwar Sadat stirred up resentment toward the Copts to establish his Islamic credentials in the late 1970s. Since then, Coptic churches and neighborhoods have been frequently targeted by Islamic extremist groups. Most recently, a Coptic church was attacked in April 2011 because of rumors that a woman was forcibly converted to Islam. Several days of Christian-Muslim violence followed.

Women and Gays

Modernization and globalization have also led to women and gays being seen as a threat to traditional and religious values. Equality for women and, increasingly, gays has been one of the products of modernization in the West. Juergensmeyer writes that religious extremists view women assuming powerful positions in the public arena is an abomination and a sign of the encroachment of evil, social disorder, and the decline of moral values. One of the crimes of liberalism for the lower income right-wing Christian extremists in the United States has been women's liberation because equality for women has been accompanied by their own economic marginalization and decline in status. At the same time, liberalism has led to greater sexual freedom for women, which was seen as a cause of the rise of abortion clinic bombings in the United States during the 1990s.[68] Thus, attacks against abortion clinics were an attack against the secular, repressive state that has permitted the decline of morality, which has led to greater reproductive rights for women.[69] Gays are particularly appalling to religious extremists in the United States. According to Michael Bray, a leader of the violent antiabortion movement, homosexuality is another sign of the degeneracy of America's secular liberal government.[70] In 1999, Christian Identity members allegedly attacked gay bars and killed a gay couple in Northern California. The perception that straight white men in United States are losing power to women and gays is another symbol of a world gone awry because of the decay in morals that is characteristic of a postmodern society.

The notion of equality for women and gays is even more toxic for Jewish religious extremists in Israel and Islamic extremists because it is viewed as being a Western concept that has been forced on them—another unwanted product of globalization. Ultra-Orthodox Jews in Jerusalem have rioted because of advertisements on bus shelters featuring scantily clad women and in opposition to a gay pride parade. Both the advertisements and the parade are seen as being an infringement of American culture on traditional

Judaism. Women who have attempted to read from the Torah at the Western Wall, Judaism's most sacred site, in Jerusalem have been met with harassment, arrest, and occasional violence. Many in the Israeli Orthodox establishment view the Women of the Wall as being a Trojan horse to introduce Jewish pluralism and establish the Reform, Conservative, and Reconstructionist strains of Judaism in Israel.[71] Islamic extremists have been equally adamant in opposing homosexuality and equality for women as unwanted Western imports. The Ayatollah Khomeini had gays in Tehran imprisoned and, in some cases, executed following the Iranian Revolution. Sayyid Qutb railed against equality for women as being one of the Western vices that was detrimental to Islam.[72] The Taliban, after taking power in Afghanistan, banned women from working and confined them to their homes unless accompanied by a male relative, claiming that women's rights was a Western innovation that is alien to Islam.

Minority Muslim Communities in Europe and the United States

Marginalization, frustrated aspirations, and inequality are also common in countries where Muslims are a minority community. There have been Muslims in Europe for centuries, but these communities grew rapidly following World War II and continue to grow in the era of globalization. The Islamic population in the United States has also increased significantly in the United States in recent years. According to Assaf Moghadam, this deterritorialization of Islam, where roughly one-third of Muslims live as minorities, has led many immigrants to view themselves as being part of a global community that is purely religious based.[73] Second- and third-generation Muslims living in Europe feel dislocated and mentally confused. Unlike their migrant parents, they have no hope of integrating into larger society. Their communities typically have high unemployment and poverty rates, and they feel as if they are purposefully being excluded and repressed because of their religion and ethnicity. They also feel torn between traditional values such as patriarchal authority, chastity, and family and the surrounding values of consumerism, hedonism, and self-interest. Because the benefits of integration and liberalism have gone unfulfilled, many turn to religion.[74] It is not surprising, given the feelings of marginalization and alienation, that many European Muslims are attracted to violent Islamic radical groups. It is estimated that 1–2 percent or approximately 200,000–500,000 of European Muslims are radicalized.[75]

The European radical Muslims, since they are minorities, are attracted by the universalist message of al Qaeda, which is not tied to a particular nation are ethic group. Olivier Roy, an expert on radical Islamic groups in Europe, writes that al Qaeda purposefully recruits Western Muslims who are educated in the sciences and technology. Roy, however, does not see attraction to violence and anger at the West as a clash of civilizations but, rather, behavior that is typical of people on the margins of society. Like many secular radicals, European Muslims are part of a generation gap because they have broken with their families and are alienated by mainstream materialistic societal values. The perpetrators of the July 7, 2005, attack on London subways and busses were mostly the children of immigrants who had clashed with their parents and traditional upbringings but then later returned to Islam. Their anger at their countries of residence was also typical of the anti-imperialist ideologies of secular European terrorist groups of the 1960s and 1970s.[76] Like their secular-radical predecessors, radical European Muslims are alienated by but never fully reject Western society. Roy writes that most of the 9/11 hijackers had left their countries of origin to study abroad. Many drank and dated and led Western lifestyles until they returned to Islam.[77] According to Roy, an honest attempt to truly integrate European Muslims might lead to an authentic native European Islam that would make radical universalist interpretations less attractive.[78]

The humiliation and marginalization felt by Muslims in places like Great Britain and France make them more sensitive to attacks on Muslims in other places. Because of media coverage and contact with *jihadists* who have fought in places like Afghanistan, Bosnia, and Iraq, they take on the suffering of their coreligionists across the globe. Thus, the combination of alienation at home and the perception that Muslims are under attack globally makes the necessity of violently defending their faith an urgent priority and solidifies their attraction to universal Islamic ideologies. They also maintain feelings of guilt for their previous Westernized lifestyles, which often included drug use, street gangs, and promiscuity. This guilt produces the sense that they should be suffering along with their fellow Muslims on the battlefields of Iraq, Afghanistan, and Palestine.[79] Thus, terrorists such as the 9/11 suicide bombers can be seen as men stuck between the Middle East and the West who had been tainted by their previous lives and felt that an extreme act of violence could serve as penitence for their sins and retribution against the society that had caused them to go awry.

The same conflicts can be seen in Muslims who study abroad or are first-generation immigrants. Mohammad Salameh, one of the conspirators in the 1993 attack on the World Trade Center, fits the profile of the marginal alienated that is typical of the age of globalization. Being a Palestinian,

Salameh was already a refugee from his homeland and then became an immigrant when he moved from a Palestinian refugee camp to Jersey City, New Jersey, for an education and financial advancement. With few skills and limited English, he ended up in a low-income immigrant neighborhood, where most of his associates were other Arabs. There, he fell under the sway of Sheik Omar Abdul Rahman at a local mosque. Twice removed from his homeland and struggling in America, Rahman's preaching against the evils of the United States was appealing to Salameh, who felt humiliated and dispossessed. Umar Farouk Abdulmutallab, who tried to set off a bomb in his underwear on a flight from Amsterdam to Detroit on December 25, 2009, was born to a wealthy Muslim family in Nigeria. Abdulmutallab led a very global life as he attended a British boarding school in Togo and graduated from University College in London in 2008. He also attended Arabic language school in Sana'a Yemen and lived in Dubai. In his postings in a Muslim online chat room, Abdulmutallab discussed his feelings of loneliness when he was abroad, his deep religious beliefs, and how his family's wealth conflicted with his Islamic values. He also, however, mentions his enjoyment of the shopping and restaurant scene, Pizza Hut, and KFC, in Sana'a and his desire to attend a prestigious American university.[80]

The rising number of attempted attacks and connections to Islamic terrorist groups by Muslims in America is also a concern. Although Muslim immigrants to the United States generally come with the intent to integrate and settle, in contrast to European Muslims who usually intended to return to their countries of origin, and, on average, are wealthier and better educated than the average American, there have been several incidents in recent years. Nidal Malik Hasan, an army psychologist, opened fire at Fort Hood, Texas, killing 12 and wounding 31 in November 2009. Faisal Shahzad, a Pakistani immigrant budget analyst, left a bomb in a car in Times Square in April 2010 that failed to explode. At his sentencing, he claimed that he was fighting a religious war against America.[81] Anwar al Awlaki, an American-born leader of al Qaeda in the Arabian Peninsula who allegedly had contact with Abdulmutallab, Hasan, and two of the 9/11 bombers, was rumored to be one of the possible successors to Osama bin Laden before being killed in September 2011. It, therefore, appears that a small number of American-born Muslims and immigrants, despite their economic and professional success, are feeling the same alienation and conflict between their religious identity and the values of the greater society that surrounds them and a strong connection to the universalist Islamic message of al Qaeda as their coreligionists in Europe. This attraction might be strengthened by rising anti-Muslim sentiment in the United States following 9/11 that is represented in opposition to the building of mosques and congressional hearings focusing on the radicalization of American Muslims.

THE LIMITS OF RELIGION-BASED TERROR
IN OPPOSING GLOBALIZATION

This chapter has outlined how rapid socioeconomic change, particularly in the Islamic world, has been an important cause of religion-based terrorism. It is important to note that the connection between change and violence is nothing new as the Industrial Revolution led to turmoil and resistance throughout Europe in the 19th century. Since change is one of the few guarantees of human existence, and change has always created winners and losers and transformed social orders, it will continue to be a cause of violence in the future. What is not guaranteed and is unlikely is religion being the ideology that is used to motivate opposition to the change and as a justification for lashing out at the forces of change. Just as the violent secular-radical movements of the 1960s and 1970s failed to rally widespread support, al Qaeda's popularity has waned in the last five years, and the democracy movement seems to be the new powerful ideological force in the Islamic world. The terrorism that plagued Indonesia following its move to democracy and a more open economy has waned, and Islamic parties have played a supportive role in the political process. Hopefully, this chain of events will be repeated in Egypt and Tunisia, and the benefits of change are distributed more equitably across nations and within countries.

Chapter 5

Psychological Causes of Religion-Based Terrorism

A simple and straightforward explanation of religion-based terrorism is that it is related to the nature of the individuals who engage in holy wars. It could be that religion-based terrorists are much more likely to be psychopaths than other individuals or share a common psychological profile. Since religion-based terrorism is deviant behavior, it would make sense that those who kill in the name of religion have deviant personalities. As detailed in the discussion of the political causes of religion-based terrorism in chapter 3, some experts, politicians, and pundits believe that groups such as al Qaeda and Hamas and individuals such as Baruch Goldstein are motivated by pure rage and a desire to kill as many people as people. At the same time, suicide bombers choose, often with joy and eager anticipation, to take their own lives along with those of their victims. Killing for the sake of killing and suicide are suggestive of profound mental illness.

This chapter will discuss possible personal and psychological determinants of religion-based terrorism. First, I will discuss the notion that religion-based terrorists are psychopaths or clinically insane. Then, I will consider whether there is a profile for religion-based terrorists. Then, I will consider the utility of various psychological explanations of terrorism in the explanation of contemporary religion-based violence. Then, I will explore the connection between religion and the techniques that terrorists use to rationalize and justify their violence. Finally, I will discuss how being part of a group influences individual behavior. Group psychology is important because an overwhelming majority of terrorists are members of terrorist organizations rather than lone wolves acting on their own, which suggests that the group plays a key role in motivating, supporting, and pressuring people to kill and die in the name of God. At the same time, groups take on personalities of their own and develop rationales for their actions that are different from those of their individual members.

A CAUTION

An important caution is necessary at the beginning of this discussion of the possible psychological roots of religion-based violence. Even if a somewhat reliable profile of a religion-based terrorist were to be produced, it is unlikely that it would provide a comprehensive explanation for religion-based terrorism because most people who fit the psychological profile are not holy warriors, just as most religious individuals do not engage in violence in the name of religion. It is also important to note that exposure to the political and socioeconomic conditions discussed in chapters 4 and 5, such as occupation and relative deprivation, could trigger people with certain types of mental illnesses or personality disorders and also have the potential to facilitate the development of mental illness and influence personality development. Psychological and personality-based explanations of religion-based violence and terrorism are also more difficult to empirically confirm and reject than political and socioeconomic ones. The latter are based on clearly identifiable variables, such as forms of government, foreign invasion, rates of economic growth, and literacy rates, that can be measured, classified, and verified.

Psychological explanations of terrorism are often based on the interpretation of individual life histories, which is unreliable because the observer is not able to interact with the subject or directly observe the subject's behavior. As will be seen, there have been a number of interviews with religion-based terrorists and suicide bombers who have been caught or who have backed out of their missions, as well as members of their families. Although these conversations provide fascinating insights into the world of religion-based terrorists and their motivations, they are usually conducted by journalists or researchers from fields other than psychology. Thus, the interviewers are not able to accurately assess the mental health of the interviewees. The limited number of interviews of religion-based terrorists and suicide bombers that has been conducted by mental health professionals must also be viewed with caution, as the small number of individuals interviewed may not be representative of the larger population of religious warriors. At the same time, most of the interviews take place in prison, where interviewees are likely to be worried that their conversations are being monitored or that the interviewer is really a government agent collecting intelligence. It is also likely that the terrorists are lying or distorting reality to protect their group's secrets or to present themselves in a favorable manner.

PSYCHOPATHY?

The most commonsensical personality-based explanation of religion-based terrorism is that the holy warriors are psychopaths or clinically insane. In short, they are similar to serial killers such as Jeffrey Dahmer, David Berkowitz ("Son of Sam"), and Charles Manson. This would appear to be a logical conclusion regarding individuals who, like their serial-killer counterparts, eagerly kill as many people as possible and/or take their own lives while doing so.

> that idea seems to have been repeated in the aftermath of nearly every major eruption of collective Violence against authority suicide bombings included. For example, immediately following the suicide bombings of Americana and French military barracks in Beirut in 1983, psychologists characterized the bombers as "unstable individuals with a death wish," although they lacked any evidence, clinical or anecdotal of the bombers' state of mind. Similarly following the Sept. 11, 2001 suicide attacks on the United States, U.S. government and media interpretations underscored the supposed irrationality and even outright insanity of the bombers again without the benefit of corroborating data.[1]

This simple and logical explanation, criminal insanity, as suggested by Scott Atran in the preceding quote is not the correct one because research has almost universally concluded that religion-based terrorists are, indeed, sane.

Jerrold Post, a psychiatrist who has completed numerous studies on the relationship between mental illness and terrorism, has concluded that terrorists, including religious ones and suicide bombers, are not psychopathic and that the thing that distinguishes terrorists, in terms of mental health, is their normality.[2] Two important reviews of the literature regarding psychopathy from the 1980s and the 1990s supported Post's conclusion as noted terrorism scholar Martha Crenshaw wrote in 1981 that "the outstanding common characteristic of terrorists is their normality" and Rex Hudson stated in a widely cited 1991 article for the Library of Congress that "the best documented generalization is negative; terrorists do not show any striking psychopathology."[3] Crenshaw's review was prior to the era of religion-based terrorism, but Hudson's work included religion-based terrorist groups such as al Qaeda, Hamas, and Hezbollah. Given that religion-based terrorism is a relatively new phenomenon, there is a small but growing number of studies on the personalities and the mental health of religious warriors and suicide bombers, all of which support the notion that religious terrorists, like their secular counterparts, are sane.

Robert Pape did not find any cases of mental illness such as depression, psychosis, and past suicide attempts among the 462 suicide bombers, both religious and secular, who launched attacks across the globe between 1980 and 2003.[4] Nasra Hassan, who studied and interviewed samples of Palestinian and Pakistani members of Islamic terrorist groups and their families, concluded that psychopathology was not characteristic of the members of either group.[5] Ariel Merari in his research on Palestinian suicide bombers in Lebanon and the Israeli-occupied territories found that none of the individuals had been hospitalized or displayed characteristics of mental illness and that none had displayed any warning signs or had been considered suicide risks.[6] Psychiatrist and former CIA case officer Marc Sageman collected data from public sources on 172 global Salafi mujahidin, including members of the Egyptian Islamic Jihad, Jemaah Islamiyah, the Moro Islamic Liberation Front, the Algerian Groupe Salafiste pour la Predication et le Combat, and al Qaeda, who were fighting to create a new Islamic world order. Of the 69 cases where descriptions of childhood personality were located, only one individual was found to have suffered childhood trauma. Sageman concluded that there was "no evidence of pathological narcissism" and "no pattern of paranoid personality disorder" in this subgroup, with the possible exception of Ayman al Zawahiri, who became leader of al Qaeda following Osama bin Laden's death.[7]

The finding that religion-based terrorists are sane individuals can be better understood when looking at some important differences between terrorists and psychopaths. Terrorists benefit either personally or as part of their groups from their activity, while psychopaths do not. This is even true for suicide terrorists, who often believe that they will go to heaven and receive rewards such as virgins. Also, the purposefulness of a psychopath's actions, if any, is entirely personal while a terrorist is group and society-minded, which is certainly true for religion-based terrorists.[8] Maxwell Taylor argues that terrorist organizations quickly weed out mentally unbalanced individuals because they are likely to harm the group's interests. Terrorists, of course, must be discrete and able to blend in with society without attracting attention.[9] Here, we need only think of the 9/11 terrorists who lived in the United States for two years without attracting any suspicion, while they were planning and preparing to hijack three commercial airliners and crash them into major U.S. landmarks, something that could not be accomplished by a psychopath.

Another reason why terrorist groups screen out individuals with apparent mental disorders is that terrorist foot soldiers need to be controlled and must be able to function in groups. Organizations like Hamas, which launches suicide bombings against Israel, need individuals who will do as they are told and follow through with the mission as planned, while people with severe personality disorders are unpredictable and, as mentioned, are individually minded. Thus, the few mentally unbalanced religion-based terrorists, such as Israeli, Noam Friedman, who fired his army-issued M-16 into a crowded Arab market in Hebron in 1996 because he did not want the city to be returned to the Palestinians in a peace treaty, have been lone wolves. Friedman was described as a delusional and unstable loner.[10] However, most lone wolves are sane, as was the case with Dr. Baruch Goldstein, who killed 30 Arab worshippers at the Cave of the Patriarchs in Hebron in 1994. Although Goldstein was a fanatic with an intense hatred of Arabs, he was also a physician who exhibited no signs of severe mental illness.

FANATICISM IS NOT MENTAL ILLNESS

The case of Goldstein, who was a hateful but sane fanatic, illustrates Taylor's point that it is important to differentiate between fanaticism and mental illness. Terrorists, by definition, are fanatics, but fanaticism is not unique terrorism. Taylor also writes that, although fanaticism does carry some characteristics of mental illness, it "is not a diagnostic category in mental illness." Thus, "commonly held assumptions about the relationship between fanaticism and mental illness . . . seem to be inappropriate."[11] In short, fanatics are usually sane and are not usually terrorists. Thus, Walter Reich's warning that "psychological accounts of terrorism are replete with explanations that ignore or blur the variety and complexity of terrorist personalities . . . a product of loose and weak thinking, a disregard for the need for evidence, and the habit, unfortunately endemic in so many areas of psychological discourse, of having a single idea and applying it to everything" must be heeded.[12] It is inappropriate to place Noam Friedman and Baruch Goldstein in the same category simply because they intended to massacre Arabs.

ANTISOCIAL PERSONALITIES?

The notion that religion-based terrorists suffer from severe mental illness or personality disorders relates to another related misconception; they have antisocial personalities. Given that these violent holy warriors are a very small minority holding fanatical views that contrast sharply with the rest of society; it is easy to see why they might be viewed as being antisocial. However, it is important to remember that the overwhelming majority of religion-based terrorists are not loners and are part of organized groups or cells. At the same time, they strongly believe that their violence is ultimately for the good of society. Like their peaceful coreligionists who give charity, engage in acts of kindness, and love their neighbors, religious warriors believe that they are serving God and working to create a better world. However, they do so by using violence to bring about a society that is governed by religious law or the World to Come. Clark McCauley reports that documents found in the luggage of the 9/11 hijackers show that the terrorists thought that their actions were an expression of their love of God, their attachment to doing good, and being soldiers in a fight against evil. These positive intentions, along with a feeling of obligation to their comrades, are similar to the motives reported by American soldiers during World War II.[13]

It is important to remember that the antisocial label is usually placed on religious warriors by members of the target society. Victims of terrorism view themselves as being innocent civilians who have done nothing to deserve the attack, so the people who are trying to kill them must be antisocial. The terrorist, however, in his or her own society, is often viewed as a hero and is rewarded for his or her actions, even if the attacker has killed himself or herself along with his or her victims. Pape writes that the deaths of Hamas suicide bombers are celebrated and that posters and graffiti honoring the departed are pasted on the walls of buildings, while Hezbollah martyrs have had streets named after them. At the same time, both Hezbollah and Hamas have charitable and social service arms that provide welfare, job training, health care, education, and child care for citizens. Both organizations are viewed by many as being more legitimate representatives of their populations than their respective governing authorities.[14] Sometimes tacit support even comes from government officials, as former Israeli prime minister Yitzhak Shamir called members of extremist Jewish underground cells in Israel who had planned attacks against Palestinians in the 1980s as being "excellent Jewish boys who had made a mistake."[15] Given the support and adulation that religion-based terrorists receive from their groups and, sometimes, from the larger societies that surround them, it is hard to consider their behavior as antisocial even though their victims, rightly, find it barbaric.

Evidence for the pro-social nature of religion-based terrorism is found in a survey of 900 Muslim youth completed by psychologist Brian Barber in

Gaza during the first Palestinian Intifada (1987–1993). Barber reports that participation in the uprising was widespread among the adolescents as 81 percent reported throwing stones and 66 percent had been assaulted and/ or fired on by Israeli troops. Participation was not associated with depression or other forms of antisocial behavior. The young men displayed strong levels of social cohesion as 87 percent helped distribute supplies to other activists, 83 percent visited families who had children killed in the violence, and 71 percent helped provide care for the wounded. Barber repeated the study during the second Intifada (2000–2002) and found that martyrdom was increasingly viewed as the most important way to contribute to the Palestinian cause.[16] Merari's study of Palestinian suicide bombers in Lebanon also points to a pro-social and even altruistic ethic as many of the terrorists claimed that suicide was not obligatory in fighting the enemy (Israel) but was of merit for Palestinian society. Like Barber, Merari concluded that the bombers were psychologically healthy, were not suffering from despair in their personal lives, and had strong hopes for a better future. They also did not view their deaths as an escape but a projection of power that was part of a long-term struggle for their people.[17]

ALTRUISM

The notion that religion-based terrorism as pro-social behavior can be better understood in the context of suicide bombing. Emile Durkheim identified four types of suicide: anomic, egoistic, fatalistic, and altruistic.[18] Egoistic suicide is when an individual takes his or her life because he or she feels detached, isolated, and hopeless. Fatalistic suicide is when an individual is heavily influenced by strong leaders, who keep their followers isolated, and is characteristic of cults such as the followers of Jim Jones in the People's Temple community in Guyana in 1978. Pape argues that suicide bombers are committing altruistic suicide and kill themselves because of a sense of duty and obligation to their community to fight the enemy. While fatalistic suicide and egoistic suicide are usually looked down on and condemned, altruistic suicide is often venerated by society.[19] Palestinian suicide bombers and the organizations that send them on their missions, as mentioned, are often adulated. A 2003 study of 80 Palestinian suicide bombers proposed that the terrorists were acting from altruistic motives and that they were strongly connected to their families, their suicide partners, and to Islamic organizations.[20] It is also important to note that the bombers believe that they are engaging in *istishad,* selfless death in the service of Allah. Pape also points out that overall suicide rates do not increase in areas where suicide terrorism is taking place and that Muslim nations, where most suicide bombings currently originate, have lower suicide rates than other nations.[21]

IS THERE A PROFILE OF RELIGION-BASED TERRORISTS?

Although religion-based terrorists are, for the most part, sane and pro-social individuals, it still could be possible that there might be a profile or common psychological mind-set for those who kill in the name of God. This also is not the case. In 1985, Jerrold Post wrote that "behavioral scientists attempting to understand the psychology of individuals drawn to this violent political behavior have not succeeded in identifying a unique 'terrorist mindset.'"[22] Rex Hudson reached the same conclusion in 1999 during the era of religion-based terrorism stating that "There seems to be general agreement among psychologists that there is no particular psychological attribute that can be used to describe the terrorist or any 'personality' that is distinctive of terrorists."[23] Most recent studies of religion-based terrorists have concluded that these individuals are usually ordinary people who are typical of the societies from which they come. Nasra Hassan's study of Pakistani Islamic suicide bombers concluded that they could best be characterized by their ordinariness and their similarity with millions of other Pakistani males and that none had easily identifiable psychological problems.[24]

The ordinariness of religion-based terrorists is best summarized in the title, "Ordinary People" of an article detailing a small sample of failed and potential Palestinian suicide bombers. Anat Berko and Edna Erez describe the individuals as being typical for the Israeli-occupied territories in terms of family background, education, and economic status. Again, all of the subjects were viewed as being psychologically fit.[25] Nasra Hassan described the Palestinian suicide bombers that she interviewed as follows, "None of them were uneducated, desperately poor, simple-minded, or depressed. Many were middle class and, unless they were fugitives, held paying jobs. They all seemed to be entirely normal members of their families. They were polite and serious, and in their communities they were considered to be model youths."[26] It is interesting to note that much of the research on the personal characteristics of religion-based terrorists and suicide bombers concludes that religion is not a significant motivating factor for holy warriors. Berko and Erez found that most of their interviewees were not religious prior to becoming suicide bombers. Hilal Khashan concluded that political Islam was not a strong predictor of suicide bombing. Merari argues that strong religious belief is neither a necessary nor a sufficient condition for suicide bombing. Finally, Assaf Moghadam, who focuses on radical Salafi Islam and *jihad,* agreed that religion is not the ultimate cause of suicide bombing.[27] Thus, we are left with the rough demographic profile discussed in the previous chapter: single, young, educated, middle-class males.

PSYCHOLOGICAL EXPLANATIONS
OF RELIGION-BASED TERRORISM

Psychological theories of terrorism, despite the lack of a clear terrorist profile, provide some interesting suggestions about the nature of religion-based terrorists. As discussed, religion-based terrorists and suicide bombers are generally rewarded and are viewed as martyrs by their surrounding societies, which relates to social learning, a theory that will be discussed later. Post, despite rejecting the notion that terrorists are psychopaths and the existence of a terrorist psychological profile, does write that terrorists are driven to commit violence because of psychological forces and that certain types of people are more likely to be drawn to terrorism. He also mentions that terrorists must create a special psychologic that enables them to engage in activities that they know are morally inappropriate.[28] Here, religion, as will be discussed, can play in an important role in developing this psychologic of rationalizations and justifications. In the section that follows, I will briefly review a small sample of psychological theories of terrorism that are relevant to religion-based terrorists.

Novelty Seeking

A somewhat obvious hypothesis is that religion-based terrorists are seeking satisfaction of an innate and, perhaps, genetically programmed desire to take risks and for stimulation. Thus, religion-based terrorists are seeking experiences that provide levels of excitement and risk that are far beyond those offered in ordinary day-to-day life.[29] This theory is supported by Mark Juergensmeyer, who shows that a significant number of Christian, Jewish, Islamic, and Sikh terrorists have served in the military before moving to the realm of dissident violence, which signifies a pattern of attraction to risky and violent activity. Juergensmeyer also notes that many of the holy warriors that he interviewed explained that their attraction to terrorism was, in part, due to the excitement that came with the operations and the thrill of planning an attack or bombing.[30] This suggests that it may be the high-risk situations and the potential for combat that motivate religion-based terrorists rather than faith. Shamir, the former prime minister of Israel from 1983 to 1984 and 1986 to 1992, related that his time in the Irgun, a violent Jewish underground organization prior to the birth of the State of Israel, was the best and most exciting part of his life.[31]

Novelty theory also helps explain why most religion-based terrorists fall into the 17–30 age range because adolescents are known to be both crime prone and risk acceptant. This age range is also a time when young men are going through the end of a period of hormonal change and physical development and experiencing anxiety about the future and sexual frustration. During this impressionable time, adolescents are more likely to develop extremist viewpoints, which harden when they enter young adulthood but mellow as they grow older. After all, Shamir opted for a career in politics rather than the military after Israel was established, and he moved into adulthood. On the other hand, those who become career terrorists, perhaps, fall into the group that is genetically predisposed to high-risk activity.[32] The explanatory power of Novelty Theory is limited because action-oriented individuals are also common in nonpolitical criminal groups, such as street gangs, and legally sanctioned organizations such as the military and the police. Consequently, political and socioeconomic factors are needed to explain whether an action-oriented individual chooses a legal, criminal, or terrorist outlet to satisfy his or her innate need for excitement.[33]

Narcissism and Splitting

There are a number of psychoanalytic theories that trace terrorist behavior back to injuries suffered in early childhood, which, subsequently, facilitate the development of a damaged adult personality. Rather than being aggressive psychopaths, terrorists are timid, emotionally scarred individuals with injured egos because of parental rejection, which causes the delay or prevention of an adult identity. Individuals with healthy personalities are able to deal with the ambiguity that they find in themselves, the world around them, and others. In contrast, those with damaged egos, even as adults, revert to immature strategies of splitting the world into the diametrically opposed categories of good and evil. In order to repair their damaged sense of self-esteem, they develop grandiose versions of themselves and narcissistic personalities. The narcissistic individual typically projects all of his or her own inadequacies onto others. To relieve himself or herself of his or her rage and self-hatred at his or her damaged self and inadequacies, he or she lashes out at an external target, who has been assigned all of his or her negative characteristics. The target becomes the source of the negative feelings that the terrorist has about himself or herself that must be destroyed.[34]

The narcissistic personality/splitting theory was confirmed by an analysis of data collected on 227 left-wing and 23 right-wing secular West Germany terrorists in the 1980s by that country's ministry of the interior. Many of the individuals came from fragmented families, had conflict with their parents, were often former Nazis, and had failed in their personal and professional lives.[35] The application of narcissistic personality/splitting theory to religion-based terrorists, particularly suicide bombers, is difficult because, as mentioned, there are few detailed interviews conducted by mental health professionals that delve into their family history and their relationship with their parents. However, the interviews and research discussed in the preceding text conducted by Berko and Erez, Hassan, Khashan, Merari, Barber, Sageman, and Post suggested that most of the religion-based terrorists came from normal families, did not have troubled backgrounds, and were often viewed as role models. On the other hand, Muslims living as minorities in the West, including members of Islamic extremist groups in Europe, do feel alienated from their parents.[36]

James Jones suggests that dysfunctional personality development and splitting could influence how individuals view God. Religious individuals who maintain an image of a wrathful God are associated with "external locus of control, anxiety and depression and immature object relations . . . a more benevolent representation of God is associated with more mature psychological development and the capacity for more mature object relations."[37] Jones goes on to conclude that individuals who view God as angry, wrathful, and punishing are more likely to rigidly split the world in to good and evil and to feel less empathy for others, which are traits that are characteristic of religion-based terrorists.[38] Jones concludes that the angry God that demands sacrifice as a means of purification is also characteristic of the apocalyptic vision of a cataclysmic struggle between good and evil that is typical of the eschatological visions of many holy warriors. Therefore, it might be that religion-based terrorists are individuals with dysfunctional personalities caused by traumatic childhoods, who are drawn to violent extremism because it provides convenient targets for them to externalize their self-loathing.

A number of the reasons why religion facilitates violence that were discussed in chapter 2 appear in Jones's conclusions about locus on control, capacity for object relations, and splitting. To review, religion divides the world into believers and nonbelievers, which allows the extremist to devalue those outside the faith. For the Jewish terrorist, the gentile is of lower status than one of the chosen people. Judaism, Christianity, and Islam also contain cosmic struggles between good and evil. For the healthy personality, this could be the struggle against sin and temptation or following religious law. For the unhealthy personality, the struggle is against a real-world enemy that presents an existential threat such as the United States, abortion providers, or the Palestinian Arabs of the West Bank. Jones also points to other reasons why religion facilitates violence, as he raises the image of the angry God who punishes those who do not follow his will and who are not willing to sacrifice themselves in his name. Finally, eschatological visions that are preceded by conflict and violence, such as the second coming of Christ and the rebuilding of the Temple in Jerusalem, cause some with grandiose egos and narcissistic personalities, such as an American who plotted to blow up the Islamic holy sites on Mt. Zion, to think that it is their duty to bring about the end of history by instigating the violence. Again, it is important to remember that it is very difficult to make a direct empirical connection between psychological development, personality, and terrorism, but there does seem to be a theoretical fit between narcissistic personalities, splitting, and religion-based violence.

Idealization

Idealization is another possibility when a child does not obtain sufficient love and approval from his or her parents. Again, the child engages in splitting but internalizes his or her badness and projects goodness onto the parent and creates an idealized version of him or her. In contrast, the healthy child and, later, adult develop a strong enough self-image to acknowledge the ambiguity that is inherent in people. We also usually create idealized versions of individuals when we first meet them, but the healthy person can move beyond that, recognize the flaws in others, and develop a more realistic assessment. In contrast, the ill-developed individual adheres to the idealized perception, ignores the flaws of authority figures, and maintains his or her idolization of those individuals. According to Jones, this idealization increases the probability that an individual might fall under the sway of a charismatic religious leader.[39] One possibility is a cult leader and another is a cleric or other individual who preaches interpretations of religion that call for violence and terrorism. Religion facilitates this idealization of authority figures because clerics are to be respected and obeyed due to their mastery of religious texts, holiness, or positions of power. It is, therefore, easy to see how someone with a damaged personality could idealize a religious leader like Rabbi Meir Kahane or Irish Protestant leader Rev. Ian Paisley and blindly follow their calls to violence.

Jones writes that the person with an ill-developed personality and negative self-image who associates good with external objects can also idealize religious texts, institutions, and ideologies. This idealized view of religions, their symbols, and leaders creates a mind-set that cannot see the ambiguities, contradictions, and multiple interpretations that are inherent in the mono-theistic faiths. Rather, the believer with the damaged self-image maintains absolutist and literal interpretations that divide the world into good and evil and encourage extremism. Jones points out that the idealized, perfect object, be it God, a cleric, or text, facilitates the denigration of the damaged self. As a result, the believer deems himself or herself as being unworthy when contrasted with the ideal external object. Another possibility is that, in ad-dition to self-denigration, this individual will project the evil onto the out-side world.[40] Again, extremist interpretations of Judaism, Christianity, and Islam facilitate this process through their division of the world into believers and nonbelievers and their call for struggle against evil.

We now have a picture of the violent religious extremist as being someone who is burdened with feelings of intense self-loathing who is seeking relief. To repair his or her self-image, he or she will identify with a group that es-pouses an idealized interpretation of religion that is not open to questioning or doubt. To further relieve him or her of his or her sense of badness, he or she, like the narcissistic splitter, projects his or her negative characteristics on to an outside group and labels them as evil. The sense of self-loathing is so profound that the outside group (another religion, race, or nation) is demonized and must be destroyed. Extremist religious groups that divide the world into good and evil and see themselves as being under constant at-tack from their enemies provide targets to demonize.[41] Idealized religious texts provide blueprints such as calls for destroying Amalek and fighting the forces of ignorance for the violence against the evil enemy. Jones's the-ory helps explain why many religion-based terrorists have been sinners or had criminal backgrounds before they returned to the faith. As discussed in chapter 4, many members of European Islamic terrorist groups and Europe-ans and North American Muslims who went to fight in *jihads* in Afghani-stan, Iraq, Bosnia, and other countries had been gang members, drank, used drugs, and strayed from religion. Nidal Malik Hasan, the army psychologist who killed 12 at Fort Hood, and Faisal Shahzad, the Times Square bomber, were both American Muslims who had adapted sinful lifestyles.[42]

Frustration/Aggression

Frustration/Aggression theory also focuses on anger and self-loathing as a cause of terrorism and political violence but attributes the rage to an indi-vidual's inability to achieve a goal in their personal life rather than improper development during childhood. The result, however, the development of a negative self-identity, is the same. According to Jeanne Knutson, the frustrated individual develops an identity that purposefully and sometimes violently rejects the role that society regards as being moral and proper. Terrorism, according to Knutson, is a result of the anger and helplessness that is caused by the terrorist's perception of a lack of alternatives and belief that the world is unfair.[43] Oots and Wiegle also view terrorists as frustrated and aroused individuals who have repeatedly experienced fight or flight syndrome. This state of arousal, which facilitates the move from potential terrorist to terrorist, is caused by physiological, political, and psychological forces. Eventually, the constant arousal, facilitated by media presentations of terrorism, leads the potential terrorist to lash out with violence to destroy the cause of his or her frustration and to achieve a political goal that has been denied.[44]

Theories of terrorism that focus on frustration and aggression overlap with relative deprivation, which was considered in chapter 4. Relative deprivation leads to violence when individual expectations exceed society's ability to fulfill those aspirations, and people feel that they are unfairly being denied what those above them have. The notion that individuals turn to religion-based terrorism when they fail to achieve personal goals rings partly true. On one hand, evidence was presented in chapter 4, which suggested that terrorists are marginal individuals with unmet aspirations in terms of careers and starting a family. Here the cases of the people who rebelled against the shah of Iran, those left behind by globalization in the Muslim world, Muslims living in Europe, and members of the right-wing Church of Creativity in the United States provide supporting evidence. At the same time, many religion-based terrorists, such as Dr. Baruch Goldstein, have been successful in the personal lives, and others, such as Palestinian suicide bombers, are highly respected in their societies. However, all terrorists have been denied a political goal, be it banning abortion, annexing the West Bank, or creating an Islamic state, and lash out at the force that appears to be denying them that goal. However, the notion that this denial creates an aroused physiological state that leads to violence has not been confirmed.

Learning Theory

Learning theory, rather than focusing on personality development and the characteristics of individuals, attributes terrorism to the influence and behavior of the society and individuals who come into contact with the potential terrorist. In the interest of space, these theories are being collapsed into one short section with the realization that there are a number of learning theories that deal with a variety of influences such as rewards and punishments, teaching, family and peers, and society. Albert Bandura, one of the leading scholars of learning theory, argues that violence and aggression are a result of observation and imitation, rather than innate personality traits. Consequently, individuals, primarily adolescents and young adults living in areas with frequent terrorist activity and political violence, observe these activities and learn to imitate them.[45] For example, Palestinian children during the first Intifada played a game where some would portray Palestinians and throw stones at another group that portrayed Israeli soldiers, who chased the stone throwers and fired imaginary weapons.[46] Adolescents and young adults can also learn that terrorism is socially acceptable from their terrorist friends and terrorist organizations and through the posters of martyrs and songs and poems that honor suicide bombing in the Israeli-occupied territories.

Post stresses the significant role that families and society play in teaching that terrorism is sociably desirable in his claim that nationalist terrorism is bred to the bone. In contrast to revolutionary and anarchic terrorism, which are condemned by the greater society, nationalist and separatist terrorism, such as Irish Catholics in Northern Ireland, is passed down from parents, who breed their children to hate. Children in these societies, according to Post, grow up with hatred in their blood because of the anger- and violence-filled cues that are transmitted from their parents and society.[47] Post's theory was supported by psychiatric evaluation of children in Northern Ireland, which found that exposure to terrorism as a child facilitated participation in terrorism as an adult.[48] The bred to the bone explanation, in addition to Catholics in Northern Ireland, appears to help explain several other cases of religion-based terrorism. Post, Sprinzak, and Denny reported that most Palestinian and Lebanese terrorists came from families that supported their children's participation in terrorist organizations, while peer involvement and increased social status were also important influences.[49] Hassan found that one-third of Pakistani religious militants came from militant families.[50] Anat Berko, in the conclusion to her book featuring interviews with Palestinian suicide bombers and their handlers, takes their greater society to task for indoctrinating them and making them into heroes. "This suicide bombing, which is a very private act, has become common Palestinian property and has led to a cult of death and killing."[51]

The terrorism taught by family, peers, and society explanation, as would be expected, works well in cases such as the Palestinians, Hezbollah in Lebanon, Catholics and Protestants in Northern Ireland, and Jewish extremists in Israel, where religion merges with nationalist and ethnic causes. However, multinational religion-based terrorist groups such as al Qaeda, which are more anarchic and revolutionary, appear to present contradictory evidence. Most of the *jihadists* who went to fight in Afghanistan and other venues came from the Middle East, Europe, and other places. Thus, their interest in the conflicts in these faraway places did not come from parents or society. In fact, most left their countries of origin because they felt alienated in their homelands and, like their socialist and left-wing radical predecessors, were disgusted by the societies that produced them. One interesting possibility is that they did their social learning from *jihadist* websites on the Internet, the atrocities that they saw against Muslims on television, and DVDs of speeches by radical clerics. It is also possible that religious warriors do their learning in religious schools and during their training as the righteousness of violence can be taught didactically. Jeff Victoroff writes that many Palestinian and Pakistani terrorists attended *madrasas,* which have increased in number and, increasingly, have taught violent interpretations of Islam.[52]

Anecdotal evidence supports the didactic explanation of religion-based terrorism as one of the al Qaeda members who participated in the bombing of the U.S. embassy in Tanzania in 1998 claimed that he had been indoctrinated as a child at his mosque about the importance of helping Muslims who were being persecuted throughout the world and that his training in Pakistan included four hours per day of ideological instruction.[53] Signs in Hamas kindergartens in Gaza read that "The children of the kindergarten are the martyrs of tomorrow."[54] Atran writes that in the Taliban early religious indoctrination is an important cause of martyrdom. *Jihad* is the first word that children learned to spell in Taliban schools. At the same time, ritual a cappella chanting and physical activities are widely used in training. "The Taliban and al Qaeda also promote ritual communion, which often includes typical primate gestures of submission and trust (kneeling, bowing, prostrating, baring throat and chest, etc.) as well as routinized, formulaic patterning of ritual and bonding (cooing, hugging, kissing, etc.)."[55] Although only a minority of Muslim terrorists have been educated in *madrasas,* it could be that nonattendees are also affected as the students bring the messages to the rest of society. It is also important to remember that most students who attend *madrasas* do not become terrorists, so other factors must also influence the small minority that engages in violence.

Psychologic

The preceding discussion of psychological based theories of terrorism suggested that certain personality characteristics and lessons learned from families, institutions, and societies might make some individuals more likely to become religion-based terrorists. Another important psychological factor, according to Post, might be the special psychologic that terrorists construct in order to rationalize and justify the acts that they are compelled to commit.[56] Bandura writes that terrorists must insulate themselves from the consequences of their behavior. In order to achieve this psychological cleansing of their activities, they use moral disengagement techniques to justify and rationalize behavior that they know is unacceptable.[57] It is important to note that the justifications that terrorists use to disengage their moral inhibitors are also used by nonterrorists to rationalize their immoral behaviors in day-to-day life. Although this implies that we all have the potential to become terrorists, it also suggests that the bad behaviors that we need to justify are partly determined by our political status, socioeconomic conditions, and our psychological health. The middle-class American students in my courses who live in a democracy are likely to be justifying plagiarizing, while an Afghan who saw members of his or her family killed by an American retaliatory bombing against the Taliban is more likely to justify a suicide attack against U.S. soldiers.

Religion can play an important role in supporting the rationalizations and justifications of terrorists, as an ideological framework links the individual to an ongoing struggle for a greater cause. It is important to remember that religion is not the only ideology that has been used to validate terrorism, as socialism, nationalism, ethnocentrism, and anarchism have all been utilized in the past. However, a review of some of the justifications and rationalizations employed by terrorists will show that they correspond with many of the aspects of religion that facilitate violence that were considered in chapter 1. Jones ties religion-based justification to its reinforcement and encouragement of feelings of shame and humiliation, which stimulate violent outbursts. According to Jones, religion provides socially acceptable channels and divinely sanctioned targets for violence by dehumanizing others and encouraging prejudices. The justifications are the final step of a process where religious teachings and practices build on and intensify the humiliation that is caused by social and political conditions. At the same time, the teachings and practices allow the developing fanatic to deny responsibility for his or her actions and provide targets who are deserving of their wrath.[58] Thus, religion does not cause the violence; rather, it is the social and political conditions, which are then manipulated by religion-based terrorist organizations in their advocacy of violent interpretations of religion that provide a justification for behavior, such as suicide and murder, that are otherwise unacceptable.

Defending Others

A common justification for terrorism and other violence is defending a constituency that is threatened by a powerful and evil force. Thus, terrorists who kill abortion providers and firebomb abortion clinics claim that they are defending unborn children, who cannot defend themselves. Not only are the unborn children at the mercy of the abortion providers, they are also threatened by the powerful U.S. government that sanctions abortion and a largely apathetic public that does nothing to stop the carnage. As noted, the antiabortion terrorists often liken themselves to Dietrich Bonhoeffer, a Lutheran minister and theologian, who was involved in plans to assassinate Adolf Hitler during World War II. The assassination of Hitler for Bonhoeffer, a pacifist, was justified by Hitler's extermination of the Jews and other groups and by the overwhelming power of the Nazi regime, which made murder the only possible way of stopping the carnage. Al Qaeda and other Islamic terrorist groups view themselves as defenders of Muslims against the United States, a dark and powerful force that represents the West's hostility to Islam. The monotheistic religious traditions include many examples of heroic figures defending the weak, as Moses stood up to the Pharaoh so that the Hebrew children could go free, Jesus died on the cross at the hands of the Romans for the sins of others, and Husayn and his forces martyred themselves at the hands of their Sunni enemies.

Displacement of Responsibility

Another common neutralization technique is the displacement of responsibility on to someone or something else. The most notorious example of the use of displacement was the Nuremberg War Crimes Trial in 1948 when many of the Nazis who helped perpetrate the Holocaust claimed innocence because they were only following orders. Religion provides numerous options for the terrorist seeking to transfer responsibility and/or authority for his or her actions. God is the most obvious choice because all religion-based terrorists believe that they are fulfilling God's will. Chapter 1 provided examples of religious warriors claiming that their actions were divinely commanded, authorized, and inspired. Thus, the holy warriors believe that they are not acting on their own accord but, rather, as a tool or conduit in the implementation of a divine plan such as the rebuilding of the Temple in Jerusalem or the second coming of Christ. Here, religion is unique in providing a supreme being whose authority is far superior to that of any human or any human-made law.

How does the religion-based terrorist know that God wants him or her to kill and/or take his or her life? Religious texts such as the Bible, *Quran*, and Torah present divinely authored or sanctioned blueprints for the violence. As discussed in chapter 1, these holy books have verses that explicitly sanction violence or can be interpreted as condoning violence. Thus, the religious warrior can believe that he or she is fulfilling the divine injunction to wipe the seed of Amalek from the face of the earth or to destroy the infidels wherever they are to be found. What does our religion-based terrorist do if he or she does not have the authority or knowledge to interpret sacred texts or to ascertain God's will? Religion provides clerics, scholars, and other leaders who are to be respected and obeyed because of their learnedness, holiness, or positions of authority. Many religion-based terror organizations are headed by clerics or have religious authorities who legitimate their activities. In Islam, *fatwas* (interpretations of religious law) that condone killing, such as the one that the late Ayatollah Khomeini issued calling for the life of novelist, Salman Rushdie, have become commonplace in recent years.[59]

Blaming the Victim

A related justification is the displacement of blame for terror and violence onto the target, which can take the form of a preemptive attack before the enemy has a chance to strike first. Palestinian terrorist groups defend their suicide bombings against civilian targets by claiming that all Israelis serve in the army and, therefore, have the potential to harm innocent Palestinians through Israel's occupation. This logic is even extended to killing Israeli children because they will serve in the army when they grow up.[60] Terrorists also blame the target for their actions by insisting that it did something to provoke or deserve the attack. Abortion providers would not be killed if they did not perform abortions. The 9/11 attacks would not have happened if the United States had not placed its troops in Saudi Arabia, propped up dictators in the Muslim world, supported Israel, or spread its secular, hedonist, antireligious culture.[61] Bin Laden frequently claimed that the *jihad* against the United States is defensive and is a result of America's hostile and aggressive behavior. The rationalization that the enemy provoked the attack is often substantiated by the claim, "what they did is far worse." The abortion provider takes thousands of lives while, his or her murderer takes only one. The damage done on 9/11 pales in comparison to what the United States and the West have done to the Muslim world from the Crusades to the Iraq War.

Religion facilitates the victim brought the attack on itself rationalizations by dividing the world into believers and nonbelievers and by focusing on the struggle between good and evil. It is much easier to convince one's self that an entity intends to do harm or to perceive its intentions as being hostile, when that group is viewed as the other. As discussed, extremists place less value on the lives of nonbelievers, and texts, theologies, and history can be used to support this claim. Thus, the Church of the Creativity can justify unprovoked attacks on Jews because of their conspiracy to control the world and their history of evil doing. Jewish extremists in Israel rationalize attacks on Palestinians with a 5,000-year history full of groups that have tried to destroy the Jews. This division of the world intensifies the need to defend the boundaries against outsiders. The imperative to struggle against wickedness also helps convince the holy warrior that the enemy deserves to be victimized because it is inherently evil and must be punished. As Juergensmeyer argues, religion-based terrorists tend to fight cosmic wars where the enemy must not only be defeated but also destroyed.[62] Thus, Rabbi Kahane wanted nothing less than the removal of all Arabs from Israel and its occupied territories and was willing to use violence, if necessary, to do so. Islamic extremists in Pakistan and Iraq have used terrorism to drive Christians from their countries.

Demonization and Euphemistic Labeling

This dialectic thinking also leads to the demonization of the opponent and euphemistic labeling. Ehud Sprinzak wrote that the final step in the process that turns law-abiding citizens into terrorists is a crisis of legitimacy, where the challenge group extends its hostility to an entire society, including citizens, and deems them a subhuman species. Terrorism can only be justified after this dehumanization has taken place.[63] Thus, Islamic terrorists refer to the United States as "the great Satan." Abortion providers are referred to as butchers, and Jews have, historically, been caricaturized with devil's horns. Juergensmeyer points out that this labeling also serves the purpose of collectivization, the portrayal of individuals in broad terms in order to deny them their humanity. Thus, all Israelis, even women and children, are the enemy for Hamas activists.[64] The enemy is also made subhuman through belittlement and humiliation. Accordingly, Ian Paisley, a Protestant leader in Northern Ireland, referred to the pope as a "black-coated bachelor." A Jewish teenager, when viewing the exposed grey brain matter of one of Dr. Baruch Goldstein's victims in a photograph, laughed and said that the picture was proof that Arabs had no brains.[65] Conversely, the terrorist provides himself or herself with a positive label such as freedom fighter or mujaheed, which further justifies his or her actions.

Everyone Else Is Doing It

A final rationalization, everyone else is doing it, relates to learning theory and group psychology. The mob mentality is when people do things, which they ordinarily would not do, such as riot and loot because other people are doing them. Individuals feel more comfortable engaging in acts that are morally reprehensible when they are part of a crowd. This concept helps explain why people without criminal records join in looting during blackouts and why ordinarily well-behaved college students set fires and damage property when their favorite sports team wins a championship. Post notes that this rationalization was common among terrorists in Northern Ireland and Palestine and that it was strengthened when young adults saw their peers being honored and celebrated for their violent activities.[66] At the most extreme level, suicide bombers are more likely to feel that participating in two activities, murder and suicide, that are strongly condemned under normal circumstances is desirable when it is happening around them. Many Palestinian suicide bombers justify their actions with the claim that "others were doing it."[67]

GROUP EXPLANATIONS OF RELIGION-BASED TERRORISM

The everyone is doing it justification provides evidence of the profound influence that society and other individuals can exert that might lead someone to engage in religion-based terrorism. Groups provide an even stronger justification and rationalization for terrorism and violence and relief from personal responsibility. The group connects the individual, through indoctrination and isolation from contracting viewpoints, to the ideology and religion, which makes the violence noble and righteous. Bandura writes that groups facilitate the displacement of responsibility by allowing members to view themselves as functionaries who, as was the case with the Nazis who implemented Hitler's final solution, were only following orders.[68] Stanley Milgrim found that many ordinary Americans were willing to administer painful electric shocks when instructed to do so by an authority figure, despite cries of pain from their victims. In the face of their own moral reservations, the subjects were able to cause pain when they believed that the responsibility rested with superiors. The tendency to defer to leadership is enhanced when the authority figure is a cleric or someone with apparent divinely ordained authority. The terrorist can also displace responsibility onto other group members and the collective as a whole.

I have emphasized that terrorism is largely a group activity and that there are few lone-wolf terrorists. There has been a trend in the age of new terrorism for terrorists to be organized in small cells or franchises that operate independently of each other.[69] Even the new terrorists are trained and indoctrinated in groups, so they are still subject to group pressures, which endure when they are sent into the field. Hudson, summarizing the work of Wilfred Bion, a pioneer in group psychology, writes:

> Every group, according to Bion, has two opposing forces—a rare tendency to act in a fully cooperative, goal-directed, conflict-free manner to accomplish its stated purposes, and a stronger tendency to sabotage the stated goals. The latter tendency results in a group that defines itself in relation to the outside world and acts as if the only way it can survive is by fighting against or fleeing from the perceived enemy; a group that looks for direction to an omnipotent leader, to whom they subordinate their own independent judgment and act as if they do not have minds of their own; and a group that acts as if the group will bring forth a messiah who will rescue them and create a better world.[70]

Therefore, groups not only shape individual action, they are also inclined toward risky and violent behavior.

Groupthink

The power of the group in shaping individual behavior is summarized in Groupthink. Irving Janis concluded that group members' strong desire for unanimity overwhelms their ability to rationally evaluate alternative options and strategies. This desire for unity leads groups to display characteristics such as risk taking, intolerance of challenges to key shared beliefs, presumptions of morality, a sense of invulnerability and extreme optimism, and perceptions of the enemy as evil.[71] Groupthink, in short, both facilitates violence and provides justifications for terrorism. The peer pressure that is common in groups, particularly violent ones, represses dissent, because individuals are uncomfortable resisting a strong majority and fear being ostracized, punished, or even killed for going against the tide. As a result, groups move toward extremism because nobody wants to be left behind in supporting the group's ideals. In a terrorist group, the ideal that members compete to support is violence.[72] Concurrently, those who wish to be leaders must demonstrate that they are the most extreme and most likely to use violence.

Loss of Individual Identity

[The power of groups in shaping individual behavior is strong enough to cause people to lose their individual identities and to define themselves and their relationship with the outside world by group dynamics rather than their own preferences.] Sprinzak contends that "It appears that, as radicalization deepens, the collective group identity takes over much of the individual identity of the members; and, at the terrorist stage, the group identity reaches its peak. This group identity becomes of paramount importance."[73] Post, Sprinzak, and Denny, in their interviews with 35 Middle East terrorists, including members of Hamas and Hezbollah, concluded that membership in a terrorist organization resulted in a merging of member's identities with the group's collective identity and goals.[74] [Group members become more obedient, and the group mind-set becomes more powerful, as individuality is subordinated to the group identity.] The marginality, desire for a purpose, and weak self-identities of many terrorist recruits facilitate their willingness to replace their individuality with the group's identity.[75] Terrorist organizations facilitate this process by separating new members from society and providing ideological indoctrination along with practical training.

The significance of the fusion of individual and group identity is supporting in Donald Kinder's finding that political behavior is motivated more by group anger than self-interest.[76] For terrorists, self-sacrifice is inspired by insults, humiliations, and degradations suffered by their group, not themselves or their threats to their self-interest. Many Muslims enlist in al Qaeda's fight against the United States despite having never experienced any direct personal harm by America. Rather, they are avenging attacks on other Muslims across the globe. Eventually, the individual's personal success and feelings of prestige are linked to his or her association with the terrorist organization and its successful performance of violent acts. The power that groups wield in defining individual identity can transcend separation and distance. It is likely that the strength of the 9/11 hijackers' bond to al Qaeda and their attachment to its ideology helped maintain their dedication to their mission when they lived in the United States when planning and preparing for the attack. At the same time, they developed no new group connections while in the United States.[77] Assaf Moghadam suggests that the Internet can also facilitate group solidarity, identity, belonging, pride, and a sense of common victimization for global jihadists.[78]

Insularity and Bonding

The fusion of individual identity and group identity helps strengthen the insularity of the religion-based terrorist organization, which produces a sense of family and strong and deep bonds between group members. Here religion facilitates the crucial bonding process, as strong ties develop between members of the group, while affiliations with the outside world are limited. Scott Atran writes that "a critical factor determining suicide terrorism is loyalty to intimate cohorts of peers, which recruiting organizations often promote through religious communion."[79] Religion provides bonding experiences such as group prayer, performance of holy rituals, and providing a sense of family, which has often been missing for many terrorists. Hamas and Hezbollah use oaths, language, and rituals to produce these bonds, a sense of comradeship, and feelings of loyalty. Juergensmeyer reports that the two members of Palestinian suicide teams sign an oath that is similar to a marriage contract.[80] A Singapore Parliamentary Report on 31 captured operatives from Jemaah Islamiyah and other al Qaeda allies in southeast Asia concluded that a secret knowledge of true *jihad* created feelings of sharing and empowerment among group members.[81] Thus, religion-based terrorists kill for comrades as well as for a cause.

Boundaries

The insular and secretive nature of terrorist organizations, particularly when they maintain a strict separation from society, restricts access to contradictory information and enhances members' perception of the group's importance in providing security and a sense of belonging. W. W. Messner writes that religion helps strengthen the boundaries between religious groups and society by idealizing those within, true believers, and demonizing those on the outside, nonbelievers and apostates. As group members become detached from reality, they become paranoid and project hostile intentions onto outsiders, which provide a stimulus and justification for violence. Religion encourages this paranoia and hostile projection through its emphasis on struggles between good and evil.[82] Finally, the insularity and boundaries facilitate the fight or flight tendency discussed earlier. The fight or flight tendency is particularly significant because the outside world is a constant threat, which serves to increase group cohesion. Given that revolutionary violence is the unifying group ideal for terrorist organizations, the absence of a threat and a battle to fight makes it difficult to justify the group's existence. Members whose self- identity and purpose are defined by the group and its struggle will push the group to continue its violence because they fear that it will be disbanded. Thus, religion-based terrorist organization might engage in violence in order to perpetuate the existence of the group and to satisfy the affiliation needs of members.

Group Self-Preservation

The notion that religion-based terrorism is partly a result of the need for terrorist organizations to stay alive is supported by two studies of suicide bombings by Palestinians from the Israeli-occupied territories, which point to the development of a corporate mentality. Pedahzur and Perliger argue that the main motive for suicide bombing during the second Intifada that began in 2000 was a struggle for status, power, and market share between local terrorist networks. One network leader compared the rivalry between groups to competition between soccer clubs for status, popularity, and fans. Competing groups even began to take credit for attacks before it was certain that members of their networks had actually carried out the bombings in order to deny their rivals' public support. Pedahzur and Perliger also trace a pattern of alternating attacks by the groups and one upsmanhship.[83]

Mia Bloom also argues that Palestinian suicide bombing is aimed at gaining public support and staying ahead of rivals. Bloom points out that suicide attacks continued from 2000 to 2006 when conditions became worse for Palestinians during that period. Suicide bombings were infrequent from 1993 to 1996 because they were not supported by the public, which believed that the Oslo Accords might improve their living conditions. However, the failure to create a Palestinian state, the expansion of Jewish settlements in West Bank, and Israeli crackdowns led to increased public support for suicide bombings. Taking their cues from the public, Palestinian groups began to compete with each other with new bombings to gain public support and to discredit Yasser Arafat and the Palestinian Authority, as Israeli responses to the attacks would delegitimize the peace process.[84] Suicide bombings were also launched to avenge Israeli actions such as the assassination of Hamas and Islamic Jihad leaders and to influence Israeli politics. For example, there was a wave of suicide bombings prior to Israeli elections in 1997, which led to the victory of a Benjamin Netanyahu and a hard-line government, which stalled the peace process.

Facilitator

A final key role of groups in religion-based terrorism is that of facilitator. The organizations identify and recruit members, and individuals are often approached by terrorist organizations rather than seeking them out. The groups also plan and facilitate the bombings, although this is less the case for transnational groups such as al Qaeda, where this is done by the attack team. Merari points to the crucial role that trainers play in developing the group bonding that was described earlier and encouraging the commitment to the terrorist cells.[85] Berko and Erez describe the role of Palestinian groups:

> The organizations that produce suicide bombing provide a complete framework: wherewithal, finances, equipment, contacts and support personnel throughout the journey. These resources comprise the infrastructure without which successful missions cannot be executed. Familiarity with prospective targets. . . . Area residents' routines and security personnel schedules are also important, as is access to and information about desirable targets including the propitious time to execute a mission. Without the support network, organization and infrastructure, an individual cannot become a suicide bomber.[86]

The group also makes sure that the operative follows through with the attack. Hassan writes that during the week before Palestinian suicide bombings, two assistants stay with the martyr to be 24 hours a day. They report any signs of doubt or wavering to a senior trainer who is called to alleviate his fears, if need be.[87] Dispatchers ensure that the recruits conform to the plans, do not have second thoughts, or change their mind and fail to carry out the attack by driving the suicide bomber to the site and producing the martyr's video, where he or she provides his or her last words.[88] Sometimes the organization will compel individuals to commit a suicide bombing by threatening to expose them as collaborators with the Israelis or claiming that it is the only way to clear the reputation of a family member that is suspected of helping the enemy. In other cases, individuals are tricked and told that they will have a chance to escape before the bomb goes off or that their task is to smuggle the bomb past security checkpoints and then it will be detonated by remote control.[89] Or, the recruit is simply not told that he or she is being trained for a suicide mission until the week of the attack.

Leadership

The final key to the group's power to motivate religion-based terrorists is the leader. Chapter 1 discussed charismatic leadership and how religion facilitates this type of authority by giving the leader a divine and messianic aura. Post writes that terrorist leaders are often viewed as being superhuman because of their sanctity, heroism, and exemplary character, which inspires blind belief from their followers.[90] Often, it is the power of the charismatic leader that molds alienated and isolated individuals into a cohesive group by providing a message, a cause, and an enemy. Osama bin Laden was the avenger who stood up to the superpower. Taliban leader Mullah Omar is the man in the shadows, who engenders loyalty by the mystery surrounding him. Rabbi Kahane was the proud Jew who was not afraid to fight and offend the gentiles. Hassan's study of Pakistani and Palestinian religion-based terrorists found that many were inspired by bin Laden and other clerics who engaged in *jihad*.[91] The power of the leader is often strengthened by the weak self-identities of group members who idealize authority figures and rebuild their self-images by associating with perfection. Thus, group members have a tendency to subordinate themselves to messiah figures, who they believe will rescue them and the world. The charismatic leader often offers a dualistic view of the world, good versus evil, which encourages the narcissistic personality to project his self-loathing onto an enemy. Finally, group members can justify their immoral actions displacing responsibility to the leaders.

Psychological theories provide interesting and intriguing suggestions about the roots of religion-based terrorism. However, their explanatory power is limited, as it has been found that holy warriors are not psychopaths or severely mentally ill. Rather, researchers have described terrorists as pro-social, typical of the societies that they come from and, for the most part, normal. Interesting propositions have been put forth regarding a connection between childhood development and social learning and terrorism that make sense but are difficult to confirm through empirical research. These theories also point to developmental issues and social learning that is characteristic of many nonterrorists. Groups make individuals more likely to engage in violence by increasing risk acceptance, subordinating personal interest to group interest, and developing bonds between members. Terrorist groups develop a culture that supports violence by limiting dissent, encouraging a fight or flight mentality, developing fortified boundaries between themselves and society, and allowing members to displace responsibility for violence on to the collective or the leaders. Religion, through its division of the world into believers and nonbelievers and emphasis on the struggle between good and evil encourages the propensity for group violence. Religion facilitates terrorism because it supports many of the neutralization techniques that terrorists use to justify killing. In short, religion assures people that the violence that they are going to commit for other reasons is morally acceptable.

_____ *Chapter 6* _____

Judaism: Religion-Based Terrorism in Israel

I will present case studies in this chapter on Judaism and in the chapters that follow on Christianity and Islam, of religion-based terrorism that will illustrate how political, socioeconomic, and psychological causes, as well as historical circumstances, combine to facilitate violent interpretations of religion. The first case study considers Jewish extremism In Israel. Here, I will be looking at the extremist fringe of the religious-Zionist movement that, since 1967, has often used violence, primarily against Palestinians, in pursuit of building and maintaining settlements in the land captured by Israel in the Six-Day War, annexation of that land to Israel, and the prevention of a peace treaty that would return any of that land to the Palestinians. The last goal has led to violence against Israelis, such as Prime Minister Yitzhak Rabin, who was assassinated because he agreed to the creation of a Palestinian state in the West Bank and Gaza in the 1993 Oslo Accords. Other Jewish extremists have attempted to destroy the Islamic holy sites on Mt. Zion or Haram al-Sharif so that the Jewish Temple from biblical times can be rebuilt in their place.

I will begin with a discussion of how Judaism has gone from being associated with pacifism in the face of oppression for the nearly 2,000-year Diaspora period between the final Roman conquest of Jerusalem in 70 CE and the birth of the modern state of Israel in 1948 to a religion that is now used, by some, to support violence and terrorism. Here, I will focus on four themes from Jewish history that influence the contemporary Jewish psyche. I will then trace the development of the radical fringe of the religious-Zionist movement from the creation of the state of Israel through the period that followed that country's shocking and overwhelming victory in the Six-Day War. I will briefly outline some of their attacks on Palestinians during the 1980s, attempts to destroy the Islamic holy sites in Jerusalem, and later events such as the assassination of Yitzhak Rabin. Throughout, I will identify crucial historical factors that explain the violence by radical religious-Zionists in Israel and consider whether Israeli democracy facilitates or inhibits terrorism.

THE FOUR THEMES OF JEWISH HISTORY IN THE DIASPORA

The ancient Israelites, like other peoples of their time, used violence to achieve political goals, as war was used to conquer the Promised Land following the Exodus from Egypt, and the ancient kingdoms of Israel and Judea were involved in frequent conflicts with their neighbors. When the biblical Jewish kingdoms were overrun by powerful enemies, terrorism and guerilla warfare were used against the occupiers as well as traitors who tried to accommodate them. The Hasmoneans (Maccabees), using guerilla tactics, successfully rebelled against the Seleucid Empire, but the Sicarii's campaign of terror against the Roman conquerors of Palestine failed, and the Jews were forced into exile. The results of the violent revolts against the Romans, including the capture of Jerusalem, the destruction of the Second Temple, enslavement, massacres, and the beginning of the Diaspora, and exile from the land of Israel, and a final uprising from 132 to 136 CE, which led to the banning of Jews from their holy city, had a profound effect on Jewish attitudes toward violence. Violence and armed insurrection were viewed as leading only to catastrophe and were to be avoided, particularly now that almost all Jews lived in the Diaspora as minorities ruled by Christians and, later, Muslims.

The calamitous revolts against the Romans and later persecution and violence by the Christians and, to a lesser extent, the Muslims who ruled them created passive Jewish communities that tried, and were forced, to separate themselves from the rest of society and to avoid instigating the wrath of the their gentile rulers. Thus, the passive ethic of Diaspora Judaism and the rejection of the warrior ethic of the biblical kingdoms are explained by the loss of a state and by conditions of powerlessness and vulnerability. The loss of the Promised Land and its central role in Judaism is the first of four important themes of Jewish history that help explain today's radical religious-Zionist terrorism. In the Torah, God made a covenant with Abraham and gave him and his descendents the land of Canaan (Israel) for eternity. The Exodus story details the miraculous return to the Promised

Land, in which the biblical kingdoms of Israel and Judea were later located. The city of Jerusalem is of particular significance because that is where the first and second temples, the centers of religious ritual and worship, stood. Thus, Judaism, unlike Christianity, holds one specific geographical location as being the most sacred place on earth, and living on that piece of land is part of the core essence of Judaism.

The importance of the land of Israel increased during the Diaspora as Jews yearned and prayed for a return to their homeland and an end to their persecution, suffering, and exile. However, the return of the Jews to their homeland, the rebuilding of the Temple, and the reestablishment of a Jewish state in the Promised Land would only happen with the coming of the Messiah (*Mashiach*) and not by human action, which could lead to disaster and God's wrath. Thus, the return to Zion became intertwined with a passive ethic and a growing emphasis on messianic redemption. This messianic vision is the second important theme of Jewish history that supports today's radical religious-Zionism. As will be seen, a transformation to a more assertive posture toward establishing a Jewish state in the land promised to Abraham and messianic redemption resulted from changing political and historical conditions that began with the Zionist movement at the end of the 19th century and intensified with the Holocaust, the birth of the state of Israel in 1948, and culminated with the 1967 Six-Day War. With the state of Israel in existence and the capture of Jerusalem and other holy sites in 1967, some began to believe that the process of messianic redemption was unfolding and that it was their obligation to help it along.

A third important theme of Jewish history is that the Jews are a righteous and outnumbered people, that is, facing calamity or destruction, but God intervenes to save them in their time of need. This scenario first occurred in the liberation from slavery in Egypt and repeated itself in the struggle with Amalekites while wandering the desert, the conquest of Jericho when the Jews began to retake the Promised Land, the battle between David and Goliath, the Maccabees' victory, and the defeat of Haman in the Book of Esther. The prophets, however, had warned that the corruption of the kings of Israel and the Temple priests would lead to God's wrath. Therefore, the Jews not being saved from the Roman onslaught was viewed as a sign of God's disfavor by the survivors and exiles. God also did not intervene in the countless other calamities including massacres, inquisitions, and pogroms that befell the Jews during the Diaspora. Anti-Semitism and persecution continued into the 20th century, even in places where Jews attempted to assimilate, and 6 million Jews were slaughtered during the Holocaust. Consequently, many Jews began to believe that God could not be counted on and that they had to take matters into their own hands, which inspired the founding and growth of the Zionist movement to create a Jewish state in the land of Israel. Ironically, the success of this endeavor would eventually cause a growing number of Jews to believe that God was, once again, rescuing the Jews in a time of need and that the period of messianic redemption had begun.

The history of persecution and maltreatment that began with the pharaohs of ancient Egypt and that continued in most places where the Jews have lived outside of the land of Israel created the fourth important theme of Jewish history; the Jews are very different from other people and, as a result, are always hated by non-Jews. Therefore, Jews should always be wary of gentiles and outsiders. The sense of difference and distrust of others was strengthened by being forced to live apart from the non-Jews who surrounded them, which also caused Jewish communities to usually be insular and isolated. This "Jews are different and despised" ethic was challenged in the late 19th century as a growing number of Jews in the West sought to end anti-Semitism by assimilating with their Christian neighbors or supporting secular-universalist movements such as socialism and communism. Others believed that the Jews would never gain acceptance from their gentile neighbors and that the only real solution to the problem of anti-Semitism was the creation of a national Jewish homeland.

ZIONISM

The latter group, led by Theodore Herzl, began the Zionist movement, which eventually led to the creation of the modern state of Israel in 1948. The Labor-Zionist ideology ran counter to three of the four themes of Jewish history discussed above, the obvious exception being the centrality of the land of Israel.[1] The Zionists believed that a Jewish state would happen only through human action, not messianic redemption or God's will, and that a Jewish homeland was the cure for anti-Semitism. Labor-Zionism was also a cautious and pragmatic ideology as represented by the Jewish Agency's (the Jewish pre-state administrative body in Palestine) decision to accept the UN 1947 partition plan, which gave the Jews half of Palestine and half to the Arabs, the withdrawal from the Sinai following the 1956 war against Egypt, and a willingness to negotiate a settlement following the Six-Day War that would have returned some of the territories gained in the conflict to the Arabs.[2]

The secular-socialist Labor-Zionist movement viewed traditional religion negatively or, at best, ambivalently because it held that Jews should strive to become a people like others, which would be accomplished through labor, agriculture, and building a modern state based on social justice and equality. In contrast, the emphasis on separation, difference, and holding to traditional observance in the ghettos of Europe only led to backwardness, persecution, and anti-Semitism. Jewish culture, history, values, and love of the land of Israel were admired, but the Jewish religion was not. The religious community largely rejected Zionism because it was in direct opposition to the notion that the return to the Promised Land and the creation of a Jewish state could take place only with the coming of the Messiah and because of the Labor-Zionist's rejection of traditional religion.[3] Most branches of Orthodox Jewry only grudgingly accepted Zionism after World War II because the Holocaust had shown that a place of refuge had been needed when Jews faced extermination.

The overwhelming majority of Israel's Orthodox community did not see the modern state of Israel as a fulfillment of a divine plan for the Jewish people or the beginning of the messianic era during the years from independence in 1948 up to the 1967 Six-Day War. In fact, the religious-Zionist National Religious Party served as a junior partner in coalition governments headed by the secular Labor Party and pragmatically focused on building its network of schools, kibbutzim (collective farming settlements), and youth movements; controlling the ministry of religion; and demonstrating that Orthodoxy was compatible with modernity.[4] One exception was Rabbi Abraham Kook, the chief rabbi in Palestine during the British Mandate period, who wrote that the Zionist movement signified the beginning of the period of redemption and the messianic era. According to Kook, the secular Labor-Zionists were doing God's work without realizing it. Thus, it was his and Orthodox Jewry's job to convince the nonreligious majority that their seemingly secular endeavor was part of a divine plan that would lead to the ingathering of all of the Jewish exiles, control of all of the land promised to the Jewish people in the Torah, a nation based on Jewish law (*Halachah*), the coming of the *Mashiach,* and the rebuilding of the temple. Kook's views were largely rejected during his lifetime by the Orthodox community.[5]

THE EFFECT OF THE 1967 SIX-DAY WAR

Israel's shocking and overwhelming triumph in the 1967 Six-Day War caused major upheavals in the country's religious and political cultures as the victory took on divine overtones and the cautious and the pragmatic ethic of Labor-Zionism was replaced by a more confident, aggressive, and expansionist outlook, as the country was in a state of euphoria and triumphalism.[6] When considering the magnitude of Israel's triumph against the armies of three countries with huge advantages in manpower and weapons, the victory took on a religious dimension, as it appeared to be a miracle from God. "There was a feeling in the country that anything was now possible. We had shown that we had the might and we knew that God was on our side. The only thing that could stop us from marching toward redemption was a lack of desire."[7] This religious interpretation of the victory was further enhanced by Israel's capture and control of three crucial parts of biblical Israel, the Western Wall of the Temple Mount, the old city of Jerusalem, and the lands of Judea and Samaria.[8] Kook's notions of Zionism being divinely ordained, messianism, and settling the holy land being the fulfillment of a religious commandment now became the foundation of the ideology that gave root to violent, extremist religious-Zionism.

After Rabbi Abraham Kook's death in 1935, his son, Tzvi Yehuda, preached his father's message regarding the divine nature of Zionism and predicted, one month prior to the Six-Day War, that a great event was about to happen. Naturally, he claimed, after the war, that the great event was Israel's victory; the unification of Jerusalem; and the capturing of the Kotel (Western Wall), Judea, and Samaria. According to Kook, it was now an imperative for every Jew to go and settle in those lands that had been promised to them, as descendents of Abraham, in the Torah.[9] In addition to giving the modern state of Israel religious meaning, the war also served to reinvigorate the other three themes of Jewish history, which had been rejected by Labor-Zionism. The return of the Jews to the homeland; the creation of the state of Israel in 1948, which had also involved a miraculous military despite overwhelming odds; and the triumph in 1967 now appeared to be evidence that after nearly 2,000 years God had finally stepped into save the Jews when they appeared to be headed for destruction. Messianism was used to explain the tragedy of the Holocaust as some believed that a period of suffering and tribulation, footsteps of the Messiah, will precede the arrival of the *Mashiach*.[10]

The Six-Day War also helped strengthen the "Jews are different and always hated" theme of Jewish history. Despite the creation of a state that resembled the other nations of the world, Israel was surrounded by Arab enemies who sought its destruction. Thus, the Jewish state, like the Jewish people, really was different, and the Jews had always survived in the Diaspora by maintaining their uniqueness and adhering to the precepts of their religion.[11] However, it was now clear that militancy, vigilance, and the aggressive pursuit of security, rather than passivity and appeasing the Gentiles, were the keys to survival. Passivity had led only to persecution, massacre, and, eventually, the Holocaust. In contrast, Israel's preemptive strike against

Egypt and Syria in 1967, its well-trained and well-armed military, and its refusal to yield to international pressure to return the land that it had captured in the war to its previous Arab owners signified that the Jews had returned to being the warrior nation marching into battle with God's support that it had been in biblical times.[12]

THE BIRTH OF THE RELIGIOUS SETTLEMENT MOVEMENT

The birth of an assertive religious-Zionist movement that aimed to settle the land captured in the Six-Day War, particularly the old city of Jerusalem and Judea and Samaria (West Bank), and more radical fringes that hoped to bring about the coming of the Messiah by reasserting Jewish control over the Temple Mount and removing all Arabs from Israel and its occupied territories were also facilitated by changes in Israel's Orthodox community. During the 1970s, the National Religious Party fell under the sway of a Young Guard, which had studied in the state's religious school system, belonged to its B'nai Akiva youth movement, served together in religious army units, and attended the same yeshivas. As a result, this generation of Israeli Orthodox Jews was more self-confident, aggressive, and less fearful of alienating the secular majority than their parents. They were also attracted to the settlement and messianic oriented ideology of the Kooks and became the backbone of the Gush Emunim movement that was launched to settle the West Bank and lobby for its annexation to Israel.[13] Ironically, Israel's being caught off guard at the beginning of the 1973 war and the anomie and disarray that followed facilitated the rise of Gush Emunim and its increasingly aggressive behavior.

The first Jewish settlers moved into the occupied territories in 1967 and illegally occupied a hotel in Hebron in order to stake their claim in a city where Jews were massacred in 1929 and where the Torah writes that Abraham, Isaac, and Jacob are buried. Kiryat Arba, a Jewish city, was soon built nearby, but the cautious and pragmatic Labor Party limited the construction of Jewish settlements to areas that were vital to Israel's security and to reestablishing those that had been lost to Jordan in the 1948 War of Independence.[14] The religious settlers, like the original Zionists who came to Palestine at the turn of the 20th century, did not foresee or even intend to cause conflict with their new Arab neighbors. The settlers thought that coexistence was possible, that the Palestinians would adjust to their presence, and that second-class status under Jewish rule was still better for the Palestinians than when they were ruled by the Jordanians and the Egyptians.[15]

An important consequence of the near catastrophe in the 1973 war and the malaise that followed was the end of the Labor Party's monopoly on power in 1977, when the Likud Party narrowly prevailed in elections. Israel's near defeat in the opening days of the October 1973 war with Egypt and Syria severely tarnished the Labor Party's reputation, and its yielding to strong international pressure to make concessions following the war made it appear defeatist. Gush Emunim took advantage of the Labor Party's decline and campaigned to be the new representative of a hopeful future, Israel's founders' pioneering spirit, and the settlement ethic. Gush Emunim, during the period following the war, held numerous marches and demonstrations calling for the settling and annexing the West Bank. To the religious right and other Israelis, the new national role model was a religious soldier wearing a knitted *kippah* (skullcap) with a weapon in one hand and prayer book in the other.[16] For many religious and some secular Israelis, Gush Emunim's campaign to settle the occupied territories was the cure for the postwar sense of defeat and vulnerability.

The Likud's Revisionist-Zionism, which shared a common outlook and key goals with Gush Emunim, also capitalized on the mood of the country. Although secular based, revisionism is more hospitable to religion than Labor-Zionism and is rooted in the territorial integrity of the land of Israel. It also has a messianic tone, which places great importance on miraculous events and stresses the uniqueness of the Jewish people and the inevitability of conflict with the gentile world.[17] The first Likud prime minister Menachem Begin and his predecessor Yitzhak Shamir were both advocates of settlement and maintaining Israeli control over the West Bank. They also saw the contemporary conflict with the Arabs and Palestinians in terms of the historical struggle for Jewish survival against hostile non-Jewish nations and peoples. Thus, the National Religious Party, which had strong support in Gush Emunim, and other smaller settlement–oriented parties helped the Likud form coalition governments in 1977 and 1981.

THE RETURN OF THE SINAI AND THE START
OF THE JEWISH UNDERGROUND

It would seem unlikely that the religious right, with its goals of settlement and annexation of the land promised to Abraham in the Torah, would need to resort to terrorism because it had an interest group with a strong voice, Gush Emunim, to lobby for its agenda; political parties in the government to pursue its agenda; and a governing coalition, headed by Likud, that shared its goals.[18] Here the question of how religious groups behave in a democracy becomes relevant. In chapter 3, I argued that representative government helps repress terrorism because there are a number of legal means that can be used to have a group's demands represented in law and government policy. Democracy provides governments legitimacy, as citizens believe that the government has the right to rule them, even if they disagree with its policies. Groups will accept defeat if they feel that they have had an opportunity to make their case and that they could prevail in the future. At the same time, terrorism is usually counterproductive in democracies because of backlash, as most people condemn the use of violence in pursuit of political goals because nonviolent channels are available to pursue agendas. On the other hand, it could be that religious radicals will use violence, regardless of the type of political system, because they answer to a higher authority and view any human-made law as illegitimate. Thus, the key question is how did the religious-Zionist movement react when it did not get its way?

This question, at first, appeared to be moot, because Begin and the Likud did as was expected and greatly expanded the construction of settlements in all of the occupied territories (West Bank, Gaza, Golan Heights, and Sinai Peninsula). On a symbolic note, Begin made it mandatory for government documents to refer to the West Bank by its biblical names, Judea and Samaria. He also went to Elon Moreh, a Jewish outpost near Nablus where settlers had been evicted eight times under the Labor government before they were finally permitted to stay in 1976, and said that "there would be many more Elon Morehs."[19] However, Egyptian president Anwar Sadat, less than six months into Begin's term, announced that he was prepared to go to Israel in pursuit of peace. A historic visit and address to the Israeli Knesset (parliament) took place in November 1977, the Camp David Accords were signed in 1978, and a peace treaty between Egypt and Israel followed in 1979. These developments were seen as a significant threat to Gush Emunim and its allies because the Camp David Accords provided a framework for the development of an autonomous Palestinian entity in the West Bank and Gaza, while the peace treaty provided for the return of the Sinai, which now had 7,500 Jewish settlers, to Egypt. Gush Emunim's friend, Begin, was willing to compromise on maintaining Jewish sovereignty over the entire biblical Land of Israel and to please Arab, Egypt, and the non-Jewish United States, neither of which could be trusted.[20]

The return of the Sinai to Egypt and the evacuation of Yamit, Israel's largest settlement in the area, were pivotal in stimulating violence by some members of the religious-Zionist settlement movement, which suggests that religious extremists are not pacified by democracy. Gush Emunim had launched a major public relations campaign and funded the Movement to Halt Retreat from Sinai, which sent thousands of protesters to Yamit to thwart the Israeli army's forced evacuation through passive resistance. However, there was solid support among Israelis for the peace process and the withdrawal, so Yamit was evacuated, and the Sinai was returned to Egypt. As a result, Gush Emunim's leadership began to believe that Begin was too soft, and a sense of uncertainty developed over the future of the settlements in the West Bank.[21] Therefore, the settler movement and the religious-Zionists made it their goals to eliminate further opportunities for peace and territorial compromise, using extralegal means if necessary.[22]

The sense of threat increased as the Palestinians began to become more militant and to respond violently to Israeli occupation. Israel's war with the Palestine Liberation Organization in Lebanon in 1982 caused further anxiety among Jewish settlers in the West Bank because they feared that the local Palestinians would rise up in support of their brethren. The birth and growth of the Peace Now movement, which opposed settlement and advocated territorial compromise, presented another threat to the religious-Zionists.[23] In 1983, Emile Grunzweig was killed by a grenade that had been tossed at demonstrators at a Peace Now rally. Another setback for Gush Emunim occurred in Israel's 1984 elections, which resulted in a joint Labor–Likud unity government with Labor's Shimon Peres, a dove and perceived enemy of Jewish settlements, serving as prime minister from 1984 to 1986. That and a severe financial crisis led to a near halt in construction of new settlements.

The sense of threat and the loss of confidence in the government translated into the launching of the Jewish Underground (Machteret) and the first widespread attacks against Palestinian Arabs. Vigilantism and harassment were used as tools to pacify and control the Palestinians. From 1980 to 1984, there were 380 attacks against Arab individuals that resulted in 23 killed, 191 injured, and 38 abducted, while there were frequent acts of vandalism on homes, cars, stores, and other property (including 41 involving places of worship).[24] Attacks by the Jewish Underground were often in response to terrorist acts committed by Palestinians. After 6 Jewish settlers were killed leaving a synagogue in Hebron, where 450 Jews live surrounded by 160,000 Arabs, the Israeli authorities deported several Arab leaders to Lebanon. The Jewish Underground, feeling that the government was not protecting them or responding harshly enough to Arab terror, booby-trapped the cars of four Arab mayors with bombs, which maimed and paralyzed the mayors of Nablus and Ramallah. An Israeli security agent was blinded when trying to defuse one of the bombs. The murder of a yeshiva student in Hebron was followed by the killing of three Arab students at that city's Islamic University. Attacks on Jewish busses led the Jewish Underground to place bombs on Arab busses that were found by Israeli security before they could explode. The cycle of Arab attacks being met by Jewish vigilantism, justified by the claim that the government was not doing enough to protect the settlers, continues today.

THE TEMPLE MOUNT FAITHFUL

A more extreme and potentially destructive violent reaction to the Camp David Accords and the evacuation of Yamit was the formation of a group that intended to blow up the Muslim holy sites, the Dome of the Rock and the al Aqsa Mosque, on the Temple Mount in Jerusalem where the Second Temple had stood. After Israel's capture of the old city of Jerusalem in the Six-Day War, the government decided that control of the Temple Mount area would remain in the hands of the Islamic Waqf, which administered the shrines, and that Israeli Jews would not be permitted to enter. This was done to assuage Arab and Muslim fears that the Jews wanted to take over their holy sites. The ban was supported by Jewish tradition because only the high priest had been permitted in the most sacred area of the Temple, the holy of holies. Given that it was not known where that area was and that there were no high priests, Jews could be prevented from entering the area.[25] Groups that formed to prepare for the rebuilding of Solomon's Temple following the Six-Day War were peaceful and were content to wait for the coming of the Messiah.[26] However, the despair caused by the Camp David Accords, the previously discussed threats to Jewish settlement and control of all of the land of biblical Israel, and the possible prevention of messianic redemption caused a small group to believe that radical action was needed to reverse the course of history and the policies of the Israeli government.[27]

Yehuda Etzion, one of the leaders of the group that conspired to blow up the Muslim holy sites, had intended to launch the attack before the evacuation of Yamit but could not find a rabbi who would approve the operation. Etzion and his conspirators were more radical than their counterparts in Gush Emunim, as they did not accept the legitimacy of the Israeli government because of its decision to let the Islamic Waqf maintain control of the Temple Mount.[28] To Etzion, the Islamic shrines were abominations that had to be removed for the redemption process to take unfold. He claimed that the Islamic authorities were desecrating the sacred land by building more shrines, digging, and undermining the foundation, which was causing humiliation to the Jews.[29] Since the secular Israeli government was not taking action, it was beholden on individual Jews to act so that the Messiah would come, the Temple would be rebuilt, and a theocratic government using the law of the Torah would be established.[30] Etzion's group, which included military veterans with expertise in explosives, had acquired grenades and bomb-making materials before they were discovered by Israeli police. Another group that was caught digging tunnels below the Temple Mount and stockpiling arms had planned to violently take control of the area and hold prayer services.

The Jewish terrorist threats to the Temple Mount between 1980 and 1984 exemplify many of the key connections between religion and terrorism that were discussed in chapter 1. The destruction of the Muslim holy sites was seen as God's will, which overrides the laws and policies of the Israeli government. The plotters hoped to bring about the coming of the Messiah and the creation of an eschatological vision, the World to Come. Clerical approval was also important as Etzion had delayed the attack because he was unable to a find a rabbi who would sanction the bombing. Failing to obtain rabbinical support, another conspirator, Dan Be'eri, turned to sacred Jewish texts to justify the planned bombing and claimed that his personal interpretation had led him to conclude that blowing up the Islamic holy sites was supported by Jewish law and tradition.[31] Given the religious motives of Gush Emunim for settling the West Bank and the Temple Mount Faithful for blowing up the Islamic holy sites and both groups' use of extralegal violence to influence or counter government policy, it would appear that these are cases of religion-based terrorism that cannot be moderated by democracy.

THE IMPORTANCE OF HISTORICAL CIRCUMSTANCES

It is still important, despite the importance of religious ideology and political setbacks, to investigate other causes of extremist religious-Zionist violence and terrorism. The use of violence to achieve redemption and control of the biblical land of Israel is as much a result of historical circumstances as it is a result of texts and theology. Earlier I discussed the significant role that the Holocaust, the creation of the modern state of Israel, the Six-Day War, the Yom Kippur War, and the Camp David Accords played in stimulating the creation of an aggressive settlement-oriented religious-Zionism. The land of Canaan (Israel) is promised to Abraham in the Torah as an inheritance for him and his descendents. The first and second temples on the Temple Mount in Jerusalem were the centers of the biblical Jewish commonwealths. Thus, the desire to control the entirety of the land promised to Abraham and the Temple Mount and live in Israel are religious imperatives for some Jews today that inspire violence. It is important to remember, however, that these obligations were put aside during the 1,900-year Diaspora period and that it was mandated by religious authorities that the return to the Promised Land could only come with messianic redemption, which could not be brought about with human action. As stated, their passive orientation was a result of exile being viewed as God's punishment, the disastrous rebellions against the Romans, and the vulnerability of living as a minority in Christian and Muslim lands.

One also has to wonder if returning to Zion and settling the land would have remained as important part of the Jewish psyche if the Jews had not been persecuted, had been allowed to integrate in the lands where they lived, and had been treated as equals. The Zionist movement was strongest in Eastern Europe, where Jews were treated the worst and suffered the most. At the same time, Jewish immigration to Israel, even among Orthodox Jews, from the United States and Canada, where Jews have gained equality, suffered the least anti-Semitism, and obtained a comfortable standard of living has been never more than a trickle.[32] In recent years, most American immigrants to Israel have been Orthodox, and a significant number of the residents of the more religious settlements in the occupied territories are from the United States. However, most North American Jews, including religious ones, are not willing to give up their comfortable lives to move to Israel, let alone to an isolated outpost on the West Banks surrounded by hostile Arabs, and take up arms to defend the right to reside on the land promised to them in the Torah. Many Israelis who move to the West Bank do so because of the comparatively low cost of housing rather than religious zeal.

It is also important to note the significance of the Zionist aspect of religious-Zionism. Gush Emunim and the settlement movement are as much a product of the original secular, socialist Zionist movement as they are of Jewish texts and theology. The original Zionist pioneers exhibited a strong love of the land, which was exemplified in the establishment of kibbutzim (farming collectives) and an emphasis on agriculture. Although they did not believe in God or the divine origins of the Torah, they still were strongly motivated by the strong historical and cultural connection between the Jewish people and their homeland.[33] Like religious settlers in the West Bank, the original settlers were rugged pioneers who often had to defend themselves and their outposts from attacks by their Arab neighbors. The emphasis on the land of Israel continued after modern Israel was created as love of the land was emphasized in school curriculums, youth movements, and scouting.[34] There was even a brief Canaanite movement that hoped to create a Hebrew-speaking nation in Israel that was divorced from the Jewish religion. Thus, the religious-Zionists viewed themselves as the inheritors of the original pioneering and settlement ethic of the country's founders and have claimed the right to defend themselves when the governing authorities did not provide adequate protection.

A FRONTIER MENTALITY AND ISOLATION

A frontier and vigilante mentality is also a cause of violence by religious-Zionists in Israel. Ehud Sprinzak wrote that the settlers who founded many of the religious-Zionist communities on the West Bank viewed themselves, as did the original Zionist pioneers, as a rugged breed of frontiersmen and doers, who took matters into their hands. It is important to remember that some of the West Bank settlements, like many Jewish settlements in pre-Israel Palestine, were, at first, illegal. Just as the original Zionists had challenged the British authorities, some of the enthusiasm and spirit of the settlement movement came from challenging the government by establishing illegal outposts, conflict with the Israeli police and armed forces that attempted to remove them, and surviving in a hostile and dangerous territory. Thus, friction with neighboring Arabs was a sustaining force, and the belief that the government was not protecting them made vigilantism and incremental violence a way of life.[35] A survey in the early 1990s found that 25 percent of Gush Emunim settlers had engaged in vigilantism and that 65 percent of residents of the settlements approved of retributive violence to keep the Palestinians in line. Many believed that not reacting was a sign of weakness and that the Arab mind and culture only respect people in power who exercise their authority through the use of force.[36] With the perception of constant Arab threat that had to be repressed and the support of their community, the vigilantes could easily justify violence as a norm.

The frequent use of retributive violence and its high level of community support harken back to the fight or flight tendency that is commonly found in groups. Gush Emunim and the religious settlers were clearly a group that defined itself in opposition to others, Arabs and Israeli Jews who opposed settlement. The boundaries between them and their Arab neighbors were clearly defined and fortified psychologically and physically with razor wire, fences, and weapons. The insularity and isolation of the more ideological settlements sharpened the sense of danger and threat and the need to respond with violence. Group solidarity was further strengthened by the separation of religious-Zionists from secular Israelis and the socialization that religious settlers underwent as youths and young adults. They attended religious public schools, yeshivas, and youth movements, which taught the importance of settling the West Bank and control of the biblical land of

Israel. Some served in special army units that allowed military service to be combined with religious study. Thus, most adapted the values of their community; developed a strong sense of loyalty, belonging, and purpose; and had little contact with those with opposing views.

The religious settlers also carried the weight of Jewish history, which taught that Jews were different and were hated for it. They lived in a Jewish state that was constantly under threat from hostile Arabs and a world that never seemed to understand the righteousness of their claim to the land. These feelings of threat and isolation were exacerbated by their choice not to live in the pre-1967 borders where they would be part of a Jewish majority, and, instead, purposefully settled in places where they would be a minority surrounded by Arabs who resented and fought against their presence. The settlers viewed the hostility to their presence from their Arab neighbors as being the usual hatred that Gentiles harbored toward Jews rather than being a result of their settlements often having been constructed on land that had been expropriated from the Palestinians, the second-class status of the Palestinians, and the military checkpoints that served to protect them caused significant hardship and humiliation to their Arab neighbors.

The isolation of the religious-Zionists in Gush Emunim and the settlements led them to generally hold the view, in contrast to Labor-Zionism, that the Jews are an abnormal people, who can't be like other nations because of their covenant with God, who chose them for a unique and divine destiny. Others did not understand that because of their chosen status and the divine commandment to possess the land of Israel, they did not have to abide by the laws of other nations. The hostility of the Palestinians and the international community's failure to recognize Israel's claim to the land was also proof of Israel's choseness and unique mission. At the same time, the historical hatred of Jews was now represented in animosity toward Israel and the settlers. They viewed the Arab–Israeli conflict and their struggles with local Palestinians as being the latest battle in the Jew's long history of being confronted by forces of evil. The Palestinians were seen as being the descendents of Israel's ancient enemies, the Canaanites, Amalekites, Midianites, and the Ishmaelites, whose only purpose was to oppose and eliminate Israelis and Jews. Thus, peace with the Arabs was impossible and the land had to be settled, with force when necessary.[37] Shlomo Aviner, a Gush Emunim leader, stated:

> We experienced the opposition of the goyim to the state of Israel even before it was established. The enmity which the peoples of the world show towards the Jewish people has been present throughout history. It's like has not been

shown to any other people . . . it goes beyond all historical or rational explanations. Various economic, sociological etc. explanations have been advanced
to explain the European holocaust. We don't deny them but they certainly do
not suffice. It simply must be recognized that there is an inner instinctual en-
mity on the part of the nations of the world toward the Jewish people.[38]

RABBI MEIR KAHANE AND KACH

The messianic, land centered Jews are different and hated by others but
will always prevail because God is on their side ideology is best exemplified
by the late Rabbi Meir Kahane and his Kach movement. Kach was notorious for instigating vigilante violence against Palestinians in the West Bank
and harassing and assaulting left-wing Israeli activists and politicians. In
1984, Kahane was elected to the Israeli parliament with the platform of
transferring all Arabs from Israel and the occupied territories—with force—
if necessary, removing the Muslim shrines from the Temple Mount, and replacing Israel's democratic political system with a theocracy based on Torah
law.[39] Kahane's paranoia and ethnocentrism were rooted in his conclusion
as a youth that African Americans in New York City were anti-Semitic and
out to hurt Jews and that another Holocaust was imminent. Consequently,
he founded and organized the Jewish Defense League (JDL) to oppose anti-
Semitism and attacks on Jews with force. The group later turned its focus
on the Soviet Union because of that country's refusal to let its Jewish population emigrate, and several bombings of Soviet targets in the United States
were attributed to the JDL.[40] Kahane's call to violence and message that
America was rife with anti-Semitism and that Jews were facing a holocaust
from African Americans and neo-Nazis were largely ignored by the greater
Jewish community. Under investigation by the FBI, Kahane, a former informant with ties to the Mafia, moved to Israel in 1971, where he identified a
more serious threat to the Jews—Arabs and Palestinians.[41]

Kahane preached a theology that Ehud Sprinzak labels "catastrophic
messianism," which reflects the messianic and Jews are hated because they
are different, and land of Israel themes of Jewish history. According to Kahane, the Messiah would come in a time of great conflict in which the Jews
would triumph. Anything that humiliated the Jews was an affront to God
and would reverse the messianic process. Thus, it was the Jews' obligation
to sanctify God's name through avenging every drop of Jewish blood and
responding to every act of Arab terror with Jewish terror.[42] The sanctification of God (*kiddush Ha'shem*) through violence represents a radical shift,
as, historically, the concept had been interpreted as taking one's own life

rather than renouncing Judaism. Kahane's violent *kiddush Ha'shem* represents the move from the minority Diaspora Jew at the mercy of the gentiles to the strong, religious Israeli Jew that has power over the Palestinian Arabs. Kahane also rationalized violence against Arabs by claiming that since Jews were victims for so long, self-defense was a demonstration of love for Israel.[43] Kahane's focus on the new empowered Jew could also be seen in his dehumanizing of Palestinians, who he claimed to respect but demonized as being an epidemic and germ that was poisoning the Jews. Secular Jews were labeled as Hellenizers who were destroying the Jewish people and had to be eradicated as the Maccabees had done to Jews who had supported the Seleucids.[44]

Sprinzak writes that Kahane was also mobilized by the peace treaty with Egypt and the evacuation of Yamit, which led him to conclude that Begin, his former hero, could not be trusted. Then he began to attack the legitimacy of the Israeli government and actively plotted violence against the Muslim shrines on the Temple Mount after Camp David.[45] Therefore, Kahane provides further evidence that religious radicals will turn on democratic institutions when they cannot achieve their objectives through legal channels. Even though Kahane turned the Kach movement into a political party, ran for office, and served in Israel's parliament, his ultimate goal was to use legitimate politics to, ultimately, bring about the fall of Israeli democracy. Kahane and Kach, however, were the radical tips of Israel's right-wing iceberg and had thousands of supporters in the settlements and within Israel. Other political parties in the Knesset at the time, such as Moledet, also called for transfer of the West Bank Palestinians. One of Israel's chief rabbis, Mordechai Eliyahu, who Kahane viewed as a spiritual mentor, eulogized him at his funeral. Kach and Gush Emunim cooperated in the Jewish Underground in the 1980s. Kahane Chai, the group formed by his followers after his death, participated with Yesha, the governing board of the West Bank settlements, in mobilizing the opposition to the 1993 Oslo Accords and campaigning to destroy the credibility of Yitzhak Rabin.[46] Kahane and Kach, legally and extralegally, have represented the interests of a small and radical portion of the Israeli population that is tied to the more mainstream right and shares many of its political objectives.

Kahane was also very much a political creature who thrived on being in the limelight and maintaining power within the JDL and Kach. Sprinzak suggests that Kahane turned to violence and causing friction with the Palestinians, in part, to remain in the news when Gush Emunim began to gain attention and to claim the mantle of being the defenders and champions of the land of Israel in the 1970s.[47] Kahane was also noted for being an autocratic leader who tolerated no dissent, dismissed those within Kach and the JDL who became too powerful or garnered too much attention, and devoted significant efforts to fundraising.[48] Kach and its violence might partly be attributed to the need of an emotionally disturbed man to satisfy his over-blown ego. At the same time, Kahane went to Israel's low-income develop-ment towns and neighborhoods and played on class and ethnic anger—not religion—to appeal for votes from Israel's Sephardim (Jews from Arab lands), who had been discriminated against by the Ashkenazim (Jews of European descent) when they immigrated in the 1950s. Kahane played on their anger and frustration and claimed that the government was favoring Israel's Arabs with generous subsidies, while they, as Jews in a Jewish state, struggled. He went as far as accusing the Labor Party and the Ashkenazim of letting Arabs seduce Jewish girls.[49]

BARUCH GOLDSTEIN

Kahane's catastrophic messianism and xenophobic worldview can also be seen in one of his followers, Baruch Goldstein, a Kach member who mur-dered 30 Arab Muslims at the Cave of the Patriarchs in Hebron in 1994. Goldstein, like Kahane, believed that the dawn of the messianic era was sub-ject to human events and would come during a period of conflict. He also shared Kahane's view that sacrifice and violence sanctified God's name and that all Arabs were threat and should be expelled from the West Bank.[50] Three events caused Goldstein to believe that messianic redemption was being threatened. The first two were the Oslo Agreements and the ongoing peace process that would have led to the creation of the Palestinian state in the West Bank along with a freeze on the construction of new settlements, which meant that Jewish control of all of the biblical land of Israel was threatened. The third was hearing an Arab youth allegedly shout "Kill the Jews" at the Tomb of the Patriarchs in Hebron on the eve of the holiday of Purim and the Israel military guards doing nothing. To Goldstein, the hu-miliation of a Jew at a holy site on a holiday needed to be met with drastic action that would reverse the setbacks to Israel's messianic destiny, which led him to return the next day and exact his revenge.[51]

Goldstein's religious motives are undeniable, but other factors helped cause his massacre. One crucial influence was living in a place where vio-lence against Arabs was a way of life and viewed positively. Goldstein, al-though a follower of Kahane, was a doctor and healer, who once treated an Arab wounded by the Israeli military, and was not a thug who took part in vigilante attacks against Arabs.[52] Even so, Kiriyat Arba, the settlement where Goldstein lived, is a Kach stronghold where most supported Kahane's conflict-oriented ideology, and Arab baiting was the norm. The support for violence against Arabs in Kiryat Arba is evident in the 1,000 people who attended Goldstein's funeral, the shrine that exists to him in the town's center, and that he is viewed as a hero and martyr. Goldstein's personal experience as the town physician and security chief exacerbated the usual sense of threat and potential catastrophe that is experienced by Jewish settlers in the West Bank, as he regularly saw cars that were damaged by stoning and those who were killed and injured by Arab attacks on settlers.[53] Thus, his massacre might have been a reaction to life under siege and living in a community that supported vigilante violence against Arabs. Finally, those who knew Goldstein report that he had become restless, bitter, and withdrawn following the murder of his hero, Kahane, and that his massacre was an act of revenge.[54]

THE ASSASSINATION OF YITZHAK RABIN

The assassination of Prime Minister Yitzhak Rabin in 1995 provides another example of an Israeli religious extremist using violence to carry out God's will and to change the policy of the country's democratic government. Yigal Amir, a religious law student who had served in a combat unit in the army, killed Rabin to stop the peace process with the Palestinians, to punish Rabin for being a traitor to the Jewish people, and to stop the spilling of Jewish blood. Amir used Jewish law to justify his actions, claiming that Rabin's agreement to the creation of a Palestinian state in the West Bank and Gaza made him a *mosser,* someone who illegally hands over Jewish property to a Gentile, and a *rodef,* someone who facilitates the murder of Jews. The penalty for both of these crimes is death. According to Yoel Lerner, an extremist who approved of the assassination, Amir's action was equivalent to disarming some who had a gun pointed at the head of the Jewish people.[55] Amir was motivated by a book commemorating the death of Baruch Goldstein, particularly a chapter on revenge and terrorism as *kiddush Ha'shem* and the importance of Jews acting strongly and powerfully to be worthy of their divine mission as the chosen people. He was also inspired by the catastrophic messianism of Goldstein and Kahane and the belief that humiliation and weakness in the Jewish state would halt the process of redemption. Consequently, revenge against enemies like the Arabs and traitors like Rabin was an expression of an individual's love of God.[56]

Amir, like Goldstein, did not have a history of violence or a background that suggested metal illness. Although some of his comrades in the military noted that he often used excessive force on Palestinians, he was never cited or disciplined and was promoted.[57] It is more likely that Amir's actions were influenced, like members of the Gush Emunim in the 1980s, by the socialization and the separation that is characteristic of the religious-Zionist community. He attended religious schools as a youth and served in an army unit that combined military service with religious study. Amir attended Kerem' D'Yavneh yeshiva, which serves the sons of religious nationalists and is focused on the settlement of the land of Israel.[58] He went on to pursue his law degree at Bar Ilan, Israel's university that is geared toward the country's Orthodox population. There, he was active in a group that supported the West Bank settlements and opposed the Oslo Agreements. He also associated with leaders of the religious-Zionist and settlement movements, such as Rabbi Moshe Levinger, who had participated in violence, allegedly including murder, against Palestinians in the past.[59]

THE CONFLATION OF NATIONALISM AND RELIGION

It is important to recognize the conflation of nationalism and religion in Israel's religious-Zionist community. As discussed, zealots like Kahane, Goldstein, and members of the Temple Mount Faith view themselves as defending the state of Israel as much as the Jewish people or religion. Amir is no different as he used the words Israel and Jewish people interchangeably when explaining his actions. "It began after Goldstein. That's when I had the idea that it's necessary to take Rabin down. I'm sorry about the words. I'm not that kind (of person). I have never murdered before, and I love this country very much; I love this people (Jewish)."[60] I have discussed how the notion that the Jews are hated and under constant threat has helped shape the psyche of the religious-Zionist and settler communities in Israel. The constant feeling of existential threat is also a product of Israel's brief history. The country has fought four major wars and many minor skirmishes with its Arab neighbors. It has endured a variety of terrorist attacks, suicide bombings, and missile strikes from Palestinian groups and Hezbollah. It is likely that the constant state of war and hostility has helped facilitate the violent actions of religious extremists like Yigal Amir to head off what they perceive to be as impending catastrophe. The Israeli government, itself, has invaded Lebanon on three occasions, destroyed an Iraqi nuclear reactor, hunted terrorists across the globe, and apprehended a flotilla bringing supplies to Gaza in its quest for security.

The Israeli government commission that investigated Rabin's assassination concluded that Amir acted alone and was not part of a conspiracy, but he, as was the case with Gush Emunim, Kahane, and Goldstein, enjoyed the support of a segment of Israel's population and was also at the tip of Israel's religious-Zionist iceberg that includes strata that act within the law and strata that flirt with the boundary of the law. So far, I have suggested the Israeli religious extremists use violence to influence government policy when they lose political battles. Sprinzak argues that the connection of the radicals to groups and institutions that share their goals but operate within the law and use legitimate politics to achieve their goals both represses and encourages violence.[61] One boundary that was not crossed after the grenade attack that killed Emile Grunzweig at the Peace Now rally until the assassination of Rabin was killing Jews because that would tarnish the settlement movement. Violence has very rarely been used against the Israeli Defense Forces, even when Yamit was evacuated, illegal outposts were removed in the West Bank, and the Jewish settlements in Gaza were abandoned in 2005. Generally, resistance has been passive, involving insults and taunts and the throwing of fruit and other objects.

RELIGIOUS EXTREMISM'S TIES TO THE MAINSTREAM

It is also the case that Israeli democracy and the radicals' connection to the mainstream empower and facilitate violence by the radical religious-Zionist fringe. Here, Israel is somewhat unique in that its terrorists often share many of the goals and objectives of its governments, particularly when the Likud is in power. As a result, Israeli governments have implemented policies that have turned a blind eye, if not encouraged, violence by the radical fringe, and courts have usually imposed weak sanctions and punishments on Jewish terrorists when they attack Arabs. Groups that don't use violence, themselves, as was the case with Rabin's assassination, have created an atmosphere that encourages extremism. The encouragement of law-breaking activity by the religious-Zionists is rooted in the Labor government's inability to develop a clear policy about what to do with the occupied territories after the Six-Day War. Unwilling to annex them and with no Arab government willing to negotiate with Israel until 1977, a military government and administration were established. With the lack of a clear policy, the failure to evict the settlers who took over a hotel in Hebron in 1968, which resulted in the construction of Kiryat Arba as a compromise, and the allowing of limited settlement, Gush Emunim was able to flout the law and create facts on the ground, which they have continued to do since.[62]

Two justice systems are responsible for law and order in the territories: the military courts that implement severe punishments for Palestinian terrorists and Israeli courts that tend to be lenient with Jewish vigilantes and terrorists. Palestinian terrorists are given long prison sentences or are deported and have their homes destroyed or sealed. In contrast, 20 of the 27 members of the Jewish Underground who were convicted in the earlier mentioned attack on Arab mayors, attempted bus bombings, and other acts of violence in 1984 were free by September 1986. Eight were pardoned for their crimes, and those who remained in jail were given furloughs for holidays and reduced sentences. In 1987, 40 of the 120 members of the Israeli parliament voted to give amnesty to members of the Underground. The Israeli president (largely a ceremonial position) at the time, Chaim Herzog, supported the amnesty as did several members of the governing Likud Party, who abstained from voting.[63] A Likud Knesset member expressed his empathy, "My heart goes out to the detainees. These boys are the pride of Israel. They are the best."[64] Political pressure was used to block the investigation of the attack on the Arab mayors.[65] These expressions of support by political officials and leniency by the courts for Jewish terrorism, while Arab terrorists were punished severely, gave the impression that the government was giving free reign to the Jewish extremists.

A reason, other than a shared to desire to build settlements and maintain control of the occupied territories, for the government's behavior was the support that the Underground had in Israeli society. An opinion poll in 1985 found that their activities had the approval of 25 percent of Israelis, 20 percent favored blowing up the Islamic sites on the Temple Mount, and 35 percent favored expelling the Arabs or denying them their rights.[66] Given that most of the Underground's supporters vote for Likud and parties further to the right, it is likely that the government was trying to mollify a key constituency. The Likud further facilitated vigilante violence against Palestinians by allowing settlements to provide for their own security and allowing settlers to perform their yearly reserve service in their settlements. Consequently, settlers performed security operations where they rampaged through Arab villages to take revenge for acts of violence such as stone throwing. The Israeli military usually did little to stop these operations, and those who committed acts of violence or destroyed property were rarely found, and charges were usually dropped when they were arrested.[67] It is also important to remember that the Israeli military has often been accused of using harsh and extreme tactics in the occupied territories when dealing with Palestinians uprisings, treating the Palestinians with disdain and disrespect, and using torture against Palestinian prisoners.[68] In short, the government sanctioned a wild-West atmosphere in the occupied territories, and the second-class status of Palestinians encouraged settler violence and terror.

It also appears that the radical tip of the right-wing religious iceberg actually moved the base to the extreme, rather than the opposite. The idea of

Jewish control over the Temple Mount, which was considered a fantasy in the 1970s, eventually became more mainstream. In 1986, 50 Israeli rabbis ruled that ordinary Jews could enter the Temple Mount and pray and that it was a sacred duty.[69] Every year on the last day of the festival of Sukkoth, Gershom Shalom led a march to the Temple Mount to pray and lay a cornerstone for the new temple. In 1990, his actions helped cause a riot by Palestinians, which lead to six Arab deaths. In 2000, Ariel Sharon, surrounded by a phalanx of soldiers, visited the Temple Mount as a precursor to Israel's 2001 elections to demonstrate Israeli sovereignty over the area. Many credit that visit as being a catalyst for the second Palestinian Intifada. Five months later, Sharon's Likud Party was victorious. Kahane's idea of transferring Israel's Arabs, which was once considered extreme, is now advocated in limited form by the Yisrael Beitanyu Party, part of the current governing coalition, which would transfer areas of Israel with high percentages of Arabs to a Palestinian state.

Extremists have also made violence against Israeli Jews more acceptable. Although Amir acted alone, the assassination of Rabin took place in the context of a campaign to destroy him personally and vitriolic rhetoric. Moshe Peled of the Tzommet political party stated that the Oslo Accords were "an act of national treachery and in treachery the rules and tools must be broken."[70] Elyakim Ha'etzni, a former parliament member and founder of Yesha, called on the army to revolt and compared Rabin to Hitler and the French Vichy government.[71] Yesha set up an Action Headquarter, led by Ya'akov Novick, who had threatened the life of the police chief of Jerusalem (no charges were filed), with the objectives of destroying Rabin's credibility and ruining him personally. Kach was actively involved in the campaign with the approval of Yesha and members of the Likud Party. A young Likud leader ordered his followers to make Rabin's life a nightmare, and the prime minister was heckled with shouts of "murderer," "traitor," and "son of a whore."[72] A group of rabbis gathered outside of Rabin's residence one month before his assassination and chanting a mystical curse, "Pulses of Fire," calling for his death.

Amir, despite the revulsion of most Israelis, still had his supporters. News of Rabin's assassination was met with cheers at Bar Ilan University, and a website was created celebrating his actions, which led to him becoming a teen idol for a group of religious girls.[73] The threats and vitriolic rhetoric were repeated when hard-line Likud prime minister Benjamin Netanyahu signed the Wye River Memorandum in 1998 that committed Israel and the Palestinians to implementing the 1995 agreement creating a Palestinian state and again, in more severe form, in 2005 when Ariel Sharon, who had left Likud to form the centrist Kadima Party, decided to evacuate the Jewish settlements in Gaza and their 7,500 settlers. As had been the case with Yamit, angry demonstrations and marches were held and soldiers implementing the evacuation were met with passive resistance, taunts, and insults, but little violence occurred. Sharon suffered a stroke and cerebral hemorrhage in 2006 and went into a coma.

It appears that a constant state of warfare and threat of terrorism and the socialization and separation of the religious-Zionist community have created an atmosphere that is conducive to catastrophic messianism and interpretations of Judaism that legitimize vigilante violence and terrorism against Palestinians and Jewish traitors. At the same time, the government's soft treatment of those who commit acts of violence against Arabs and allowing a wild-West environment in the West Bank further encourage Jewish vigilante violence and terrorism. As a result, Jewish extremists have often felt comfortable resorting to violence against Palestinians when government decisions and policies work against their goal of settlement and annexation of the West Bank and Jewish control of the Temple Mount because they perceive that they have the tacit support of a significant minority of Israel's population and political elites. Violence against Jews and the Israeli army is a line that has rarely been crossed, with the glaring exception of the assassination of Yitzhak Rabin. However, the latest generation of religious-Zionists has increasingly used violence when resisting removal by Israeli soldiers.

The failure to settle the conflict between Israel and the Palestinians is likely to facilitate violence by religious radicals on both sides. As will be discussed in chapter 8, Palestinian opposition to Israeli occupation has grown more severe and become more religiously rooted over the past 25 years. The Likud government, as of January 2012, remains committed to building and expanding West Bank settlements, despite American and international opposition. Each new settlement creates a new point of friction and conflict with the Palestinians, which further radicalizes Palestinian resistance and, subsequently, Israeli harsh responses. At the same time, Jewish settlers become more emboldened with each new victory and fact created. In contrast, the 1993 Oslo Agreements and their widespread support actually led to an interlude of passivity and relative quiet for Israel's religious radicals, and Gush Emunim dissolved during this period.[74] Unfortunately, a series of suicide bombings by Hamas and the opportunity created by the failure to fully implement the Oslo Agreements reinvigorated Israel's religious warriors. Given the current stalemate, threat of Palestinian terror, and a hardline Likud government that views the religious-Zionists as a key ally, Jewish vigilante violence and terrorism should continue in the near future.

Christianity: The Troubles in Northern Ireland and Antiabortion Terrorism in the United States

Christianity, in contrast to Judaism and Islam, appears to be in an era of relative peace, as, currently, there are few acts of terrorism and violence in the name of Christ. Most recent cases of Christian religion–based violence have involved conflicts with Muslims in Bosnia, Lebanon, the Philippines, Nigeria, Indonesia, and other places. As was discussed in chapter 4, these clashes are rooted in political and economic grievances such as demands for independence; autonomy; and more equitable distributions of political power, resources, and wealth. Ultimately, the conflict in Bosnia was resolved with that country gaining its independence, and the Lebanese civil war ended with a power-sharing agreement that more fairly represented the populations of the country's religious groups. Contemporary examples of religion-based violence and terrorism by Christians against Christians are limited to the troubles in Northern Ireland. Thus, I will look at this case to determine the extent to which religion was responsible for the violence between Protestants and Catholics. Christianity, unlike Islam, is not often used as an ideology for dissident violence against secular regimes. Here, I will look at the example of radical antiabortion terrorists in the United States.

WHY IS THERE SO LITTLE RELIGION-BASED TERRORISM IN THE CHRISTIAN WORLD?

Before proceeding to the case studies, I will briefly consider explanations as to why Christianity is in this period of relative peace. It might be, as some contend, that Christianity is an inherently peaceful religion. It is important, however, to remember the historical instances of violence motivated by Christianity such as the Crusades, the Inquisition, and the Thirty Years War, as well as religiously motivated attacks against Jews in the Christian world that continue to this day. It can be argued that the paucity of contemporary Christian terrorism and violence is a result of the early development of a separation between religion and politics in Christianity, as Jesus said "Render unto Caesar the things which are Caesar's, and unto God the things that are God's."[1] Yet, Christianity eventually became the state religion of the Roman Empire. The notion that Christians should accept secular authority is called into question by St. Augustine, who wrote in the *City of God* that there is overlap between the earthly city and the godly city and that the temporal city should facilitate the creation of the City of God on earth.[2] At the same time, most European, Catholic kings in the Middle Ages claimed divine right, rule ordained by God, and the authority to control the affairs of both church and state within their kingdoms. However, the pope, as Christ's representative on earth, asserted that he not only had control over the affairs of the church but also those of the state, including the right to depose of Catholic kings. Ultimately, this struggle for power was resolved with the Concordant of Worms, which gave kings the power to invest bishops with secular, but not religious, authority and to call on them for military support.

The Protestant Reformation is often credited as being the beginning of the modern separation of church and state.[3] According to Martin Luther, there is an earthly kingdom, which was ruled by law and included that which could be seen or felt by the body, and a heavenly kingdom, which includes faith in Christ alone. In addition to separating the spiritual and the temporal, Luther argued in *On Secular Authority* that there could be no coercion of religious belief and that civil government's role is to keep the peace and protect life and property but not to interfere in spiritual matters.[4] The separation of church and state became one of the cornerstones of the Liberal political philosophy that became the foundation of the American, French, and other revolutions against monarchies and other authoritarian forms of government in the West. As a result, opposition to despotism in the Christian world was secular-based, and there was little demand for religion-based government. In contrast, Islam has not had a similar reformation; a lack of religion-based government is a key grievance of many Islamic terrorists, and Islamic law extends into the realm of the temporal as well as the spiritual. As discussed in chapter 6, Orthodox Jewish terrorists in Israel call for the replacement of Israel's largely secular-based government with a religious one based on Torah law.

The Protestant Reformation and the subsequent separation of church and state are important causes of the decline of religion-based terrorism and violence in the Christian world in both predominantly Protestant and Catholic nations. However, it is interesting to note that the violent fringe of the antiabortion movement in the United States is largely Protestant and claim Luther and other reformation theologians as ancestors. Members of this group advocate Dominion and Reconstructionist theologies, which call for a theocracy in the United States based on bible law. The Rev. Ian Paisley, a leader and inspirational figure for Protestant militants in Northern Ireland, has also called for the intertwining of church and state. Protestant evangelicals in Africa have led violent campaigns against witches and homosexuals that have led to murders. Some of their theology is also taken from the writings of key figures of the Protestant Reformation such as Luther and John Calvin. Once again, radicals are able to find justifications for violence in the same teachings that are used by the mainstream to call for religious tolerance. Consequently, nonreligious factors are needed to explain the relative lack of religion-based terrorism in the Christian world.

One possible explanation is that most nations of the Christian world, including those in North America, most of Europe, Australia, New Zealand, and much of Latin America are democracies. In contrast, many of the most fundamentalist and intolerant forms of Christianity are occurring in Africa in countries with authoritarian governments or where democracy is unstable. Almost all of the terrorism in the Christian world since World War II, however, has been leftist, socialist, and Marxist based, which suggests that Christianity, because of the legacy of the Protestant Reformation, is not viewed as an ideology that is useful for motivating violent resistance to unfair government. Rather, Christianity has motivated nonviolent campaigns for political change during the civil rights movement in the United States and in opposition to authoritarian government in Latin America. Another explanation rests in the West's role as a colonizer during the 18th and 19th centuries, its continued military and economic dominance in the 20th century, and American world hegemony following the fall of the Soviet Union.

Bernard Lewis, as discussed, argued that the roots of Islamic rage are its subordinate position to the West after being the leading global civilization for centuries. In contrast, most individuals in the Christian world are generally satisfied with the global pecking order, as they usually have been the colonizers and the occupiers, while Muslims, Hindus, Sikhs, Buddhists, Animists, and other faiths have been the colonized and the occupied. The modernization and globalization processes discussed in chapter 4 originated in the West and have facilitated the spread of Western culture and, until recently with the rise of Japan, China, India, and other Asian nations, have largely benefitted Western Christian nations. It is also important to note that most of the wars between Christian nations and nations with other faith traditions in past 200 years have been initiated by the Christians, although for primarily nonreligious reasons. In short, Christians generally live in countries that provide legal channels for the pursuit of political demands and in a world where their nations are not threatened and are often privileged. The threat of Muslim terrorism, however, has led to violence against Muslim in the United States and Europe and an increased tendency, by some, to portray the war on terror as a conflict between Christianity and Islam.[5] In Norway, Anders Breivik, a Christian who killed 77 people in July 2011, wrote a rambling 1,500 page manifesto that discussed his hatred of Muslims and fear that they are taking over Europe. If Christians continued to feel threatened by Islam, a rise in retributive Christian terrorism and violence is likely.

THE TROUBLES IN NORTHERN IRELAND

The violent conflict between Catholics and Protestants in Northern Ireland from 1969 to 1998 exemplifies the multidimensional nature of religion-based violence and terrorism. Although religion played an important role in solidifying and sharpening the divisions between Catholics who wanted Northern Ireland to unify with Ireland and Protestants who wanted it to be annexed by Great Britain, several of the causes of religion-based terrorism outlined earlier including colonialism, occupation, ethnic division, discrimination, and inequality are of equal or greater importance. Northern Ireland represents a very rare case of violent conflict between Catholic and Protestant Christians in the last 300 years. If Protestants and Christians have lived in peace in all other parts of the world, it is unlikely that the theological and organizational differences between the two forms of Christianity are significant enough to cause the bloodshed and terrorism that plagued Northern Ireland. In the end, the two sides were able to agree to a peace agreement and share power despite their enduring religious differences.

Historical Background

The contemporary Troubles in Northern Ireland can be traced back to the Norman invasion of 1172 and the assumption of control of Ireland by the kings of England. For the next 500 years, the English ruled Ireland from walled fortresses, while the Irish peasants controlled the countryside. The Irish clans and tribes were divided, which prevented them from removing the occupiers. The Irish were devoutly Catholic, and the church became the primary unifying force in the fragmented society. As a result, the church would play an important role in the Irish nationalist movement that developed in the 19th century. The beginning of the conflict between Catholics and Protestants and Irish resistance to British occupation have their roots in King Henry VIII's separation from the Catholic Church and creation of the Church of England (Anglican). Naturally, the devoutly Catholic Irish resisted British attempts to spread Protestantism in Ireland. The expropriation of prime agricultural land and the displacement of natives, the subsequent settlement by English and Scottish Protestants, and the creation of the Plantation of Ulster generated the ethnic and religious cleavage that exploded in 1969 in Northern Ireland. The division was sharpened by the Plantation's expansion and further displacement of Catholics. In 1649, Oliver Cromwell led an invasion of Ireland to put down a Catholic revolt and suppress attacks on Protestants. Thousands of Catholics were massacred, and hatred of the British and the Protestants intensified. The cleavage between the Protestants and Catholics strengthened in 1689 when James II, a Catholic challenger for the British throne, used Ireland as a base to revolt against King William.[6]

The Protestants in Ireland, as would be expected, supported King William, and a group of skilled workers, "The Apprentice Boys," held off the Catholics forces of James II during a siege at Derry. Eventually, they were relieved by William's army, which defeated the Catholics in 1692 at the Battle of Boyne River ending the revolt and solidifying English control over Ireland. As a result, Protestant loyalties remained with Britain, while Catholics viewed the English as occupiers and aspired to Irish independence. From that point on, the Irish Catholics fought to remove the British occupiers and struggled against the Irish Protestants, who disproportionately controlled wealth and land, staffed the government apparatus and the military, and were viewed as an extension of the occupying force. The ethnic division between Catholics and Protestants was heightened by Protestant marches each year, often through Catholic neighborhoods in Northern Ireland, commemorating and celebrating their victory in the 17th century.[7] Also, Catholics had suffered from frequent famine and starvation during British rule, while the Protestant plantations prospered and exported crops for profit. The presence of the large Protestant population in Northern Ireland led to the partition of the island in 1922, as the 26 southern counties gained independence, while the 6 northern counties gained home-rule and remained part of the United Kingdom. The struggle between Catholics and Protestants was now concentrated in Northern Ireland, where Catholics sought unification with the Irish Free State (later renamed the Republic of Ireland), while the Protestant majority, fearful of becoming a minority in a unified Ireland, pressed for the continuation of home rule and inclusion in the United Kingdom. The second-class status of Catholics in Northern Ireland continued during the period of home-rule, as they were politically and economically oppressed by the Protestant government. The government bureaucracies and the police forces, Royal Ulster Constabulary (RUC) were almost exclusively Protestants. Consequently, the RUC became a tool for the maintenance of Protestant dominance and was feared and hated in Catholic neighborhoods. John McGarry and Brendan O'Leary write that the situation in Northern Ireland was similar to that in the American South where a majority group used its power to control a minority group through disenfranchisement, economic discrimination, cultural oppression, police repression, and discriminatory administration of justice.[8] The result was a Protestant dominance and sense of entitlement because of their loyalty to the British government, while Catholics were shut out of desirable skilled labor occupations, were relegated to low-wage positions, and lived in inferior housing. By 1969, Catholics and Protestants lived in segregated working class ghettos that were maintained by ethnic cleansing and fire bombings.[9]

The entrenchment of ethnic animosity, Protestant feelings of besiegement, and British ambivalence that were characteristic of Northern Ireland were evident in an attempt in 1965 by liberal Northern Ireland prime minister Terence O'Neill to institute reforms that would provide more opportunities for Catholics. The British, unwilling to commit the resources for direct intervention to aid the Catholics, instead, pressured O'Neill to make changes. O'Neill, however, faced resistance from hardliners in his Protestant community, which feared that any power for Catholics would lead to a decline in their own status. Richard Rose writes that the reforms were too little and too late to satisfy Catholics and that O'Neill was eventually defeated by the Protestant hardliners.[10] Consequently, the Catholics formed the Northern Civil Rights Organization and attempted to employ the strategies of the American civil rights movement such as marches, demonstrations, and nonviolent resistance in a campaign for equal rights within Northern Ireland. In 1969, the Catholics began a series of marches and demonstrations, which were banned by the Northern Ireland Protestant authorities. Protesters were often harassed and attacked by the RUC and its part-time reserve force, the B-Specials.[11] Civil rights protesters were gassed and beaten by the RUC and B-Specials in a march from Londonderry to Belfast in July 1969. On August 15, Protestants, during their annual marches commemorating their 17th century triumphs, were stoned by Catholics. Police pursuing the Catholics were met by barricades and Molotov cocktails. The Protestants, aided by the RUC and B-Specials, attacked Catholic neighborhoods and full-scale rioting ensued.[12]

The 1969 Demonstrations and Riots

The 1969 riots marked a crucial turning point in Northern Ireland, as the British were finally forced to intervene and send troops to control the violence. At first, the Protestants welcomed the intervention because they believed that the British would be an impartial arbiter and that they would no longer be at the mercy of the RUC and the B-Specials. The British, however, took a very heavy-handed approach to restoring order and ignored rules of engagement, which led to conflict with the Catholics and their Provisional Irish Republican Army. The occupiers began to imprison those suspected of violence without trials, conduct trials without juries, and invade homes in search of suspects and weapons. In 1972, a British paratrooper unit broke up a Catholics civil rights march in Londonderry with excessive force killing 13 demonstrators. The event, known as "Bloody Sunday," helped facilitate the rise of the extremist Provisional IRA, and soon violence was used by Catholics against the Protestants and British troops. Catholic anger was further fueled when the government commission that investigated the shooting exonerated the British soldiers who were involved. The British also shut down the Northern Ireland parliament at Stormont, which strengthened the hand of Protestant extremists, who began to act against British forces, as well as the Catholics.[13]

The failure of the Catholic civil rights marches, the violence in 1969, and the British occupation ended the period where the conflict was viewed as a campaign for equality and fairness in Northern Ireland and transformed it into an ethnic clash between Catholics and Protestants and a Catholic struggle against occupation. During the 1960s, the Irish Republican Army had taken a more Marxist, class struggle approach, refrained from using Catholic and nationalist rhetoric, and emphasized the achievement of equal rights as British citizens. This strategy led to a split in the IRA and the formation of the Provisional IRA, which called for an ethnic struggle against the Protestants and later the British occupiers. According to Connor Cruise O'Brien, the Provisionals, despite their claim that they did not hate Protestants, appealed to fierce nationalism and Irish Republicanism and a call for blood shaped their agenda.[14] The oppression by the British led to the reuniting of the Official IRA and the Provisionals and a focus on fighting the British army and removing its soldiers from Irish soil. Each British crackdown and overreaction to acts of civil disobedience strengthened the hands of extremists on both sides, and Catholic hopes of being full citizens in Northern Ireland disappeared.[15] The result was 25 years of intercommunal violence and terrorism, attacks on British forces, bombings in Great Britain, and disciplinary violence against suspected traitors and collaborators by both sides.

The Role of Religion

The presentation of the historical background of the Troubles in Northern Ireland has offered a number of causes for the violence and terrorism including colonialism, occupation, ethnicity, discrimination, and religion. There is disagreement over religion's role as a cause of the conflict in Northern Ireland. Connor Cruise O'Brien argues that religion played an important role, as Catholicism has historically been intertwined with Irish nationalism. The Catholic Church was a major supporter of the rebellion against the British in 1916, and Irish nationalism was propagated by the Christian Brothers order. The 1937 constitution made the Catholic Church the guardian of the faith in Ireland, including the six counties under British control. It was during the revolutionary period that the notion of becoming a martyr by dying for the cause of independence became a part of the nationalist movement.[16] According to O'Brien, religion elevates anyone who is willing to die or kill for the republic to a Christ-like figure. Bobby Sands, a Provisional IRA member who died in a prison hunger strike in 1982, saw himself as following in a line of Irish martyrs whose sacrifices were similar to those of Jesus, who also did not save himself when offered the opportunity by the Roman authorities that persecuted him. Sands had been encouraged by a priest to take up arms for his oppressed people.[17]

Adversaries, as is always the case in a holy war, are agents of the anti-Christ and must be shown no mercy. Consequently, Protestants, British soldiers, traitors, and even British civilians have been killed indiscriminately and treated ruthlessly. The notion that religion strengthens the emotional mystique of Irish nationalism, for which some are willing to die, was seen at IRA funerals where religious symbols, such as the crucifix and the rosary, were blended with nationalist emblems such as the tricolor flag representing a unified Ireland.[18] Although some priests, both in Northern Ireland and the Republic, supported the IRA and failed to denounce its violence, the Catholic hierarchy condemned IRA violence and called terrorism counterproductive to achieving an equitable resolution to the conflict. Catholic clergy were not involved in IRA violence and were not leaders of the nationalist movement. Religious nationalism was not taught in Catholic schools but propagated itself in the home, where religion and nationalism merged.[19]

The influence of religion on the Protestant side is more difficult to assess because the community is fragmented into different denominations. Mainline Protestant churches, such as the Church of England and the Presbyterian Church, although unionist, have not supported violence. Much attention has been paid to Rev. Ian Paisley, a fundamentalist who formed his own church, the Free Presbyterian, because the mainstream Presbyterian Church was too moderate. Paisley calls for a theocracy and openly mixes unionism with religion, as his church flies the flags of Ulster and Britain and has plaques honoring those who died fighting for the United Kingdom. He has referred to the Vatican as a demonic force, and one of the goals of his World Congress of Fundamentalists is to expose the crimes of the papacy. He is also extreme politically, as he founded the Democratic Unionist Party when the Unionists were becoming too moderate, and he labeled Protestant leader, David Trimble, as being a traitor for accepting the Good Friday Agreement.[20] For Paisley, religion was a tool to produce extremism, which would counteract more moderate Protestant elites who made conciliatory gestures toward the Catholics.[21] Another Protestant militant, Billy Wright, said that religion provides moral sanction for violence encounters and that he has "the right to defend and die for what we believe is the truth."[22] Thus, religion was mixed with unionism and used to justify violence in the far right of the Protestant community. Fundamentalists, however, were a very small part of the Protestant community as only 0.8 percent of Protestants (roughly 12,400 individuals) were members of Paisley's Free Presbyterian Church in 1991.[23]

It is difficult to label religion as being the primary cause of the violence in Northern Ireland. As mentioned, the Catholic hierarchy condemned violence, as did most Protestant clergy.[24] Also, the Second Vatican Council in the early 1960s had repudiated the notion that Protestants are heretics and that the Catholic Church is the only path to salvation. Although Northern Ireland is the most religiously observant place in Europe in terms of church attendance, secularization took place during the Troubles, as church attendance declined, the divorce rate rose, and the number of children born out of wedlock increased.[25] It is hard to argue that the Unionists wanted to become a part of Great Britain for religious reasons because that country is highly secular and its Anglican Church is hardly fundamentalist. It is important to add that cultural matters are often merged with religion, as Catholics and Protestants in Northern Ireland, as well as pundits and commentators, usually identify cultural characteristics, rather than theological issues, when discussing key differences between the two communities. Catholics are usually labeled as being willing to submit to authority and hierarchy, while Protestants are more independent minded. Protestants are influenced by charismatic clerics, while Catholics owe allegiance to the Vatican. Protestants are fragmented, but Catholics are a unified community.[26] It is these cultural differences rather than the relatively minor theological disagreements that separate Protestants and Catholics that were usually played on to ferment ethnic hatred.

It is important to note that there was an effort to marginalize religion during the height of the violence, as key political parties and organizations on both sides shunned religious names and terminology and maintained purely political objectives. Both sides rarely targeted clerics and houses of worship for violence. Of greatest importance, most Northern Irish did not view the conflict as being rooted in religion as only 13 percent of Protestants and 12 percent of Catholics labeled religion as being the primary cause of the troubles in a 1986 survey, while political and constitutional issues were ranked as being most important by 35 percent of Protestants and 32 percent of Catholics.[27] The fact that intermarriage is extremely rare has often been pointed to as evidence of the salience of religion in the conflict, but this statistic is also influenced by the segregation between Catholics and Protestants in housing, education, and social life. In short, the barriers that prevent intermarriage are more based on ethnic affiliation than church policy, as non-religious Catholics and Protestants also do not intermarry.[28]

Religion in Northern Ireland is best identified as being a factor that strengthened the ethnic divide between Protestants and Catholics and helped unify each community. Michael Burleigh writes that religious rhetoric was used by wealthy Protestant landowners to gain the support of the working class for the Unionist cause, while Catholic appeals to religion were often rooted in past injustices committed by Protestants.[29] McGarry and O'Leary conclude that religion was less important than national political identity, distribution of political and economic power, and historical experience in dividing Catholics and Protestants. They add that theological differences between Catholicism are minor, but the differences between the secular, civil religions were major, as each community worshipped its own nation in an exclusionary manner.[30] At the same time, ethnic and racial partitions in other parts of the world that have not been supported by a religious divide have also led to violence. In the end, the religious division in Northern Ireland remained after the Good Friday Agreements were reached. It was not secularization or ecumenism that ended the conflict but each community's willingness to compromise on its exclusive national vision.

Colonialism, Settlement, and Occupation

The original cause of the Troubles that created two national visions in Northern Ireland, as discussed, was British colonization and occupation because there would have been no Troubles if the British had not conquered Ireland and transplanted its citizens onto the most fertile land in the north of the island. All occupations are inherently unstable, and the British, as would be expected, granted Southern Ireland, where Catholics and Republicans were the overwhelming majority, independence because controlling the south became too difficult after World War I. The role of colonization and occupation in Northern Ireland is more nuanced, as the Protestant majority wanted to remain part of the United Kingdom. The Protestants could not be considered colonizers or British settlers in 1969 because they had been living in Ireland for more than 300 years and had developed a unique Irish identity. The British, however, were responsible for facilitating the Protestants' sense of entitlement because they had received preferential treatment during the long period of occupation, while the Catholics were second-class citizens in their own land. As loyal British citizens, the Protestants viewed their domination of the home rule government from 1922 to 1972 as their right. They also used the political and economic advantages that they enjoyed during home rule to keep Catholics out of government positions, the police, and desirable professions.[31]

Ian Lustick argues that the large-scale settlement in the 16th and 17th centuries is an important antecedent of the conflict in Northern Ireland that erupted in 1969. Because the settlers were given preferential treatment and became the dominant class, England never earned the loyalty of the natives and was not able to co-opt the local elite. The settlers also saw it as being in their interest to keep the locals politically and economically subordinate. Consequently, settlers interfered with and prevented British conciliatory policies such as Catholic emancipation in the early 19th century, an attempt to gain loyalty and stability when the French were threatening to attack Ireland. Lustick goes on to blame the intransigence of the settlers for preventing Ireland from being incorporated into Great Britain, which would have meant equal rights for Catholics but a reduction of their own power and influence.[32]

The settlers purposefully used their dominance to ferment Catholic opposition and violence, which was then used to justify the denial of equal rights for Catholics and real democratization. As a result, a caste system was created that left the dispossessed natives with a lasting legacy of bitterness and hopes for a golden age after the settlers were removed, which made political accommodation, even years later, difficult.[33] Richard Rose concludes that Northern Ireland was a fragmented society both internally and externally because the Protestant settlers had been separated from the host country long enough to develop their own interests and to resist British control.[34] The settlers helped cause internal fragmentation by insisting on including areas with large Catholic populations in Northern Ireland. If these areas had been allowed to remain in the Irish Free State, the partition may have been tenable to Ireland and the Catholics.

British and Irish Policies

The British are not without blame as their policies, as well as those of the Irish government after independence in 1922, served to foment the conflict in Northern Ireland. Britain chose not to employ either of the two strategies that would have likely prevented the conflict in Northern Ireland, near complete subjugation of the local population, as was the case in Australia and North America, or integration of Ireland into Great Britain, as was the case with Scotland. Again, the second policy was largely prevented by the intransigence of the Protestant settler population. Britain, however, chose a policy of neglect as Ireland and, later, Northern Ireland was viewed as another far away colony rather than a neighbor. During the period of home rule in Northern Ireland, Britain's major political parties did not attempt to organize there, which might have facilitated a sense of connection to the mother country.[35] Like all colonial overlords, Great Britain's actions were based on its own interests. Conciliatory gestures were made during times of threats such as the early 1800s. Otherwise, the British did not want to allocate funds and resources to a people that many viewed as being atavistic. As would be expected, the British were more interested in exploiting than integrating Northern Ireland and did not make significant efforts to share markets or establish a fair legal system and allowed the Protestants to resist Catholic demands for equal rights.[36]

Serious errors were made by the British in the period leading up to the outbreak of hostilities in 1969. Westminster's policy was not to intervene in Northern Ireland and to let the home rule parliament at Stormont handle local affairs. They mistakenly counted on O'Neill to control the Protestant right-wing and make changes fast enough to prevent the outbreak of violence. The inaction by Britain's Labor Party continued in 1968 when the IRA was planning disturbances to commemorate the Easter massacre, and it also had become clear that sectarian violence was inevitable without reform.[37] Britain did not act and, according to Connor Cruise O'Brien, was hoping to shed its responsibility for Northern Ireland and disengage. Therefore, it had no real will to take on the IRA and defeat them. Britain's lack of intervention to hasten reform alienated the Catholics and its apparent tolerance of the IRA caused the Protestants to conclude that their militias needed to take matters into their own hands.[38] The British lack of will to pressure the Protestants for a fair distribution of political power, government resources, and jobs killed hopes for accommodation, as parochial boundaries remained strengthened by the class divide. Once the military was sent in to intervene, their heavy-handed tactics and flouting of the law and due process further alienated the Catholic community, which came to view the British army as an ally of the Protestants and caused the IRA to make removal of the occupying force one of the objectives of its violence.

The Irish also contributed to the conflict as they allowed the IRA to operate within their borders as long as its violent activities were limited to Northern Ireland. At the same time, the British had turned a blind eye to the Protestant Orange Lodges and allowed them to arm themselves illegally. In essence, Northern Ireland was an ethnic frontier and a site of contested sovereignty between two competing communities with allegiances to different countries. Ireland's desire for unity, as represented in articles six and seven of its constitution, and Britain's allowance of a political system in Northern Ireland that ranked its culture over Ireland's encouraged the Catholic Republicans and the Protestant Unionists to pursue their exclusive nationalistic agendas.[39] This external support sharpened the conflict during the 1960s, which eventually led to more British and Irish interference on behalf of their proxies and more violence. The importance of the British and Irish role in sustaining the conflict is evident in the key parts that the two countries played in helping produce the Good Friday Agreements and power sharing, once they decided that pressuring the Catholics and Protestants to reach a peace agreement was in their best interests.

External Influences

Other nations also helped to sustain the violence as Libya, the Soviet Union, and Irish Americans channeled funds for weapons to the IRA, while the Protestants received aid from South Africa (before the end of white rule) and right-wing Europeans. Adrian Gaulke argues that the international illegitimacy of Northern Ireland was also a significant factor because it was accepted in the international community that former colonies should be decolonized whole rather than partitioned, which created pressure for a united Ireland. Being on the wrong side of world opinion enhanced the Protestants' sense of isolation and siege mentality, which caused them to become more nationalistic and strengthened extremists such as Paisley. At the same time, the Republicans were emboldened by being viewed as an oppressed group that was engaged an anticolonial struggle.[40] It is important to note that Libya, the Soviet Union, and South Africa were out of the picture when the Good Friday Agreement was reached and that another important external actor, the United States, played an important role in pushing the two sides toward an agreement.

Ethnic Nationalism

Ethnic nationalism was the key cause of the Troubles in Northern Ireland because the volatility of the conflict and the use of terrorism and violence was a product of the competing national claims, which were supported by other important divides including political power, religion, and economic class. McGarry and O'Leary accurately describe the Troubles, like most other violent conflicts, as a struggle for land, power, and recognition. This was an ethno-nationalist fight between groups with different visions for the same piece of land. The Catholics wanted to be ruled by their own nation, Ireland, and the Protestants wanted their state, Great Britain, to protect their community. The Catholics and Protestants were kinship groups, almost extended families with shared ancestry, which viewed themselves as being in a hostile world where an attack on one was an attack on all. Thus, individuals were eager to make sacrifices for the well-being of the whole.[41] According to Rose, this strong ethnic partition translated into a highly mobilized society where individuals' primary loyalty was to their ethnic communities. The preponderance of Republican Rebels and ultra-Loyalists meant that few felt ambivalent about political matters and fewer felt allegiance to the governing authorities, which created a highly charged and confrontational political environment. Rose also contends that the nonbargainability of religiously rooted conflict was a factor.[42] However, the fact that a bargain was reached means that this could not have been a true religious conflict.

The divisions including religion, political power, and economic class divisions that supported the ethno-national partition also made accommodation and power sharing difficult. All political and economic conflicts pitted Catholics against Protestants, whereas in stable democracies, people from different ethnic and religious groups join together to advocate for single issues where they share the same position. These cross-cutting cleavages vary from issue to issue and prevent the creation of a permanent conflict between the same two groups, as was the case in Northern Ireland.[43] Nationalism also influenced the civil rights and inequality dimension of the conflict because the Catholics desire to be part of Ireland, which was supported by Ireland's government, allowed the Protestants to claim that the Catholics had to be disenfranchised and denied their rights because of their irredentism.[44] Although the Catholics demanded civil rights and equality, like African Americans in the South, very few African Americans had nationalist aspirations, while most Irish Catholics did. Even if London had not ignored what was going on in Northern Ireland, as Washington did in the South, the Catholic demand for Irish reunification would have remained, whereas African Americans were satisfied with equal rights and integration. Thus, the evolution of Catholic demands and Irish policy away from reunification played a key role in bringing about the Good Friday Agreements.

Cross-cutting cleavages that weaken an ethnic partition, according to Arend Lijphart, is only one of a number of conditions that are necessary for elite bargaining and consensus and the formation of a governing coalition that represents all segments of society, where power is allocated proportional to representation in the population, that did not exist in Northern Ireland. Protestant and Catholic elites were often pressured toward extremism by their followers and, subsequently, had little leeway to bargain with each other. Rather than facing a common external enemy that unified them, Catholics' and Protestants' outside threats, Great Britain and Ireland, respectively, supported their local adversaries. At the same time, the groups were geographically isolated; were socially, politically, and economically unequal; had no tradition of accommodation; and had no sense of national solidarity. Finally, the Protestants could dominate the Catholics because they represented two-third of the population and had held the upper hand since the founding of the Ulster Plantations in the 16th century. Therefore, they felt no incentive to bargain and share power.[45] Thus, the obstacles that needed to be overcome to reach an agreement were numerous. Religion was only one of many factors that separated the combatants and served to support the differing national visions. In the end, it was the national visions that changed, not the religions.

ANTIABORTION VIOLENCE IN THE UNITED STATES

Religious Motivations

Antiabortion violence in the United States is another case of religion-based terrorism in a democracy and a rare instance of Christian terrorism that is not part of an ethnic conflict or a clash with Muslims. Antiabortion terrorism has involved the murder of abortion providers, harassment, fire-bombing of clinics, vandalism and destruction of property, acid attacks, and anthrax hoaxes. A number of killers of abortion providers and clinic bombers have claimed to be part of the Army of God, a leaderless group whose members are not in contact with each other and which seems to exist only on paper.[46] It would appear that antiabortion terrorists are purely motivated by religion. Matthew Goldsby and James Simmons said that their bombing of a Pensacola abortion clinic in December 1984 was a birthday present for Jesus.[47] Michael Griffin, who killed abortion provider Dr. David Gunn in 1993, claimed that God told him to do so and had presented him with the opportunity when he saw Gunn outside of his clinic. Griffin justified his actions with a quote from the Bible "Whoever sheds man's blood, by man his blood shall be shed."[48] Militant antiabortion leader, Randall Terry, claimed that "God does not wave a magic wand. We are his body—his hands and feet. He uses people who work as if it all depends on them while praying as if it all depends on God"[49] Paul Hill, another abortion provider murderer, has called for a holy war for God against abortion that involves killing supreme court justices and the use of chemical and biological weapons.[50]

Clerics, including Terry and Michael Bray, who were convicted for fire-bombing a Wilmington DE abortion clinic and were viewed as being an inspiration for other antiabortion radicals, have been leaders and members of violent antiabortion groups. Many antiabortion extremists are part of the Christian Reconstructionist movement and espouse Dominion theology, which asserts that Christians must fight for God's rule over everything, that society must be rebuilt around the church and Bible law, and that the separation of church and state was a mistake. In a Reconstructionist government, abortion providers, adulterers, and homosexuals would be subject to the death penalty; schools would be run by the church; and women would be subservient to men.[51] Reconstructionists view Reformation era theologians Martin Luther, John Calvin, and John Knox as being ideological inspirations and claim that Calvin and his followers believed that God wanted them to control society on earth, while Knox wanted the elect who had been saved to punish the wicked sovereign. Thus, people like Bray believed that they could use weapons to influence politics and take the law in their own hands because they were acting in the name of the Lord.[52] Millennial and apocalyptic notions also motivate antiabortion radicals, as they portray themselves as the army of good facing off against the forces of Satan and abortion as an atrocity that is a sign of Armageddon. Killing an abortion doctor fuels the forces of good while disrupting evil.[53] Paul Hill, who murdered abortion provider, Dr. John Britton, believed that his divine interaction would inspire the righteous to rise up to end abortion and bring about the apocalypse.[54]

Antiabortion terrorists provide further evidence that religions have multiple interpretations because they are a miniscule minority in the greater population of American Christians and pro-life advocates. The overwhelming majority of individuals who wish to ban abortion do not use violence and the Army of God is limited to approximately 200 individuals, of which an even smaller number have engaged in acts of terrorism. The preacher at the staunchly pro-life church attended by Goldsby and Simmons said that their actions contradicted scripture, which was against violence, and that they should have shown love to the abortion providers.[55] Reconstructionists and Dominionists, as mentioned, trace their roots to Reformation theologians, Luther, Calvin, and Knox. At the same time, these theologians and the Reformation are credited with producing a theology that actually facilitated the separation of church and state. Many Reconstructionists including Gary North, a leader of the movement, reject violence and have condemned killing abortion providers. The dominate strain in American millennialism prior to the 1980s argued that Christians should avoid politics and wait for Christ's return rather than trying to build a society that would facilitate the second coming.[56]

What causes this small minority to cling to a questionable interpretation of 16th-century Protestant theology that is used to justify violence against abortion providers and clinics? Many of the political and socioeconomic explanations of religion-based terrorism offered in chapters 3 and 4 do not appear to fit. Antiabortion terrorists live in a democracy that is a dominant military power, leader of the world economy, and whose culture influences others. They have the opportunity to change policy through elections, interest groups, and legal action. They are not part of a persecuted ethnic minority, and they have not been denied their rights or been discriminated against. Most come from solid middle-class origins, are well educated, and have jobs and families. A study of 15 individuals convicted for crimes against abortion clinics including bombing, arson, and kidnapping found that they were best described as middle-class, hardworking, and normal white males, who believed that their actions would change the law. Most had the resources to take care of their family while they were in prison. Many were first-generation city dwellers or lived in the fringes of urban areas, which suggests that they, like their Muslim terrorist counterparts, might have been marginal individuals caught between old lifestyles and the contemporary cosmopolitan world.[57] As will be discussed, many were troubled by the increasing power of women and gays and secular humanism and the overall decline of traditional values.

Historical Background: From Civil Rights to Religious Fundamentalism

The antiabortion movement, as was the case with the campaign to set-tle and annex the land Israel captured in the Six-Day War, started out as a peaceful protest movement that grew to include violent extremist elements and terrorism when it failed to achieve its objective. The Catholic Church and the National Right to Life Organization led the antiabortion movement following the Supreme Court *Roe v. Wade* decision in 1973 that legalized abortion, and they tried to frame the debate as being over the human rights and civil liberties of fetuses, which were viewed as having the same rights as people. Thus, the tactics of the civil rights movement such as political ac-tion, demonstrations, and acts of civil disobedience were used.[58] Many of the early leaders of the Right to Life movement were former leftists from the 1960s and veterans of the antiwar movement, who made banning abortion their cause in the 1970s.[59]

Social and culture changes are important to understanding antiabortion terrorism, as the appearance and growth of the conservative religious right in the later 1970s had an important influence on the antiabortion move-ment. The religious right was a response to what some felt was the degra-dation of American culture in the 1960s and 1970s by leftists and secular humanists. Banning abortion was crucial to the religious right and, conse-quently, the struggle against abortion began to focus more on God as the au-thor of life and the supremacy of God's law and became tied to other moral issues such as homosexuality, sexual promiscuity, pornography, prayer in the schools, and stopping America's overall moral decay.[60] This religioniza-tion was accompanied by more assertive direct action, as groups such as the American Life League and Pro-Life Action went beyond political and legal action and rallies and began to block entrances to clinics, harass providers, and assertively preach to women who were seeking abortions.

Operation Rescue, headed by Randall Terry, a preacher from upstate New York, organized antiabortion protests across the country in the late 1980s that often mobilized thousands of people and usually led to hostile confrontations with clinic defenders, counterdemonstrators from the pro-choice movement, and the police. Major acts of violence also became more common in the 1980s. In August 1982, clinic owner Dr. Hector Zevallos and his wife were kidnapped by members of the Army of God and held at gunpoint until he made a tape calling for the end of abortion and promised to close his clinic. Zevallos and his wife were also physically assaulted during their time in captivity. In December 1984, an abortion clinic in Pensacola, Florida, was bombed and destroyed. Between January 1983 and March 1985, there were 319 acts of violence against 238 reproductive health centers and their staff.[61]

The move toward a more aggressive and religious orientation in the pro-life movement was partly a result of the institutionalization and co-optation that takes place in many protest movements. National Right to Life and other mainstream pro-life groups became players in the political system and increasingly were run by lobbyists, legal experts, and administrators. As a result, National Right to Life had to bargain, negotiate and compromise, and settle for incremental victories. The religious fundamentalists who were entering the movement quickly became impatient and disillusioned with incremental change and increasingly resorted to the more confrontational tactics described earlier. For these true believers, abortion was a moral issue with no room for middle ground. Thus, they turned to direct action, trying to prevent abortion by persuading women not to have abortions, harassing doctors into not performing them, and closing down abortion clinics.[62] Many of the more moderate activists, who had been involved in early protests, left because they disapproved of the more strident and aggressive demonstrations.[63]

The rise of the New Right, as mentioned, was largely a reaction to the culture of the 1960s and early 1970s, which they felt represented the decline of American culture and values. The religious conservatives saw abortion as being tied to other threats such as the Equal Rights Amendment (ERA) (for women), gay rights, sexual liberation, hedonism, drugs, and secular humanism. Television evangelists such as Jerry Falwell and Pat Robertson argued that Christian Conservatives had been too passive during the 1960s and that it was time to engage in cultural warfare. Opposition to abortion became part of this battle and pro-life groups, such as the Pro-Life Action League and, later, Operation Rescue, expanded the campaign from defending the unborn to pursuing the broader religious conservative agenda. Their dualistic and militant ideology led to the more aggressive and hostile tactics such as blocking entrances to clinics and harassing providers.[64] Carol Mason writes that the religious right was particularly threatened by the increasing power of women and the feminization of America, which was preventing men from taking their rightful positions as leaders of families and society. Michael Bray claimed that America was suffering from a testosterone deficiency, which was a product of an emasculated church. Thwarting women's self-determination and reproductive freedom was an important step toward disempowering women and keeping them in their rightful place at home pregnant, raising children, and subservient to their husbands.[65]

Antigovernment Sentiment and the Militia Movement

The appearance of fundamentalist, confrontational, and sometimes violent antiabortion groups was also related to the rise of antigovernment and military-oriented sentiment following the Vietnam War. The notion that America had lost the Vietnam War because the government had tied the hands of the military became popular in right-wing circles. Many were also reacting to what they perceived as the emasculation and feminization of American men. Consequently, the militia movement was born in the 1970s, as groups of men became weekend warriors and trained for the day when the government would come to take away their weapons and for the return of the real man to his prominent place in American society. Many of the militia members and supporters of the Promise Keepers organization, which sought to restore the traditional American family where women and children were subservient to their husbands, were also strongly antiabortion and viewed the government's sanctioning of legalized abortion as part of a greater conspiracy against men and true Americans.[66] The antigovernment, military-minded ethic is seen in Leo Bozell's Society for a Christian Commonwealth. Bozell called the fight for life America's Armageddon and a holy war against satanic culture and an agnostic government that conspired against Christians at the highest levels.[67]

The White Supremacy Movement

The rise of the militant antiabortion movement was also tied to the growth of the white supremacist movement and the Church of the Creativity. Eric Rudolph, who set off a bomb in Atlanta during the 1996 Olympics, was also responsible for bombings at two abortion clinics and a lesbian bar. Rudolph was a member of the racist Christian Identity movement and a Holocaust denier. To him, the real holocaust was the abortions that were performed by Jewish doctors on Christian babies. Larry Pratt, who raised 150,000 dollars for Operation Rescue, was also tied to white supremacist groups. Ku Klux Klan members and skinheads were also visible participants in protests at abortion clinics. White supremacists also believe in government conspiracies against white men and maintain that Jews and lesbians are using abortion to weaken the white race. Mason writes that abortion providers are often portrayed as Jews out to make money by exterminating babies, while their lesbian nurses use abortion to weaken the power of men. Some believe that abortion is a gay plot to kill babies and use their fetal tissue for stem cell research so that gays could spread AIDS and destroy America.[68] White supremacists often use the example of Phineas, who killed an Israelite male and a Midianite woman for their intermarriage, as a role model. Like Phineas, they will alleviate God's anger at sin by spilling the blood of the sinner, abortion providers.

The Election of Ronald Reagan

The cultural shift in America to the right was strengthened by Ronald Reagan's victory in the 1980 presidential election and the defeat of the ERA. Reagan had courted the evangelical Christian vote, and the movement of this group to the Republican Party is often viewed as being a cause of his victory. Incumbent Jimmy Carter, a born-again Christian, had supported a women's right to choose, while Reagan had come out strongly against abortion.[69] Falwell, Robertson, and other right-wing Christian leaders had mobilized their supporters and encouraged them to abandon their political passivity. Even though most Americans rejected the agenda of the religious right and had voted for Reagan because of the economy and a perception that America's status in the world had declined, the religious conservatives saw Reagan's victory as a triumph against secularism and expected that their agenda, particularly banning abortion, would soon become law.[70] The success of their new found political assertiveness and the resulting triumphant mood also led antiabortion forces to feel that it was time to aggressively pursue ending abortion in America. At the same time, the number of clinic bombings and arsons rose significantly during Reagan's first term and remained high during his second.[71]

Religious Extremists in a Democracy

The rise in the number of acts of violence against abortion clinics during Reagan's first term raises the question as to whether democracy represses or encourages religion-based terrorism. Pro-life groups have used violence even though they have not been shut out of the political system and have seen many favorable outcomes in legislation and court decisions including limits being placed on abortion such as parental consent, waiting periods, and restrictions on late-term abortions. State legislatures introduced between 425 and 620 bills annually between 1990 and 2000 that would restrict or ban abortion.[72] The discussion of Jewish terrorism in Israel in chapter 6 found that governing coalitions supported their objectives of settling and annexing the West Bank, had offered them tacit support, and had not cracked down on them when they broke the law, as long as their violence was directed at Palestinians. The more moderate mainstream had often facilitated and sometimes encouraged the activities of the violent fringe. It might be that Reagan's support for banning abortion and endorsement of pro-life groups encouraged the radicals' acts of violence. At the same time, reproductive health clinics and workers suffered from the brunt of the violence, while there were few costs for federal and state governments—at first. Finally, protest movements, both secular and religious, even in democratic nations, usually include violent fringe elements, as was the case with the civil rights and antiwar movements in the United States in the 1960s.

Mainstream antiabortion groups such as National Right to Life and religious institutions such as the Catholic Church usually condemn acts of violence by radicals. However, Dallas Blanchard and Terry Prewitt argue that the violent extremist wing of the antiabortion movement can only operate with an approving audience. "The clear tendency of moderates has been to deny the legitimacy of violence, such as arson and bombings, while at the same time, welcoming it and using it to add to their own public exposure."[73] Usually, moderates will offer a general condemnation of violence but not the specific act that took place. Catholic bishops condemn antiabortion violence but say that it is caused by abortion itself and that violence begets violence. Joseph O'Keefe, an early leader of the Right to Life movement who called for peaceful resistance during 1970s, later stated that he admired violence by members of the Army of God and that he found their actions courageous. He justified his support for violence by claiming that it was acceptable to respond to violence against people by destroying property.[74]

Pro-life Action League leader Joseph Scheidler also did not engage in violence but encouraged and inspired those who did. Scheidler was in contact with clinic bombers, John Brockheft and Don Anderson, and supported their actions because they produced results like closing clinics but did not kill people.[75] Paul Hill, who later murdered abortion provider Dr. James Britton, went on the *Phil Donahue Show* and said that the murder of Dr. David Gunn was as good as killing Dr. Joseph Mengele, a Nazi doctor who performed horrendous experiments on concentration camp prisoners, and called for executing abortionists. Scheidler wrote to Hill to offer him encouragement and support for defending Gunn's murder. Hill had earlier received a reward for being "the most active right to lifer" in Mississippi from National Right to Life.[76] John Burt, who often brought an aborted fetus in a jar to demonstrations, said that he couldn't help it if what he did inspired someone to "go off the deep-end" and that he would blow up a clinic himself, but he was scared of getting caught.[77] The lack of condemnation from President Reagan was also important. There was a rise in violence following his publication of an essay in 1983 expressing his desire to ban abortion. He did not speak out against violence against abortion providers and clinics until three years after he had been asked to in 1982. Don Anderson, one of the kidnappers of Dr. Zevallos and his wife, stated that bombers were encouraged by the lack of condemnation from Reagan and thought that they had the green light from the president. Pensacola clinic bombers, Goldsby and Simmons, claimed that they were acting on behalf of the president.[78]

A Supportive Environment

The legal and borderline legal activities of pro-life groups, such as blockading clinics, harassing clinic staff, and street corner preaching, in combination with informational and publicity campaigns that included manuals on how to close abortion clinics, websites with the names and addresses of abortion providers, graphic depictions of aborted fetuses, films showing late-term abortions, and effigies of providers created a hostile and emotionally charged atmosphere that was aimed at closing clinics, persuading women not to have abortions, and convincing providers to stop performing abortion, also encouraged violence. Although the *Army of God Manual* did not encourage acts of violence, it did describe how to burn down a clinic and kill providers. The *Nuremberg Files* website did not instruct people to go hunt down abortion providers, but it did provide the addresses of those who were guilty of the crime of providing abortions.

The 1984 Pensacola bombing took place in the midst of confrontational sit-ins and demonstrations featuring James Burt parading with his jar containing an aborted fetus. Bombers Goldsby and Simmons had been influenced by graphic films depicting abortions and highly charged antiabortion rhetoric at their evangelical church and at demonstrations.[79] Operation Rescue's Summers of Mercy in the late 1980s, where hundreds of protesters were arrested for blockading clinics, corresponded with a sharp rise in bombings and acts of arson.[80] It might be that the attempts to transform people through preaching, which took a very hostile tone that included calling people by name, yelling, threatening, protesting at people's home, and blocking entrances to clinics, encouraged extreme actions such as clinic invasions, assaults, and vandalism.

Frustration with Friends

The discussion of Jewish extremism in Israel also found that extremists used violence when governments were in power that shared their objectives because they felt frustrated and betrayed when their moderate allies, who had raised their hopes, did not produce results in law or policy. Citing relative deprivation theory, Alesha Doan proposes that continued frustration will eventually lead to violence, which might explain the surge in antiabortion terrorism during Ronald Reagan's presidency.[81] The turn to violence due to impatience and frustration with the political process is particularly relevant with abortion, a moral issue where compromise is unacceptable. Reagan's actions, despite his strong statements and essay opposing abortion, were mostly symbolic, such as not covering abortion in federal employee health insurance. He showed a reluctance to take on *Roe v. Wade* and did not actively fight for the Hatch Amendment, which would have left the legal status of abortion to the states. The Family Protection Act, a 25-point Conservative wish list for social issues, did not make it to the House floor. Reagan appointed Sandra Day O'Connor, despite her lack of commitment to overturning *Roe v. Wade,* to the Supreme Court. Reagan later appointed Anthony Kennedy, who became the swing vote for maintaining legal abortion, after staunch abortion opponent Robert Bork was withdrawn without a confirmation hearing because of strong Democratic opposition in the Senate.[82]

The antiabortion movement viewed Reagan's landslide reelection victory in 1984 as another mandate for social change but was, again, disappointed when little progress was made on abortion. Consequently, religious conservatives felt betrayed and increasingly turned to direct action to prevent abortion. Randall Terry called for upping the ante with aggressive confrontation because the politicians were not doing anything. Terry's Operation Rescue began a series of rescues in cities across the country where protesters would crawl on their knees to block clinic doors.[83] The rescues gave the participants a sense of doing something tangible to compensate for the failure of the politicians because they could claim each abortion prevented, each clinic closed, even for a day, and each provider who stopped performing abortions because of the rescues was a victory. The radical fringe was possibly encouraged by the success of the rescues, as there were 319 acts of violence against 238 clinics between 1983 and 1985. The election of pro-life George H. Bush in 1988 and Supreme Court decisions requiring waiting periods and parental consent in the early 1990s corresponded with a drop in violence.

Hatred of Enemies: Clinton

It would be expected that antiabortion terrorism would increase when Bill Clinton, who was pro-choice, held the presidency from 1993 to 2001. Although Clinton's election coincided with a decline in demonstrations and blockades, this was largely due to lawsuits won by clinics and pro-choice organizations against Operation Rescue, which helped cause that organization's demise. Antiabortion rhetoric and violence, however, continued to increase, as there were three murders of abortion providers, seven attempted murders, and a sharp increase in arsons and bombings from 1994 to 1998. Some felt that opportunities for legal protest being shut down by a hostile government, particularly after the Freedom of Access to Clinic Entrances Act (FACE) that made preventing access to an abortion clinic a federal crime, allowed clinic staff to sue for damages, and levied heavy fines for violations was passed in 1994, pushed antiabortion activists into violence. Neal Horsley, who posted the Nuremberg Files website, claimed that the rise in antiabortion violence in the 1990s was directly caused by FACE and the lawsuits.[84] It might also have been an angry reaction to political setbacks such as FACE and Clinton's reversal of policies banning abortions at U.S. military bases overseas, ending the Title X gag rule on abortion counseling, and banning fetal tissue research. At the same time, many members of the religious right felt a deep personal hatred for Clinton and his wife, Hillary, who they viewed as being a radical feminist. Bray referred to Bill Clinton as being a Hitler-like neo-pagan and stated that an armed revolution was needed to depose him.[85]

Rational Actors

It appears that antiabortion terrorists, like all extremists, are rational actors who use violence when other means of achieving their goal appear to have failed and whose behavior is greatly affected by a number of factors, not just religious zeal. The rational actor model poses another possibility—antiabortion terrorists use violence because it works. When viewed in light of their goals of reducing the number of abortions, providers, and clinics, violence does appear to have been successful. The government, until the passage of FACE in 1994, had imposed few consequences on the protest groups, while the costs of their demonstrations and harassment were burdened by the targets—the clinics, the providers, and the patients. Clinics and doctors were largely left to provide for their own security, while the aggressive tactics, militant rhetoric, harassment, and violence created an environment of fear and panic that altered people's behavior.[86] Accordingly, harassment has been named by reproductive health clinics as the factor that is most important in preventing the providing of services and the hiring of staff. For some, having their names on wanted posters, nooses on their front lawns, and being harassed when out in public are too high a cost to bear. Thus, there has been a steady decline in the abortion rate, the number of abortion providers, and the number of clinics since 1990.[87]

The cost for the use of extralegal actions was minimal because the radical extremists have usually not been shunned or banned from the pro-life movement and have rarely been strongly condemned. The other institutions that could place heavy costs on extremist antiabortion forces, law enforcement and the justice system, were slow to act, so those who committed antiabortion violence had reason to believe that they would receive lenient treatment from the justice system, which encouraged further illegal activity and violence.[88] Pro-choice activists, Patricia Baird-Windle and Eleanor Bader, argue that law enforcement and the justice system often did not respond to requests for assistance and action from clinics. Police have been reluctant to make arrests and the FBI, under Reagan and Bush, would not get involved because they argued that there was no evidence that there was a criminal conspiracy and that attacks on abortion clinics could not be considered terrorism. FBI director William Webster stated in 1984 that the agency did not put as much efforts into investigating clinic bombings as it did for "true acts of domestic terrorism."[89] The police in Granite City, Illinois, told a clinic that had been bombed that they don't deal with abortion clinics. Police in suburban St. Louis did little to stop illegal protests, and those who were arrested spent little time in jail and were not prosecuted. A clinic in Everett, Washington, that had been fire bombed was told by investigators that the fire had been purposefully set by clinic staff and that they would not investigate, a claim that has also been made by the investigators in Florida and North Dakota and by the Bureau of Alcohol Tobacco and Firearms.[90]

There is evidence that suggests that illegal antiabortion activity is affected by legal action and a strong response from the criminal justice system. Operation Rescue's activities sharply declined in the early 1990s after several cities that experienced rescues grew weary of the costs that they were enduring and began arresting and prosecuting lawbreakers. Lawsuits by the National Women's Health Organization based on federal laws relating to organized crime and antitrust succeeded in gaining injunctions against Terry and Scheidler as well as the awarding of damages.[91] As mentioned, the number of violent incidents following FACE sharply declined, and there were no murders of abortion providers between 1998 and the killing of Dr. George

Tiller, the last provider of late-term abortions, in 2009, shortly after pro-choice Barack Obama took office.[92]

Group Identity

Group identity and social isolation also facilitate antiabortion violence. Doan argues that antiabortion groups made extremism and illegal behavior rational by creating tight bonds, stressing commonality, rewarding supporters of the group's goals, and punishing those who do not. Consequently, those who became part of groups that protested abortion clinics in the 1980s and 1990s became absorbed in the goals of creating fear and panic through harassment that would change people's behavior, while some took this to an extreme and used violence.[93] Participation in demonstrations also provided a network for militants and solidified their commitment to using violence. Many perpetrators of violence against abortion clinics and providers in the 1990s, including Shelly Shannon who would attempt to kill Tiller in 1993, met during Operation Rescue's massive demonstrations in Atlanta in 1988. Blanchard and Prewitt also label group membership as being a crucial factor in facilitating antiabortion violence because of reinforcement of values and isolation from those who might disagree or present contradictory opinions. Communities of interest are monolithic and reinforcing, especially when they provide people's only social interaction. All family members and close contacts of Goldsby and Simmons were members of their church and antiabortion groups.[94]

Inspirational leaders also play an important role in antiabortion terrorism. Jessica Stern argues that religion-based terrorism is dependent on inspiration leaders who provide moral suasion. Followers have a strong need for authority and someone who they can admire and to whom they can submit. Stern found that Bray, Hill, and others were held in awe by young antiabortion radicals.[95] Former FBI agent Jerry Reiter writes that radical antiabortion groups "are a millennialist cabal led by older public figures such as Don Trehman, Joseph Scheidler, and John Burt who manipulate younger impressionable men, like Michael Griffin and John Salvi, in a psychological dynamic between an older more established bully and a younger easily impassioned doofus used as a pawn."[96] Michael Bray was a mentor and inspiration to clinic bomber Thomas Spinks and encouraged him to engage in more bombings and use bigger bombs.[97]

Psychological Influences

The importance of inspirational leaders relates to the life histories of some antiabortion terrorists, as many admit that their violence is penitence for past sins and unsavory lifestyles. Thus, they confess their sins to inspirational leaders and seek to please them by being dedicated followers. Michael Bray was an Eagle Scout, All-American boy who went to the Naval Academy but was kicked out because he violated rules, had poor grades, and was a discipline problem. Prior to being saved, he had drifted aimlessly for several years. Randall Terry was a dope smoking, juvenile delinquent with a drinking problem who dropped out of high school and fell in with a group of New Agers before he found Jesus. Thus, antiabortion violence is penitence for past sins or replacing one addiction with another, which is reflected in the need to up the dose from picketing to harassment to violence.[98] Past inadequacies might also have led to narcissistic personalities and splitting as a sense of self-hatred and low self-esteem causes the projection of negative characteristics on to others, such as abortion providers. Diminished self-esteem also leads to a fear of nonbeing, which makes abortion an existential crisis. Antiabortion activists often present women seeking abortions with the question, "What if your mother had aborted you?" which for them is a poignant threat.

Fear and hatred of women is also a psychological characteristic of antiabortion terrorists. Many see abortion as a threat to traditional religious assumptions about women being subservient to men. Abortion gives women control and the option of not assuming their traditional role as child-bearers and mothers. Psychologist Dr. Phyllis Chesler argues that men who have been humiliated or ruled by tyrannical males will often scapegoat the harm caused by males onto females. They then prove their worth to their adopted mentors or heavenly fathers by engaging in violence against women.[99] Blanchard and Prewitt claim that antiabortion violence is a religious substitute for rape and another tool for establishing male dominance. The justifications that men use for antiabortion violence, such as blaming the victim and claiming that the offense is not serious enough to warrant serious punishment, are similar to those used by rapists. Like rapists, most antiabortion terrorists view themselves as nice guys and demonstrate feelings of inadequacy.[100] Their sense of insecurity, as is the case with most violent men, leads to violence against women. Prior to his murder of Dr. David Gunn, Michael Griffin's wife obtained a restraining order against him after he abused and battered her and her mother-in-law.

Christian antiabortion terrorism in the United States exemplifies how religion combines with other factors to produce violence. These warriors for Christ, who justify their violence with theology and biblical texts, are a miniscule minority in the Protestant and pro-life populations. Their Reconstructionist, Dominion, and millennial theologies are espoused by a minority and have nonviolent interpretations that they have chosen to reject. Antiabortion terrorists are one of three extremist fringes, along with racist hate groups and antigovernment militias, of a right-wing, conservative reaction against what they believed were the leftist, permissive, hedonistic, and secular-humanist excesses of the 1960s and 1970s. Their violence was likely encouraged by the inflammatory rhetoric; hostile, aggressive, and borderline legal tactics of antiabortion groups; and the lack of strong condemnation and even encouragement by antiabortion activists. Like their Jewish counterparts in Israel, they react with violence when political allies fail to fully meet their objectives and when adversaries institute laws and policies contrary to their interests. It appears that most religiously motivated actors are satisfied with using legitimate politics and the legal system in a democracy and will accept defeat but the radical fringe will not. Finally, groups, again, appeared to be an important facilitator of religion-based terrorism, and it was suggested that certain psychological factors such as guilt for previous sins, narcissistic personality, and harm done by parents during childhood might have also helped create violent personalities.

_____ *Chapter 8* _____

Islam: Hamas,
Hezbollah, and al Qaeda

The contemporary era of religion-based terrorism is primarily associated with Islam, as approximately 60 percent of global terrorist incidents in 2010, according to the United States State Department, were committed by Sunni extremists, while Muslims also usually bear the brunt of these attacks as a majority takes place in Islamic countries.[1] The current wave of Islamic terrorism began with the Lebanese Civil War in the 1970s, the murder of Anwar Sadat in 1982, and the suicide attack against U.S. and French forces in Beirut by a Shiite militant in 1983. At the same time, the rise of the Islamic Republic in Iran, under the rule of the late Ayatollah Ruhollah Khomeini, served as an inspiration to radicals across the Islamic world. Since then, terrorist attacks by Muslims have occurred across the globe. This chapter will consider some proposed theological connections between Islam and terrorism. I will then offer case studies that represent three varieties of Islamic-based terrorism. The Palestinian group, Hamas, will be used to exemplify the importance of occupation and how a nationalist struggle became religionized. Hezbollah, in Lebanon, will illustrate the significance of ethnic conflict, political and social inequality, and resistance to foreign invasion. Al Qaeda will demonstrate how global power imbalance, history, and globalization created the global jihadist movement.

Bernard Lewis warned of the dark cloud that was the return of political Islam in the 1970s, while Samuel Huntington's "Clash of Civilizations?" labeled Islam as having "bloody borders" and being a likely cause of conflict in the 21st century.[2] Numerous books on political Islam and Islam and terrorism were published in the 1980s and 1990s that investigated the origins of what appeared to be fanatical rage that was ingrained in Islam and its adherents' collective psyche. The attacks on September 11, 2001, caused the intensification and widening of the debate as to whether Islam was a religion of violence or peace. The political and Christian right often argues that Islam is a violent religion and that the roots of Islamic terrorism are in the faith itself. Liberal and moderate Muslims and the political left contend that the Salafi, Wahhabi, and other forms of Islam favored by terrorists represent extremist or incorrect interpretations of the faith. To me, this debate is of little relevance because religions can be interpreted in an almost infinite number of ways, and texts and traditions are often contradictory and can be used to justify peace and violence. In this regard, Islam is no different than Judaism, Christianity, and other religions.

RELIGIOUS FACTORS ASSOCIATED WITH ISLAMIC TERRORISM

Some point to *jihad* as being indicative of Islam's violent nature, but Judaism and Christianity also have notions of just wars and have inspired holy wars throughout their histories. *Jihad* was also found to have nonviolent connotations, and its violent manifestation is generally viewed as being a defensive struggle. Some argue that Islam was spread through the sword and that Islamic terrorists represent the latest round in a campaign to convert non-Muslims to Islam. However, Judaism and Christianity, at times, were also spread through violence, and the wars of Islamic conquest in the seventh and eight centuries also had political, social, and economic roots.[3] It is important to reiterate that Western nations have usually been the aggressors in wars between Islamic and other nations and peoples in the colonial and post–World War II eras. Terrorism, including the 9/11 attacks, has been used by Muslims as a tool to resist what is believed to be Western military, economic, and cultural aggression rather than as a means of spreading Islam.

More serious consideration must be given to the intertwining of religion and politics in Islam and the lack of an Islamic Reformation. The Christian Reconstructionists discussed in the previous chapter do call for America to be ruled by a government rooted in Christian principles and Bible law and the amalgamation of church and state, but they represent a very small, radical fringe in American Christianity. The Protestant Reformation, as discussed in chapter 7, helped facilitate the separation of church and state and, eventually, the near-complete elimination of religion-based war and terrorism in the Christian world. In contrast, the call for religion-based government and the use of *Sharia* has widespread support throughout the Islamic world and is advocated by moderates who seek to achieve that goal through legitimate politics. As mentioned in chapter 3, Islamic parties have participated in elections in countries such as Indonesia, Turkey, and Algeria and have sought to participate in others.

Although only a very small minority of nations with predominantly Muslim populations have governments that combine religious and political authority and use *Sharia,* Islam has not had a reformation, and God's realm and *Sharia* extend into areas such as governance, criminal law, banking, and religious practice that have largely been left to secular authorities or the individual in the Christian world. Protestant Christianity never developed this type of comprehensive legal code, and Catholic Cannon law has long been relegated to the affairs of the Church and its members and has left matters of governance to secular authorities. Thus, nations implementing and following religious law is not a core element of modern Christianity and motivates very few Christian terrorists, while for many Muslims, the use of *Sharia* and the maintenance of a society that follows its precepts will ultimately lead to the perfection of humankind. Consequently, the goal of most Islamic terrorists is to create national governments or a world government, in the case of the late Osama bin Laden, that are rooted in Islam and that use *Sharia.* Bin Laden and others who call for violence in the name of Islam claim that the separation of religion and state is a Western invention that has led to the corruption and decline of the Islamic world. In order to return Islam to its past greatness, the Caliphate, the political, and religious leader during the two early Islamic empires must be restored; political leaders must be guided by religious principles; and *Sharia* must be implemented. On the other hand, the number of Muslims living as minorities continues to grow, which signifies that some place greater importance on economic advancement by living in Europe, while others are content living in a multicultural society such as the United States.

Muslims across the globe are angry, but it is not the unique nature of their religion that makes them angry or prone to violence at this particular historical moment. Rather it is the political and socioeconomic forces described in detail in chapters 3 and 4. As was seen in chapter 7, Israel has a disproportionately large cohort of angry Jews, who are using religion to justify politically motivated violence. In chapter 7, I showed that many of the world's Christians live in free societies and in the West, which has dominated the world militarily, culturally, and economically in the modern era. Those in the United States who feel threatened by hostile forces such as women's rights and America's moral decline have, at times, reacted with violence. Others have documented angry Sikhs and Hindus who use violence in the name of religion.[4] Islam, with its historical legacy of mixing religion and state and comprehensive legal system, does provide a native and culturally authentic solution to the political and socioeconomic grievances of aggrieved Muslims. It is important to note, however, that the Islamic solution became popular only after imported ideologies such as Socialism and Liberalism failed in places like Egypt and Iran and, as will be discussed, Palestine. The most radical solution offered by al Qaeda is attractive only to a small minority and has seen its popularity diminish. Finally, many Muslims, despite their anger, have increasingly used peaceful methods to press their grievances as was seen in the demonstrations against authoritarian government throughout the Middle East in 2011.

HAMAS

The rise of Hamas in the Palestinian struggle for a state, opposition to Israeli occupation of the West Bank and sealing off Gaza, and its upping of the ante of violence to include suicide bombings and shooting missiles at civilian targets represent the religionization of a struggle that had largely been nationalist and secular. As discussed in chapter 6, the same religionization also took place on the Israeli side following the Six-Day War and the capture of the old city of Jerusalem and the West Bank. The struggle for Palestinian independence is rooted in the birth of Israel in 1948 and its subsequent war with its Arab neighbors. Many Palestinians fled their homes during the fighting, as they were encouraged to leave by the leaders of the Arab nations, who assured them that they would return after the Jews were defeated. Others were forced to leave by Israeli armed forces. Many of the refugees went to the West Bank and Gaza, which were controlled by Jordan and Egypt, respectively. Following Israel's victory, which included capturing most of the land set aside by the UN for a Palestinian state, the Palestinians left the struggle to the Arab nations, which again assured them that Israel would be defeated and that they would soon return to their homes. The cataclysmic defeat of the Arab armies in the 1967 Six-Day War and the subsequent Israeli occupation of the West Bank, Gaza, and East Jerusalem convinced the Palestinians that they had to take ownership of their struggle for independence. The Palestine Liberation Organization (PLO), which had formed in 1964, began to launch raids and terrorist attacks against Israel from its bases in Jordan.

Historical Roots

The PLO's dominant Fatah movement was secular nationalist and had no real ideology so as to accommodate the small leftist and communist groups that played important parts in the Palestinian movement in the 1960s and 1970s. The PLO originally called for the replacement of Israel with a secular, democratic state and the return of the Palestinian refugees to their homes. Three crucial events led to a decline in the power and status of the PLO and created an opportunity for Hamas to grow and win followers. Israel's 1982 invasion of Lebanon led to the relocation of the PLO and its leadership from that country to Tunisia, which weakened its influence in the West Bank and Gaza and its ability to directly confront Israel. The beginning of the first Intifada (uprising) against Israel was largely led by Palestinians in the occupied territories, and Hamas used the uprising to demonstrate that it was on the front lines against the Israelis while the PLO leadership was 1,500 miles away living in luxury in Tunisia. Finally, the PLO began to move toward a more conciliatory position recognizing Israel's right to exist and calling for a peaceful, negotiated solution to the conflict. This move strengthened Hamas's claim to be the Palestinian group that was standing up to Israel and that would not give away their legitimate right to their entire homeland.[5]

Hamas's roots are in the Egyptian Muslim Brotherhood, a group founded to foster a return to Islam and the creation of Islamic state in response to the decline of the Islamic world and its dominance by the West. Ironically, the Israelis allowed the Brotherhood, which had been banned by the Egyptians, to organize in Gaza following their capture of that area and the West Bank in 1967. During the 1970s, Hamas was viewed as a counterweight that would siphon support from Israel's primary enemy at the time, the PLO. Consequently, Hamas was given a license to operate as a religious and charitable organization and was even provided funds by the Israeli government.[6] Thus, the transformation of the Palestinian struggle from secular national to religious was originally facilitated and encouraged by Israel. Naturally, this support ended when Israel discovered that Hamas was acquiring weapons and preparing for an armed struggle. At that point, the Brotherhood and, later, Hamas avoided confrontation and violence as they argued that transforming backward Palestinian society and bringing it back to Islam was necessary for successful opposition to Israeli rule. The Islamist leadership also claimed that a campaign by a corrupt and deviant society would fail and that provoking the Israelis would jeopardize the organization.[7] During this time, Hamas built strong network of mosques, schools, health clinics, youth groups, and charitable organizations that slowly won the hearts and minds of the occupied Palestinians. Later, Hamas was able to tap into this network of supporters when it moved to an armed struggle. The rehabilitation period lasted until 1987, as the Islamists came under criticism for not confronting the Israelis when the Intifada began.[8]

Hamas was officially formed in 1987. The group's charter calls for armed struggle against Israel, the destruction of the Jewish state, and the creation of an Islamic nation based on the *Quran* in all of Palestine. Although Hamas has religious and nationalistic origins, it appears that the struggle against occupation more than religion has caused Hamas's use of terrorism and violence. The group has been very adept at adapting its strategy to realities on the ground, as it has used violence when it is perceived to be politically advantageous. Hamas's decision to begin armed confrontation against Israel was forced by the first Intifada, when the group's leadership realized that they would lose credibility if they did not participate. Their rivals, Islamic Jihad, instigated the Intifada when some of its members escaped from prison and engaged in a shootout with Israeli soldiers. Hamas, therefore, had no choice but to participate in the explosion of outrage that followed in the Jabaliya refugee camp when an Israeli truck driver ran over four Palestinian workers, as it did not want to lose credibility.[9]

Oslo Presents an Opportunity

Hamas's participation in the Intifada along with its social services increased its status and reputation in the occupied territories. The Oslo Agreements between Israel and the PLO in 1993, which called for the ultimate creation of a Palestinian state after a five-year period during which the Palestinian Authority (PA) was to demonstrate that it could control violence against Israel and its settlements and that it was competent to govern, offered Hamas another incentive to engage in terrorism and armed confrontation. If Hamas accepted the Accords, it would have played a subservient role to the PLO in the PA. By rejecting the peace agreements, continuing the armed struggle, and calling for regaining of all of Palestine, Hamas offered a competing vision to that of the PLO and framed itself as the real champion of the Palestinian people that would not compromise in order to gain recognition by Israel and the United States. Hamas also relieved itself of any responsibility for the success of the PA and the Oslo Accords and dedicated itself to ensuring that the peace process failed and that a Palestinian state was not created in the West Bank and Gaza. Consequently, Hamas and Islamic Jihad began a campaign of suicide bombings and other attacks against Jewish settlements in the West Bank and within Israel. A series of bombings prior to Israel's 1996 elections helped facilitate the victory of the hawkish Benjamin Netanyahu, who was against Palestinian independence, over the dovish Shimon Peres, who had vowed to implement the Oslo Accords.[10]

These attacks forced Yasser Arafat and the PA to crackdown on Hamas and Islamic Jihad, which served to boost the popularity of the Islamists as the peace process was increasingly viewed as a failure. The number of Israeli settlements in the occupied territories doubled, the issue of the return of displaced refugees was not addressed, little progress was made toward the creation of a Palestinian state, and there was no improvement in the daily lives of Palestinians. Thus, Hamas could claim that the peace process, which it had helped to derail, was a failure and Yassir Arafat was to blame. Eventually, the Israelis attacked Arafat's compound, as terrorist attacks continued against Israel, and he was forced to flee to Paris. Oslo, in short, destroyed the credibility of the PLO, made it appear to be weak, and allowed Hamas to claim the mantel of the true defender of the Palestinians and that armed struggle was the only way to gain a state. Also, Israel and the West's refusal to deal with Hamas further strengthened its credibility and claim to be the authentic voice of the Palestinians.[11]

Hamas again showed its ability to adapt its strategy and ideology to political realities by participating in elections for the Palestinian Leadership Council of the Palestinian Authority in 2006. The group had previously stated that it would not participate in Palestinian Legislative Council elections because the PA was illegitimate and armed struggle was the only path to liberate Palestine. Hamas, however, realized that it had a chance to win because of increasing disillusionment with Fatah, which was seen as being corrupt, incompetent, and unable to end the occupation or improve the daily lives of Palestinians. Consequently, Hamas's strategy of resistance along with its reputation of being honest and for delivering much needed social services and aid facilitated its shocking victory in the elections. It was the frustration with Fatah and the desire for new leadership that caused many, including Christians and leftists, to vote for Hamas.[12] Following its victory, Hamas considered negotiating with Israel, which it had previously refused to do, and offered the Israelis a long-term truce.[13]

Politics over Religion?

The question as to whether Hamas is primarily a political or religious organization does not have a clear answer. Khaled Haroub best describes

Hamas as an Islamist movement with religious foundations and a nation-alist agenda based on a struggle for liberation against a foreign occupier. Haroub, however, concludes that "at this highly politicized juncture (2006) of Hamas's life, it has been clearly evident that the political vigorously oc-cupied the driver's seat."[14] Hamas's religious orientation is obvious based on its organization in mosques, propagation of Islamic observance and lifestyle, provision of religious education rooted in the *Quran*, campaign against vice in the streets, and goal of an Islamic state in all of Palestine through *jihad*. Hamas's late cofounder and co-leader Abdul Aziz al Rantisi argued that martyrdom operations (suicide bombings) are an obligation for Muslims that they should choose with joy.[15] It is interesting to note that Hamas's predecessor, the Muslim Brotherhood, was almost exclusively a re-ligious organization that, as mentioned, focused on the religious rehabilita-tion and transformation of Palestinian society. Hamas only turned to active confrontation and violence after it began to integrate political goals such as displacing the PLO as the dominant force in the occupied territories and expelling the Israelis.

Al Rantisi and other Hamas leaders, despite the virulently anti-Jewish language that is in Hamas's charter, maintain that their conflict is with Israel and not the Jewish people or religion, for which they claim that they hold no animosity. Accordingly, suicide bombings and missile strikes are used because of Israel's occupation of Palestine and campaign to destroy Islamic nationalism, not hatred of Jews.[16] Dr. Mohammed Zahar, an early Hamas leader, blamed Israel for religionizing the conflict because Israel made Judaism its state religion. According to Zahar, the Israelis also declared war on Islam, closed mosques, and attacked defenseless worshippers.[17] Dr. Eyad Sarraj, a Gaza psychiatrist, not only acknowledges the importance of Hamas's religious roots and mission but also mentions the importance of historical conscious. He believes that Hamas's strident and violent opposi-tion to Israel is as much a reaction to the setbacks and defeats that Muslims and Arabs have endured over the past 500 years, which suggests a deeply held psychological need to nullify these setbacks by violently confronting Western enemies.[18] Consequently, it is not surprising that Hamas leaders frequently describe Israel as a tool used by the West and the United States to spread globalization, to continue colonialism, and to subjugate the Islamic world economically with consumerism and strip it off its cultural roots.[19]

The ascendancy of political expediency over religious zeal is evident in Hamas's increasing political pragmatism. Hamas has limited its terrorism to Israel and the occupied territories in order to avoid provoking third-party nations. The group has frequently clashed with al Qaeda militants in

Gaza, who criticized Hamas for engaging in legitimate politics.[20] Hroub argues that Hamas has made a gradual move from idealistic naiveté to pragmatic realism. The group's original goal of creating an Islamic utopia from the Mediterranean to the Jordan has been replaced by more short-term and intermediate objectives such as making the costs of Israel's occupation unbearable, stopping the expansion of Israeli settlements, and defeating the PLO in the internal struggle for the hearts and minds of Palestinians. Hamas did not emphasize an Islamic state or the total liberation of Palestine in the 2006 elections but, rather, focused on reform, providing services, and ending corruption, as it had to modify its message to appeal to a broad spectrum of Palestinian society, particularly those who were disgusted with Fatah.[21] Some inside Hamas have suggested that there is a faction that wants to change the group's charter, but the international isolation and nonrecognition following its electoral victory in 2006 has strengthened the hand of the militant faction.[22] It is important to remember that the original PLO charter also did not recognize Israel and also called for armed struggle until victory.

Israeli Occupation

The most significant cause of Hamas's violence and terror is opposition to Israeli occupation. Hamas officials such as Sheik Saleh al Arouria, a leader of Hamas's military wing, usually list nationalism and resistance to occupation, rather than creating an Islamic state as being the group's most important cause.[23] Hamas also follows a long history of nonreligious Palestinian terrorism and violent opposition to Israel. The secular-nationalist PLO used terrorist tactics such as hijacking and attacks on Israeli civilians until Arafat determined that negotiation provided the best chance of gaining a Palestinian state. Hamas only became the champion of armed resistance following Egypt and, later, Jordan's peace treaties with Israel and exit from the Arab-Israeli conflict, the PLO's flight from Lebanon and acceptance of a negotiated settlement and two-state solution, and the Oslo Accords. Therefore, armed struggle, along with social services, morality, and honesty, and religion is what differentiate Hamas from Fatah. Since the first Intifada, the group has tried to raise the cost of occupation for the Israelis to a point where it is no longer bearable. The failure of the Oslo Accords, the rapid expansion of Israeli settlements, and the increasing desperation of the Palestinians have led to an increased severity of Hamas violence as the second Intifada, beginning in 2000, featured suicide bombings and missiles rather than stone throwing.[24] Leftist Palestinian groups and militant branches of

Fatah, such as the al Aqsa Martyrs Brigade, have also used suicide attacks during the second Intifada.

The radicalization of Hamas and other Palestinian groups and their use of suicide bombings, missiles strikes, and other extreme acts of violence are partly a result of the increasing severity and duration of Israeli occupation. Hamas leader Ismail Abu Shanab claims that the offenses against Palestinians began with Jewish immigration from 1917 followed by almost 100 years of land expropriation, eviction of Palestinians, and frustration, humiliation, and suffering caused by occupation. To Shanab, violent demonstrations of power are deterrence, and it is an Islamic duty to struggle against occupation and serve God by defending one's land.[25]

Al Rantisi argued that the 50-year occupation is slavery, victimization of women and children, and an act of war that has killed thousands of Palestinians. Hassan Salameh, who organized a series of suicide attacks in 1996, claimed that his fight was with the Israeli government. Although his motivations were partly religious, it was seeing his people "murdered in the soul by the occupation" that was his primary inspiration.[26] A trainer said, "Much of the work is already done by the suffering these people have been subject to. . . . Only 10 percent comes from me. The suffering and living in exile away from their land has given the person 90 percent of what he needs to become a martyr."[27]

The humiliation of occupation is a key factor in motivating Hamas suicide bombers. Nasra Hassan reports that "Over and over I heard them [militants] say, 'The Israelis humiliate us. They occupy our land, and deny our history.'"[28] Most Palestinians have experienced restrictions on their ability to work and travel; loss of property; and have endured long waits, searches, and humiliation by Israeli soldiers at checkpoints. Many have been detained and served time in Israeli prisons, where accusations of torture and abuse are common. Palestinians are also at the mercy of the Israelis in every sphere of economic life, as obtaining a permit, working in Israel, and transporting and exporting goods require a struggle with a hostile Israeli bureaucracy and military. According to el Sarraj, martyrdom is an attempt by the humiliated to regain power and respect for themselves and their parents. Many Palestinians saw their parents humiliated and don't want to feel the same helplessness, so they take revenge.[29]

Humiliation, Despair, and Revenge

The humiliation is fortified by the despair of their living conditions as three-quarters of Palestinians in Gaza live below the poverty line on two dollars per day and health conditions are substandard. Thirty percent of children under the age of five suffer from malnutrition, and the infant mortality rate was 40 deaths per 100 live births in 2001. Unemployment rates in Gaza are between 40 and 50 percent.[30] Jessica Stern found an "epidemic of despair" in Gaza and an "inescapable feeling of depression here (Gaza), of utter humiliation and despair" that was "missing the consumerism and entrepreneurial spirit seen in the rest of the developing world."[31] Given this despair and hopelessness, the 12,000 to 15,000 dollars in compensation provided for a suicide bomber's family and the promise of virgins in paradise are important motivators, as martyrdom offers hope of a better existence and help for one's family. The desperation, along with the frequent clashes with the Israeli army and police and the resulting casualties, creates a desire for revenge that motivates many Hamas activists. A study of Palestinian suicide bombers during the second Intifada found that revenge for the death or injury of a friend or relative, for the Palestinians in general, and for affronts to Islam inspired approximately 60 percent of the bombers.[32] Ami Pedhazur and Arie Perliger also found that many suicide bombers had spent time in Israeli prisons or had seen loved ones killed or harmed by the Israelis. Israel's killing of Yehiya Ayash, a leader of Hamas's military arm, in 1996 stimulated the formation of several suicide bomber cells and attacks on Israel.[33] Anat Berko writes that Hamas often recruits at funerals for those killed by the Israeli army.[34]

The humiliation, despair, and desire for revenge that pervade Palestinian society in the occupied territories, along with the efforts of Hamas, combine to socialize young Palestinians into a culture of violence. Mark Juergensmeyer argues that Hamas provides a family for disgruntled Palestinians who cannot find a job, got married, have sex, and start a family.[35] Many suicide bombers have spent time in Israeli prisons and/or come from refugee camps where they meet Hamas leaders who become mentors. Palestinian youth also become supporters of Hamas through its network of mosques, schools, youth groups, and charitable organizations. There is also social pressure to become an activist and join Hamas, as one suicide bomber stated that, "Joining Hamas was the natural thing to do, all the young people were enlisting. Nobody wanted to feel ostracized."[36] Many militants were recruited into Hamas by school friends and other associates. As discussed in chapter 5, suicide bombers are viewed as heroes and celebrated by society with songs, poems, and posters praising their sacrifices. Consequently, the cult of suicide bombing has spread through contagion, developed a momentum of its own, and become part of popular culture to the point where children play a *shahada* (martyr) game that emulates a suicide bombing.[37] Both Brian

Barber and Ariel Merari found that suicide bombers in the second Intifada believed that martyrdom was the best thing that an individual could do to help Palestinian society and that what they were doing was strongly supported by their community.[38] Berko concludes that suicide bombing has become a common Palestinian property and part of a cult of death and killing.[39]

Strategic Calculation

Hamas attacks and suicide bombings are also a product of military and strategic calculations, as they often follow Palestinian casualties caused by Israel. The first suicide bombing against Israel was in 1994 in response to Baruch Goldstein's mass murder of Arabs praying at the Cave of the Patriarch in Hebron. Other events, such as the shooting of Palestinians praying at the Dome of the Rock by Israeli police and the deportation of 415 Hamas and Islamic Jihad members, were followed by car bombings and attacks on Israeli settlers in the West Bank. Assassinations of Hamas leaders have usually been followed by missile strikes.[40] Hamas claims that it only began to attack Israeli civilians after Palestinian civilians were harmed by Israel so that Israelis would feel the pain that they have endured for years.[41] Israeli responses to suicide bombings are usually harsh, involve collective punishment, and lead to civilian casualties, which helps motivate more anger and potential bombers. Suicide bombings are also chillingly cost-effective and require little training or preparation, making them a logical strategic choice for Hamas organizers. At the same time, the psychological trauma caused to the Israelis, knowing that they are not secure within their borders, is profound. As discussed in chapter 5, Hamas, other Palestinian militias, and local cells also carry out bombings because of competition for support and to maintain relevance and popularity. Thus, an attack by one group will be followed by one from its rivals. Groups will even take credit for a rival's bombing in order to increase market share.[42]

HEZBOLLAH

The Lebanese Shiite group Hezbollah, like Hamas, began as a rejectionist opposition organization and then moderated its religious ideology in order to participate in legitimate politics. Hezbollah, as is the case with Hamas, owes its existence to Israeli occupation and has also built support by providing services and welfare to a downtrodden community. Violence has been one of several tools that Hezbollah has strategically used to go from being a marginal group in Lebanon to the country's dominant political force that carries the flag of resistance against Israel in the Arab and Muslim worlds. Hezbollah's use of terror and violence has also been influenced by Lebanon's unique political environment and the experience of that country's Shiite population. Lebanon's Shiites had been a marginalized and oppressed group until Hezbollah began to assert itself during Israel's 18-year occupation of southern Lebanon. The Shiite legacy of persecution and martyrdom began with a lost battle against the Sunnis over the Caliphate shortly after Muhammad's death. Since then, the Shiites have often been a persecuted minority in much of the Islamic world. Lebanon's Shiites fled to the area to escape harassment by Sunnis in Arabia but were eventually stripped of most of their land because the Ottoman Empire viewed them as being agents of Shiite Persia.

The French forcibly included the Shiite areas in the Bekaa Valley and the Coastal Plane when they created Lebanon for their Maronite Christian protégées. Although the Shiites were recognized as an official religious community under the French and were allowed to create their own religious courts, they were marginalized and languished in poverty in comparison to the Christian and Sunni communities. Their inferior status was perpetuated by Lebanon's confessional political system, which was based on a flawed 1932 census. The majority of seats in parliament and the presidency were earmarked for Christians, while the Sunnis controlled the prime minister position. The Shiites were left with the comparatively powerless speaker of parliament and were excluded from top positions in the military and government bureaucracies.[43] As a result, the Shiite communities were poor, uneducated, underdeveloped, and dominated by feudal landlords who neglected their constituents. Several events including the Iranian Revolution, the death of Musa al Sadr, the creation of a Palestinian state within a state in southern Lebanon, and the Lebanese Civil War served to politically mobilize Lebanon's Shiites and to create a situation where their rising expectations could not be met by the Christian-dominated confessional political system.[44]

Iranian Influence

A number of Lebanese Shiite clerics studied in Najaf, Iraq, from 1950 to 1970, when it was a center of Shiite learning. Many fell under the sway of the late Iranian leader Ayatollah Khomeini who preached that Islamic values were being pushed out by Western influences such as socialism, liberalism, consumerism, and hedonism and that an Islamic state was necessary to redeem and reinvigorate Muslim societies. Many of these clerics, including Musa al Sadr, took this message, which was prominent in early Hezbollah proclamations, back to Lebanon and maintained close ties with the Iranians.[45] Al Sadr became the religious leader and champion of the Lebanese Shiites, formed the Council of the South in 1959 to develop neglected Shiite regions, and created the Movement of the Deprived in 1974 to pressure the government for reform and to mobilize the masses. Al Sadr's mysterious death during a trip to Libya in 1978 was reminiscent of the 12th hidden imam who Shiites believe has mysteriously disappeared and will return as the messiah.[46] The Iranian Revolution in 1979, which led to an Islamic government in a Shiite nation, was an inspiration for Lebanon's dispossessed Shiites. Khomeini and the Iranians provided Lebanon's Shiites with a sense of dignity and respect and a road map for their own success. Khomeini also exported his bitter hatred toward Israel and the West to his Lebanese brethren. Iran's Revolutionary Guard would soon make its way to Lebanon to train Hezbollah and make it a tool in its quest to become the hegemon in the Middle East.[47]

Lebanon's Civil War

The outbreak of Lebanon's civil war in 1975 also served to mobilize Lebanon's Shiites, as they were now the country's largest sectarian community, but were still shut of power and lagged economically behind the Christian and Sunni communities.[48] Lebanon's Shiites were originally attracted to secular universal movements such as socialism, Arab Nationalism, and Ba'athism, which sought to end the confessional system, and along with Sunnis, Druze, and Palestinian militias, participated in the Lebanese National Front against the Christians. As was the case throughout the Muslim world, the failure of these secular organizations to solve Lebanon's problems left the door open for an Islamic alternative.[49] The PLO state within a state in southern Lebanon, which had been established following that organization's expulsion from Jordan, soon soured Shiite relations with the Palestinians. The Shiite suffered greatly under the Palestinians, who took Shiite jobs, confiscated Shiite land and property, and brutalized the local population in their de facto state in southern Lebanon. The Shiite also bore the brunt of Israeli reprisals for PLO raids into Israel, including a full-scale invasion in 1978. Consequently, the secular oriented Shiite militia, Amal, which had originally been trained by the PLO and fought against the Christians during the civil war, began to engage in armed resistance against the Palestinians.[50]

Israeli Invasion, 1982

Most Shiites welcomed Israel's full-scale invasion in 1982 to drive the PLO out of Lebanon, as they were tired of being caught in the cross fire between the two warring parties and of the Palestinian's brutal rule. Also, the opening of the border with Israel brought prosperity to Shiite communities.[51] Israel's continued presence and occupation of southern Lebanon, however, turned out to be a catalyst that helped create Hezbollah and facilitated its domination of the Shiite community and its becoming the most powerful political and military force in Lebanon. Former Israeli prime minister Ehud Barak remarked that "When we entered Lebanon . . . there was no Hezbollah. We were accepted and showered with rice and flowers by the Shiites in the south. It was our presence there that created Hezbollah. It was staying and occupying that created them." The late Yitzhak Rabin succinctly stated that "We let the genie (Hezbollah) out of the bottle."[52]

The Shiites, when it became clear that the Israel had no intention of leaving south Lebanon, began to resist. Israel responded with an iron fist as young men were conscripted into Israel's proxy Christian militia, the South Lebanon Army (SLA), hundreds were accused of being militants and were imprisoned, villages were sealed off, electricity and water were cut off, curfews were enforced, and an economic blockade was put in place. Eventually, Israel's iron-fisted attempts to pacify the South under the control of the SLA led to the destruction of 7 villages, damage to 82 more, 19,000 deaths, and 35,000 injuries.[53] The Shiites were also weary of Israel's plans to leave a Maronite-dominated government in Beirut, which would mean continued political marginalization. In October 1983, an Israeli military convoy interrupted an Ashura procession, a sacred festival in Shiite Islam, and refused to retreat, causing a riot. In the melee that followed, 2 people were killed and 15 were injured, which prompted the head of the Higher Shiite Council to issue a *fatwa* calling for resistance against Israel.[54] The Israeli invasion also caused a massive Shiite migration to the poor southern suburbs of Beirut, which became fertile Hezbollah recruiting grounds. Violent struggle against Israel, even after it withdrew from Lebanon in 2000, would become the strategy that took Hezbollah to the top of Lebanon's political system, made it the country's most powerful military force, and made it a threat to stability in the Middle East.

A final factor relating to the Israeli invasion and occupation that facilitated the rise of Hezbollah and its use of violence was the decline of the secular oriented Shiite militia Amal, which had never fulfilled its expectations in improving the lot of Lebanon's Shiites. Amal had welcomed the

Israeli invasion, participated in the Christian-led National Salvation Committee when Israel laid siege to Beirut during the summer of 1982, had
fought Israel's enemy the PLO, and had provided no material support to
the Shiites in the Belt of Misery in Beirut's southern suburbs. Amal eventually abandoned its radical ideology for patronage and backroom politics
and lost the support of the Shiite community, which led to it being routed
by Hezbollah in an intrasectarian civil war in 1987.[55] With the resentment
caused by years of marginalization in Lebanon's political system and economy, the model of Iran's Shiite Islamic revolution, a hatred of the occupying Israelis and their Western supporters, and the support of Lebanon's
Syrian overseers, Hezbollah was ready to rise to power and fill the vacuum
created by Amal.

Hezbollah's Birth

Hezbollah made its public debut in February 1985 when it published
its manifesto. As mentioned, many of its founding members were clerics
who had studied in Najaf and were inspired by Khomeini and the Iranian
Revolution. Other founders were disenchanted with Amal's secular orientation and its accommodation with the Israelis and the Christian-dominated
government. According to Sheik Naiim Qassem, a former Amal cleric who
helped found Hezbollah, the inspiration of Iran was of key importance, and
the group originally intended to create a *Sharia*-based state and an Iranian
style Islamic government.[56] The group's manifesto rails against the West for
its hatred of Islam, its colonialism and imperialism going back to the Crusades, and its desire to impose its ideology on the Middle East. The United
States is singled out as being the root of the problems in the Islamic world
because of its desire to control the region's economy and oil and its support
for Israel. Hezbollah originally refused to participate in the confessional
political system but did encourage its supporters to vote for parties that
supported an Islamic system.[57] Although Hezbollah activists killed several
members of opposing Shiite groups and enforced Islamic law in its enclaves
in Beirut and the Bekaa Valley by closing liquor stores and forcing women
to dress modestly, it has always claimed that it would not force Islamic government on Lebanon. The group's spiritual mentor Mohammed Fadlallah
argued that the conditions are not right for an Islamic state in Lebanon because of the country's diverse religious population and the lack of consensus. Consequently, Hezbollah activists would first have to convince people
to choose Islam and lead by example, while respecting Lebanon's pluralist
nature.[58]

Charity and Social Services

Hezbollah, like Hamas, has used charity and social service, in addition to opposition to Israel, to broaden its base of support. According to Thanassis Cambanis, many of Hezbollah's followers are true faithful who believe the group's credo that faith in God, resistance, and hard work will restore pride, dignity, and self-determination to the dispossessed Shiites. Others are won over to the group, and their allegiance is maintained through social services, education, and job training, which provide hope for a better future.[59] Hezbollah originally gained support by going into The Belt of Misery, the Shiite suburbs of south Beirut that were ignored by the government, and providing food, shelter, health care, and schooling with money from Iran. The Lebanese government was happy to be relieved of the burden of caring for these areas and was content to let Hezbollah take care of their Shiite brethren. At the same time, the Shiite rival militia, Amal, had done little for the poor.[60] Although Hezbollah can be heavy-handed when encouraging supporters to volunteer time and labor for community service projects, providing a safety net for the needy and strengthening the community have created a strong social fabric and a rebuilt south Beirut that engenders pride and loyalty.[61]

Attacks on Westerners in Early 1980s

Many in the West associate Hezbollah with the suicide bombings against the Multinational Force (MNF, primarily the United States and France) that was sent to Beirut in 1983 to restore order after massacres by Israel's Christian allies at the Sabra and Shatila Palestinian refugee camps in 1983, the bombing of the U.S. embassy in Beirut in the same year, and the kidnapping of several Americans and Westerners during the 1980s. All of these events, however, took place prior to Hezbollah's formal founding in 1985, and credit for the bombings and many of the kidnappings was taken by a group that referred to itself as Islamic Jihad. That group was closely tied to Iran and was believed to be supported by the clerics that founded Hezbollah, who denied responsibility for the attacks but expressed approval. Husayn al Masawi argued that the bombings were a response to Western occupation and intervention on behalf of Israel in its attempt to create a Christian client state.[62] Although the MNF entered Lebanon as peacekeepers, they eventually shelled Muslim and Druze militias, which President Ronald Reagan claimed were tools of Syria and the Soviets in support of the Lebanese army. Consequently, the MNF lost its neutrality, became another militia in the civil war, and, as a result, a target.[63] Hezbollah's association with the attacks and the kidnappings helped fuel their popularity because they became to be seen as a group that would defend Lebanon against Western occupiers and influence.

A Turn to Moderation and Pragmatism

Hezbollah, despite its association with kidnappings and suicide bombings, halted its use of both practices early in its existence as part of its effort to be seen as a resistance army rather than a terrorist group. This attempt to change Hezbollah's reputation was part of a prolonged public relations campaign after its early radical days to be seen as patriotic Lebanese nationalists rather than Iranian style fundamentalist terrorists.[64] By 1986, Hezbollah had begun to alienate itself from the residents of South Lebanon, who suffered from the Israeli reprisals for attacks on their troops and who were not pleased when the militants banned alcohol, music, parties, and coffee shops causing Lebanese tourists to avoid Hezbollah-controlled areas. In the 1990s, the group began to adopt a more conciliatory and tolerant approach, emphasizing its desire for intercommunal harmony and that it did not wish to turn Lebanon into an Iranian style Shiite theocracy. Thus, Hezbollah limited its use of violence to Israeli targets and avoided clashes with other Lebanese sectarian militias. The only Lebanese group that had been a target of Hezbollah attacks during the civil war was Shiite rival, Amal. The group's leaders and clerics also began to speak to foreign journalists and insisted that they had nothing against the West, but only the imposition of its culture and political objectives on the Middle East.[65]

Conflict with Israel as a Reason for Being

Hezbollah's turn to a more moderate and pragmatic approach to Lebanese domestic politics has been accompanied by an unwavering and total commitment to violent confrontation with Israel. According to Thanassis Cambanis, perpetual war with Israel made Hezbollah the most powerful force in Lebanon and has mobilized thousands under its banner of resistance. Hezbollah's longtime leader, Hassan Nasrallah, has acknowledged that the perception of an Israeli threat has created an opportunity for the group both in the Shiite community and within Lebanon. Anger against Israel unifies the movement, prevents internal struggles, rallies its Shiite supporters, and wins the respect of Lebanon's other religious communities.[66] Thus, continuing the conflict with Israel remains in Hezbollah's best interest and also allowed it to maintain the only independent militia following the end of the civil war. As mentioned, Hezbollah rose to prominence because of its resistance to Israel's occupation of southern Lebanon in the 1980s, and every Israeli attempt to destroy the group has served to increase its popularity and its number of supporters. Collective punishment against Shiite villages caused hatred to be directed against Israel rather than spark uprisings against Hezbollah. Deporting and targeting Hezbollah leaders for assassination have turned them into martyrs rather than cutting off the head of the dragon. Massive retaliation for Hezbollah attacks on Israeli civilians, such as the bombing of a UN base where civilians had sought refuge during Operation Grapes of Wrath in 1996 that killed 63 civilians, earned Hezbollah support and sympathy from all of Lebanon's sectarian groups. Consequently, Hezbollah was able to successfully argue that it needed to remain armed following the end of the civil war because it was a liberation army fighting to end the occupation of Lebanese soil.[67]

Hezbollah's pragmatic and public relations minded approach can be seen in its armed conflict with Israel. It moved away from suicide bombing in order to be seen as a liberation army rather than an extremist terrorist organization. Hezbollah was responsible for less than one-third of suicide bombings against Israeli troops in Lebanon and had largely discontinued these attacks by 1990. The group also made several informal agreements with Israel during its occupation of South Lebanon, as Hezbollah agreed to limit its operations to Israeli troops within Lebanon and not to attack military or civilian targets within Israel if Israel refrained from targeting Lebanese civilians. After Israel's withdrawal in 2000, the border between Israel and Lebanon was relatively peaceful until 2006.[68] These agreements allowed Hezbollah to claim that it was fighting a defensive *jihad* targeted against an occupying military force, while doing its best to protect Lebanese civilians from harm. Also, the end of Israeli occupation in 2000 did not lead to a massacre or acts of revenge against Lebanese Christians who had been members of the SLA or who had supported the Israelis. Those who did not flee to Israel or emigrate to the West served short prison sentences and then were largely left alone.[69]

The importance of the struggle against Israel as a reason for Hezbollah's existence, its dominance of Lebanese domestic politics, and the maintenance of party unity and passion is exemplified in the continuation of hostilities following Israel's withdrawal of its troops in 2000. Because evicting the Israelis from Lebanese soil was Hezbollah's justification for remaining armed, the end of the conflict would mean that the group would lose one of its central purposes and unifying forces, as well as reducing its ability to influence Lebanese domestic politics. Consequently, Hezbollah claimed that the Israeli withdrawal was not complete because it retained control of a

small disputed piece of territory, the Shebaa Farms, and that armed resistance needed to continue.[70] In 2006, Hezbollah provoked a full-scale Israeli
invasion by kidnapping two Israeli soldiers near the border, which led to
Israeli reprisals and counterreprisals and a 30-day war. Israel's bombing
campaign included Hezbollah military forces and political headquarters in
South Lebanon and Beirut as well as targeting Lebanese government buildings and crucial infrastructure. Hezbollah fired missiles into several Israeli
cities including, for the first time, the large port city of Haifa. More than
1,100 Lebanese civilians were killed, and much of the rebuilding that had
been done following the end of the civil war and Israel's occupation was,
once again, destroyed.

Hezbollah's kidnapping of the Israeli soldiers and instigating of the subsequent bombardment and invasion demonstrate how the group uses the
threat of Israel to rally its base and as a tool to win domestic political battles, as well as Israel's tendency to fall into its traps. Prior to the war, a
Lebanese TV comedy had mocked Hezbollah and its pretexts for not disarming. According to Richard Norton, this touched the raw nerves of a for-
mally marginalized community that had to regain its honor and reestablish
that its militia was essential for the defense of Lebanon.[71] Michael Totten
writes that the United Nations had recently concluded that Hezbollah's Syrian patrons were responsible for the assassination of Lebanon's Western
leaning prime minister Rafik Hariri and that the provocation was an attempt to deflect anger onto Israel.[72] At the onset, public opinion in Lebanon
was against Hezbollah and the war, but Israel's massive retaliation and the
resulting civilian casualties and destruction, once again, played into Hezbollah's hands, and most Lebanese soon supported Hezbollah, while the
Lebanese army remained on the sidelines. At the end of the war, Hezbollah
was able to claim victory and bring pride and honor to its supporters simply
by surviving and holding off the Israeli army and by being seen as the leader
of Arab resistance to Israel. In order to extend the state of perpetual war,
Hezbollah has switched its focus from defending Lebanon to helping in the
liberation of Palestine and bringing about the end of Israel.[73]

Dominance of Lebanese Politics

The successful war against Israel in 2006 left Hezbollah as the dominant
force in Lebanon, as its militia was far more powerful than the Lebanese
army, and it had created a state within a state in south Beirut and south
Lebanon, where there is literally no sign of the Lebanese government. It had
gone from being a conspiratorial terrorist group that rejected participation

in politics, to a backbench opposition, to the kingmakers in Lebanese politics. Concurrently, Hezbollah's clerical leaders have adjusted their interpretation of Islam to political conditions, just as they moved away from their endorsement of suicide bombing when it became clear that those missions were damaging the group's reputation. The political system, which had been deemed corrupt and oppressive in the 1980s, was declared acceptable following the Taif agreement in 1989 that ended the civil war. At the same, Hezbollah has displayed a skilled hand at playing politics by maintaining its militia, when all others disarmed following the civil war. It has also shown a ruthless side by shutting down the investigation into Hariri's death; staging massive demonstrations to counter the Cedar Revolution by a coalition of pro-Western Druze, Sunnis, and Christians; and maintaining its dominance after the Syrian forces that had been present since the civil war departed in 2005. In 2008, Hezbollah sent its fighters into the streets and used violence against Christians, Druze, and Sunnis to shut down their challenge to Hezbollah's de facto control of the government and demand that it disband its militia. Clearly, Lebanon's once marginalized Shiites, although they will not force a Shiite theocracy on Lebanon's diverse population, will not tolerate any challenge to their newly established position of power.

AL QAEDA

It would seem that the acts of terrorism and mayhem inspired by the late Osama bin Laden and committed by al Qaeda and its affiliates can be attributed to sheer religious fanaticism. Bin Laden and his followers have been engaged in a *jihad* to defend Islam and Muslims against a variety of enemies including the United States, its Western allies, Israel, the former Soviet Union, the Saudi ruling family, other corrupt and *kefir* (apostate) regimes in Islamic nations, and countless other nations that oppress Muslims. He presents the conflict as being between Islam and Christian Crusaders, Jews, and other infidels. He espouses a Salafi vision of Islam that includes a return to the society that existed at the time of the Prophet Muhammad, the implementation of *Sharia* law, and the unification of the Islamic world under a new Caliphate. Early in his struggle, bin Laden sought out prominent Muslim clerics to support his violent actions with *fatwas* and later began to issue his own. In short, bin Laden's appeals for *jihad* and a return to a pure Islam are parts of classical Islamic jurisprudence and are an acceptable part of Islamic traditions and history.[74]

Bin Laden's interpretation of Islam, although legitimate, is one of many competing Islamic visions and one for which few are willing to dedicate and sacrifice their lives. Violent *jihad* is even a minority strain in the Salafi movement, as others either withdraw from corrupt contemporary society or attempt to bring about change through preaching and living their lives as examples of pure Islam. At the same time, bin Laden and key associates, such as his successor Ayman al Zawahiri, have altered their interpretations of Islamic law and tradition according to the necessity of circumstances. Consequently, bin Laden cooperated with Shiites, who Salafi generally view as heretics, Chinese criminal gangs, former Red Army and KGB officers, and Western banks. In 1998, he, for the first time, justified the killing of Muslim civilians, following the bombing of the U.S. embassies in Kenya and Tanzania.[75] Once again, factors relating to politics, economics, social change, and personality will provide an understanding as to why bin Laden's version of Islam is appealing to some at this point in history and why conditions are ripe for using Islam to justify violence. Also, bin Laden's talents included political astuteness, an awareness of global and regional issues, and how changes in the political and social environment were negatively affecting the lives of many Muslims.[76] Al Qaeda's terrorism should not be seen as mindless religious fanaticism but a military response to a steady decline in the power of the of the Muslim world relative to the West, United States world hegemony and foreign policy, corrupt and autocratic regimes in the Muslim world, globalization, and bin Laden's personality and lifestyle.

Fighting Back against the Western Crusaders

The hostility to globalization discussed in chapter 4 that is present in segments of the Muslim world is a good place to begin when understanding al Qaeda's war against the United States, the West, and apostate Muslim regimes. Islam, for 1,000 years, was a dominant civilization militarily, economically, and culturally, and it expanded into Christian lands. Then the tables were turned, and the European colonial empires penetrated much of the Muslim world with their cultures, ideas, laws, way of life, militaries, and settlers. The dominators became the dominated and the advanced became the backward. This reversal of fortune produced a scar on the Muslim psyche that has grown over the years.[77] Abdel Bari Atwan writes that "People in the West do not often fully understand the deep connection many Muslims feel with their past, and how bitterly many lament the lost glory of the *umma*. This sense of historical loss is all too often combined with a contemporary experience that is defined by disappointment and humiliation."[78] Therefore, bin Laden's Salafi-based notions of going back to the time of glory of the *umma*, before the Islamic world had been divided into artificial nations by the Western powers and reestablishing the Caliphate when Islam was practiced correctly, appeal to many Muslims. This raises the question as to why using violent *jihad* to restore Muslim glory is popular enough for bin Laden to rally thousands of militants and the support of millions of others.

The decline of the Muslim world was accompanied by military defeat by the European powers followed by colonial domination, Muslim nations being used as pawns in the Cold War by the United States and the Soviet Union, and, finally, U.S. world hegemony, which has involved a number of military incursions in the Islamic world. According to bin Laden, Western hostility to Islam began with the Crusades, when Christian armies attempted, repeatedly, and often with great brutality and civilian casualties, to recapture the Holy Land from the Muslims. Although they failed and the Crusades came during the period of Muslim world dominance, bin Laden and other Muslims see contemporary American-led military campaigns in painted the Middle East as part of a long history of Christian attacks on Muslims. As a result, he built on the collective Muslim psyche that is scarred by anger at the West and exploits massacres of Muslims in today's world by linking them to historical battles between Muslims and their enemies and invoking broad Muslim grievances going back to the Crusades.[79]

Al Qaeda is best seen as a movement that has formulated a broad and coherent set of grievances against the West and the Western dominated political system and as an attempt to regain honor and to relieve humiliation. Bin Laden viewed his struggle as being a defensive one that has been forced on Muslims by the West's arrogance, barbarity, and ruthlessness.[80] He painted a picture of a Muslim world that is under frequent attack from the West, led by the United States, and pointed to the Soviet attack on Afghanistan; Russia's atrocities in Chechnya; Israel's occupation of Palestine; the war against Bosnian Muslims; U.S. attacks on Iraq, Sudan, and Afghanistan; and countless other atrocities against Muslims as evidence. The notion that the United States is intent on destroying Muslims and their religion and that its political leaders are modern version of the European Catholic nobility makes the appeal for resistance to restore Islam's dignity through a defensive *jihad* a potent rallying call. The great disparity in power between the United States, Israel, and the West and the Muslims that they oppress makes taking up the fight even more noble and a responsibility for all who are able.[81]

The Soviet Invasion of Afghanistan

Al Qaeda, although best known for its global *jihad* against the United States and its allies, traces its roots to the Soviet Union's invasion of

Afghanistan in 1979 to aid a client regime. Bin Laden first went to Afghanistan at the invitation of Abdullah Azzam, who had taught him Islamic thought at King Abdulaziz University in Saudi Arabia and was the ideologue of the Mujahedeen resistance fighters. Bin Laden quickly saw the necessity of fighting to liberate Muslim lands from foreigners and went on to use his wealth to supply equipment, volunteers, and arms to the Afghan rebels.[82] Eventually, bin Laden joined the Mujahedeen, fought on the front lines, was wounded, and nearly escaped death on numerous occasions. The campaign to push the Soviets out of Afghanistan was crucial in shaping bin Laden's worldview. The brutality and ruthlessness of the Soviet occupation involved atrocities such as rape, burning civilians alive, raising villages, and machine gunning peasants. These actions confirmed the notion of a barbaric infidel enemy that was out to destroy Islam.

The eventual success of the Mujahedeen, the withdrawal of the Red Army, and the breakup of the Soviet Union that soon followed convinced bin Laden, his supporters, and many others that a superpower could be brought to its knees through a righteous struggle because a lightly armed group of guerillas had defeated a powerful army. This was the first successful military operation against infidels by Muslims following disappointments and humiliation at the hands of enemies such as Israel and India.[83] In contrast to past lost campaigns, this successful one had been waged in the name of Islam. The war also planted the seeds of al Qaeda because many of the Arabs that bin Laden brought to Afghanistan to fight became loyal disciples who later followed him to Saudi Arabia, Sudan, and back to Afghanistan and became career jihadists. Others returned to their home countries and spread the word about the glory of *jihad,* their success, the righteous man who had led them, and started local Islamic insurgency movements. Bin Laden also met insurgents from other countries such as Egypt, Yemen, Algeria, Kashmir, and the Philippines that would later become al Qaeda affiliates. Afghanistan was also where he developed the plan for a worldwide *jihad* that would not be limited by national borders.[84]

Afghanistan also marked the beginning of bin Laden becoming a folk hero in the Muslim world to the point where he enjoyed the support of up to 60 percent of those polled in some Arab countries and had higher approval ratings in Saudi Arabia than ruling family. It was the perception that he was a champion of revolution, the David who took on Goliath, and that he brought hope and dignity after centuries of decline and humiliation that made him popular, not his Salafi interpretation of Islam or call for the use of *Sharia* law. Bin Laden was the wealthy man who was willing to give up all of his luxuries to live in austerity in caves and fight on the front lines, while surviving numerous bombardments, assassination attempts, and injuries further enhanced bin Laden's larger than life status.[85] Bin Laden's militant and masculine approach that involved taunting America and the West put him in sharp contrast with the leaders of Arab and Muslim nations such as his native Saudi Arabia, Egypt, Pakistan, and Jordan who appeared to be weak and subservient to the West. Finally, the frequent demonization of bin Laden by American leaders and the media made him even more of a folk hero. According to Peter Bergen, he became a combination of Robin Hood and the Pied Piper leading his loyal small band followers into *jihad* against the mighty superpower.[86]

Saudi Arabia

Bin Laden's native country, Saudi Arabia, also played an important role in causing his hatred of the West and facilitating his development of a global *jihad* against Christians and Jews. He came from a wealthy and well-connected family that controlled the cement manufacturing industry in that country, and he was able to use that wealth to bring fighters to Afghanistan and provide them with jobs in the industries that he later developed in Sudan, where they also trained for future operations. It is likely that his family's connections delayed the Saudi government from taking action against him when he began to criticize and agitate against the royal family. Saudi Arabia uses Islamic law, adheres to the strict and puritanical Wahhabi variant of Islam, and its royal family claims to be the guardians of Islam's holy places. Despite majoring in economics and public administration, bin Laden still had mandatory classes in Islamic thought, where he was taught by Azzam and Mohammed Qutb, the brother of Sayyid Qutb, one of the founding ideologues of today's radical Islam. Thus, he was instructed about the importance of *jihad* at a government institution, which led to his journey to Afghanistan at the invitation of his former teacher. On his return from Afghanistan, he soon became disenchanted with the Saudi ruling family—which claimed to represent pure Islam, implement strict Islamic law, and protect the holy cities of Mecca and Medina—and concluded that these claims were false and that the regime was corrupt and apostate. The Saudi regime quickly became concerned because bin Laden's popularity and his call for reform were a threat to their Islamic legitimacy.[87]

It is important to note, when determining whether the conflict between bin Laden and the West is rooted in religious and civilizational differences, that most of al Qaeda's attacks have taken place in Saudi Arabia and other Muslim nations and the intensity of his hatred for the Saudi ruling family.[88]

Like many others who use terrorism in the name of Islam, bin Laden is the product of a corrupt, authoritarian society. Bin Laden and other young Saudis saw a ruling family that squandered the country's oil wealth on their own luxuries, a regime where bribery was required to get anything done, and an authoritarian government that denied civil rights and used torture to repress dissent and imprisoned religious scholars who dared criticize the regime. Bin Laden was particularly appalled by the Saudi's close ties with the United States, which he claimed was looting the country and polluting its values. When his calls for reform were not answered, he accused the regime of being traitors to Islam and claimed that it was the duty of good Muslims to rebel.[89] Ironically, the government had helped create the insurgency movement because it had encouraged young men to fight in the *jihad* in Afghanistan and had given them financial support. Like bin Laden, most had been taught about the duty of *jihad* in state schools and universities and returned to guest houses that had jihadist literature.

American Troops in the Arabian Peninsula

The Saudi regime's decision to invite the American military to Arabian Peninsula and to station troops there after Saddam Hussein's Iraq attacked and occupied Kuwait in 1990 was the final catalyst of both bin Laden's revolt against the Saudi regime and the global *jihad* against the United States. After the Iraqi invasion, bin Laden sent a letter to the royal family offering to arm and train 100,000 men, including his Mujahedeen from the Afghan campaign, to evict the Iraqis from Kuwait. Bin Laden's offer was ignored and then ridiculed, and he was finally told not to interfere. This denial was a cause of great humiliation, particularly since he was under house arrest, while the Crusaders defended Islamic holy land. He later said that the decision to refuse his offer was the "shock of his life," because the government had invited infidel troops onto the Arabian Peninsula near the holy places in Mecca and Medina for the first time since the inception of Islam. Bin Laden pointed to verses from the *Quran* and sayings of the prophet that forbade Christians, Jews, and atheists from the land of the Holy Places. For bin Laden, inviting 500,000 foreign troops, including females, to colonize and occupy the Arabian Peninsula, a transgression that even the French and British had avoided during the colonial era, meant that the government had allowed the desecration of the holy cities, committed an unforgivable sin, and lost all legitimacy.[90]

The American occupation also intensified his hatred for the United States as his formal declaration of *jihad* in 1996 was against the "Americans occupying the sacred places," which he labeled as the worst disaster since the death of the prophet. His statement on forming the World Islamic Front for *jihad* against Jews and Crusaders in 1998 that set the stage for the 9/11 attacks listed the seven-year occupation of the Peninsula, which humiliated and frightened Muslims, as a central grievance. At the same time, the Americans had gone too far in the war against Saddam and with later economic sanctions, which created millions of victims.[91] Soon bin Laden fled to Sudan and began organizing and training *jihadist* groups to make American taste the bitter fruit of its arrogance and aggression. He also set up a network of clerics and scholars who issued *fatwa* stating that it was obligatory for all Muslims to fight the American invaders. Consequently, there were numerous attacks by al Qaeda and affiliated groups on American armed forces and government installations across the globe including the 1993 bombing of the World Trade Center, a trucking bomb at a U.S. military housing complex in Saudi Arabia in 1996, explosions at U.S. embassies in Kenya and Tanzania in 1998, the bombing of the USS *Cole* in Yemen in 2000, and the attacks on 9/11.

Hatred of the United States and Its Allies

The United States, as the lone remaining Western superpower after the fall of the Soviet Union, was now public enemy number one for bin Laden and al Qaeda. With the position of global hegemon, America became the inheritor of the 1,000 years of Muslim anger and resentment toward the Christian West dating back to the Crusades. The United States, like all of the great powers that preceded it, has acted globally to defend its perceived interests and to maintain its hegemony. Consequently, it intervened in Iraq to combat a threat to its access to oil, which was highly offensive to bin Laden. His disdain for the United States was furthered by other policies and actions that it undertook in the Muslim world to protect and further its interests. Bin Laden's first grievance was that the Americans had exploited the Mujahedeen, abandoned them after the Soviets had left Afghanistan, and purposefully caused divisions so that an Islamist government would not take power.[92] High on the list of America's crimes was its support for Israel. Bin Laden viewed the presence of a Jewish state on Islamic holy land (Jerusalem is the third holiest city in Islam.) as illegitimate and an abomination. He also labeled Israel's treatment of the Palestinians under its occupation as criminal and genocide. America, because it was controlled by the Jews, was viewed as having a double standard that allowed Israel to occupy Palestine and commit atrocities but attacked Iraq when it occupied Kuwait.[93]

The United States' support, again to protect its access to oil, for the corrupt and apostate Saudi regime, as well as other dictators and autocrats in the Muslim world, is also prominent on bin Laden's list of grievances. He argued that without American military, technological, and political support, the corrupt House of Saud would fall like a house of cards. The United States has also supported autocratic regimes that have frequently violated human rights in Egypt, Jordan, Morocco, Tunisia, Yemen, Algeria, and other Muslim countries because they are/were believed to be/have been bulwarks against Islamic fundamentalism and instability. To bin Laden and others, this policy reeked of a double standard where freedom and democracy were desirable everywhere but in the Islamic world.[94] Finally, the United States is guilty of countless other atrocities that targeted and killed civilians, such as dropping atomic bombs on Japan at the end of World War II, the Vietnam War, the bombing of Sudan and Afghanistan in response to the attacks on the U.S. embassies in Kenya and Tanzania, and sanctions on Iraq for trying to develop weapons of mass destruction.[95] Allies have also been targeted because of their support for American policies. Four commuter trains were bombed in Madrid, Spain, in March 2004 and London's subways and busses were bombed in July 2005 because both countries had sent troops in support of America's invasion of Iraq in 2003. Both countries were told that the bombings would stop if they changed their policies.

Al Qaeda's use of violence and terrorism is part of a campaign to get America, its allies, and the Saudis to change their policies. The anonymous author of *Through Our Enemies' Eyes: Osama bin Laden, Radical Islam and the Future of America* makes an intriguing argument that Osama bin Laden is similar to John Brown, an abolitionist who led a raid on a federal installation at Harpers Ferry, Virginia, before the Civil War in order to end slavery, and the leaders of the American Revolution. Bin Laden and his followers, like Brown and the Minutemen, believed that they had protested the evil ways of an oppressor and tried to get it to change its ways without using violence. The oppressor, however, ignored their demands and crossed a line where the righteous rebels had to use violence to get the attention of their powerful adversaries.[96] Subsequently, each offense had to be met with a devastating response and, given the overwhelming power of the adversary, terrorism becomes a justifiable means of resistance. Consequently, the truck bomb in Dharan, Saudi Arabia, was a response to the occupation of the Arabian Peninsula. The attacks on the U.S. embassies were a response to U.S. troops intervening in Somalia. Bombings at Israeli tourist resorts in Africa were a response to that country's treatment of the Palestinians. The attacks on the USS *Cole* were a response to the cruise missiles launched into Sudan and Afghanistan.

Al Qaeda and bin Laden gained further support each time that the United States retaliated for their attacks. The use of cruise missiles and drones from hundreds of miles away was viewed as a sign of cowardliness and reluctance to fight on the battlefield. Although the U.S. invasion of Afghanistan following 9/11 weakened al Qaeda in Afghanistan, it strengthened support in Pakistan when the United States sent drones into that country in pursuit of insurgents. Civilian casualties caused by the bombing of al Qaeda and Taliban targets have led Afghans to resent the American presence and to join the rebels. The U.S. invasion of Iraq in 2003 to allegedly punish Saddam Hussein for his weapons of mass destruction, which were never found, led to the formation of an al Qaeda cell in that country, where it previously had not been a presence. Anger over the invasions of Afghanistan and Iraq facilitated support for bin Laden and an increase in recruits in the mid-2000s. Statements by George Bush that God had instructed him to attack Iraq and al Qaeda and former head of the U.S. interim administration in Iraq, Paul Bremer, that the United States dominated the scene and could impose its will on the country reminded Muslims of the Crusades and the period of colonial occupation.[97]

Globalization

The chaos, disruption, and interconnectedness of the contemporary era of globalization also facilitated the rise of bin Laden and al Qaeda. The decline of the Soviet Union and other Communist nations, such as the former Yugoslavia, provided new opportunities to support and join Muslim rebels in places such as Chechnya and Bosnia. Failed states and weak governments that cannot control their borders or what goes on within their borders have provided havens for bin Laden to raise funds, procure arms, send out propaganda, and communicate with affiliates, as well as opportunities for al Qaeda operations. Bin Laden was welcomed in Sudan, a poor nation that was torn by a brutal 25-year civil war between its northern Muslim and southern Christian and Animist regions, as he started businesses, helped equip the army, and paid good salaries to workers. In turn, he was allowed to set up training camps and begin waging global *jihad* until he was forced to leave because of pressure from the United States. Bin Laden took advantage of the anarchy in Somalia to train and advise the militia that attacked American peacekeepers that had been sent to relieve starvation in 1993 during a civil war but became involved in the conflicts between warring parties. After

Sudan, bin Laden found safe haven in Afghanistan under the Taliban, who were trying to maintain their grip on power following a 10-year civil war after the departure of the Soviets. Bin Laden, of course, was in Afghanistan when 9/11 took place, and the subsequent American led invasion was intended to bring him to justice. Yemen, another weak state that has been torn by civil war and insurrection, has also been an al Qaeda hotbed with the attack on the USS *Cole* and other bombings, kidnappings, and assassinations. Anwar al Awlaki, an American citizen who was rumored to be a possible successor to bin Laden, was killed in Yemen in September 2011.

Globalization has also led to the deterritorialization of Islam as approximately one-third of Muslims live as minorities. Many transplanted Muslims view themselves as being part of a global religious-based community and, as a result, are receptive to bin Laden's Salafi message of a global *umma*, free of national boundaries.[98] At the same time, the humiliation and marginalization felt by Muslims in places like Great Britain and France makes them more sensitive to attacks on Muslims in other places. As Olivier Roy writes, they are angered by discrimination, hostility, suspicion, and a lack of opportunity in their home countries, as well as their parents for accepting second-class status. Contact with Arab jihadists in Europe, who fought in Afghanistan but could not return home, and the media expose them to suffering of other Muslims across the globe and the glory of battle against the powerful enemies and oppressors of Islam. This combination of alienation, anger, and the perception that Muslims everywhere are under attack makes defending their faith an urgent priority and draws them to violent *jihad*. Many also feel guilty because of their partly Westernized lifestyles including drug use, street gangs, and promiscuity, which produces a sense that they should be fighting with Muslims in Iraq and Afghanistan.[99]

A terrorist organization that engages in violence and mayhem worldwide is only possible in today's era of globalization. Satellite phones, e-mail, and websites made it possible for bin Laden to communicate with followers without being traced. Because of the Internet, he did not have to depend on the media to get his message out and could speak directly to his followers and supporters. At the same time, the releases of bin Laden's videos became media events in themselves with experts offering their interpretations of his true intent, which enhanced his importance and perceived power. The ability to transfer money electronically and the ease of money laundering made it easier for him to finance operations across the globe. Al Qaeda is set up like a multinational corporation with franchises throughout the world that act independently. Local cells plan and implement their own attacks without direction from a centralized hierarchy, which makes monitoring and infiltrating the organization very difficult. The ease of global travel and the sheer volume of international trade mean that al Qaeda operatives can travel the world with ease and send weapons and supplies across borders undetected. Bin Laden was also able to recruit well-educated, well-traveled, and talented jihadists from across the world, like the 9/11 hijackers, who could fit in anywhere and could master complex skills such as piloting aircraft.

Conclusion

What's Next?

I began this work by discussing how religion is often seen as a dark, irrational, and uncontrollable force that causes irrational behavior, violence, and terrorism. I hope that I have shown that religions are vague, amorphous, and contradictory ideological frameworks that can be and have been used to justify and rationalize a whole range of behaviors and actions ranging from the extremely harmful suicide bombing, to the mundane, what people eat, and to the benevolent acts of charity and tolerance. I have argued that it is primarily political, socioeconomic, and psychological forces that cause a very small number of individuals to choose interpretations of their faiths that justify and sanction violence. A good way to better understand the relationship between religion and violence and terrorism is to look at some of the emotions and feelings: humiliation, shame, loss of self-worth, and revenge that are characteristic of those who kill in the name of God. Is it religion that causes people to feel these emotions or is it other factors? It is the nonreligious forces listed in the preceding text, as well as factors relating to holy warriors' personal lives, which cause these emotions. Religion, like nationalism, ethnic pride, communism, anarchism, and even liberalism, offers the ideological framework that justifies the channeling of these emotions into organized violence.

EMOTIONS THAT PRODUCE VIOLENCE

Humiliation motivates many forms of violence, not just terrorism. Students at the high school where I taught years ago often responded to insults and other perceived acts of humiliation with violence or threats of violence. Psychologists, who have worked in prisons, conclude that most acts of inmate violence were preceded by the aggressor suffering some form of humiliation by another prisoner.[1] Violent crime rates in the United States have often increased when unemployment rates rise and individuals can no longer provide for their families. The discussion of Hamas and Palestinian terrorism in chapter 8 described how the Israeli occupation causes humiliation on a daily basis at checkpoints and at the hands of Israeli soldiers and bureaucrats. Catholics in Northern Ireland faced the same humiliation by Protestants and British soldiers. Baruch Goldstein's attack on Muslims praying at the Cave of the Patriarchs in Hebron followed being taunted and humiliated by Muslims the day before at a site that was sacred for Jews. Authoritarian governments, such as the Saudi regime, also cause humiliation, as they take away freedom and self-determination and force individuals to submit to their authority through fear and intimidation. Violence and striking back at the oppressor serve as powerful means of reestablishing honor and self-empowerment when freedom and autonomy have been taken away by domestic and external oppressors.

Shame is another emotion that has the potential to trigger violence. Psychologist Thomas Scheff argues that men, in particular, are socialized to deny shame and that this repressed emotion often can erupt in rage and violence.[2] Scheff's book, *Bloody Revenge: Emotions, Nationalism and War*, focuses on national level leaders such as Hitler, but a shameful past is also characteristic of many religion-based terrorists. In chapter 7, I showed that a number of militant antiabortion activists, such as Randall Terry, had led sinful lives involving drugs, promiscuity, and laziness, before they found God and dedicated themselves to Jesus and intimidating abortion providers. Chapters 5 and 8 discussed al Qaeda recruits from the West and other Islamic militants who felt shame and guilt for their secular lifestyles and un-Islamic behavior such as drinking and premarital sex. As a result, they concluded that fighting for Muslims who are being oppressed across the globe would reestablish their righteousness and absolve them of their sins. Religion does teach the importance of feeling shame for sinning, but it offers a number of nonviolent means of redemption such as confession, prayer, making amends, and changing one's ways. The use of violence to redeem one's self is a product of socialization, oppression, or, perhaps, a deeper psychological disorder.

Feelings of marginality, despair, and deprivation have also been shown to be characteristic of religion-based terrorists. In chapter 4, I showed that the Iranian Revolution and the growth of violent Islamic political groups in

Egypt were partly a result of the rising expectations caused by modernization, education, and contact with the outside world that were not met. At the same time, groups that have seen a decline in their status, such as the heterosexual, Caucasian, male, Christians who are attracted to the Church of Creativity in the United States, turn to chauvinistic and ethnocentric religious ideologies that offer the possibility of restoring them to their perceived rightful dominant roles in society. Rabbi Meir Kahane touched on the threat of Israeli Arabs, not a return to Torah law, when appealing to Israel's Sephardic community, which had been discriminated against by Israel's Ashkenazi establishment. A number of studies cited in chapter 5 detailed the conditions of despair and hopelessness among Palestinians in the West Bank and Gaza, which produce suicide bombers. Religion does not cause these feelings of isolation, deprivation, and marginality; social and political and economic conditions do. Assertive and violent interpretations of religion do offer an option for regaining lost status, but so do nationalism, ethnocentrism, and communism. Religion also offers other options for self-assertion such as accepting one's lot in life, working hard to better one's status, and the nobility of accepting suffering as one's destiny.

Revenge, of course, is the most powerful emotional motivation for religion-based terrorists. It has been documented throughout this work that revenge for some wrong doing links all of the terrorists and terrorist groups that have been considered. Osama bin Laden believed that his *jihad* against the Christians and Jews was defensive and a response to all of the atrocities committed by West against Muslim over the past 1,000 years. Yigal Amir had no choice but to assassinate Yitzhak Rabin because the prime minister had betrayed the Jewish people by signing a peace treaty with the Palestinians that ceded Jewish land. Abortion providers are murdered as vengeance on behalf of the innocent fetuses that will be slaughtered and cannot defend themselves. It is important to note that the targets of religion-based terrorism almost always retaliate after they have been victimized. Israel and Hezbollah have been engaged in a war of strikes and counterstrikes for close to 20 years. Palestinian suicide bombings are often followed by the assassination of Hamas leaders. The United States launched cruise missiles into Afghanistan in response to al Qaeda's bombing of U.S. embassies in Kenya and Tanzania. There are countless examples in religious texts, traditions, and histories of revenge being justified and even glorified. Christianity, Judaism, and Islam all have concepts of defensive just wars. On the other hand, the texts, traditions, and histories also call for restraint and turning the other cheek. The violent examples became more attractive for those who believe that they have been harmed for no apparent reason.

PERSONAL LIVES AND COERCION

There are two important exceptions to the argument that religion-based terrorists are acting on emotions that are produced by political, socioeconomic, and psychological forces and then use religion to justify their actions. These are the individuals who are dissatisfied with their personal lives or who are tricked or compelled by others. There have been a number of instances where individuals have joined terrorist groups to escape what they viewed as intolerable situations in their personal lives. Anat Berko and Edna Erez, in their study of Palestinian suicide bombers, describe women who were looking for excitement and to get out of their homes and to escape their controlling fathers. Other women simply wanted to have the opportunity to be around men. One potential bomber related that she had been upset because her father would not let her marry the man of her choice. Other suicide bombers have been blackmailed, as they have been told that they or their families will be exposed as Israeli collaborators.[3] The 15,000-dollar reward paid to the bomber's family on his or her death motivates others in Gaza's impoverished slums.

There have also been a number of cases where suicide bombers have been tricked or deceived and led to believe that they will not die as part of their missions. A Palestinian female who wanted excitement and secret contact with men related that

> I did not think it was going to be like that. I did not think I will die and I did not want to die. They (the recruiters and dispatchers) planned that I will be a suicide bomber. I did not ask for that. They offered me the explosive belt and other things. But I did not agree. At first they did not force me. But things developed and the situation got to where it got. I was a spoiled child and did not plan to die. . . . The dispatcher told me that I would be going on a suicide mission "*istishhad*" (self-sacrifice) on Monday. He said to me, "Get yourself ready, and be prepared." . . . I was very surprised that he was ordering me to be a "*shahida*" (a female martyr). I hadn't planned to die in this way. At first I thought he was joking, but now, he wasn't joking. He said—"you prepared, you practiced, you know us, you're active in the organization and you have to do this."[4]

Ariel Merari documented cases of Lebanese suicide bombers who were deceived and told that they were only smuggling their bombs past checkpoints and did not know that their handlers would set off their explosives by remote control. Others were told that their bombs had 10-minute delays when they did not, while others, like their Palestinian counterparts, were coerced as threats were made against their families.[5]

IS THIS NEVER ENDING?

Now that I have presented my argument as to how faith becomes lethal, it is time to consider whether the current wave of religion-based terror will, as was proposed by some following 9/11, be never ending. One clue comes from current president Barack Obama who stated that the war on terror was winding down when justifying the downsizing of the U.S. military in a press briefing on January 5, 2012. Obama's conclusion was based on the end of the war in Iraq, the coming departure of U.S. troops from Afghanistan, and the killing of Osama bin Laden and other al Qaeda leaders.[6] These events, however, represent only relate to a small sample of the world's religion-based terrorism. It is important to note that although al Qaeda has been weakened and the military's role in fighting terrorism might be reduced, the United States still appears to be laying the foundation for a long-term campaign because the 2011 Defense Authorization Act "allows the military greater authority to detain and interrogate U.S. citizens and non-citizens and deny them legal rights protected by the Constitution."[7]

Trends

Some trends appear to be positive as the end of the war in Iraq takes away an important theater of engagement, as will the drawing down of U.S. troops in Afghanistan. At the same time, Obama's conciliatory gestures and efforts to reach out to the Muslim world seem to have reduced animosity toward the United States. The peace treaty in Northern Ireland has held, and Palestinian suicide bombings in Israel have almost been eliminated in recent years. The use of anecdotal evidence, however, in drawing conclusions about the future of religion-based terrorism is very unreliable. For example, the United States has not suffered a major terrorist attack since 9/11, but that does not mean that there have not been attempts. Noteworthy failed attacks include the "underwear bomber," who tried to bring down a flight from Amsterdam to Detroit on December 25, 2009, and Faisal Shahzad, whose bomb failed to detonate in Times Square in May 2010. Countless other plots were discovered before they were launched. Statistics provide an unclear answer because the number of terrorist attacks worldwide (excluding Iraq) has very slowly increased on a yearly basis during the past decade, but the number of deaths that they have caused has begun to decline. At the same time, Sunni Muslim groups continue to be responsible for almost half of the world's terrorism.[8]

Reason for Optimism

It does seem likely that the current wave of religion-based terrorism, just like the previous three waves, will run its course. Religion, of course, will not disappear, nor will terrorism. There will always be groups and individuals with grievances against enemies that have a preponderance of military, political, and economic power. However, some of the groups and individuals that use religion to express their grievances and to justify acting on them with violence will, ultimately, fail. Many will fail because they are being pursued and fought by governments with greater resources. Only recently, Marxist rebels and Tamil separatists caused mayhem and instability in Columbia and Sri Lanka, respectively. Now both have been defeated and given up their armed struggles. To some extent, violent Islamic extremist groups have been contained, but not eliminated, in many countries such as Morocco, Algeria, and Jordan. Right-wing Christian extremist groups and antiabortion groups in the United States have largely been controlled through law enforcement. Osama bin Laden's death at the hands of U.S. Navy Seals in May 2011 dealt a severe blow to al Qaeda.

Other religious extremist groups will fail because their goals are unattainable, and all but the most dedicated core members will give up the fight or the group will eventually moderate goals and tactics. It is almost guaranteed that there will not be a global Islamic *umma* ruled by a new Caliphate in the next 50 years. Most al Qaeda cells have been and are now engaged in nationalist struggles in Iraq, Yemen, Afghanistan, and other places. At the same time, the extremist-minded foreign al Qaeda fighters have often come into conflict with local insurgents, as was the case in Iraq. Hezbollah moderated its goal from a Shiite theocracy through armed struggle to dominating Lebanon's confessional and democratic political system, while tolerating other religious groups and secular lifestyles outside of its enclaves in South Beirut and the Bekaa Valley. Hamas also entered legitimate politics in Palestine, signed a truce with its Fatah rivals, and drops hints that it is ready to negotiate a long-term truce with Israel. Finally, Protestants and Catholics in Northern Ireland gave up their exclusive visions of annexation to Great Britain or Ireland to enter a power-sharing agreement.

It is also possible that some religion-based terrorist groups will stop using violence because they have achieved their objectives. Most of the nationalist struggles involving terrorism, beginning with the American Revolution, ended when the rebellious group defeated the colonial overlords. Although violence has rarely brought Islamic governments to power, with the notable exception of the Taliban, which had established control over most of

Afghanistan and established a theocracy before they were dislodged by the American invasion in 2001. Hamas defeated Fatah in a civil war in Gaza in 2006–2007, and the two groups later signed a reconciliation agreement that left that territory under Hamas control. Zionist extremists have witnessed an exponential increase in the number of Jewish residents and settlements in the West Bank. The peace process between Israel and the Palestinians is at a stalemate, and it is likely that most of the Jewish settlements would be annexed to Israel if an end to the conflict is ever negotiated.

Another important consideration is the grievances that motivate religion-based terrorists. In short, will they be ameliorated or will they continue to exist? One hopeful sign is the Arab Spring of 2011 and the call for democracy that has spread throughout the Muslim world in countries such as Tunisia, Egypt, Syria, Bahrain, and Yemen. At the same time, Islamist parties in Egypt, Tunisia, and Morocco prevailed in democratic elections in the fall of 2011. An important question that surfaced in chapter 3 is what happens when these groups take control of their political system?[9] If allowed to rule, will they resort to state-sponsored terrorism to stay in power, like their more secular nationalist-oriented predecessors, and create Saudi style Islamic states governed by *Sharia* law that repress dissent? Or, will they maintain the democratic process that brought them to power and protect the rights of religious minorities and less religiously oriented citizens? Turkey and Indonesia, as discussed in chapter 3, offer evidence that Islamic parties have remained supportive of democracy in victory and defeat. In Indonesia, the United Development Party (PPP) and the National Mandate Party (PAN) have accepted electoral setbacks and acted as a loyal opposition.[10] The Justice and Development Party (AK) in Turkey, although rooted in religious values, recognizes secularism as a key foundation of democracy.[11] In its nine-year reign of leading Turkey's government, it has advocated for religious rights rather than trying to create a religious state and religionize society.

The discussion of Hamas and Hezbollah in chapter 8 showed that both groups moderated their political platforms in order to compete in legitimate politics. They also, however, have used violence to control dissenters and in their drive for political power. Hamas fought pitched street battles with the secular nationalist Fatah for control of Gaza from 2006 to 2007. Hezbollah clashed with Shiite rival, Amal, in a civil war in 1987 and forced changes to Lebanon's political system through street demonstrations and violence in 2006–2008. Both groups have also continued to use armed struggle with Israel as a means of unifying their followers. Islamic political groups participating in legitimate politics and winning elections create a role reversal, as they become the powers that be and the defenders of the status quo. Hezbollah discovered this with Lebanon's Cedars Revolution from 2006 to 2008, when they were held responsible for the assassination of Prime Minister Rafik Hariri and the continued presence of Syrian troops in the country. If Islamic democratically elected governments fail to provide for their citizens or engage in costly and unsuccessful military adventure, they will be challenged by groups with alternatives to religion-based government, as was the case in Lebanon.

The viability of religion-based terrorism in democracies is also dependent on how extremists are dealt with. Although extremist Jewish settlers and eschatologists in Israel were sometimes reigned in and repudiated by their more mainstream allies, their violence was often ignored, tacitly approved, supported, and even encouraged by political parties and regimes that shared their goals of settling the West Bank and preventing the formation of a Palestinian state. At the same time, groups opposed to trading land for peace helped create the heated atmosphere that existed at the time of the murder of Yitzhak Rabin and the withdrawal from Gaza under Ariel Sharon. A generation of extremist religious settlers known as hilltop youth have begun to confront the Israeli army and have increasingly assaulted Palestinians and vandalized their property in defending their settlements, both legal and illegal. Is this another genie that is out of the bottle or will the pro-settlement Likud-led government crack down? Antiabortion groups in the United States, such as Operation Rescue, helped create the volatile atmosphere that facilitated violence in the 1990s with their massive protesters and harassment and vilification of abortion providers. Again, those who committed violence thought that they had the tacit approval of pro-life politicians and leaders. The passage and enforcement of laws restricting their activities eventually led to a reduction in violence against abortion clinics and providers.

The end of U.S. military operations in Afghanistan and Iraq should serve to reduce Islamic terrorism against the West. As discussed in chapters 3, 4, and 8, Muslims viewed these wars and other American-led military activities in the Islamic world as the continuation of a 1,000-year campaign by the Christian West against Islam. The resentment caused by these wars in the Muslim world was labeled as an important cause of *jihadism* across the globe in the mid-2000s. Limited Western intervention on behalf of the Libyan rebels who toppled Muammar Qaddafi, support for the pro-democracy movements in the Middle East, and Barack Obama's attempts to reach out to the Muslim world (along with having a father who was born a Muslim) have also improved America's standing in the Islamic world. It is also likely that in the long term, as America's power declines and China becomes an increasingly prominent player in world affairs, anger and resentment in the Muslim world toward the West will decline.

Two remaining trouble spots, which could possibly cause terrorism, are Iran and the Israeli–Palestinian conflict. Iran continues to develop the technology for producing nuclear weapons. Although Iran insists that their nuclear ambitions are peaceful, Israel has stated that it will use whatever means are necessary to stop them, while some politicians in America have also called for using force against Iran. A war involving Israel and Iran would be catastrophic as Hezbollah and Hamas would likely launch missiles against Israeli civilian targets. The United States would also be likely to intervene creating the potential for a conflict with Muslims pitted against the Israel and the West. The continuation of the Israeli-Palestinian conflict provides opportunities for extremists on both sides. Extremist Israeli settlers and Palestinian militants, both religious and nationalist, will continue to use the atrocities of the other side to justify their violence. Israeli extremists will continue to defy the government and confront the army as long as the possibility of derailing a settlement exists. Palestinians will continue to suffer the humiliation, degradation, and despair of occupation, which will create more militants. At the same time, U.S. support of Israel and, by default, the occupation will continue to damage America's standing in the Muslim world.

Muslim parties participating in elections and leading governments will weaken some of the anger and resentment felt toward modernization and globalization in the Islamic world. As discussed in chapter 4, much of the hostility toward these processes is a result of their being associated with Western ideologies and cultural values such as consumerism, secularism, and hedonism and their being viewed tools for the West to dominate the Islamic world. Muslim governments, such as Saudi Arabia, and even terrorists, such as Osama bin Laden, have shown a willingness to take advantage of some aspects of globalization such as ease of travel, technology, communications, media, and international banking and commerce. When democratically elected Islamic governments provide their countries with these benefits of globalization, they will be stripped of their Western ideologies and, consequently, negative connotations. Modernization and globalization also fostered resentment because of the inequalities and the loss of status for some that they produced. However, the popularity of the Muslim Brotherhood, Hamas, and Hezbollah is partly due to their provision of education, employment, job training, and social services. They also have reputations of being honest and trustworthy, in contrast to the corrupt and patronage-based authoritarian regimes, both religious and secular, that they seek to replace. It is possible that Islamic parties might lead to governments that do a better job of taking care of their citizens, reducing inequality, and where merit, rather than connections, leads to success. Consequently, modernization and globalization could be seen as opportunities rather than tools of Western dominance.

WHAT CAN BE DONE?

Is there anything that can be done to reduce the popularity and attractiveness of interpretations of religion that facilitate and encourage violence? Little can be done about religion because the texts, traditions, and histories that justify violence will always be present. It is a waste of time to try to discredit them as being wrong or flawed because, as established in chapter 2, the texts are vague, amorphous, and contradictory and can be used to justify almost anything. As discussed throughout the book, defensive war and violence are acceptable in Judaism, Christianity, and Islam, and there will also be individuals such as Sheik Ahmed Yassin, Meir Kahane, and Paul Hill, who will provide their clerical seal of approval for the defensive struggles of religion-based terrorists. Calling for the encouragement of peaceful and moderate interpretations of religion will also not do much good when there are political, socioeconomic, and psychological conditions that produce violence. Hence, it is these conditions that can and should be changed.

The United States and its allies should continue actively supporting the groups that are protesting against authoritarianism and calling for democracy in the Islamic world. Good will was created when the United States finally called for former Egyptian president Hosni Mubarak to step down and when ambassador to Syria Robert Ford met with opposition protestors in that country. This support counters the grievance that America wants participatory government everywhere but in the Islamic world. As discussed earlier, democracy has the potential to moderate extremism and offers rewards, such as political power, for supporting the status quo. Islamic parties running governments would be pressured to focus on providing for the needs of their citizens and the mundane affairs of running a nation. Again, the crucial question is whether religious parties would respect the democratic process if they came to power and respect the rights of religious minorities and secularly minded individuals. Here, it is important to note that Islamic democracy would differ from Western Liberal democracy, as there might be greater emphasis on obligations to community and society than on individual rights and limited government. There is also the fear that these regimes would not be dependable allies like their authoritarian predecessors but there are steps that can be taken to maintain mutually beneficial relations.

The end of the war in Iraq and the withdrawal of troops from Afghanistan will facilitate the process of alleviating resentment against the United States and the West in the Islamic world. Given the blowback from Iraq and Afghanistan, the United States and its allies should be as restrained as possible in further military operations and troop deployments in the Muslim world. Despite former president George W. Bush's logic that the war in Iraq meant that "We are fighting them (al Qaeda) over there instead of over here," the reality is that the presence of the U.S. military in a locale simply provides terrorists with more targets and more support.[12] The biggest concern in this regard is Iran's development of nuclear weapons. An Iran with nuclear weapons is certainly undesirable but appears to be unavoidable. Covert actions, such as sabotage and the assassination of key personnel, are delaying that outcome with some success. Overt military operations by the United States or Israel, as discussed earlier, would be disastrous and could ignite a full-scale war in the region. The United States has also acted wisely in suspending drone attacks on al Qaeda in Pakistan because they have caused significant civilian casualties due to error.

One way that the United States and the West could diminish its footprint in the Middle East and the Islamic world is to reduce its dependence on foreign oil. Although America imports most of its oil from Canada, Mexico, and Venezuela, Saudi Arabia is our second largest source of foreign oil. The first Iraq War in 1989–1990 was launched to ensure that Iraq did not control Kuwait's oil or threaten the Saudis, which led to the stationing of troops on the Arabian Peninsula and helped intensify Osama bin Laden's hatred of the United States. America and its allies' need for oil is an important cause of our support of the autocratic and corrupt Saudi regime and other dictators in the Persian Gulf. The United States and United Kingdom were very restrained in their response to Bahrain's monarchy's use of live ammunition in suppressing pro-democracy protests because that country provides the base that is home for the Navy's fifth fleet.[13] The fleet would not need a base in the Persian Gulf if it did not need to counter Iran's threat to our oil-producing allies. All American presidents since Richard Nixon have promised to reduce the country's dependence on foreign oil. Forty years after Nixon's original proclamation, accomplishment of that goal remains elusive.

The United States, with the Quartet on the Middle East (United States, United Nations, European Union, and Russia), needs to take bold action to bring about a resolution to the Palestinian–Israeli conflict that guarantees

Israel's security and creates a viable Palestinian nation. This, of course, is easier said than done as all previous efforts have failed. The current Israeli Likud government is building and expanding settlements in the West Bank, and one of the two major parties in the Palestinian camp, Hamas, does not recognize Israel and is committed to its destruction. Successful resolution of the conflict would eventually enervate Palestinian and Israeli extremists, weaken Hezbollah (as it would now have no excuse for military actions against Israel), and alleviate Muslim resentment for America's alleged pro-Israel bias. If Obama is elected to a second term, he will have the capacity to pressure Israel to halt construction of Jewish settlements in the West Bank because he would not have to worry about alienating Jewish and Christian American supporters of Israel, which he is currently avoiding in the year leading up to the 2012 elections. Hamas might also be pressured to join the peace process to avoid being politically isolated, as 10 years of suicide bombing and missile strikes have not brought the Palestinians in the West Bank any closer to real statehood. Thus, Hamas might face opposition if it, again, tries to sabotage an agreement that created a Palestinian state.

It is also important for Israel to crackdown on Jewish extremists such as the hilltop youth. Israeli governments have, at times, ignored, tolerated, or even given their tacit support for violence by religious-Zionist extremists in the West Bank. The situation has become increasingly volatile, as vigilantism against Palestinians has become commonplace, and a line appears to have been crossed as violence has been used to resist the Israeli Defense Force. It would seem unlikely that such action will be taken by a pro-settlement Likud-led government that includes hypernationalist parties, Yisrael Beitanyu (Israel, our home) and Habayit Hayehudi (the Jewish home), and Shas (Sephardic Torah Guardians), a religious party. At the same time, Israel's main security concern remains the Palestinians. Delaying taking action against Jewish extremists has led them to become more numerous and bolder in their actions. Further delay will lead to an even greater reduction in the probability of a negotiated settlement with the Palestinians and a possible civil crisis if one does occur. The United States' use of the legal system, civil suits, and law enforcement against antiabortion extremists is evidence that such a crackdown could be effective.

WHAT'S NEXT?

Terrorism will always exist because there will always be groups of people with political, social, or economic grievances that are not addressed by existing political structures. At the same time, change will also result in some groups losing status and the perception that the loss is because of the rise of another group. Change in the form of modernization, globalization, and whatever is to follow will raise the hopes of individuals, but some of these aspirations will not be met. In short, we, like the generations that preceded us, live in a world where people's needs are not being met, where they are threatened by powerful and uncontrollable forces, and where they are being treated unfairly and denied their dignity. Religion and other ideological frameworks such as nationalism, socialism, democracy, anarchism, and capitalism have all been proposed as ways of building a world where these conditions do not exist. Each has failed and then been challenged by one of the others. The question that remains to be answered is what is the next ideology that will be used to justify violent attacks on the status quo after religion-based violence fails to meet its adherent's expectations?

Notes

INTRODUCTION

1. The first attempt to bomb the World Trade Center in 1993 by a group of Islamic extremists did not succeed in bringing down the towers and had a relatively low death count of six individuals.

2. This is what George Bush said during an address to a Joint Session of Congress and the American people on September 20, 2001.

3. So warned noted Orientalist, Bernard Lewis, in an address to the Jerusalem Conference in August 2009.

4. Both sides in the Cold War agreed on a policy of mutually assured destruction (MAD), where it was assumed that nuclear arsenals would not be used because it would mean that the world would be destroyed.

5. Bernard Lewis, "The Return of Islam," *Commentary* (January 1976): 39–49.

6. See, Daniel Lerner, *The Passing of Traditional Society* (Glencoe, IL: Free Press, 1958) and Donald Smith, *Religion and Political Modernization* (Boston, MA: Little and Brown, 1970).

7. Samuel Huntington, "The Clash of Civilizations," *Foreign Affairs* (Summer 1993): 22–49.

8. A sample of some of Huntington's critics can be found in the responses to his article in the September–October 2003 issue of *Foreign Affairs*.

9. Huntington, "The Clash of Civilizations," 22–49.

10. Mark Juergensmeyer, *The New Cold War: Religious Nationalism Confronts the Secular State* (Berkeley, CA: University of California Press, 1993).

11. For example, see Francis Fukuyama, *The End of History and the Last Man* (New York: Free Press, 1992).

12. Juergensmeyer, *The New Cold War*, 8.

13. Susanne Rudolph and Lloyd I. Rudolph, "Modern Hate," *New Republic* (December 1993): 9.

14. Bruce Hoffman, "Holy Terror: The Implications of Terrorism Motivated by a Religious Imperative," *Studies in Conflict & Terrorism* 18 (1995): 271–84. Of course, most Islamic legal scholars would disagree with this contention, a point that will be taken up in chapter 3.

15. See Norman Podhoretz, *World War IV: The Long Struggle against Islamofacism* (New York: Doubleday, 2007).

16. Hoffman, "Holy Terror," 271–84.

17. Gilles Kepel, *The Revenge of God: The Resurgence of Islam, Christianity, and Judaism in the Modern World* (University Park, PA: Pennsylvania State University Press, 1994), 5.

18. Kepel, *The Revenge of God,* 1–12.

19. Kepel, *The Revenge of God,* 11.

20. Kepel, *The Revenge of God,* 11.

21. Kepel, *The Revenge of God,* 12.

22. See Mark Juergensmeyer, *Terror in the Mind of God: The Global Rise of Religious Violence* (Berkeley, CA: University of California Press, 2003) and Jessica Stern, *Terror in the Name of God: Why Religious Militants Kill* (New York: Harper Collins, 2003).

23. These books include Sam Harris, *The End of Faith* (New York: W. W. Norton, 2004) and Christopher Hitchens, *God Is Not Great: How Religion Poisons Everything* (New York: Twelve, 2007). Comedian and commentator Bill Maher presents his case against religion in the 2008 film, *Religulous.*

24. Harris, *The End of Faith,* 11–12, 26. It is important to note that all of the conflicts that are listed as pitting religion against religion also pit nationality against nationality.

25. Assaf Moghadam, *The Globalization of Martyrdom* (Baltimore, MD: Johns Hopkins University Press, 2008), 254.

CHAPTER 1

1. Magnus Ranstorp, "Terrorism in the Name of Religion," *Journal of International Affairs* 50 (Summer 1996): 41–63.

2. These words are commonly attributed to Pope Urban II, but it is unclear whether he uttered the phrase or the crowd shouted them in response to the pope's speech.

3. J. Harold Ellens, "The Violent Jesus," in *The Destructive Power of Religion: Violence in Judaism Christianity and Islam,* ed. J. Harold Ellens, Volume 3 (Westport, CT: Praeger, 2004), 50–51.

4. J.P. Larsson, *Understanding Religious Violence* (Burlington, VT: Ashgate Publishing Company, 2004), 119–21.

5. Mark Juergensmeyer, "Sacrifice and Cosmic War," *Terrorism and Political Violence* 3 (Autumn 1991): 114.

6. Jessica Stern, *Terror in the Name of God: Why Religious Militants Kill* (New York: Harper Collins, 2003), 167–71.

7. Ellens, "The Violent Jesus," 5.

8. Sayyid Qutb, *Milestones,* trans. Hasan Budral (Karachi: International Islamic Publishers, 1981), 2–7.

9. "Full Text of bin Laden's Message," *BBC News World Edition,* http://news.bbc.co.uk/2/hi/middle_east/2455845.stm.

10. Stern, *Terror in the Name of God,* 167.

11. Larsson, *Understanding Religious Violence,* 115.

12. Jonathan Fox, "The Effects of Religion on Domestic Conflicts," *Terrorism and Political Violence* 10 (Winter 1998): 47.

13. The name, Israel, was given to Jacob, following his struggle with an angel, because he had struggled with God. From this it can be derived that Jacob's descendents, the Children of Israel, should also be a people who struggle with God. Also, Abraham tried to bargain with God in order to save the people of Sodom and Gomorrah, and Moses resisted God when he was told that he had been selected to lead the Hebrew slaves from their bondage in Israel.

14. Mark Juergensmeyer, *Terror in the Mind of God: The Global Rise of Religious Violence* (Berkeley, CA: University of California Press, 2003), 47–48.

15. Another meaning of the same three-letter root is peace.

16. Peter Berger, *The Sacred Canopy: Elements of a Sociological Theory of Religion* (New York: Doubleday, 1969), 23–25.

17. Regina Schwartz, *The Curse of Cain: The Violent Legacy of Monotheism* (Chicago, IL: University of Chicago Press, 1997), 12.

18. David Rapoport, "Fear and Trembling: Terrorism in Three Religious Traditions," *The American Political Science Review* 78 (1984): 672–73.

19. Lloyd Steffen, *Holy War, Just-War: Exploring the Moral Meaning of Religious Violence* (Lanham, MD: Rowman and Littlefield Publishers, 2007), 15–16.

20. Juergensmeyer, *Terror in the Mind of God,* 139.

21. It is written in the Bible that Abraham, Isaac, and Jacob are buried in the Cave of the Patriarchs. The site is holy to both Muslims and Jews because Muslims view the Hebrew Bible as being a holy book and Abraham as their forefather. Abraham's first son, Ishmael, is noted as being the founder of the Arab people. There are separate prayer spaces for Muslims and Jews, who are given access for prayer services at different times.

22. Juergensmeyer, *Terror in the Mind of God,* 139.

23. Stern, *Terror in the Name of God,* 51–55.

24. Jews believe that the *Torah* is God's only revelation. Christians accept the divinity of the Hebrew Bible as well as the New Testament. Muslims accept both as being divine, as well as the *Quran.* The word torah in Biblical Hebrew, literally, means instruction.

25. Charles Kimball, *When Religion Becomes Evil* (New York: Harper Collins Publishers, 2002), 45.

26. Schwartz, *The Curse of Cain,* 123.

27. See Albert Martin, *War and the Christian Conscience: From Augustine to Martin Luther King* (Chicago, IL: Henry Regnery, 1971) for a discussion of Christian just-war theory.

28. Niebuhr was advocating for using war against Hitler and the German Nazi regime. See Reinhold Niebuhr, *Why the Christian Church Is Not Pacifist* (London: Student Christian Movement Press, 1941).

29. Juergensmeyer, *Terror in the Mind of God,* 24–27.

30. Mark Gopin, "Judaism: The Limits of War and Conflict Resolution," http://www.gmu.edu/depts/crdc/docs/j_limitsofwar_and_cr.html.

31. Stern, *Terror in the Name of God,* 91–92.

32. For a discussion of the history and doctrine of *jihad,* see Michael Bonner, *Jihad in Islamic History: Doctrine and Practice* (Princeton, NJ: Princeton University Press, 2006).

33. Kimball, *When Religion Becomes Evil,* 100.

34. Quoted in Charles Selengut, *Sacred Fury: Understanding Religious Violence* (Walnut Creek, CA: Altamira Press, 2003), 7.

35. R. Scott Appleby, *The Ambivalence of the Sacred: Religion Violence and Reconciliation* (Lanham, MD: Rowman and Littlefield Publishers, 2000), 83–85.

36. Hector Avalos, *Fighting Words: The Origins of Religious Violence* (Amherst, NY: Prometheus Books, 2005), 106–111.

37. Appleby, *The Ambivalence of the Sacred,* 84.

38. See Max Weber, *Max Weber: The Theory of Social and Economic Organization,* trans. A. M. Henderson and Talcott Parsons (New York: The Free Press, 1947).

39. *Quran,* 2:154.

40. Quoted in Stern, *Terror in the Name of God,* 122.

41. Stern, *Terror in the Name of God,* 55.

42. Joe Thomas, "Smiling Unrepentant Anti-Abortion Extremist Is Executed in Florida," *Agence France-Presses,* September 4, 2003.

43. Stern, *Terror in the Name of God,* 50–51.

44. See www.baruchgoldstein.com. One can also find a YouTube video of Israeli Jews in a neighborhood where many Palestinian homes have been expropriated celebrating the anniversary of Goldstein's death and massacre.

45. Ellens, "The Violent Jesus," 2–4. Numerous evangelical preachers have speculated about when the Armageddon followed by the return of Christ will take place. The book, *Left Behind,* describes life on earth after all the Christians have gone to heaven following the rapture. The movie, *2012,* showed what would happen when the world ended according to the prognostications of the Mayan calendar.

46. Jews do not believe that Jesus was the Messiah.

47. Howard Sachar, *A History of Israel: From Zionism to Our Time* (New York: Knopf, 1976).

48. Kimball, *When Religion Becomes Evil,* 100.

49. The West Bank contains the cities of Nablus, Hebron, and Bethlehem, all of which are mentioned in the Bible and have important religious significance. This area was also part of the land promised by God to Abraham in the book of Genesis.

50. For a discussion of the religious-Zionists, see Ian Lustick, *For the Land and for the Lord: Jewish Fundamentalism in Israel* (New York: Council on Foreign Relations, 1988).

51. Kimball, *When Religion Becomes Evil,* 102.

52. Juergensmeyer, *Terror in the Mind of God,* 27–29.

53. See Gary North, *Backward Christian Soldier: An Action Manual for Christian Reconstruction* (Tyler, TX: Institute for Christian Economics, 1984). North has published more than 20 books on Christian Reconstructionist theology.

54. John Esposito, *Islam and Politics* (Syracuse, NY: Syracuse University Press, 1984), 34.

55. Mark Juergensmeyer, *Global Rebellion, Religious Challenges to the Secular State from Christian Militants to al Qaeda* (Berkeley, CA: University of California Press, 2008), 256.

56. Juergensmeyer, *Global Rebellion, Religious Challenges to the Secular State from Christian Militants to al Qaeda*, 256.

57. Ellens, "The Violent Jesus," 2.

58. Steffen, *Holy War, Just-War*, 103.

59. Ranstorp, "Terrorism in the Name of Religion," 52.

60. Kimball, *When Religion Becomes Evil*, 135.

61. Quoted in Kimball, *When Religion Becomes Evil*, 136.

62. Quoted in Juergensmeyer, *Terror in the Mind of God*, 156.

63. Quoted from *Al-Jazeera* broadcast, 1825, GMT, October 7, 2001.

64. Juergensmeyer, "Sacrifice and Cosmic War," 214.

65. Juergensmeyer, "Sacrifice and Cosmic War," 214.

66. Bruce Hoffman, "Holy Terror: The Implications of Terrorism Motivated by a Religious Imperative," *Studies in Conflict & Terrorism* 18 (1995): 255.

67. Deuteronomy 16: 18.

68. Hoffman, "Holy Terror," 255.

69. Amir Taheri, *Holy Terror: The Inside Story of Islamic Terrorism* (London: Sphere Books, 1987), 5.

70. Schwartz, *The Curse of Cain*, 5.

71. The notion of choseness is found frequently in Jewish liturgy. God is often praised for choosing the Jews from among the nations.

72. Jeff Sharlet, "Jesus Killed Mohammed: The Campaign for a Christian Military," *Harper's Magazine*, May 2009, 31–43.

73. Samuel Huntington, "The Clash of Civilizations?," *Foreign Affairs* (Summer 1993): 22–49.

74. Larsson, *Understanding Religious Violence*, 105.

75. Avalos, *Fighting Words: The Origins of Religious Violence*, 103–104.

76. Quoted in Kimball, *When Religion Becomes Evil*, 119 from *The 700 Club*, November 17, 1993.

77. Quoted in Stern, *Terror in the Name of God*, 59.

78. Berger, *The Sacred Canopy*, 184.

79. Max Weber, *Economy and Society: An Outline of Interpretive Sociology*, ed. Guenther Ross and Klaus Wittich (Berkeley, CA: University of California Press, 1978), 422–24.

80. See Rene Girard, *Violence and the Sacred*, trans. Patrick Gregory (Baltimore, MD: Johns Hopkins University Press, 1977).

81. This can be seen in the Eucharist and the self-flagellation done by Shiite Muslims to commemorate the death of Hussein. Ancient Judaism replaced pagan human sacrifice with animal sacrifice, which was replaced by additional prayers said in Sabbath and festival morning services.

82. Juergensmeyer, "Sacrifice and Cosmic War," 111.

83. See Freiherr von Gottfried Wilhelm Leibniz,*Theodicy: Essays on the Goodness of God, the Freedom of Man, and the Origin of Evil*, ed. Austin Farrer, trans. E. M. Huggard (La Salle, IL: Open Court Pub. Co., 1985). The book of Job tells the story of a man of true faith, who does not lose faith in God, despite suffering

great hardship, including the loss of his family. Ultimately, Job is rewarded for his steadfastness.

84. Quoted in Appleby, *The Ambivalence of the Sacred*, 26.

85. These attacks include the shooting at Fort Hood by Nidal Malik Hasan, the attempted bombing of Northwest Airlines flight by Umar Farouk Abdulmutallab, and the attempted Times Square Bombing by Faisal Shahzad.

86. Stern, *Terror in the Name of God*, 51.

87. Juergensmeyer, *Terror in the Mind of God*, 19–29.

88. Selengut, *Sacred Fury*, 12.

CHAPTER 2

1. David Rapoport "The Four Waves of Rebel Terror and September 11," *Current History* 100 (December 2001): 419–25.

2. Mark Juergensmeyer, *Global Rebellion, Religious Challenges to the Secular State from Christian Militants to al Qaeda* (Berkeley, CA: University of California Press, 2008), 16.

3. Rapaport, "The Four Waves of Rebel Terror and September 11," 425. Also, Juergensmeyer writes that the Enlightenment and the narrowing of religion's role in society were rooted in the excessive power of the clergy and the fanaticism associated with the 16th- and 17th-century wars of religion. See Juergensmeyer, *Global Rebellion, Religious Challenges to the Secular State from Christian Militants*, 16.

4. Bin Laden, ironically, addressed Bush's claim in a September 2007 video where he stated that he and his followers love freedom, while it is America that seeks to enslave the world.

5. For a history and discussion of the Great Purges, see Robert Conquest, *The Great Terror: A Reassessment* (New York: Oxford, 1991) and J. Arch Getty, *Origins of the Great Purges: The Soviet Communist Party Reconsidered, 1933–1938* (Cambridge: Cambridge University Press, 1985).

6. The CIA assisted in the overthrow of Salvador Allende in Chile in 1973 and Mohammed Mosaddegh of Iran in 1953. Both were viewed as threats to U.S. interests because of their socialist leanings. Mosaddegh was replaced by the Shah Mohammed Pahlavi. The legacy of the 1953 coup was a rallying point for the 1979 Iranian Revolution, which ultimately led to today's Islamic Republic. The Iran-Contra scandal involved the illegal funding of the Nicaraguan Contras, who were fighting to overthrow Daniel Ortega's socialist regime. Funds for the Contras were arranged by members of the Reagan administration who illegally sold arms to Iran through Israeli middlemen.

7. Regina Schwartz, *The Curse of Cain: The Violent Legacy of Monotheism* (Chicago, IL: University of Chicago Press, 1997), 5.

8. See Lucy S. Dawidowicz, *The War against the Jews 1933–1945* (New York: Bantam Books, 1976) for a discussion of the ethnic, nationalist, and religious origins of the Holocaust.

9. There has been debate as to whether Hale actually said the words in question. Rather, he said "I am so satisfied with the cause in which I have engaged that my only regret is that I have not more lives than one to offer in its service."

10. The historical significance of the willingness to die for freedom and liberty in the United States can be seen on New Hampshire's license plate, which includes the motto, Live free or die.

11. See the opening of Sam Harris, *The End of Faith* (New York: W. W. Norton, 2004), 11–12 for a portrayal of the suicide bomber driven to fanaticism by religion.

12. David Martin, *Does Christianity Cause War?* (Oxford: Clarendon University Press, 1997), 10.

13. Theories of Marx and Friedrich Engels are spelled out in several works including *The Communist Manifesto, Das Kapital, and A Contribution to the Critique of Political Economy*. Selections from these and other writing can be found in Eugene Kamenka, editor, *The Portable Marx* (New York: Penguin Books, 1983).

14. Karl Marx, "Critique of the Gotha Programme," in *The Portable Karl Marx*, ed. Eugene Kamenka (New York: Penguin Books, 1983), 333–55.

15. See Vladimir Lenin, "What Is to Be Done?" in *Essential Works of Lenin*, ed. Harry Christman (Mineola, NY: Dover, 1987), 53–126.

16. Guevara was named in *Time* magazine's list of the 100 most influential people of the 20th century. Two of his most noteworthy works are Che Guevera, *The Motorcycle Diaries* (London: Verso, 1996) and Che Guevera, *Guerilla Warfare* (Lincoln, NE: University of Nebraska Press, 1985). See John L. Anderson, *Che Guevara: A Revolutionary Life* (New York: Grove Press, 1996) for a discussion of Guevara's life and works.

17. Timothy McVeigh, who bombed the Mura federal building in Oklahoma City, was found with a worn copy of *The Turner Diaries* when he was arrested. The American right-wing terrorist group, Bruder Schweigen (the Silent Brotherhood), was based on the fictional group in *The Turner Diaries*.

18. Janet Wallach and John Wallach, *Arafat in the Eyes of the Beholder* (Rocklin, CA: Prima, 1992).

19. See, Charles Kimball, *When Religion Becomes Evil* (New York: Harper Collins Publishers, 2002) and R. Scott Appleby, *The Ambivalence of the Sacred: Religion Violence and Reconciliation* (Lanham, MD: Rowman and Littlefield Publishers, 2000).

20. For an example, see the essay on Islam and *jihad* at *Islamic Insight*, http://www.islamsight.org/default_article.asp?Rec=5.

21. It is important to note that I am not arguing that today's religious terrorist groups are the equivalents of Abraham, Jesus, Muhammad, and their followers. Rather, my purpose is to argue that being a small and radical group does not disqualify that group from membership in the larger religious community.

22. Schwartz, *The Curse of Cain*, 8.

23. This line is from *The Merchant of Venice*, Act I, Scene 3. In Matthew IV, Satan reads scripture to Jesus in order to tempt him.

24. Schwartz, *The Curse of Cain*, 8.

25. Walter Laqueur, *The New Terrorism: Fanaticism and the Arms of Mass Destruction* (New York: Oxford University Press, 1999), 47.

26. Lloyd Steffen, *Holy War, Just War: Exploring the Moral Meaning of Religious Violence* (Lanham, MD: Rowman and Littlefield Publishers, 2007), 9.

27. J. Harold Ellens, *The Destructive Power of Religion: Violence in Judaism, Christianity and Islam*, Volume 3 (Westport, CT: Praeger, 2004), 9.

28. The promise originally appears in God's covenant with Abraham (Abram at the time) in Genesis 12:7. Entitlement to the land is later mentioned in a conversation with Jacob in Genesis 28:13. Moses is told to take possession of the land in Deuteronomy 1:8.

29. See Ian Lustick, *For the Land and for the Lord: Jewish Fundamentalism in Israel* (New York: Council on Foreign Relations, 1988).

30. Exodus 15:3–6.

31. Joshua 24:11–13.

32. Chronicles I 28:2–3.

33. Jeremiah 27:17.

34. John Ferguson, *War and Peace in the World's Religions* (New York: Oxford University Press, 1978), 83.

35. Zachariah 4:6.

36. Isaiah 2:4.

37. This rabbinic period produced the *Talmud* and collections of commentaries on the *Tanakh* known as *Midrash*.

38. Mark Gopin, *Between Eden and Armageddon* (New York: Oxford University Press, 2000), 67–68.

39. For more examples, see Ferguson, *War and Peace in the World's Religions*, 86–97.

40. Gopin, *Between Eden and Armageddon*, 68–69. Some consider the chief rabbinate of the state of Israel as replacing the Sanhedrin court.

41. Ferguson, *War and Peace in the World's Religions*, 101.

42. Matthew 5:44.

43. Matthew 5:38–39.

44. Matthew 12:1–17.

45. Matthew 21:12–17.

46. J. Harold Ellens, "The Violent Jesus," in *The Destructive Power of Religion: Violence in Judaism, Christianity and Islam,* ed. Harold Ellens, Volume 3 (Westport, CT: Praeger, 2004), 34.

47. Ellens, "The Violent Jesus," 24–27.

48. Matthew 10:34–39.

49. Albert Martin, *War and the Christian Conscience: From Augustine to Martin Luther King* (Chicago, IL: Henry Regnery, 1971), 53.

50. Martin, *War and the Christian Conscience,* 68.

51. Martin, *War and the Christian Conscience,* 72.

52. Niebuhr was advocating for using war against Hitler and the German Nazi regime. See Reinhold Niebuhr, *Why the Christian Church Is Not Pacifist* (London: Student Christian Movement Press, 1941).

53. Mark Juergensmeyer, *Terror in the Mind of God: The Global Rise of Religious Violence* (Berkeley, CA: University of California Press, 2003), 24–27.

54. David Cook, *Understanding Jihad* (Berkeley, CA: University of California Press, 2005), 163.

55. The distinction between greater *jihad* and lesser *jihad* is attributed to a *Hadith* (saying of the Prophet Muhammad). "The Prophet returned from one of his battles, and told us, 'You have arrived with an excellent arrival, you have come from the Lesser Jihad to the Greater Jihad—the striving of a servant (of God) against his desires.'"

56. Ferguson, *War and Peace in the World's Religions,* 132–33.

57. For example, People of the Book were excluded from lesser *jihad* if they accepted the authority of the Islamic state and paid a tributary tax.

58. See Bernard Lewis, *The Political Language of Islam,* (Chicago, IL: University of Chicago Press, 1988); David Cook, *Understanding Jihad* (Berkeley, CA: University of California Press, 2005); and Reuven Firestone, *Jihad: The Origin of Holy War in Islam* (New York: Oxford, 1999).

59. *Quran* 8:39–40.

60. *Quran* 2:190.

61. It is estimated that Muhammad participated in 27 military campaigns and deputized others. See Cook, *Understanding Jihad,* 6 for a discussion.

62. Cook, *Understanding Jihad,* 164.

63. Like their Christian counterparts in the United States, today's Islamic terrorists would argue that conventional authority figures are illegitimate because they support regimes that implement secular laws and maintain policies that are against religion.

64. Cook, *Understanding Jihad,* 164.

65. *Quran* 2:256.

66. *Quran* 8:61.

67. For more on Sufism, see Idries Shah, *The Sufis* (Garden City, NY: Doubleday, 1971) and James Fadiman and Robert Frager, *Essential Sufism* (San Francisco, CA: Harper San Francisco, 1997).

68. Abul Ala Maududi, *Come Let Us Change the World,* ed. and trans. K. Siddique (Lahore: Salama Saddique, 1971).

CHAPTER 3

1. Bernard Lewis, "The Roots of Muslim Rage," in *The New Global Terrorism: Characteristics, Causes, Controls,* ed. Charles Kegley (Upper Saddle River, NJ: Prentice Hall, 2003): 194.

2. Lewis, "Roots of Muslim Rage," 200.

3. All three are quoted in "Understanding Terrorism," *Harvard Magazine,* January–February 2002, 36–49.

4. For a discussion of the new terrorism, see Walter Laqueur, *The New Terrorism: Fanaticism and the Arms of Mass Destruction* (New York: Oxford University Press, 1999). See Bruce Hoffman, "Holy Terror: The Implications of Terrorism Motivated by a Religious Imperative," *Studies in Conflict & Terrorism* 18 (1995): 251–84 for a comparison between the new religious terrorism and traditional terrorism.

5. David C. Rapoport, "The Four Waves of Rebel Terror and September 11," *Current History* 100 (December 2001): 419–25.

6. Rapoport, "The Four Waves of Rebel Terror and September 11," 422.

7. Three of the four remaining hijackers were also from authoritarian nations; two were from the United Arab Emirates, and one was from Egypt. The fourth was from Lebanon, which is a marginal democracy.

8. Freedom House is an independent nongovernment organization that monitors and supports the expansion of democracy across the world. Its determination of

the state of freedom in the nations of the world includes separate scores for political rights and civil liberties. Scores for the two dimensions range from 1 to 7, with one being the most free and seven being the least free. The data cited here are for 2010. For further information, see www.freedomhouse.org.

9. Seymour Lipset, *Political Man: The Social Bases of Politics* (London: Heinemann, 1983), 64.

10. See John Locke, *Second Treatise on Government*, ed. C. B. Macpherson (Indianapolis, IN: Hackett, 1980).

11. Ted Gurr, "Terrorism in Democracies: When It Occurs, Why It Fails," in *The New Global Terrorism: Characteristics, Causes, Controls,* ed. Charles Kegley (Upper Saddle River, NJ: Prentice Hall, 2003), 202.

12. H.H.A. Cooper, "What Is a Terrorist? A Psychological Perspective," *Legal Medical Quarterly* 1 (1977): 8–18.

13. Gurr, "Terrorism in Democracies," 213.

14. Gurr, "Terrorism in Democracies," 214.

15. Syrian Islamic Action Front, *Program of the Syrian Islamic Action Front* (Beirut: N.P., 1981).

16. Under Morocco's new constitution, Justice and Development Party will now select the nation's prime minister and form a coalition government. Previously the king held both of these powers.

17. Lolita Baldor, "US Worries about Terrorism on Upswing in Indonesia," *Washington Times,* November 7, 2010, http://www.washingtontimes.com/news/2010/nov/7/us-worries-about-upswing-terrorism-indonesia/?page=all.

18. Adrian Vickers, *A History of Modern Indonesia* (New York: Cambridge University, 2005), 218–19.

19. Rapoport, "The Four Waves of Rebel Terror and September 11," 419–25.

20. See Robert Pape, *Dying to Win: The Strategic Logic of Suicide Terrorism* (New York: Random House, 2005).

21. See James Reinhart, *Apocalyptic Faith and Political Violence* (New York: Palgrave, 2006).

22. Don Higginbotham, *The War of American Independence: Military Attitudes, Policies, and Practice,* 1763–1789 (Boston, MA: Northeastern University Press, 1983).

23. John Esposito, *Islam and Politics* (Syracuse, NY: Syracuse University Press, 1984), 61–95.

24. For detailed histories of the Israeli–Palestinian conflict, see James Gelvin, *The Israeli Palestinian Conflict: One Hundred Years of War* (New York: Cambridge University Press, 2005) and Mark Tessler, *A History of the Israeli–Palestinian Conflict* (Bloomington, IN: Indiana University Press, 2009).

25. For more on the Soviet war in Afghanistan, see Gregory Feifer, *The Great Gamble: The Soviet War in Afghanistan* (New York: Harper, 2009) and M. Hassan Kakar, *Afghanistan: The Soviet Invasion and the Afghan Response, 1979–1982* (Berkeley, CA: University of California Press, 1995).

26. The word *mujahedeen* means "one who engages in *jihad*" in Arabic.

27. "The Afghan-Pakistan Militant Nexus," *BBC News,* December 9, 2009, http://news.bbc.co.uk/2/hi/south_asia/7601748.stm.

28. "Our Man in Afghanistan," *Newsweek,* July 25, 2009, http://www.news week.com/2009/07/25/our-man-in-afghanistan.html.

29. Al Qaeda did not have a presence in Iraq until after the American invasion.

30. John McCain frequently took Barack Obama to task in the 2008 presidential campaign for not admitting that the surge was working. The media also supported the notion that the surge had reduced violence in Iraq. See Michael Duffy, "The Surge at Year One," *Time,* January 31, 2008, http://www.time.com/time/magazine/article/0,9171,1708843,00.html and Dexter Filkins, "Exiting Iraq, Petraeus Says Gains Are Fragile," *The New York Times,* August 21, 2008, http://www.nytimes.com/2008/08/21/world/middleeast/21general.html.

31. Patrick Cockburn, "Violence Is Down but not because of America's 'Surge,'" *The Independent,* Sunday, September 14, http://www.independent.co.uk/news/world/middle-east/iraq-violence-is-down-ndash-but-not-because-of-americas-surge-929896.html.

32. For more on Israel's invasion of Lebanon in 1982, see Ze'ev Schiff, *Israel's Lebanon War* (New York: Simon and Schuster, 1984).

33. Samuel Huntington, "The Clash of Civilizations?" *Foreign Affairs* 72 (Summer 1993): 40–41.

34. Jonathan Fox, "Counting the Causes and Dynamics of Ethnoreligious Conflict," *Totalitarian Movements and Political Religions* 4 (Winter 2003): 122–23.

35. "Genocide in Rwanda," United Nations Human Rights Council, http://www.unitedhumanrights.org/genocide/genocide_in_rwanda.htm.

36. Jonathan Fox, "The Effects of Religion on Domestic Conflicts," *Terrorism and Political Violence* 10 (Winter 1998): 57.

37. See Minorities at Risk Project, "Minorities at Risk Dataset." (College Park, MD: Center for International Development and Conflict Management, 2009), http://www.cidcm.umd.edu/mar.

38. Fox, "Counting the Causes and Dynamics of Ethno-religious Conflict," 123.

39. Ted Gurr, "Why Minorities Rebel," *International Political Science Review* 14 (1993): 166–201.

40. Fox, "Counting the Causes and Dynamics of Ethnoreligious Conflict," 137.

41. Clifford Geertz, *The Interpretation of Culture* (New York: Basic Books, 1973), 123–25.

42. Anthony Smith, "Ethnic Election and National Destiny: Some Religious Origins of Nationalist Ideals," *Nations and Nationalism* 5 (Fall 1999): 331–355 and Anthony Smith, "The Sacred Dimension of Nationalism," *Millennium* 29 (2000): 791–814.

43. United States Holocaust Museum, "Jasenovac," *Holocaust Encyclopedia,* April 1, 2010, http://www.ushmm.org/wlc/en/article.php?ModuleId=10005449.

44. Patrick Ball, Ewa Tabeau, and Philip Verwimp, *The Bosnian Book of the Dead: An Assessment of the Database* (Sussex: Households in Conflict Network, 2007), 4–5.

45. Paul Mojzes, *Yugoslavian Inferno: Ethnoreligious Warfare in the Balkans* (New York: Continuum, 1995), 125.

46. Mojzes, *Yugoslavian Inferno,* 125–51.

47. Mojzes, *Yugoslavian Inferno,* 128–49.

48. Mojzes, *Yugoslavian Inferno,* 141.

49. Francine Friedman, *The Bosnian Muslims: Denial of a Nation* (Boulder, CO: Westview Press, 1986), 179.

50. Susan Woodward, *Balkan Tragedy: Chaos and Dissolution after the Cold War* (Washington, DC: Brookings Institution, 1996), 6–15.

51. Sumir Ganguly, *Conflict Unending: India–Pakistan Tensions Since 1947* (Washington, DC: Woodrow Wilson Center Press, 2001), 88.

52. Asian Center for Human Rights, *2009 Human Rights Report: India* (New Delhi: Asian Center for Human Rights, 2009), 86.

53. "Behind the Kashmir Conflict: Abuses by Indian Security Forces and Militant Groups Continue," *Human Rights Watch,* July 1, 1999, http://www.hrw.org/en/reports/1999/07/01/behind-kashmir-conflict.

54. Jessica Stern, *Terror in the Mind of God: Why Religious Militants Kill* (New York: Harper Collins, 2003), 116.

55. Ganguly, *Conflict Unending,* 88–92.

56. Olivier Roy, *Globalized Islam: The Search for a New Ummah* (New York: Columbia University Press, 2004), 293.

57. Quoted in Maggie Michael, "Bin Laden: Palestinian Cause at Heart of al Qaeda's Mission," *USA Today,* May 16, 2008, http://www.usatoday.com/news/world/2008–05–16-bin laden_N.htm.

58. Greg Bruno and Julia Jeffrey, "Profile: Al Qaeda in Iraq," *Council on Foreign Relations,* April 26, 2010, http://www.cfr.org/publication/14811/profile.html.

59. National Intelligence Council, "Trends in Global Terrorism: Implications for the United States, April 2006, http://www.dni.gov/nic/special_global_terrorism.html.

60. Peter Bergen and Paul Cruickshank, "The Iraq Effect: The War on Iraq and Its Impact on the War on Terrorism." *Mother Jones,* March 1, 2007, http://motherjones.com/politics/2007/03/iraq-101-iraq-effect-war-iraq-and-its-impact-war-terrorism-pg-1.

61. Hugh Thomas, *The Spanish Civil War* (New York: Modern Library, 2001), 942.

CHAPTER 4

1. Assaf Moghadam, *The Globalization of Martyrdom* (Baltimore, MD: Johns Hopkins University Press, 2008), 68.

2. Allen Krueger and Jitka Malekcova, "Education and Poverty, Political Violence and Terrorism: Is There a Causal Connection?" *Journal of Economic Perspectives* 17 (Fall 2004): 119–44.

3. Nasra Hassan, "Suicide Terrorism," in *The Roots of Terrorism,* ed. Louise Richardson (New York: Routledge, 2006), 29–43.

4. For examples, see Seymour Martin Lipset, "Some Social Requisites of Democracy, Economic Development and Political Legitimacy," *American Political Science Review* 53 (1959): 69–105; Karl Deutsch, "Social Mobilization, Political Change, and Development," *American Political Science Review* 55 (1961): 493–514; and W. W. Rostow, *The Stages of Economic Growth* (Princeton, NJ: Princeton University Press, 1958).

5. For a description of how this process played out in a Turkish village in the 1950s, see Daniel Lerner, *The Passing of Traditional Society* (Glencoe, IL: Free Press, 1958).

6. See Donald Smith, *Religion and Political Development* (Boston, MA: Little and Brown, 1970).

7. Gilles Kepel, *The Revenge of God: The Resurgence of Islam, Christianity and Judaism in the Modern World* (University Park, PA: The Pennsylvania State University Press, 1994), 11.

8. Mark Juergensmeyer, *Global Rebellion, Religious Challenges to the Secular State from Christian Militants to al Qaeda* (Berkeley, CA: University of California Press, 2008), 253.

9. James Reinhart, *Apocalyptic Faith and Political Violence* (New York: Palgrave, 2006), 24.

10. Sayyid Qutb, *Milestones*, trans. Hassan Budral (Karachi: International Islamic Publishers, 1981), 73.

11. Llewellyn Howell, "Is the New Global Terrorism a Clash of Civilization: Evaluating Terrorism's Multiple Sources," in *The New Global Terrorism: Causes, Characteristics, Controls*, ed. Charles Kegley (Upper Saddle River, NJ: Prentice Hall, 2003), 177–78.

12. James C. Davies, "Towards a Theory of Revolution," *American Sociological Review* 27 (1962): 5–18.

13. Ted Gurr, *Why Men Rebel* (Princeton, NJ: Princeton University Press, 1970), 24.

14. Ted Gurr, "A Causal Model of Civil Strife: A Comparative Analysis Using New Indices," *American Political Science Review* 62 (1968): 1104–24.

15. See Jerrold Greene, *Revolution in Iran* (New York: Praeger, 1982).

16. Kepel, *The Revenge of God: The Resurgence of Islam, Christianity and Judaism in the Modern World*, 5–9.

17. Jewish extremists, such as the late Rabbi Meir Kahane, share Khomeini's view of secularism as being an ideological force that seeks to destroy religion. Christian Reconstructionists in the United States see the same threat from the secular society that surrounds them. See Mark Juergensmeyer, *The New Cold War: Religious Nationalism Confronts the Secular State* (Berkeley, CA: University of California Press, 1993), 18–19.

18. Juergensmeyer, *The New Cold War*, 21.

19. Bernard Lewis, *The Political Language of Islam* (Chicago, IL: University of Chicago Press, 1988), 88.

20. "Transcript of Osama bin Laden Tape 2007" Middle East Web, September 8, 2007, http://www.mideastweb.org/log/archives/00000622.htm.

21. Tom Coghlan, "Resurgent Taliban Vow to Disrupt 'Joke' Presidential Election," *The Times*, October 7, 2008, http://www.timesonline.co.uk/tol/news/world/asia/article4894496.ece.

22. Mark Juergensmeyer, "Sacrifice and Cosmic War," *Terrorism and Political Violence* 3 (Autumn 1991): 107.

23. Juergensmeyer, *The New Cold War*, 21.

24. See Ruhollah (Ayatollah) Khomeini, *Islam and Revolution: Writings and Declarations*, trans. Hamid Algar (Berkeley, CA: Mizan Press, 1981), 281.

25. Iran maintains that its nuclear reactors are for peaceful purposes, while the United States, its European allies, and Israel claim that Iran is trying to develop the capability to produce nuclear weapons.

26. See R. H. Dekmijian, *Nasser's Egypt* (Albany, NY: SUNY Press, 1971).

27. Arab Socialism and Pan-Arabism were ideologies that called for the unity of the Arab world and the implementation of a socialist economy that, unlike European socialism, was not atheist and had a spiritual component. Both Arab Socialism and Pan-Arabism called for resistance to imperialism and the influence of the United States and the West. At the apex of the Pan-Arab and Arab Socialism movements, Nasser led a confederation of Egypt and Syria known as the United Arab Republic from 1958 to 1961. For more on Nasser and Pan-Arabism and Arab Socialism, see P. J. Vatikiotis, *Nasser and His Generation* (London: Croon Helm, 1978).

28. Vatikiotis, *Nasser and His Generation,* 115.

29. For a discussion of the significance of the Arab defeat in the Six-Day War and the various responses, including Islam, see Fuad Ajami, *The Arab Predicament* (Cambridge: Cambridge University Press, 1982).

30. Mohammed (Sheik) Kiskh, *The Defeat and the Ideological Invasion* (Beirut: n.p., 1969).

31. Qutb, *Milestones,* 87.

32. Mohammed Heikal, *Autumn of Fury* (New York: Random House, 1983), 107.

33. Heikal, *Autumn of Fury,* 132.

34. Yahya Sadowski, "Egypt's Islamist Movement: A New Political and Economic Force," *Middle East Insight* 5 (1989): 37–45.

35. Saad Ibrahim, "Anatomy of Egypt's Militant Islamic Groups," *International Journal of Middle East Studies* 12 (1980): 423–45.

36. The protests that eventually brought down the regime of President Zine el Abidine Ben Ali in Tunisia were sparked by Mohamed Bouazizi, a fruit and vegetable vendor who set himself on fire after being harassed by police and local officials in the town of Sidi Bouzid. Bouazizi could not afford a permit or to pay bribes, so he was bullied and fined by police. Because he was not accepted into the military and could not find a job or afford college, he walked 12 miles each day to the center of town to sell his wares.

37. Robert Keohane and Joseph Nye, "Globalization: What's New? What's Not? And So What?" *Foreign Policy* 118 (Spring 2000): 108.

38. Thomas Friedman, *The Lexus and the Olive Tree* (New York: Farrar, Straus, and Giroux, 2000), 34.

39. Friedman, *The Lexus and the Olive Tree,* 364.

40. Friedman, *The Lexus and the Olive Tree,* 329.

41. Quoted in John Voll, "Fundamentalism in the Sunni Arab World," in *Fundamentalism Observed,* ed. M. E. Marty and R. Scott Appleby (Chicago, IL: University of Chicago Press, 1994), 360.

42. Paul Smith. *The Terrorism Ahead* (Armonk, NY: M. E. Sharpe, 2008), 66.

43. Quoted in Jessica Stern, *Terror in the Name of God: Why Religious Militants Kill?* (New York: Harper Collins, 2003), 40–41.

44. Mark Strauss, "Antiglobalism's Jewish Problem: Globalization at Work," *Foreign Policy* 139 (November–December 2003): 62.

45. Quoted in Chris Hedges "Tehran Journal," *New York Times,* August 16, 2001, A2.

46. Friedman, *The Lexus and the Olive Tree,* 384.

47. Benjamin Barber, *Jihad vs. McWorld* (New York: Ballantine Books, 2001), xi.

48. Edward Gresser, "Blank Spot on the Map—How Trade Policy Is Working against the War on Terror," *Progressive Policy Institute Policy Report* (February 2003): 1–2.

49. Gresser, "Blank Spot on the Map—How Trade Policy Is Working against the War on Terror," 1.

50. Barber, *Jihad vs. McWorld,* vii.

51. Barber, *Jihad vs. McWorld,* vii.

52. Friedman, *The Lexus and the Olive Tree,* 368.

53. Cited in Friedman, *The Lexus and the Olive Tree,* 375.

54. John Esposito, *Holy War: Terror in the Name of Islam* (New York: Oxford University Press, 2002), 73–75.

55. See Bernard Lewis, *Islam and the West* (Oxford: Oxford University Press, 1993); Bernard Lewis, *What Went Wrong: Western Impact and Middle East Responses* (New York: Oxford University Press, 2002); and Bernard Lewis, "The Roots of Muslim Rage," in *The New Global Terrorism: Characteristics, Causes, Controls,* ed. Charles Kegley (Upper Saddle River, NJ: Prentice Hall, 2003), 194–201.

56. Lewis, "The Roots of Muslim Rage," 194–201.

57. Smith, *The Terrorism Ahead,* 68.

58. Bruce Lincoln, *Holy Terrors: Thinking about Religion after September 11* (Chicago, IL: University of Chicago Press, 2003), 238.

59. Samuel Huntington, "The Clash of Civilizations?" *Foreign Affairs* (Summer 1993): 48.

60. Hamas Communiqué, January 22, 1991.

61. Barber, *Jihad vs. McWorld,* 215.

62. Mike Mousseau, "Market Civilization and Its Clash with Terror," *International Security* 23 (Winter 2002/2003): 5–29.

63. Mark Juergensmeyer, *Terror in the Mind of God: The Global Rise of Religious Violence* (Berkeley, CA: University of California Press, 2003), 196.

64. Michael Barkun, *Religion and the Racist Right: The Origins of the Christian-Identity Movement* (Chapel Hill, NC: University of North Carolina Press, 1994), 7.

65. This type of thought is best represented in the *Protocols of the Elders of Zion,* a fraudulent Russian text published in 1903 that described a secret meeting where the Jews plotted to control the world by subverting Christian morality through control of the economy and the press.

66. Susanne Rudolph and Lloyd I. Rudolph, "Modern Hate," *New Republic* (December 1993): 26–28.

67. Stern, *Terror in the Name of God,* 75–78.

68. Juergensmeyer, *Terror in the Mind of God,* 202.

69. Juergensmeyer, *Terror in the Mind of God,* 36.

70. Juergensmeyer, *Terror in the Mind of God,* 203.

71. Israel's Ministry of Religion does not recognize Reform, Conservative, and Reconstructionist Judaism, which represent 85 percent of the Jewish community in

the United States. Vandalism, arson, and other acts of desecration have occurred at a number of non-Orthodox synagogues in Israel.

72. Sayyid Qutb, *This Religion of Islam*, trans. Islamdust (Palo Alto, CA: al-Manar Press, 1967), 82.

73. Moghadam, *The Globalization of Martyrdom*, 118.

74. Farhad Khosrokhavar, *Suicide Bombers: Allah's New Martyrs*, trans. David Macey (London: Pluto, 2005), 155–56.

75. Timothy Savage, "Europe and Islam: Crescent Waxing: Cultures Clashing, *Washington Quarterly* 27 (Summer 2004): 31–33.

76. Olivier Roy, "Terrorism and Deculturation," in *The Roots of Terrorism,* ed. Louise Richardson (New York: Routledge, 2006), 160–63.

77. Roy, "Terrorism and Deculturation," 161.

78. Roy, "Terrorism and Deculturation," 166.

79. Khosrokhavar, *Suicide Bombers,* 151.

80. Phillip Rucker and Julie Tate, "In Online Posts Apparently by Detroit Suspect, Religious Ideals Collide," *Washington Post,* December 19, 2009, accessed http://www.washingtonpost.com/wp-dyn/content/article/2009/12/28/AR2009122802492.html?sid=ST2009122802585.

81. "Times Square Bomber Gets Life Sentence. "*MSNBC.com,*" October 5, 2010, http://www.msnbc.msn.com/id/39513363/ns/us_news-security/t/times-square-bomber-gets-life-sentence/.

CHAPTER 5

1. Scott Atran, "Genesis of Suicide Terrorism," *Science* 299 (2003): 1535–36.

2. See Jerrold M. Post, "Individual and Group Dynamics of Terrorist Behavior," in *World Congress of Psychiatry, Psychiatry: The State of the Art* (New York: Plenum, 1985), 93–106; Jerrold M Post, "Terrorist Psycho-Logic: Terrorist Behavior as a Product of Psychological Forces," in *Origins of Terrorism: Psychologies, Ideologies, Theologies, States of Mind,* ed. Walter Reich (Cambridge, England: Cambridge University Press, 1990), 25–40; and Jerold Post, "The Psychological Dynamics of Terrorism," in *The Roots of Terrorism,* ed. Louise Richardson (New York: Routledge, 2006), 17–28.

3. Martha Crenshaw, "The Causes of Terrorism," *Comparative Politics* 13 (1981): 390; Rex Hudson, *The Sociology and Psychology of Terrorism: Who Becomes a Terrorist and Why?* (Washington, DC: Library of Congress, 1999), 30.

4. Robert Pape, *Dying to Win: The Strategic Logic of Suicide Terrorism* (New York: Random House, 2005), 210. There was one case, a Chechen female, of probable mental retardation.

5. Nasra Hassan, "An Arsenal of Believers," *New Yorker,* November 19, 2001, 40.

6. Ariel Merari, "Psychological Aspects of Suicide Terrorism," in *Psychology of Terrorism,* ed. Bruce Bonger et al. (New York: Oxford University Press, 2007), 109.

7. Marc Sageman, *Understanding Terror Networks* (Philadelphia, PA: University of Pennsylvania, 2004), 62–98.

8. Maxwell Taylor, *The Terrorist* (London: Brassey's, 1988), 92.

9. Taylor, *The Terrorist,* 92.

10. Serge Schmemann, "An Unbalanced Loner with a Rifle," *New York Times,* January 2, 1997, A.8.

11. Taylor, *The Terrorist,* 92.

12. Walter Reich, "Understanding Terrorism: The Limits and Opportunities of Psychological Inquiry," in *Understanding Terrorism: Psychologies, Ideologies, Theologies, and States of Mind,* ed. Walter Reich (Baltimore, MD: Johns Hopkins University Press, 1990), 262.

13. Clark McCauley, "Psychological Issues in Understanding Terrorism and the Response to Terrorism," in *Psychology of Terrorism,* ed. Bruce Bonger et al. (New York: Oxford University Press, 2007), 18.

14. Pape, *Dying to Win,* 172–80.

15. Robert Friedman, "Inside the Jewish Terrorist Underground," *Journal of Palestine Studies* 15 (Winter 1986): 199.

16. Brian Barber, *One Heart, so Many Stones* (Palgrave: New York, forthcoming).

17. Ariel Merari, "Psychological Aspects of Suicide Terrorism" in *Psychology of Terrorism,* ed. Bruce Bonger et al. (New York: Oxford University Press, 2007), 107–9.

18. Emile Durkheim, *Suicide: A Study in Sociology,* trans. John Spaulding and George Simson (New York: Free Press, 1951), 210–19.

19. Pape, *Dying to Win,* 172–80.

20. A. Pedahzur, A. Perliger, and L. Weinberg, "Altruism and Fatalism: The Characteristics of Palestinian Suicide Terrorists," *Deviant Behavior* 24 (2003): 405–23.

21. Pape, *Dying to Win,* 181–85.

22. Jerrold M. Post, "Individual and Group Dynamics of Terrorist Behavior," in *Psychiatry: The State of the Art,* ed. World Congress of Psychiatry (New York: Plenum, 1985), 103.

23. Hudson, *The Sociology and Psychology of Terrorism,* 60.

24. Nasra Hassan, "Suicide Terrorism," in *The Roots of Terrorism,* ed. Louise Richardson (New York: Routledge, 2006), 38–39.

25. Anat Berko and Edna Erez, "Ordinary People and Death Work: Palestinian Suicide Bombers as Victimizers and Victims," *Violence and Victims* 20 (2005): 603–23.

26. Hassan, "An Arsenal of Believers," 40.

27. See Berko and Erez "Ordinary People and Death Work," 603–23; Hilal Khashan, "Collective Palestinian Frustration and Suicide Bombing," *Third World Quarterly* 24 (2003): 1049–67; Merari, "Psychological Aspects of Suicide Terrorism," 106; and Assaf Moghadam, *The Globalization of Martyrdom* (Baltimore, MD: Johns Hopkins University Press, 2008), 255.

28. Jerrold Post, *Leaders and Their Followers in a Dangerous World* (Ithaca, NY: Cornell University Press, 2004), 127–28.

29. Jeff Victoroff, "The Mind of the Terrorist: A Review and Critique of Psychological Approaches," *The Journal of Conflict Resolution* 49 (February 2005): 28.

30. Mark Juergensmeyer, *Terror in the Mind of God: The Global Rise of Religious Violence* (Berkeley, CA: University of California Press, 2003), 192–94.

31. Kati Marton, *A Death in Jerusalem* (New York: Arcade, 1996), 53.

32. See Victoroff, "The Mind of the Terrorist," 28 for a review of novelty theories of terrorism.

33. For example, a Palestinian youth would not have the option of joining the military and may lack the connections to get into the police or has suffered from their corruption, while Palestinian terror groups are in constant need of recruits and are respected in society. An American low-income minority youth, who is apolitical and sees little hope for a better economic future while growing up in a gang-infested area, might join a street gang. A white, American middle-class youth, who has been raised to love his or her country and to respect the military, would be likely to enlist in the armed forces.

34. For a review of the literature on splitting and narcissistic rage, see Hart, *The Sociology and Psychology of Terrorism,* 20–21. Also, see Post, "Terrorist Psycho-Logic," 27–29, and Robert Robins and Jerrold Post, *Political Paranoia: The Psychopolitics of Hatred* (New Haven, CT: Yale University Press, 1997), 97.

35. Post, "Terrorist Psycho-Logic," 27–28.

36. Olivier Roy, "Terrorism and Deculturation," in *The Roots of Terrorism,* ed. Louise Richardson (New York: Routledge, 2006), 160–63.

37. James Jones, "Why Does Religion Turn Violent? A Psychoanalytic Exploration of Religious Terrorism," *The Psychoanalytic Review* 93 (2006): 167–90.

38. Jones, "Why Does Religion Turn Violent?," 178.

39. See James Jones, *Terror and Transformation: The Ambiguity of Religion in Psychoanalytic Perspective* (New York: Taylor and Francis, 2002), 64–79.

40. Jones, *Terror and Transformation,* 64–79.

41. Jones, *Terror and Transformation,* 64–79.

42. Hasan was serving in the U.S. army, and Shahzad was a budget analyst who lived in a Connecticut suburb.

43. Jeanne Knutson, "Social and Psychodynamic Pressures toward a Negative Identity," in *Behavioral and Quantitative Perspectives on Terrorism,* ed. Yonah Alexander and John Gleason (New York: Pergamon, 1981), 105–52.

44. Kent Oots and Thomas Wiegele, "Terrorist and Victim: Psychiatric and Physiological Approaches from a Social Science Perspective," *Terrorism: An International Journal* 8 (1985): 1–32.

45. See Albert Bandura, *Aggression: A Social Learning Analysis* (New York: Prentice Hall, 1973).

46. "Suicide Bombers: Dignity, Despair, and the Need for Hope. An Interview with Eyad El Sarraj," *Journal of Palestine Studies* 31 (Summer 2002): 72.

47. Jerrold Post, "The Socio-Cultural Underpinnings of Terrorist Psychology: When Hatred Is Bred to the Bone," in *Root Causes of Terrorism,* ed. Tore Bjorgo (New York: Routledge, 2005), 55–69.

48. Rona Fields, "Child Terror Victims and Adult Terrorists," *Journal of Psychohistory* 7 (1979): 71–76.

49. Jerrold Post, E. Sprinzak, and L.M. Denny, "The Terrorists in Their Own Words: Interviews with Thirty-Five Incarcerated Middle Eastern Terrorists," *Terrorism and Political Violence* 15 (2003):171–84.

50. Hassan, "Suicide Terrorism," 38–39.

51. Anat Berko, *The Path to Paradise: The Inner World of Suicide Bombers and Their Dispatchers,* trans. Elizabeth Yuval (Westport, CT: Praeger Security International, 2007), 171.

52. Victoroff, "The Mind of the Terrorist," 16.

53. Post, "The Socio-Cultural Underpinnings of Terrorist Psychology," 61.

54. Khashan, "Collective Palestinian Frustration and Suicide Bombing," 1055.

55. Atran, "Genesis of Suicide Terrorism," 1536.

56. Post, "Terrorist Psycho-Logic," 56.

57. Albert Bandura, "Mechanisms of Moral Disengagement," in *Origins of Terrorism: Psychologies, Ideologies, Theologies, States of Mind,* ed. Walter Reich (Cambridge: Cambridge University Press, 1990), 161–62.

58. Jones, "Why Does Religion Turn Violent?," 167–90.

59. Khomeini viewed Rushdie's novel, *Satanic Verses,* as being an act of apostasy because of its portrayal of the Prophet Muhammad. The publication of a satirical cartoon depicting the Prophet Muhammad in a Danish newspaper in 2005 led to the issuing of several *fatwas* sanctioning violence against the paper and Denmark, rioting across the Muslim world, attacks on Christians in Iraq and Pakistan, and assaults on Western embassies in Muslim nations.

60. Berko, *The Path to Paradise,* 172–73.

61. McCauley, "Psychological Issues in Understanding Terrorism and the Response to Terrorism," 18. Surveys in Muslim nations found that 76 percent of Muslims labeled U.S. policies as the primary cause of the 9/11 attacks.

62. Juergensmeyer, *Terror in the Mind of God,* 148–66.

63. Ehud Sprinzak, "The Process of Delegitimization: Towards a Linkage Theory of Political Terrorism," in *Terrorism and Public Policy,* ed. Clark McCauley (London: Frank Cass, 1991), 50–68.

64. Juergensmeyer, *Terror in the Mind of God,* 175–76.

65. Juergensmeyer, *Terror in the Mind of God,* 177, 186.

66. Post, "The Socio-Cultural Underpinnings of Terrorist Psychology," 56.

67. See Berko and Erez. "Ordinary People and Death Work," and Hassan, "An Arsenal of Believers"; and "Suicide Bombers: Dignity, Despair, and the Need for Hope: An Interview with Eyad El Sarraj."

68. Bandura, "Mechanisms of Moral Disengagement," 173–75.

69. See Walter Laqueur, *The New Terrorism: Fanaticism and the Arms of Mass Destruction* (New York: Oxford University Press, 1999).

70. Hudson, *The Sociology and Psychology of Terrorism: Who Becomes a Terrorist and Why?,* 35. Also, see Wilfred Bion, *Experiences in Groups* (London: Tavistock, 1961).

71. See Irving Janis, *Victims of Groupthink* (Boston, MA: Houghton-Mifflin, 1972).

72. McCauley, "Psychological Issues in Understanding Terrorism and the Response to Terrorism," 22.

73. Ehud Sprinzak, "The Psychopolitical Formation of Extreme Left Terrorism in a Democracy: The Case of the Weathermen," in *Origins of Terrorism: Psychologies, Ideologies, Theologies, States of Mind,* ed. Walter Reich (Cambridge, England: Cambridge University Press, 1990), 79.

74. Jerrold Post, E. Sprinzak, and L.M. Denny, "The Terrorists in Their Own Words: Interviews with Thirty-Five Incarcerated Middle Eastern Terrorists," *Terrorism and Political Violence* 15 (2003): 171–84.

75. Post, "Terrorist Psycho-Logic," 35.

76. Donald Kinder, "Opinion and Action in the Realm of Politics." in *The Hand-book of Political and Social Psychology,* ed. D. Gilbert, Volume 2 (New York: McGraw Hill, 1998), 778–867. Kinder found that African Americans in the civil rights movement and whites who opposed forced bussing were motivating by per-ceived harm to their ethnic group rather than to themselves.

77. McCauley, "Psychological Issues in Understanding Terrorism and the Response to Terrorism," 20.

78. Moghadam, *The Globalization of Martyrdom,* 257.

79. Atran, "Genesis of Suicide Terrorism," 1538.

80. Juergensmeyer, *Terror in the Mind of God,* 206.

81. Singapore Home Ministry, *White Paper: The Jemaah Islamiyah and the Threat of Terrorism* (Singapore: Ministry of Home Affairs, 2003).

82. W. W Messner, *The Cultic Origins of Christianity: The Dynamics of Religious Development* (Collegeville, MN: The Liturgical Press, 2000), 13–15.

83. Ami Pedahzur and Arie Perliger, "The Changing Nature of Suicide Attacks: A Social Network Perspective," *Social Forces* 84 (June 2006): 1993–1995.

84. See Mia Bloom, *Dying to Kill: The Allure of Suicide Terrorism* (New York: Columbia University Press, 2005) and Mia Bloom, "Palestinian Suicide Bombing: Public Support, Market Share, and Outbidding," *Political Science Quarterly* 119 (2004): 61–88.

85. Merari, "Psychological Aspects of Suicide Terrorism," 101–15.

86. Berko and Erez, "Ordinary People and Death Work," 607.

87. Hassan, "Arsenal of Believers," 56–61.

88. Berko and Erez, "Ordinary People and Death Work," 607.

89. Ariel Merari, "The Readiness to Kill and Die," in *Origins of Terrorism: Psy-chologies, Ideologies, Theologies, States of Mind,* ed. Walter Reich (Cambridge, En-gland: Cambridge University Press, 1990), 195–96.

90. Post, *Leaders and Their Followers in a Dangerous World,* 188.

91. Hassan, "Suicide Terrorism," 38–39.

CHAPTER 6

1. For a time, there was room for compromise on location as Herzl, at one point, suggested that it might be easier to win British approval for a Jewish state in, what is today, Uganda, rather than Palestine.

2. Charles Leibman and Don Yahiya, *Civil Religion in Israel* (Berkeley, CA: Uni-versity of California Press, 1983), 30–58.

3. Leibman and Yahiya, *Civil Religion in Israel,* 48–60.

4. Charles Leibman and Don Yahiya, *Religion and Politics in Israel* (Blooming-ton, IN: Indiana University Press, 1987), 103–30.

5. Leibman and Yahiyah, *Religion and Politics in Israel,* 121–30.

6. Mark Juergensmeyer, *The New Cold War: Religious Nationalism Confronts the Secular State* (Berkeley, CA: University of California Press, 1993), 65.

7. Yehoshefat Harkabi, *Israel's Fateful Hour* (New York: Harper and Row, 1988), 162.

8. Harkabi, *Israel's Fateful Hour*, 160–63. The Sinai Peninsula, Gaza, and the Golan Heights were also captured, but these areas are of less religious significance. The Western Wall (Kotel), the holiest site for Jews, is one of the support walls of the foundation of the Second Temple and the only part of the structure that still exists. Judea and Samaria contain the cities of Bethlehem, Hebron, and Nablus, all of which have biblical significance.

9. Ian Lustick, *For the Land and for the Lord; Jewish Fundamentalism in Israel* (New York: Council on Foreign Relations, 1988), 28–31.

10. See Lustick, *For the Land and for the Lord*, 86, for a discussion of this proposition from Menachem Kasher.

11. Harkabi, *Israel's Fateful Hour*, 160–72.

12. Leibman and Yahiya, *Civil Religion in Israel*, 79.

13. Leibman and Yahiya, *Religion and Politics in Israel*, 103–30.

14. Howard Sachar, *A History of Israel: Volume II* (New York: Oxford University Press, 1987), 16.

15. Ehud Sprinzak, *The Ascendency of Israel's Radical Right* (New York: Oxford University Press, 1991), 88.

16. Gilles Kepel, *The Revenge of God: The Resurgence of Islam, Christianity, and Judaism in the Modern World* (University Park, PA: Pennsylvania State University Press, 1994), 157–61.

17. Leibman and Yahiya, *Civil Religion in Israel*, 79.

18. During the 1980s, 12 members of the Knesset were Gush Emunim leaders. A group called "The Lobby," which exerted pressure on behalf of Gush Emunim, included 38 Knesset members (out of 120) as supporters. See Lustick, *For the Land and for the Lord*, 10.

19. Quoted in Kepel, *The Revenge of God*, 161.

20. Kepel, *The Revenge of God*, 161.

21. Kepel, *The Revenge of God*, 161–62.

22. Lustick, *For the Land and for the Lord*, 66.

23. Mark Juergensmeyer, *Terror in the Mind of God: The Global Rise of Religious Violence* (Berkeley, CA: University of California Press, 2003), 67.

24. Lustick, *For the Land and for the Lord*, 66.

25. Kepel, *The Revenge of God*, 164.

26. Lustick, *For the Land and for the Lord*, 68.

27. Kepel, *The Revenge of God*, 164–65.

28. Ehud Sprinzak, *Brother against Brother: Violence and Extremism in Israeli Politics from the Altalena to Rabin's Assassination* (New York: Free Press, 1999), 160.

29. Sprinzak, *The Ascendency of Israel's Radical Right*, 264.

30. Sprinzak, *Brother against Brother*, 162.

31. Kepel, *The Revenge of God*, 168.

32. There are approximately 100,000 Jews of North American origin in Israel, while roughly 6,000,000 remain in the United States and Canada. An overwhelming majority of new immigrants to Israel since the country's founding were fleeing persecution or poverty in their native lands. Most of Israel's Sephardim (Jews from Arab lands) were forced from their homelands after Israel was created, while many of Israel's approximately 1.5 million Jews from the former Soviet Union emigrated

to escape persecution under the communist regime and the economic chaos that followed the fall of communism.

33. Howard Sachar, *A History of Israel: Volume I* (New York: Knopf, 1976), 18–20.

34. See the introduction to Meron Benvenisti, *Conflicts and Contradictions* (New York: Villard, 1986).

35. Sprinzak, *Brother against Brother,* 169.

36. Sprinzak, *The Ascendency of Israel's Radical Right,* 92.

37. Lustick, *For the Land and for the Lord,* 74–79.

38. Quoted in Lustick, *For the Land and for the Lord,* 82.

39. Kahane was able to be elected because Israel has a proportional representation system where seats in the parliament are allocated based on the percentage of the votes that each party receives. As a result, Kahane won a seat with approximately 26,000 votes.

40. Robert Friedman, *The False Prophet: Meir Kahane—from FBI Informant to Knesset Member* (New York: Lawrence Hill Books, 1990), 83–128.

41. Sprinzak, *Brother against Brother,* 184.

42. Sprinzak, *The Ascendency of Israel's Radical Right,* 122–25.

43. Sprinzak, *The Ascendency of Israel's Radical Right,* 235.

44. Michael Karpin and Ina Friedman, *Murder in the Name of God: The Plot to Kill Yitzhak Rabin* (New York: Harry Holt and Company, 1998), 45.

45. Sprinzak, *Brother against Brother,* 189.

46. Karpin and Friedman, *Murder in the Name of God,* 47.

47. Sprinzak, *Brother against Brother,* 191.

48. See Friedman, *The False Prophet* and Sprinzak, *The Ascendency of Israel's Radical Right,* 243–45.

49. Sprinzak, *The Ascendency of Israel's Radical Right,* 242.

50. Sprinzak, *Brother against Brother,* 240–44.

51. Juergensmeyer, *Terror in the Mind of God,* 51.

52. Sprinzak, *Brother against Brother,* 240.

53. Juergensmeyer, *Terror in the Mind of God,* 50.

54. Karpin and Friedman, *Murder in the Name of God,* 44.

55. Jessica Stern, *Terror in the Name of God: Why Religious Militants Kill* (New York: Harper Collins, 2003), 90–91.

56. Sprinzak, *Brother against Brother,* 261–62.

57. Karpin and Friedman, *Murder in the Name of God,* 19.

58. Karpin and Friedman, *Murder in the Name of God,* 19.

59. Karpin and Friedman, *Murder in the Name of God,* 17.

60. Karpin and Friedman, *Murder in the Name of God,* 19.

61. Ehud Sprinzak, "Gush Emunim: The Type of the Iceberg," *Jerusalem Quarterly* 31 (Summer 1987): 28–47.

62. Stern, *Terror in the Name of God,* 103.

63. Lustick, *For the Land and for the Lord,* 11.

64. Quoted in Sachar, *A History of Israel: Volume II,* 165. As mentioned in chapter 5, Prime Minister Yitzhak Shamir referred to the Underground members as "good Jewish boys who had made a mistake."

65. Sachar, *A History of Israel: Volume II,* 164.

66. Lustick, *For the Land and for the Lord,* 14.

67. Karpin and Friedman, *Murder in the Name of God,* 42–43.

68. These accusations have come from Israeli and Jewish groups such as Peace Now, Rabbis for Human Rights, and B'tselem, an Israeli Human Rights organization.

69. Sprinzak, *The Ascendency of Israel's Radical Right,* 268.

70. Quoted in Karpin and Friedman, *Murder in the Name of God,* 64.

71. Karpin and Friedman, *Murder in the Name of God,* 66.

72. Karpin and Friedman, *Murder in the Name of God,* 71–76.

73. Karpin and Friedman, *Murder in the Name of God,* 16.

74. Sprinzak, *Brother against Brother,* 216–17.

CHAPTER 7

1. Matthew 22:21. Jesus was responding to the question as to whether Jews should pay their tributary taxes to the Roman occupiers of Palestine.

2. Noah Feldman, "Religion and the Earthly City," *Social Research* 76 (2009): 989–1000.

3. For example see James Madison "To F.L. Schaeffer," in *Letters and Other Writings of James Madison,* Volume 3 (Philadelphia, PA; J.B. Lippincott, 1865), 262–63.

4. See Martin Luther and John Calvin, *On Secular Authority,* trans. Harro Hopfl (Cambridge, UK: Cambridge University Press, 1991), 1–46.

5. See Jeff Sharlet, "Jesus Killed Mohammed: The Crusade for a Christian Military," *Harper's Magazine* (May 2009): 31–43.

6. See Giovani Costigan, *A History of Modern Ireland* (Indianapolis, IN: Bobbs-Merrill, 1980) for a discussion of the historical roots of the conflict in Northern Ireland.

7. Jonathan White, *Terrorism* (Belmont, CA: Thomson Wadsworth, 2003), 81.

8. John McGarry and Brendan O'Leary, *Explaining Northern Ireland* (Cambridge, MA: Blackwell, 1995), 314.

9. Michael Burleigh, *Sacred Causes* (New York: Harper Collins, 2007), 383–84.

10. Richard Rose, *Governing without Consensus: An Irish Perspective* (Dublin: Gill and Macmillan, 1988), 171–79.

11. Burleigh, *Sacred Causes,* 389–91.

12. Connor Cruise O'Brien, *Ancestral Voices: Religion and Nationalism in Ireland* (Chicago, IL: University of Chicago Press, 1995), 162.

13. Burleigh, *Sacred Causes,* 374–75.

14. Cruise O'Brien, *Ancestral Voices,* 157–59.

15. White, *Terrorism,* 88–89.

16. Cruise O'Brien, *Ancestral Voices,* 112–17.

17. Cruise O'Brien, *Ancestral Voices,* 168–69.

18. Cruise O'Brien, *Ancestral Voices,* 170.

19. Cruise O'Brien, *Ancestral Voices,* 190.

20. Mark Juergensmeyer, *Terror in the Mind of God: The Global Rise of Religious Violence* (Berkeley, CA: University of California Press, 2003), 39–41.

21. Burleigh, *Sacred Causes,* 387.

22. Quoted in Juergensmeyer, *Terror in the Mind of God,* 41.

23. McGarry and O'Leary, *Explaining Northern Ireland,* 202.

24. Paisley renounced violence in 1989 and his ties to the Ulster Resistance paramilitary.

25. McGarry and O'Leary, *Explaining Northern Ireland,* 189.

26. Juergensmeyer, *Terror in the Mind of God,* 38.

27. McGarry and O'Leary, *Explaining Northern Ireland,* 191–96.

28. McGarry and O'Leary, *Explaining Northern Ireland,* 212.

29. Burleigh, *Sacred Causes,* 384.

30. McGarry and O'Leary, *Explaining Northern Ireland,* 212.

31. McGarry and O'Leary, *Explaining Northern Ireland,* 334.

32. See Ian Lustick, *Unsettled States, Disputed Lands* (Ithaca, NY: Cornell University Press, 1993), 57–80, 121–86.

33. McGarry and O'Leary, *Explaining Northern Ireland,* 335.

34. Rose, *Governing without Consensus,* 74.

35. McGarry and O'Leary, *Explaining Northern Ireland,* 312.

36. McGarry and O'Leary, *Explaining Northern Ireland,* 331.

37. Rose, *Governing without Consensus,* 121–29.

38. Cruise O'Brien, *Ancestral Voices,* 166.

39. McGarry and O'Leary, *Explaining Northern Ireland,* 328–29.

40. Adrian Gaulke, *Northern Ireland: The International Perspective* (Dublin: Gill and MacMillan, 1988), 17–20.

41. McGarry and O'Leary, *Explaining Northern Ireland,* 354–55.

42. Rose, *Governing without Consensus,* 289.

43. Edward Augur, *In Search of Political Stability: A Comparative Study of New Brunswick and Northern Ireland* (Montreal: McGill-Queen's, 1981), 184–85.

44. McGarry and O'Leary, *Explaining Northern Ireland,* 314–15.

45. Arend Lijphart, "The Northern Ireland Problem: Cases, Theories, and Solutions," *British Journal of Political Science 5* (Summer 1975): 83–106.

46. Alesha Doan, *Opposition and Intimidation: The Abortion Wars and Strategies of Political Harassment* (Ann Arbor, MI: The University of Michigan Press, 2007), 209.

47. Dallas Blanchard and Terry Prewitt, *Religious Violence and Abortion: The Gideon Project* (Gainesville, FL: University of Florida Press, 1993), ix.

48. Gunn was referring to Genesis 9:6. James Risen and Judy Thomas, *Wrath of Angels: The American Abortion Wars* (New York: Basic Books, 1998), 339.

49. Quoted in Patricia Baird-Windle and Eleanor Bader, *Targets of Hatred: Antiabortion Terrorism* (New York: Palgrave, 2001), 89.

50. Baird-Windle and Bader, *Targets of Hatred,* 151.

51. Baird-Windle and Bader, *Targets of Hatred,* 140–42.

52. James Risen and Judy Thomas, *Wrath of Angels: The American Abortion Wars* (New York: Basic Books, 1998), 81–82.

53. Carol Mason, *Killing for Life: The Apocalyptic Narrative of Pro-Life Politics* (Ithaca, NY: Cornell University Press, 2002), 6, 22.

54. Jerry Reiter, *Live from the Gates of Hell: An Insider's Look at the Antiabortion Underground* (Amherst, NY: Prometheus Books, 2000), 172–75.

55. Blanchard and Prewitt, *Religious Violence and Abortion*, 158–63.

56. Mark Juergensmeyer, *Terror in the Mind of God: The Global Rise of Religious Violence* (Berkeley, CA: University of California Press, 2003), 28–29.

57. Blanchard and Prewitt, *Religious Violence and Abortion*, 208.

58. Doan, *Opposition and Intimidation*, 66.

59. Risen and Thomas, *Wrath of Angels*, 63.

60. Mason, *Killing for Life*, 16–21.

61. Baird-Windle, and Bader, *Targets of Hatred*, 114.

62. Doan, *Opposition and Intimidation*, 31.

63. Baird-Windle and Bader, *Targets of Hatred*, 4–5.

64. Mason, *Killing for Life*, 152–53.

65. Mason, *Killing for Life*, 44.

66. Mason, *Killing for Life*, 4–14.

67. Mason, *Killing for Life*, 141.

68. Mason, *Killing for Life*, 30–39.

69. Risen and Thomas, *Wrath of Angels*, 120.

70. Blanchard and Prewitt, *Religious Violence and Abortion*, 34.

71. Blanchard and Prewitt report that 42 percent of the 102 clinic bombings and arsons that took place between 1977 and 1987 occurred during Reagan's first term and that 47 percent occurred during his second term, while only 12 percent took place during Carter's one term in office. See Blanchard and Prewitt, *Religious Violence and Abortion*, 179.

72. Doan, *Opposition and Intimidation*, 23.

73. Blanchard and Prewitt, *Religious Violence and Abortion*, 34.

74. Risen and Thomas, *Wrath of Angels*, 76, 94.

75. Risen and Thomas, *Wrath of Angels*, 114–15.

76. Risen and Thomas, *Wrath of Angels*, 345.

77. Blanchard and Prewitt, *Religious Violence and Abortion*, 258.

78. Blanchard and Prewitt, *Religious Violence and Abortion*, 270.

79. Blanchard and Prewitt, *Religious Violence and Abortion*, 194.

80. Baird-Windle and Bader, *Targets of Hatred*, 156.

81. Doan, *Opposition and Intimidation*, 20–21.

82. Risen and Thomas, *Wrath of Angels*, 30–31.

83. Baird-Windle and Bader, *Targets of Hatred*, 81.

84. Mason, *Killing for Life*, 3.

85. Juergensmeyer, *Terror in the Mind of God*, 23.

86. Doan, *Opposition and Intimidation*, 26–30.

87. Doan, *Opposition and Intimidation*, 117.

88. Risen and Thomas, *Wrath of Angels*, 140–44.

89. Baird-Windle and Bader, *Targets of Hatred*, 53, 84.

90. Baird-Windle and Bader document a number of cases of inaction by law enforcement, the criminal justice system, and elected officials in *Targets of Hatred*.

91. Baird-Windle and Bader, *Targets of Hatred*, 100.

92. Doan, *Opposition and Intimidation*, 105.

93. Doan, *Opposition and Intimidation*, 20–21.

94. Blanchard and Prewitt, *Religious Violence and Abortion,* 264–66.

95. Jessica Stern, *Terror in the Name of God: Why Religious Militants Kill* (New York: Harper Collins, 2003), 275.

96. Reiter, *Live from the Gates of Hell,* 172.

97. Risen and Thomas, *Wrath of Angels,* 90.

98. Baird-Windle and Bader, *Targets of Hatred,* 13.

99. See Baird-Windle and Bader. *Targets of Hatred,* 12–13, for a discussion of their interview with Dr. Chesler.

100. Blanchard and Prewitt, *Religious Violence and Abortion,* 210–11.

CHAPTER 8

1. US State Department Office of the Coordinator for Counterterrorism, *Country Reports on Terrorism 2010,* last modified August 18, 2011, http://www.state.gov/s/ct/rls/crt/2010/170266.html.

2. Bernard Lewis, "The Return of Islam." *Commentary.* (January 1976) and Samuel Huntington, "The Clash of Civilizations?," *Foreign Affairs* (Summer 1993): 22–49.

3. See Fred Donner, *The Early Islamic Conquests* (Princeton, NJ: Princeton University Press, 1981).

4. See Mark Juergensmeyer, *The New Cold War: Religious Nationalism Confronts the Secular State* (Berkeley, CA: University of California Press, 1993) and *Terror in the Mind of God: The Global Rise of Religious Violence* (Berkeley, CA: University of California Press, 2003).

5. Khaled Haroub, *Hamas: A Beginner's Guide* (London: Pluto Press, 2006), xii.

6. Zaki Chehab, *Inside Hamas* (New York: Nation Books, 2007), 20.

7. Beverley Milton-Edwards and Stephen Farrell, *Hamas* (Cambridge, UK: Polity Press, 2010), 10.

8. Haroub, *Hamas,* 14.

9. Haroub, *Hamas,* 11.

10. Chehab, *Inside Hamas,* 219–24.

11. Milton-Edwards and Farrell, *Hamas,* 10–12.

12. Milton-Edwards and Farrell, *Hamas,* 16.

13. Chehab, *Inside Hamas,* 5.

14. Haroub, *Hamas,* vi.

15. Juergensmeyer, *Terror in the Mind of God: The Global Rise of Religious Violence,* 74.

16. Juergensmeyer, *Terror in the Mind of God,* 74.

17. Milton-Edwards and Farrell, *Hamas,* 14–15.

18. Milton-Edwards and Farrell, *Hamas,* 16–17.

19. Jessica Stern, *Terror in the Name of God: Why Religious Militants Kill* (New York: Harper Collins, 2003), 33.

20. Milton-Edwards and Farrell, *Hamas,* 13–14.

21. Haroub, *Hamas,* 20–21, 39.

22. Milton-Edwards and Farrell, *Hamas,* 14.

23. Milton-Edwards and Farrell, *Hamas*, 15.

24. Yonah Alexander, *Palestinian Religious Terror: Hamas and Islamic Jihad* (Ardsley, NY: Transaction Publisher 2002), 43.

25. Stern, *Terror in the Name of God*, 39.

26. Stern, *Terror in the Name of God*, 57–59.

27. Quoted in Joyce Davis, *Martyrs: Innocence, Vengeance, and Despair in the Middle East* (New York: Palgrave, 2003), 154.

28. Nasra Hassan, "An Arsenal of Believers," *New Yorker*, November 19, 2001, 39.

29. "Suicide Bombers: Dignity, Despair, and the Need for Hope. An Interview with Eyad El Sarraj," *Journal of Palestine Studies*, 31 (Summer 2002): 73.

30. Matthew Levitt, *Hamas* (New Haven, CT: Yale University Press, 2006), 6.

31. Stern, *Terror in the Name of God*, 36.

32. Robert J. Brym and Araj Bader, "Suicide Bombing as Strategy and Interaction: The Case of the Second Intifada," *Social Forces* 84 (2006): 1974.

33. Ami Pedahzur and Arie Perliger, "The Changing Nature of Suicide Attacks: A Social Network Perspective," *Social Forces* 84 (June 2006): 1994.

34. Anat Berko, *The Path to Paradise: The Inner World of Suicide Bombers and their Dispatchers*, trans. Elizabeth Yuval (Wesport, CT: Praeger Security International, 2007), 1–2.

35. Juergensmeyer, *Terror in the Mind of God*, 194.

36. Quoted in Stern, *Terror in the Name of God*, 47.

37. Robert Pape, *Dying to Win: The Strategic Logic of Suicide Terrorism* (New York: Random House, 2005), 172–80.

38. Brian Barber, *One Heart, So Many Stones* (New York: Palgrave, Forthcoming) and Ariel Merari, "Psychological Aspects of Suicide Terrorism," in *Psychology of Terrorism*, ed. Bruce Bonger et al. (New York: Oxford University Press, 2007), 101–15.

39. Berko, *The Path to Paradise*, 171.

40. Israel neither confirms nor denies its involvement in these assassinations. Hamas has used these assassinations as justification for ending truces with Israel.

41. Juergensmeyer, *Terror in the Mind of God*, 75.

42. See Ami Pedahzur and Arie Perliger, "The Changing Nature of Suicide Attacks: A Social Network Perspective," *Social Forces* 84 (June 2006): 1987–2008 and Mia Bloom, "Palestinian Suicide Bombing: Public Support, Market Share, and Outbidding," *Political Science Quarterly* 119 (2004): 61–88.

43. Hala Jaber, *Hezbollah: Born with a Vengeance* (New York: Columbia University Press, 1997), 8–10.

44. Amal Saad-Ghorayeb, *Hizbullah: Politics and Religion* (London: Pluto Press, 2002), 8–10.

45. Martin Kramer, "The Moral Logic of Hezbollah," in *Origins of Terror: Psychologies, Ideologies, Theologies and States of Mind*, ed. Walter Reich (Baltimore, MD: Johns Hopkins University Press), 135.

46. Jaber, *Hezbollah*, 11.

47. Michael Totten, *The Road to Fatima Gate* (New York: Encounter Books, 2011), 101–2.

48. Amal Saad-Ghorayeb, *Hizbullah*, 8–10.

49. A. Richard Norton, *Hezbollah: A Short History* (Princeton, NJ: Princeton University Press, 2009), 15–16.

50. Norton, *Hezbollah*, 17–22.

51. Jaber, *Hezbollah,* 14.

52. Quoted in Norton, *Hezbollah,* 20.

53. Saad-Ghorayeb, *Hizbullah,* 10–12.

54. Jaber, *Hezbollah,* 18.

55. Norton, *Hezbollah,* 45.

56. Jaber, *Hezbollah,* 48.

57. Jaber, *Hezbollah,* 61.

58. Norton, *Hezbollah,* 41, 158.

59. Thanassis Cambanis, *A Privilege to Die: Inside Hezbollah's Legions and Their Endless War against Israel* (New York: Free Press, 2010), 16.

60. Jaber, *Hezbollah,* 146–8.

61. Norton, *Hezbollah,* 111–2.

62. Kramer, "The Moral Logic of Hezbollah," 136–41.

63. Jaber, *Hezbollah,* 76–79.

64. Judith Harik, *Hezbollah: The Changing Face of Terrorism* (London: I. B. Tauris, 2004), 3.

65. Saad-Ghorayeb, *Hizbullah,* 3 and Jaber, *Hezbollah,* 29–33.

66. Cambanis. *A Privilege to Die,* 2–7.

67. Norton, *Hezbollah,* 73.

68. Norton, *Hezbollah,* 83–85.

69. Cambanis, *A Privilege to Die,* 5, 263.

70. The disputed area had belonged to Syria prior to 1967 Six-Day War. Israel had made overtures to Syria to return the territory, which it refused. Michael Totten, *The Road to Fatima Gate* (New York: Encounter Books, 2011), 96–97.

71. Norton, *Hezbollah,* 133.

72. Totten, *The Road to Fatima Gate,* 95.

73. Cambanis, *A Privilege to Die,* 7–8.

74. Khalid Abou el-Fadl, "Holy War Versus *Jihad,*" *Ethics and International Affairs* 14 (2000): 133–40.

75. Anonymous, *Through Our Enemies' Eyes: Osama bin Laden, Radical Islam and the Future of America* (Washington, DC: Brassey's, 2003), 55–57.

76. Magnus Ranstorp, "Interpreting the Broader Context and Meaning and of bin Laden's *Fatwa,*" *Studies in Conflict and Terrorism* 21 (Fall 1998): 321–30.

77. See Bernard Lewis, *Islam and the West* (Oxford: Oxford University Press, 1993) and Bernard Lewis, "The Roots of Muslim Rage," in *The New Global Terrorism: Characteristics, Causes, Controls,* ed. Charles Kegley (Upper Saddle River, NJ: Prentice Hall, 2003), 194–201.

78. Abdel Bari Atwan, *The Secret History of al Qaeda* (Berkeley, CA: University of California Press, 2008), 64.

79. See Ranstorp, "Interpreting the Broader Context and Meaning of bin Laden's *Fatwa,*" 321–30 for examples.

80. Anonymous, *Through Our Enemies' Eyes.*

81. Mahmood Monshipouri, "The West's Modern Encounter with Islam: From Discourse to Reality," *Journal of Church and State* 40 (Winter 1998): 25–26.

82. Bari Atwan, *The Secret History of al Qaeda*, 43–44.

83. Anonymous, *Through Our Enemies' Eyes*, 89–90, 106–7.

84. Anonymous, *Through Our Enemies' Eyes*, 89–90, 92, 107.

85. Bari Atwan, *The Secret History of al Qaeda*, 39–44.

86. Peter Bergen, *Holy War Inc: Inside the Secret World of Osama bin Laden* (London: Weidenfeld and Nicolson), 37.

87. The Saudis offered to let bin Laden return from exile in Sudan if he would sign a statement agreeing that the regime was fully implementing *Sharia* and that the ruling family was faithful Muslims. He refused. Bari Atwan, *The Secret History of al Qaeda*, 52.

88. Bergen, *Holy War Inc*, 243.

89. Anonymous, *Through Our Enemies' Eyes*, 49–52.

90. See Anonymous, *Through Our Enemies' Eyes*, 114–17 and Bari Atwan, *The Secret History of al Qaeda*, 44–46.

91. Bergen, *Holy War Inc*, 102–4.

92. Anonymous, *Through Our Enemies' Eyes*, 52.

93. Anonymous, *Through Our Enemies' Eyes*, 17.

94. Bari Atwan, *The Secret History of al Qaeda*, 58.

95. The cruise missiles that were sent to Sudan, one of the world's poorest nations, destroyed a pharmaceutical plant that produced half of that country's medicines. The plant was alleged to produce biological and chemical weapons.

96. Anonymous, *Through Our Enemies' Eyes*, 10.

97. Both are quoted in Bari Atwan, *The Secret History of al Qaeda*, 181, 199.

98. Assaf Moghadam, *The Globalization of Martyrdom* (Baltimore, MD: Johns Hopkins University Press, 2008), 118.

99. Olivier Roy, "Terrorism and Deculturation," in *The Roots of Terrorism,* ed. Louise Richardson (New York: Routledge, 2006), 160–66.

CONCLUSION

1. James Jones, "Why Does Religion Turn Violent? A Psychoanalytic Exploration of Religious Terrorism," *The Psychoanalytic Review* 93 (2006): 167–90.

2. See Thomas Scheff, *Bloody Revenge: Emotions, Nationalism, and War* (Boulder, CO: Westview Press, 1994).

3. Anat Berko and Edna Erez, "Ordinary People and Death Work: Palestinian Suicide Bombers as Victimizers and Victims," *Violence and Victims* 20 (2005): 603–23.

4. Quoted in Berko and Erez, "Ordinary People and Death Work," 612.

5. Ariel Merari, "The Readiness to Kill and Die," in *Origins of Terrorism: Psychologies, Ideologies, Theologies, States of Mind,* ed. Walter Reich (Cambridge, England: Cambridge University Press, 1998), 194–96.

6. Office of the Press Secretary, "Remarks by the President on the Defensive Strategic Review," January 5, 2012, http://www.whitehouse.gov/the-press-office/2012/01/05/remarks-president-defense-strategic-review.

7. David Nakamura, "Obama Signs Defense Bill, Pledges to Maintain Legal Rights of U.S. Citizens," *Washington Post,* December 31, 2011, http://www.

washingtonpost.com/politics/obama-signs-defense-bill-pledges-to-maintain-legal-rights-of-terror-suspects/2011/12/31/gIQATzbkSP_story.html.

8. National Counterintelligence Center, *2010 Reports on Terrorism* (Washington, DC: National Counterintelligence Center, 2011).

9. Although Islamic parties prevailed in Moroccan elections, that country's political system remains, for the most part, under the control of the monarchy.

10. Care must be used when extrapolating from the examples of Turkey and Indonesia because both countries have long histories of secular-nationalist rule and armies that view themselves as being guardians of that legacy.

11. See the party's website, http://eng.akparti.org.tr/english/partyprogramme.html.

12. "President Bush Links War in Iraq to War on Terrorism," *PBS News Hour,* May 24, 2007, http://www.pbs.org/newshour/bb/white_house/jan-june07/terrorism_05-24.html.

13. Mehdi Hasan, "Let Them Eat Doughnuts: The US Response to Bahrain Oppression," *The Guardian,* July 11, 2011, http://www.guardian.co.uk/commentisfree/2011/jul/11/west-averts-eyes-brutes-bahrain.

Index

About the Author

DANIEL E. PRICE is an Assistant Professor of criminal justice and home-land security at Westfield State University where he teaches course on terrorism, comparative criminal justice, and international crime. His previous works include *Islamic Political Culture, Democracy, and Human Rights: A Comparative Study* and articles in *Journal for the Scientific Study of Religion* and *Presidential Studies Quarterly.*